RODALE'S
GOOD-TIMES
ALMANAC

RODALE'S GOOD-TIMES ALMANAC

By the Editors
of Rodale Press

Rodale Press, Emmaus, Pennsylvania

Printed in the United States of America

Editor in Chief: *William Gottlieb*
Managing Editor: *Margaret Lydic Balitas*
Editor: *Paula Bakule*
Contributing Editor: *Carol Hupping*
Editorial Assistance: *Stacy Brobst*
            Valerie Patterson
Book Designer: *Anita G. Patterson*
Book Layout: *Lisa Farkas*
Copy Editor: *Mary Green*
Illustrations: *Robin Brickman pp. 188, 189*
       Jack Crane pp. 52, 61, 126, 128, 146, 147, 180, 249, 271, 280, 287, 374
       Leslie Flis pp. 8, 79
       Tom Quirk pp. 188, 189
       The Bettman Archive pp. i, 28, 58, 92, 134, 176, 214, 244, 276, 310, 342, 370
       All other illustrations are from the Dover Pictorial Archive Series.

If you have any questions or comments concerning this book, please write:
     Rodale Press
     Book Reader Service
     33 East Minor Street
     Emmaus, PA 18098

Library of Congress Cataloging-in-Publication Data

Rodale's good-times almanac / by the editors of Rodale Press.
     p.   cm.
Includes index.
ISBN 0-87857-835-8 hardcover
  1. Almanacs, American.   I. Rodale Press.
AY64.R63   1989
031.02—dc20   89-6408
                                                                  CIP

Distributed in the book trade by St. Martin's Press

2 4 6 8 10 9 7 5 3 1   hardcover

CONTENTS

INTRODUCTION

LET THE GOOD TIMES ROLL

You're about to discover a totally new and different type of almanac. Almanacs usually evoke feelings of nostalgia for what we imagine was a simpler, easier way of life—a time when most readers needed a reliable weather forecaster, a few hints on curing warts, and a few concise proverbs to live by. Modern-day almanacs fall into two categories: the fact-filled tome (where you can look up the number of active volcanoes in Chile) or the nostalgic collection of humor and weather forecasts (where you can still read how much snow should fall in Nebraska during the month of December). *Rodale's Good-Times Almanac* bypasses the reference tome and the nostalgic compendium to bring you a rollicking mix of both fact and fancy.

In *Rodale's Good-Times Almanac* you'll find a healthy dose of lighthearted, little-known facts. (What's the origin of Sadie Hawkins Day? What unfamous American invented the first alarm clock?) You'll find descriptions of colorful, unique events and places to visit. (How about the National Hollerin' Contest at Spivey's Corner, North Carolina? Or the Storytelling Weekend at Greenup, Kentucky?) And you'll find the answers to questions from your favorite quiz show. (Which U.S. President had a grandson who also became President?) But you'll also find what we at Rodale pride ourselves in providing—good, clear, practical advice on how to get the most out of every day of your life. And we've organized this information on a month-by-month basis so that you get it at the time it's most useful to you. In the areas of gardening, health, and home, you'll find *Rodale's Good-Times Almanac* jam-packed with clear, concise, savvy advice and information, including:

 Five secrets of success in starting garden seeds.

 How to design and install your own drip irrigation system.

☞ The most outstanding sources for old-fashioned, heirloom seeds and plants.

☞ A ten-step action plan to conquer insomnia forever.

☞ How to select the best room humidifier for treating a cold.

☞ How to develop your own unique sense of humor.

☞ Six things you should ask yourself about your current home insurance policy.

☞ The quickest and easiest ways to repair leaking downspouts and gutters.

☞ Three low-cost items that keep your house cool without air conditioning.

☞ What federal agency can help you if you have a dispute with a creditor.

And here's one last tip on getting the most from this book: Don't put it on your bookshelf. Keep it next to your bed, in the kitchen, or in the bathroom. Its purpose is to entertain you at idle moments, to give you ideas for solving common household problems, and to open your eyes to the infinite possibilities for living a positive, happy life. Pick up this book whenever you can spare a moment to lift your own spirits. And let the "good times" roll!

Paula Bakule
Editor

JANUARY

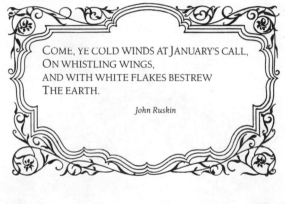

COME, YE COLD WINDS AT JANUARY'S CALL,
ON WHISTLING WINGS,
AND WITH WHITE FLAKES BESTREW
THE EARTH.

John Ruskin

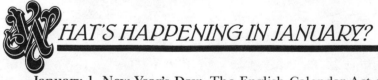

WHAT'S HAPPENING IN JANUARY?

January 1, New Year's Day: The English Calendar Act of 1751 moved New Year's Day from March 25 to January 1. Before 1751 Great Britain followed the more ancient Julian Calendar. Our modern calendar, called the Gregorian Calendar, comes from a calendar devised by Aloysious Lilius, a Naples physician and astronomer. Pope Gregory XIII officially adopted this calendar for all the Christian world in 1582, but it was not recognized in Great Britain until 1751.

January 15, Birthday of Martin Luther King, Jr.: Martin Luther King, Jr., a black clergyman from Atlanta, Georgia, was a dedicated leader in the civil rights struggles of the 1960s. Martin Luther King Day is now an official holiday in 24 states. In Alabama, Martin Luther King Day and Robert E. Lee Day are celebrated together on the 21st.

January 17, Birthday of Benjamin Franklin: This outstanding statesman, scientist, and public servant influenced every aspect of public life during the birth of our country. He helped to draft the Declaration of Independence, published *Poor Richard's Almanack*, founded the University of Pennsylvania, served as our first ambassador to France, and invented the lightning rod.

January 19, Birthday of Robert E. Lee: The celebrated Confederate general Robert E. Lee shares quite a bit of history with that other famous Virginian, George Washington. Robert E. Lee's father, General "Light-Horse Harry" Lee, served under Washington during the Revolutionary War, and Lee married Mary Anne Randolph Custis, the great-granddaughter of Martha Washington.

January 23, Pie Day: Make your bottom piecrust crisp by brushing it with melted butter or egg white before filling.

January 28, Swap-A-Brown-Bag-Lunch Day: To keep yourself perky all afternoon, eat a high-protein lunch rather than a high-carbohydrate one. Go easy on the bread and the pastries. Emphasize low-fat dairy products, such as low-fat cheese and yogurt, nuts, fish, chicken, turkey, or meat. Brown-bag lunches need not only mean sandwiches. They can mean anything that is packable, nutritious, and satisfying. See how many appetizing lunch combinations you can make by mixing and matching items from each of the menu groups shown in the box.

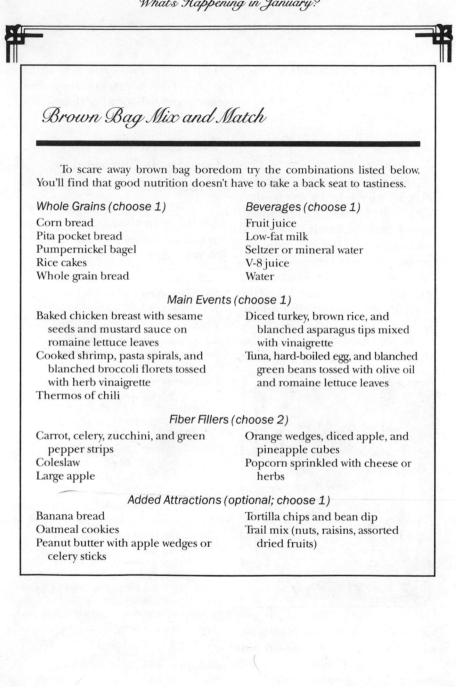

Brown Bag Mix and Match

To scare away brown bag boredom try the combinations listed below. You'll find that good nutrition doesn't have to take a back seat to tastiness.

Whole Grains (choose 1)

Corn bread
Pita pocket bread
Pumpernickel bagel
Rice cakes
Whole grain bread

Beverages (choose 1)

Fruit juice
Low-fat milk
Seltzer or mineral water
V-8 juice
Water

Main Events (choose 1)

Baked chicken breast with sesame seeds and mustard sauce on romaine lettuce leaves
Cooked shrimp, pasta spirals, and blanched broccoli florets tossed with herb vinaigrette
Thermos of chili

Diced turkey, brown rice, and blanched asparagus tips mixed with vinaigrette
Tuna, hard-boiled egg, and blanched green beans tossed with olive oil and romaine lettuce leaves

Fiber Fillers (choose 2)

Carrot, celery, zucchini, and green pepper strips
Coleslaw
Large apple

Orange wedges, diced apple, and pineapple cubes
Popcorn sprinkled with cheese or herbs

Added Attractions (optional; choose 1)

Banana bread
Oatmeal cookies
Peanut butter with apple wedges or celery sticks

Tortilla chips and bean dip
Trail mix (nuts, raisins, assorted dried fruits)

January Is National Soup Month

Soup may be our most perfect food. It's easy to make, can contain just about anything, can be low in fat and calories, needs no salt, and can be made in large quantities for freezer storage. To keep your soup within these healthy boundaries, refrigerate your stock and skim the fat solids from the top before adding the final ingredients; avoid cream- or cheese-based soups; and flavor with herbs and spices instead of salt.

Soup-saver's tip: Whenever you make soup stock, set aside a portion to freeze in ice cube trays. Empty the frozen stock cubes into a plastic freezer bag. Later you can defrost individual cubes to flavor steamed vegetables, to baste broiled meats and fish, or to perk up plain boiled rice.

The Third Week of January Is National Pizza Week

The American love affair with this Italian treat means that each of us eats, on the average, seven whole pizzas a year.

30-Minute Pizza

This homemade pizza is more than delicious—it's faster to make from scratch than a speeding delivery truck can make it to your door. It takes less than 30 minutes to mix the whole-grain dough, assemble one 11-inch pizza, and bake it.

½ package quick-rise dry yeast
½ cup lukewarm water (about 110°F)
1 tablespoon vegetable oil
½ teaspoon honey
1¼ cups whole wheat flour
¼ teaspoon garlic powder
¼ teaspoon onion powder
½ cup thick tomato sauce
1 cup shredded mozzarella cheese

Preheat oven to 475°F. In a medium bowl, add yeast to lukewarm water. Stir in oil, honey, flour, garlic powder, and onion powder, and mix thoroughly. Allow dough to rest for 5 minutes. Coat a pizza pan or baking sheet with vegetable cooking spray. Place dough on it and shape into an 11-inch round crust. Carefully spread sauce over crust and sprinkle evenly with cheese. Bake for 12 minutes.

One 11-inch pizza

IN THE GARDEN

TURN YOUR GARDEN INTO THE NEW AMERICAN GARDEN

January is that time of year when gardeners have the luxury of planning and dreaming of the garden to come. It is the time when the toil of the past year's garden is forgotten and only its pleasure is remembered. It is the time when seed catalogs become the favored bedtime reading—the time when all things seem possible.

As you plan for the new gardening year, you may want to use a completely new style of gardening. It's a style that makes better use of leisure time, combines beauty with practicality, and emphasizes quality instead of quantity.

Pleasure and Plenty

The new American garden is more than a convenient, backyard vegetable plot, more than the traditional neat lawns and trimmed shrubs of suburbia, and more than the pampered specimens of a rose fanatic. It is a style of gardening that breaks with many old gardening traditions and that integrates beauty, usefulness, and easy maintenance into a new way to garden.

The new American garden dispenses with the old notion that similar plants should always be grouped together in the same bed. Herb gardeners now plant bright annuals among the rosemary and thyme; vegetable gardeners incorporate perennials into a vegetable plot; and rose fanciers use herbs as borders for rosebeds. In addition to tossing out the old conventions of which plants belong together, gardeners are also moving toward more natural, low-maintenance landscapes by installing easy-to-grow native plants instead of exotic, nonhardy hybrids.

American gardeners are also discovering that gardening adds extra pleasure to every part of life. Gardeners who enjoy cooking now tuck herb gardens next to the kitchen door in order to have fresh basil for a favorite tomato sauce. Gardeners who love flowers install a cutting garden for an endless supply of fresh flowers for the dinner table. Vegetable fanciers experiment with exotic vegetables, such as baby corn or striped eggplant, and fruit fanciers plant heirloom apples, such as 'Esopus Spitzenburg'.

And after they've spent the time and effort to create these gardens, Americans still want to have the time to enjoy what they've made. As a result they carefully select varieties of flowers, vegetables, and ornamentals that are disease and insect resistant as well as drought tolerant and cold hardy. Endless weeding, watering, and pinching are out. Low-maintenance techniques utilizing small bed size, mulch, and drip irrigation are in.

Expert Advice for the New American Gardener

Bob Thomson, host of WGBH-Boston's nationally broadcast "Victory Garden," says, "The philosophy of gardening has changed. . . . People are growing food because they want to, not because they have to. . . . And it's not only the quality of the food that's important. There's a symbiotic relationship between people and plants. We garden because it makes us feel good."

How to enjoy it more: Being in a garden makes us feel good, so why not provide a quiet spot to sit and enjoy it all? A well-placed garden bench near shrubs and flowers or near vegetables and fruit trees invites us to get out into our gardens purely for pleasure. A birdbath or garden sculpture can make the spot even more restful. If you are unable to find garden furnishings in your local stores, you can find these items in many garden-supply catalogs.

Sam Cotner, a horticultural expert with Texas A&M Extension Service, says, "There's more of a landscape design element to gardening today. There's a move toward patio gardening and more interest in container gardening, growing crops in barrels and railroad-tie beds; more dwarf fruit trees in containers planted for their ornamental effect as well as their fruit."

Patio planting strategy: Herbs planted in the ground or in boxes along the perimeter of a patio can soften its hard edges and provide an attractive transition from wood or masonry to lawn. Having herbs growing close to your house will also remind you to cut and use them more often. Herbs that provide a particularly attractive or fragrant patio border include: chives (with purple flowers), garlic chives (with white flowers), parsley, lemon balm, spearmint, rosemary, lavender, and creeping lemon thyme.

For successful container gardening, select compact, bush-type vegetable varieties. Use pots, tubs, or plant boxes that have good drainage, and a potting soil that's lightened with peat moss, perlite, vermiculite, or sand. Water the plants daily and fertilize about once a week.

Some decorative varieties you might like to try include: 'Sweet Banana' peppers (small, long peppers that range in color from yellow to orange to red), alpine strawberries (small, bushy, runnerless plants covered with tiny red berries), and early-yielding cherry or patio tomatoes like 'Tiny Tim' or 'Pixie II'. In choosing annual flowers for planters, be sure to select a dwarf variety. Marigolds, nasturtiums, petunias, verbenas, zinnias, impatiens, and coleus are among the many annuals that thrive in containers.

Roger Kline, Cornell University extension agent, says that crops are changing: "It used to be you could hold up the largest tomato in your garden to impress your neighbors. Now you're more likely to hold up a sugarloaf chicory and ask them if they know what it is."

How to add excitement: Introduce some newcomers to the tried-and-true varieties you always plant. From 'Royal Burgundy Purple Pod' beans to 'Moon and Stars' watermelon, there's an abundance of delicious and beautiful vegetables available to you. An easy way to receive a wealth of novelty seed catalogs is to subscribe to several good gardening magazines. You'll find catalog ads for many small mail-order seed companies in the classified sections. After you've ordered a few of these specialty catalogs, you'll find others appearing unsolicited in your mailbox. If you are interested in heirloom varieties, you'll find information about heirloom seeds in the April chapter of the almanac.

Rosalind Creasy, a California landscape designer and the author of several books on edible landscaping, comments, "I expect to see the American vegetable garden change from a row of tomatoes, a row of beans, and maybe a couple of rows of corn for preserving, to a garden that's much more an organic part of life."

Tips for a beautiful mix and match: Combine flowers, herbs, and vegetables to make a richly textured and colored garden landscape. When planning your mixed beds, consider compatible cultural needs, blooming and harvest times, and complementary colors and heights. To get you started, the illustration on page 8 gives a plan. It was designed and planted by Mary Anne Nunez at the Rodale Farm in Maxatawny, Pennsylvania. All varieties are easy to grow from seed and are available from many seed houses.

Quotations from the expert gardeners in "Turn Your Garden into the New American Garden" were reprinted, with permission, from National Gardening, May, 1987. National Gardening is the monthly publication of the National Gardening Association, 180 Flynn Avenue, Burlington, VT 05401.

FOOLPROOF ANNUALS FOR YOUR GARDEN

As you plan your January seed order, include the annuals that never fail to please because they *always*

VEGETABLES

1. Snap bean 'Royal Burgundy'
2. Chard 'Rainbow'
3. Pepper (green) 'Lady Bell'
4. Pepper 'Summer Sweet'
5. Tomato 'Celebrity'
6. Tomato 'Lemon Boy'
7. Zucchini 'Gold Rush'
8. Zucchini 'Green Magic Hybrid'

FLOWERS

9. Daylily 'Stella D'Oro'
10. Dusty–miller 'Silverdust'
11. Geranium 'Cardinal Orbit'
12. Lily 'Regale'
13. Marigold 'Inca Yellow'
14. Petunia 'Red Devil'
15. Sanvitalia 'Mandarin Orange'
16. Strawflower 'Bright Yellow'
17. Zinnia 'Torch'

HERBS

18. Parsley 'Paramount'
19. Basil 'Spicy Globe'

Gardens
like the one shown
here provide both food
and beauty in the same spot.

come up and *always* flower. These foolproof annuals are beloved by experienced gardeners for their glorious color and style variations. New gardeners love them for their absolute reliability. Whether your garden is new or long established, you can depend on these annuals for color and cover the entire summer.

Alyssum

This low-growing ground cover celebrates spring with an early-blooming carpet of white, pink, or violet flowers. Alyssum prefers full sun but will tolerate light shade and will grow well even in poor soil. In midseason, you can initiate a new round of fresh flowers by lightly shearing the entire plant.

Alyssum should be direct-seeded outdoors early in spring. If you do wish to start plants indoors, be sure to set them out early (they can take the cool weather and soil) and treat them gently so as to disturb their roots as little as possible.

Impatiens

Impatiens turns an otherwise shady and dull spot into a profusion of color—coral, purple, white, or pink—for the entire growing season. There's probably no other flower that is so shade tolerant. As a matter of fact, impatiens does better in shade than in sun.

Start seeds indoors at least six weeks before planting time. Do not cover seeds with soil because light hastens germination. If you prefer to purchase plants, you will find that you can propagate several additional plants from one purchase. Simply take several 3-inch cuttings and suspend them in a jar of water. Keep them out of direct sun. Your cuttings will produce a root system within three weeks. Once established in a shady bed, plants need very little care except for deep watering during dry spells.

Marigolds

These never-fail flowers for sunny spots are disease and insect resistant and grow in almost any soil where there is good drainage.

Seeds of the French and Signet varieties can be sown right in the garden, where they'll germinate in about a week. Seeds of the triploid varieties, which have a low germination rate, and the tall American varieties, which have a long growing season, should be started indoors. After the plants are established, leave them alone. They don't need rich soil or lots of water.

Petunias

Petunias offer big, showy blooms all summer long even when other annuals are fading out in the summer heat. These annuals come in single and double blooms of purple, red, blue, pink, yellow, and white and are also available in striped or bicolored forms. They should be started indoors at least ten weeks before your last frost date. Because the seeds need light to germinate, do not cover them with soil. Set out plants in a sunny spot with reasonably fertile soil. Petunias need regular watering to thrive. Feed them several times throughout the summer and remove flowers as they fade.

Zinnias

Zinnias can be sown right in the garden and sprout within a week if the soil is warm enough. After you direct-seed zinnias, be sure to keep weeds from crowding out the young plants, and keep the seedlings well watered. Then they'll go on flowering most of the summer, even in hot, dry weather. When you water, keep water away from the blossoms and leaves to avoid mildew. Some varieties, notably the hybrids, are more mildew resistant than others. Zinnias vary from 6-inch plants bearing 1-inch flowers to gigantic 4-foot specimens with 5-inch blooms. All varieties make excellent cutting flowers.

ALMANAC GARDENING CALENDAR

In each month of the almanac, you will find a handy calendar of garden activities given by frost-free zone numbers. Whether you are a novice or an old hand at gardening, there's something here for you. If this is your first season at gardening,

Did You Know? Curious Gardening Facts

☞ Tree sap does not rise in the spring. As the weather warms, it moves outward, from the center of the trunk, limbs, and branches, to their surfaces.

☞ Hot peppers produce a chemical that protects against soil-borne fungi. Chemicals called capsaicinoids give hot peppers their pungency and also protect the seeds during their long germination period.

☞ Vitamin C and sugar continue to increase as a tomato ripens on the vine. These elements are destroyed when tomatoes ripen off the vine. No wonder a supermarket tomato can't compare with the homegrown version!

☞ The mosquito level in your backyard is unaffected by an electric bug zapper. Entomolgist Phillip Pellitteri of the University of Wisconsin found that mosquitoes account for less than 1 percent of the insects killed by electric bug lights. Mosquitoes are more attracted to heat and carbon dioxide than to ultraviolet light.

☞ Strong-flavored onions store better than sweet ones. Sweet-flavored onions lack the sulfur compounds that help fend off decay.

☞ Beet seedlings always need to be thinned because each "seed" is really a cluster of tiny seeds that will all sprout in one spot.

☞ When a yellow jacket is squashed, a chemical is released that signals nearby yellow jackets to attack. Think twice before you strike.

page through the garden calendar in every month of the almanac to discover how gardening really is a year-round pleasure. If you have gardening experience, use this reminder to jog your memory and perhaps inspire you to try something new in your garden this year.

Which Is Your Zone?

The gardening calendar gives information according to the frost-free zone numbers shown on the map on page 12. You can find your zone number by looking at the frost-free zone map. Another good way to find the approximate number of frost-free days in your garden is to call your local extension agent or the horticulture department of a local university.

You can also determine your zone number yourself without the aid of the map. Part of the art and craft of gardening is close observation of nature (including weather patterns) in your particular garden. The most dedicated gardeners keep records of these observations over a number of gardening seasons and from these records develop a calendar exactly suited to their particular garden. From several seasons of such observations, you can determine for yourself the average number of frost-free days in your garden and your correct zone number. This zone number will serve as a reference point while you hone your own skills at the art and craft of gardening.

Zone 1

Plan annual, perennial, and vegetable beds for spring planting. Go through seed packages from last year to see what must be reordered. Test the viability of left-over seeds by wrapping them in a moist paper towel. Keep them moist by covering with plastic or a dish towel. If less than 70 percent have germinated after seven to ten days, buy new seed. Order your seeds as soon as possible to be sure of getting the varieties you want. Fertilize window-grown herbs and greens lightly every two weeks. The last week of January, start seeds of container-variety tomatoes. In windy areas, shovel snow over exposed perennials, berries, and grapes to help them survive the cold.

Zone 2

Order seeds for annual, perennial, and vegetable beds. To receive them in time for early planting, be sure to include cool-weather vegetables (Brassica family). Save wood ashes, a source of calcium, phosphorus, and potash, in a dry, covered container for a spring soil amendment. If you set out your live Christmas tree, make sure to keep it watered. If your house is dry, mist houseplants often. Take advantage of a January thaw to prune apple, pear, cherry, and plum trees. Save peach tree pruning until March.

Zone 3

After checking your garden records for the past season, plan your vegetable, annual, and perennial beds. Order seeds as early as possible, remembering especially cole crops and onions, which need to be started indoors by late February. Clean and sharpen tools, and build or repair cold frames, cloches, irrigation systems, and trellises. Spread manure on the garden, especially on the asparagus bed and on

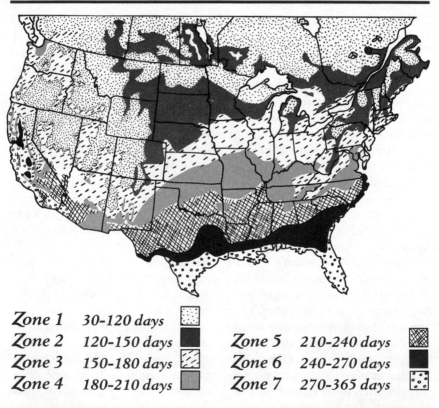

Zone 1	*30-120 days*			
Zone 2	*120-150 days*	**Zone 5**	*210-240 days*	
Zone 3	*150-180 days*	**Zone 6**	*240-270 days*	
Zone 4	*180-210 days*	**Zone 7**	*270-365 days*	

Zone Map

Note that the zone map above is based on the average number of frost-free days in each zone. Your zone number using this map is not the same as your zone number on a hardiness zone map. Hardiness zone maps are based on the average minimum temperature for each zone. The information in the almanac gardening calendar is based on the map shown here.

peonies. It will leach into the soil during thaws. Check perennial beds for signs of heaving. Cover exposed roots with soil or compost and mulch. Inspect stored bulbs, tubers, and corms for signs of rotting or sprouting. Inspect fruit trees, bushes, and brambles, pruning only winter-damaged branches and canes. Provide food and water for birds, which feed on overwintering orchard pests.

Zone 4

Early in the month, work out your garden plans for the coming season on graph paper and order seeds. Consult your notes from last year and plan for crop rotation—especially for tomatoes and brassicas —as well as succession planting. In mild areas, plant cool-season crops such as onions, peas, lettuce, radishes, and spinach. In Arizona, sow tomatoes in flats by the tenth of the month. Prepare potting mixes and flats for next month's indoor sowings. Plan for ornamental purchases by working out a long-term improvement plan for your property on graph paper. Remove heavy snow from evergreens, but leave icy branches undisturbed. Check perennials and bulbs for heaving, and push heaved plants gently back into the ground. Cover these with mulch, straw, or evergreen branches.

Zone 5

Draw up a vegetable garden plan that includes spring *and* sum-mer crops. Order seeds as early as possible. If it's possible in your region, plan for three succession crops instead of the usual two. Indoors, sow cabbage, celery, onion, and parsley seeds early in the month. Late in the month, begin moving these seedlings to a cold frame. In the West, prepare raised beds for late-winter vegetable plantings. Set out live Christmas trees as early as possible and keep them watered and mulched. Rake mulches away from spring-flowering bulbs after green shoots appear. Indoors, sow seeds of pansies, dianthus, snapdragons, and other hardy annuals. Dormant roses and lilies may be planted throughout the month. Begin pruning peaches, apples, pears, and plums. Apply dormant-oil spray to fruit trees and mulch figs heavily to protect against hard freezes. Prepare beds for strawberry plantings and cover the beds with mulch. Wrap the trunks of young trees to prevent sunscald.

Zone 6

Plant onion sets, leeks, peas, spinach, beets, and carrots. Sow tomatoes, eggplant, peppers, chard, and cole crops in flats in a cold frame or indoors. Order asparagus crowns for February planting. Buy roses, shrubs, trees, and other ornamentals now for the best selection. Plant them in large holes for a vigorous spring start. For greatest success, transplant any existing trees and shrubs during this month. Take cuttings of vines and other woody plants for rooting. Water lawns, shrubs, and trees during dry periods to make them more cold tolerant. Sow anemones, ranunculus, and pentstemons by midmonth. Later in the month, plant dianthus, snapdragons, pansies, salvias, and poppies. Prune chrysanthemums now for spring bloom. Purchase and plant fruit and nut trees. Spray trees with dormant-oil spray whenever temperature stays above 40°F. Spread manure, compost, and rock fertilizer around bases of trees and brambles. Hold off pruning fruit trees until early next month. Prune grapevines. Wrap the trunks of newly planted trees to prevent sunscald.

Zone 7

At the beginning of the month, turn in green manure crops (rye, clover, vetch) or turn in a few inches of livestock manure. Plant brassicas, Asian greens, carrots, beets, lettuce, parsley, spinach, and turnips early this month. In cooler parts of this zone plant asparagus, rhubarb, and horseradish. Start flats of herbs. Toward the end of the month begin hardening off tomato, pepper, and eggplant seedlings that were started in December. In warmer parts of the zone, these vegetables can be set out during January, but keep covers handy in case of a surprise frost. Start seeds of marigolds, rudbeckias, portulacas, and African daisies. In the cooler parts of the zone, set out calendulas, pansies, schizanthus, sweet Williams, nemesias, and primroses. In the warmer tier, set out petunias, delphiniums, candytufts, pinks, salvias, and snapdragons. Prune trees, vines, and bush fruits. Do not prune citrus until after the last frost. Spray all fruit and nut trees with dormant-oil spray.

IN GOOD HEALTH

COLD SEASON KNOW-HOW

It's that season of the year again —the time when fatigue from the past holiday celebrations catches up with us, the time when we spend more of our time indoors with other folks, the time when we fear that those other folks may be giving us a cold. Before you begin to notice that old scratchy feeling in your throat, here's some information and advice to help you through it all.

Catching a Cold

For years, people have assumed that colds were spread chiefly by contact with viruses sprayed into the air by sneezing or coughing cold sufferers. While airborne particles are one source of infection, scientists have found that the hands are also an important means of transmission, especially for rhinovirus colds.

Rhinoviruses (the viruses that cause 25 to 30 percent of all adult colds) are produced or "shed" in highest concentrations in nasal secretions. They can survive up to three hours outside the nasal passage, on inanimate objects or skin. Researchers at the University of Virginia have found that under natural conditions, rhinoviruses from nasal secretions can be transferred easily from the hands of an infected person to those of another—by shaking hands, for instance—or to a surface such as a doorknob or telephone, which is then touched by another. By touching one's eyes or nose with the fingers, something most people do several times a day, the susceptible person can be "self-inoculated."

The same investigators have found that few colds result from exposure to rhinoviruses spread by kissing, or by being sprayed with particles produced by coughing or sneezing. All cold viruses do not behave like rhinoviruses, however, and some appear to be transmitted more easily by airborne particles. University of Illinois scientists found that using aspirin to treat colds increases the amount of virus shed in nasal secretions, thus making the cold sufferer more of a hazard to others.

Although many people believe that a cold results from exposure to cold weather, or from getting chilled or overheated, these conditions have little or no effect on the development or severity of a cold. Nor is susceptibility apparently related to factors such as general health, nutrition, or enlarged tonsils or adenoids. Colds may be related to excessive fatigue, stress, allergic disorders affecting the nasal passages or pharynx, and menstrual cycles. Stress and cigarette smoking seem to make symptoms more severe.

How to Reduce Your Chances of Catching a Cold

Hand washing is the simplest and most effective way to keep from getting rhinovirus colds. Not touching the nose or eyes is another. Promptly disposing of used tissues, and cleaning surfaces with a virus-killing agent, such as a chlorine (household bleach) solution or phenol/alcohol disinfectant, might prevent spread of infection. If possible, you should avoid close, prolonged exposure to persons who have colds.

Development of a vaccine that could prevent the common cold has reached an impasse because of the discovery of many different cold viruses. Each virus carries markers on its surface called antigens. These antigens trigger your body to produce specific protective proteins (antibodies). These antibodies destroy the virus by hooking up to the antigen marker on its surface. Because there are so many different cold viruses, each with its own specific antigens, there is presently little prospect of producing a single cold vaccine that fights them all.

What to Do When You Get a Cold

Get plenty of rest. If you can't stay home during the day to rest, at least go to bed early.

Drink plenty of fluids. The best thing for your cold is to keep mucus thinned so that it carries viruses away from vulnerable nasal tissues. Encourage free mucus flow by drinking 8 ounces of hot liquid every two hours; cold drinks may impede mucus flow. Hot chicken soup or any other clear soup is good.

Use a humidifier in your bed-room at night. This helps to keep your throat and nasal passages moist so that mucus may flow more freely. This simple measure will make you more comfortable so that you can get a good night's sleep.

Go easy on the exercise. Studies have indicated that regular exercise when you're healthy increases your body's production of germ-fighting white blood cells and also may help to discourage colds by elevating body temperature. But once you've got a cold, slow down and let your body rest. Strenuous exercise at this point may do more harm than good by tiring an already-stressed body.

Take aspirin or an aspirin substitute if necessary to relieve aches and pains. Antibiotics do not kill viruses; they should be used only for rare bacterial complications, such as sinusitis or ear infections, that can develop as secondary infections. The use of antibiotics "just in case" will not prevent secondary bacterial infections.

Take nonprescription cold remedies with care. Decongestants, cough suppressants, and antihistamines may relieve some cold symptoms but will not prevent, cure, or even shorten the duration of illness. Moreover, most have some side effects, such as drowsiness, dizziness, insomnia, or nausea.

If your child or teenager has

a cold, do not give aspirin for respiratory or influenzalike symptoms. The American Academy of Pediatrics reports that the use of aspirin may cause the development of Reye's syndrome (a severe neurological disorder) in children recovering from influenza.

Information in "Cold Season Know-How" is based on "The Common Cold" by the National Institute of Allergy and Infectious Diseases and "What You Need to Know to Prevent a Cold," Body Bulletin, May, 1985, Rodale Press, Inc.

CAN YOU LOSE WEIGHT DRINKING DIET SODA?

One of the most popular (and most easily broken) New Year's resolutions is to lose weight. If you're like most dieters, you resort to the strategy of eating less than normal, feeling hungry, and then staving off hunger by drinking a diet soda. By drinking one 12-ounce diet drink instead of a regular sweetened drink, you "save" about 160 calories. The Center for Science in the Public Interest (a consumer advocacy group in Washington, DC) reports that if you drank one diet soda a day, theoretically you could lose—or avoid gaining—almost 17 pounds a year.

But the statistics suggest that despite their low-calorie lure, many people aren't substituting diet drinks for regular ones; they're drinking both. In 1985 diet soda sales were over three times higher than they were back in 1975, while sales of regular sodas jumped 47 percent. And the percentage of overweight Americans remained about the same during that 10-year period.

All this may prove to you that there is no one thing that is going to significantly help you lose weight. A weight-loss program needs to be based on changes in what you eat and in your attitudes about food and exercise. A steady loss of about one or two pounds a week is a healthy and realistic goal. To lose one pound a week, you must either decrease caloric intake by about 500 calories a day or burn up those 500 calories by increasing physical activity. To get you thinking about specific ways you can reduce the calories you eat each day, short of just plain eating less, take a look at the calorie-saving substitution table, prepared by the U.S. Department of Agriculture, on page 18.

Saving Calories: Some Ideas to Get You Started

Instead of:	Try:	Calories Saved:
3 oz. well-marbled meat (prime rib)	3 oz. lean meat (eye of round)	140
½ chicken breast, batter-fried	½ chicken breast	175
½ cup beef stroganoff	3 oz. lean roast beef	210
½ cup home-fried potatoes	1 medium baked potato	65
½ cup green bean-mushroom casserole	½ cup cooked green beans	50
½ cup potato salad	1 cup raw vegetable salad	140
½ cup pineapple chunks in heavy syrup	½ cup pineapple chunks in juice	25
2 tbsp bottled French dressing	2 tbsp low-calorie French dressing	150
⅐ 9-inch apple pie	1 baked apple	185
3 oatmeal-raisin cookies	1 oatmeal-raisin cookie	125
½ cup ice cream	½ cup ice milk	45
a Danish pastry	half an English muffin	150
1 cup sugar-coated corn flakes	1 cup plain corn flakes	60
1 cup whole milk	1 cup 1% low-fat milk	45
7-fluid-oz. Tom Collins	6-fluid-oz. wine cooler made with sparkling water	150
1-oz. bag potato chips	1 cup plain popcorn	120
¹⁄₁₂ 8-inch white layer cake with chocolate frosting	¹⁄₁₂ 10-inch-tube angel food cake	185

POST-HOLIDAY BLUES, OR ARE YOU SAD?

That letdown feeling that comes after the Christmas/New Year's crush may be more than just the result of too much celebrating. Researchers at the National Institute of Mental Health (NIMH) in Bethesda, Maryland, have a name for the midwinter blues; it's called SAD, or Seasonal Affective Disorder, and it's thought to be the result of sunlight deprivation. Evidence that the winter blahs syndrome is not related to the holiday season also comes from Australia, where winter begins in June. Researchers from down under find the same midwinter symptoms of sleep disturbance, eating disorders, and loss of libido that afflict sufferers in the United States. People who suffer from SAD typically experience lethargy, craving for sugars and starches, weight gain, and greater need for sleep as well as a loss of interest in sex. Current research at NIMH has focused on exposure to artificial sunlight as a means of relieving this type of depression.

How to Fight Back When the Blues Strike You

If you experience a mild case of winter blahs every year, plan to fight back with some specific tactics.

Don't let cold weather curtail your exercise routine. Exercise has proven beneficial in combating garden-variety depression. If you live in an area where winters are severe, sign up for an indoor exercise class at your local YMCA, swim at an indoor pool, take a daily hike around the inside of a shopping mall, schedule regular workouts at a local health club, or purchase that stationary bicycle you've had your eye on.

Avoid the revenge of the binge. Excess pounds you gain will, in the end, make you more depressed than you were to begin with. Resolve to keep your normal healthy eating patterns intact for the winter season. Focus on whole grains, fresh vegetables and fruits, lean meats or fish, and low-fat dairy products. One tactic for fighting the urge to binge is to keep score. Every time you successfully fight back a binge urge, reward yourself with a point on your personal score sheet. A set number of points wins you some time for a pleasure or hobby you normally don't take time for.

THE ALMANAC WALKING-FOR-FITNESS GUIDE

Our most frequent New Year's resolution is to begin an exercise program. This year, why not make that resolution a reality by participating in a sport you can do for the rest of your life—for no money, with no injuries, and with no equipment (except one good pair of shoes).

Walking is the number two participatory sport in the United States; only swimming attracts more people. Almost 60 percent of walkers are over 35 years old, and their frequency of walking increases with age. But walking is not just for grandparents; high percentages of new participants are under 12 and between 18 and 24. These people

Walker's Daily Log

Date	Hours or Miles	Comments: Places, Experiences, Weather, Body Responses
M		
T		
W		
T		
F		
S		
S		
M		
T		
W		
T		
F		
S		
S		
		2 Weeks' Total
		Year to Date

Walking Tip for January

Plan to make a long winter walk more enjoyable by carrying a small thermos of herb tea, hot cider, or hot grain coffee. Cupping your gloved hands around a hot drink midway through your walk will warm your fingers while the hot drink provides its own sort of comfort. Some nuts and dried fruit tucked into your coat pocket can round out your midwalk snack and send you home in good spirits.

have discovered a natural, easy way to maintain fitness through the benefits of walking. Here's how:

Brisk walking is good for the heart and lungs. It improves circulation, strengthens the heart, and increases lung capacity. If you walk at a brisk pace, you will cover about 4 miles in one hour.

Walking helps keep weight down. Walking one mile at a brisk pace burns up about 100 calories in a person of average weight. An hour of walking at a moderate pace (3 miles per hour) can burn between 250 and 400 calories depending on your body weight.

Bone density improves as you walk. This makes walking a good preventive activity for those at risk for osteoporosis.

Walking reduces stress and acts as a natural tranquilizer. It's cheaper than pills and has no unwanted side effects. You'll also find you sleep better because you're more relaxed.

Walking is easy on joints and rarely causes injury. It can be the exercise of choice for those suffering from back problems, arthritis, or old athletic injuries.

To make your walking program successful and fun, the almanac provides you with a walking tip for every month and a sample log page for January. Use this log page as a model for your own walker's diary, and write to the *Prevention* Walking Club, 33 East Minor Street, Emmaus, PA 18098, for more information on walking. Happy Walking!

AT HOME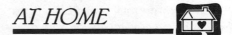

HOME INSURANCE — RIGHT POLICY, RIGHT COVERAGE

January is a good time to take inventory, a good time to review all those personal decisions you've made that serve to keep your life in order. It is a good month to review your finances in anticipation of tax time, to review your will (or make one if you haven't already done so), and to review your insurance policies.

Like most people, when you bought your home insurance policy, you probably chose your options carefully, bought the policy, and put it away with other important papers for safekeeping. If you haven't changed policies recently or had something stolen or damaged, then you may no longer be familiar with your policy, and you may not be certain that it's providing you with the best coverage for your needs. For peace of mind you may want to dig out that policy and review it yourself or with your broker, with these questions in mind:

Is your home insured for at least 80 percent of its replacement cost; that is, the amount it would cost to rebuild it today? You must be insured for at least this amount or your insurance company will not pay for your total repair bills. Don't confuse replacement cost with market value (what you would sell your home for today).

Do you have enough insurance on your personal belongings, valued as used goods? Would you prefer to insure these items for their full replacement value rather than their "depreciated" or actual cash value? Your possessions will be valued as used goods unless you pay for more expensive, full replacement cost insurance. Remember, too, that you should have an inventory of your possessions, including photographs, if possible.

Do you have special "floater" coverage for especially valuable items such as jewelry, antiques, furs, silver, and collections? Most policies put low ceilings on the amount they will pay for loss of these items unless you have paid for special coverage.

If you own your own home, are you insured for all risks (HO-3 and HO-5 policies) or only specified risks (HO-1 and HO-2 policies)? Most experts agree that an HO-3 policy, the right choice for most homeowners, provides adequate coverage at an affordable price. Condominiums and cooperative apartment owners, as well as renters, should buy policies especially designed for these types of homes.

Do you have a realistic amount of liability insurance? Liability insurance is not the place to skimp on coverage. Buy enough liability insurance to protect you against unforeseen injuries to someone else on your property.

Do you have the highest deductible you can afford to pay out-of-pocket if you have a loss? High deductibles, while obligating you to pay smaller claims yourself, also mean lower premiums.

If you plan to shop for new coverage, ask the following three questions about any insurance company you are considering:

1. Do they sell "plain English" policies that are easy to read?

2. Have any of your friends had claims experience with the company, and if so, were they satisfied?

3. Does the insurance company offer any special discounts for senior citizens; for special locks, fire, or theft protection; for having more than one insurance policy with them; or for anything else that might matter to you?

Residential insurance policies offered by almost all companies are very similar. It pays to shop for price. Decide on the type and amount of coverage you need and then compare.

Your Homeowners Policy May Cover More Than You Think

Many people are surprised about the amount of protection that their homeowners policy offers. Here is a list of all the things usually covered under your homeowners policy; be aware that they may vary slightly from state to state and by various policy provisions and dollar amounts of insurance that you purchase.

☞ Your house, including rental units that are part of the building and any attachments to the building, like a garage

☞ Any structures on your grounds that are not attached to your house; for example: a garage, tool shed, pool cabana, or gazebo

☞ The lawns, trees, and shrubs on your grounds

☞ Vacant land that you own or rent, with the exception of farmland

☞ Cemetery plots or burial vaults that you own

☞ Personal possessions that you or members of your household own or use anywhere in the world

☞ The contents of your house and of any structures on your grounds as well as any possessions that guests bring to your house (coverage usually does *not* include the possessions of any tenants living in your house)

☞ Any items friends have lent to you that you are keeping on your property

☞ Your living expenses, if your house is uninhabitable due to damage

☞ Rental payments, if you normally rent part of your house but it is uninhabitable due to damage

☞ Legal responsibility for unauthorized use of your credit cards, checks forged under your name, or counterfeit currency accepted in good faith

☞ Settlements, medical expenses, defense, and court costs involved in claims brought against you for bodily injury to others or damage to the property of others, which occurs on your grounds

"Home Insurance—Right Policy, Right Coverage" reprinted from "Information on Auto and Home Insurance," by the American Association of Retired Persons. Used by permission.

Preheat oven to 350°F. Grate the rind from 1 orange and reserve. Peel and section both oranges and remove the membranes from each segment. Coarsely chop segments. In a 2-quart casserole, heat butter until it foams. Add onions and celery, and cook over low heat until onions are transparent.

Add rice, almonds, and reserved orange rind, and cook, stirring constantly, for several minutes or until rice is golden. Add orange juice and stock, bring to a simmer, and then stir in orange pieces. Cover and bake for 1 hour, or until rice is tender and liquid has been absorbed. Fluff with 2 forks.

4 servings

YOUR JANUARY SHOPPER'S TIP

The best buys in produce this month are carrots, grapefruit, and oranges. Here's a simple but hearty recipe to take advantage of this month's citrus crop.

Rice Pilaf with Oranges

2 navel oranges
2 tablespoons butter or margarine
1 cup minced onions
1 cup minced celery
1 cup brown rice
½ cup chopped or slivered almonds
2 cups orange juice
1 cup chicken stock

YOUR HOME MAINTENANCE CHECKLIST

Throughout the almanac you'll find checklists like the one here, to remind you of tasks that probably need to be done around your house. Use it as a guide to preventive home maintenance or as a supplement to your own list of tasks to make your home run smoothly. For selected, nonroutine chores throughout the year, you'll find tips throughout the almanac offering straightforward advice for doing the job right.

☞ For forced-air heating systems, check and clean air filters monthly throughout the entire heating season.

☞ Vacuum the baseboard elements of an electric heating system monthly during heating season.

☞ Drain your hot water heater to remove sediment and to clean the electric heating element.

☞ Check the operation of your electric or gas hot water heater.

☞ Check your outdoor gutter system after a snowstorm for ice dams, which can force water back under roofing shingles.

Hot Water Tank Know-How

To clear any hot water tank of sediment that accumulates in the bottom of the tank, simply open the draincock at the bottom and draw off a pailful of water.

If you have an electric water heater, you may drain it completely to flush out scale, rust, and sediment. *First, shut off power to the heater at the fuse box or circuit breaker.* Attach a garden hose to the draincock and place the other end in the yard or on a cellar drain. Drain the tank completely; then remove the heating elements. To loosen accumulated mineral deposits, soak the element in a vinegar solution (made from one cup of vinegar to each gallon of water), and scrape off mineral deposits.

For an electric hot water heater, check its operation by manually opening the safety valve (temperature-pressure relief valve) at the top of the tank on the hot water line. Wear gloves and use a bucket to catch the water that will come out. Be sure the valve returns to its original position.

For a gas hot water heater, shut it off and then check the exhaust vent and air shutter openings for dirt and obstructions. Inspect the burner unit for dust and dirt. Clean the burner of lint and dust and vacuum air passages to the burner.

Gutter Ice Dams

Snow that melts from the roof and then refreezes in your gutters can cause backed-up water to soak through your roof sheathing. If left uncorrected, the collected water can eventually damage interior ceilings and walls. On a well-insulated roof, the water from melting snow stays melted as it travels from the roof ridge all the way past the soffit to the gutters. Ice dams are caused by an uneven roof temperature that allows snow to melt at the top of the roof and then refreeze as it reaches the soffit area. You may correct this problem by properly insulating your roof from the ridge board to the soffit or by installing electric heating strips. The heating strips are available in hardware stores and are attached to roof shingles in several rows at the bottom edge of the roof. The strips prevent runoff water from freezing and forming an ice dam as it reaches the soffit.

EVENTS AND FESTIVALS

Each month in this section of the almanac, you'll find a collection of celebrations, jamborees, and festivals. We selected these special events because they're fun and because they form a colorful part of American hometown life. We hope the selection will make you smile or better yet, help you plan a trip to one of the events. But whether you're an armchair traveler or a real one, the collection here is meant to entertain and maybe plant some ideas for your own unique hometown celebration. Happy traveling!

Mummers' New Year's Day Parade
Philadelphia, Pennsylvania
January 1. Parade of spectacularly costumed Mummers, string bands, clowns, and marchers all doing the Mummers' strut. Prizes awarded for costumes, clown acts, and string band performances. A Philadelphia tradition. Information: Philadelphia Convention and Visitors Bureau, 1515 Market Street, Suite 2020, Philadelphia, PA 19102.

The Sewer Bowl
Mahone Bay, Nova Scotia
January 1. An annual offbeat football game held on the traditional American football bowl day. Following a parade through Mahone Bay, the Plungers and the Flushers face each other on the gridiron. Information: Department of Tourism, Box 456, Halifax, Nova Scotia, B3J 2R5.

Grand American Coon Hunt
Orangeburg, South Carolina
Early January. A competitive show of coon hounds from all over the United States and Canada. Spectators and sportsmen await the naming of the Grand American Champion Coon Hound. Information: Chamber of Commerce, Box 328, Orangeburg, SC 29116.

Old Christmas
Prestonsburg, Kentucky
Early January. Held at Jenny Wiley State Resort Park, this one-day event celebrates Christmas in the tradition of the eastern Kentucky mountains. Folk songs, square dancing, storytelling, hot cider, and gingerbread. Information: Kentucky Department of Parks, Capitol Plaza Tower, Frankfort, KY 40601.

John Beargrease Sled Dog Marathon
Duluth, Minnesota
Mid-January. A 500-mile sled dog endurance race held annually in honor of John Beargrease, a Chippewa mail carrier who carried mail by dogsled along the Minnesota North Shore before the turn of the century. Information: Larry Anderson, Executive Director, Box 500, Duluth, MN 55801.

Annual Canadian-American Ben Ames Williams Bonspiel
Belfast, Maine
Mid-January. A three-day event featuring food, drink, and curling competition. Curling is a popular north-country sport similar to shuffleboard. Played on an ice rink, the game features a 42-pound granite stone puck propelled toward a scoring target. Information: Belfast Curling Club, Jeffery Dutch, 8 Cottage Street, Belfast, ME 04915.

National Western Stock Show
Denver, Colorado
Mid-January. The world's largest indoor rodeo and stock show. Information: National Western Stock Show, 1325 East 46th Avenue, Denver, CO 80216.

Aspen/Snowmass Winterskol
Snowmass Village, Colorado
Mid-January. Ski and snowshoe races, ice sculpture contest, hot-air balloon races, fireworks in Aspen. Information: Snowmass Resort Association, Box 5566, Snowmass Village, CO 81615.

Art Deco Festival
Miami, Florida
Mid-January. Celebrate the 1930s with a walking tour or tram ride through the pastel, wedding-cake-style buildings of Miami's art deco district. Vintage car show, costumes, and antiques, all from the 1930s. Entertainment plus the annual Moon-Over-Miami Ball (period costumes required). Information: MDPL, Bin L, Miami Beach, FL 33119.

Cowboy Poetry Gathering
Elko, Nevada
Late January. Poetry readings by contemporary cowboys and cowgirls who continue the cowboy song tradition by composing poetry about their world. Information: Tara McCarty, Box 888, Elko, NV 89801.

Rattlesnake Roundup
Whigham, Georgia
Last Saturday in January. Snake hunt, snake handling, and snake cuisine for the fearless. Arts and crafts, entertainment, and food of all types for the enjoyment of all. Prizes for the most snakes and the largest snake. Information: Whigham Community Club, Myron R. Prevatte, Box 499, Whigham, GA 31797.

FEBRUARY

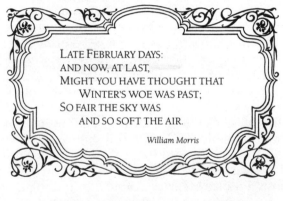

LATE FEBRUARY DAYS:
AND NOW, AT LAST,
MIGHT YOU HAVE THOUGHT THAT
WINTER'S WOE WAS PAST;
SO FAIR THE SKY WAS
AND SO SOFT THE AIR.

William Morris

WHAT'S HAPPENING IN FEBRUARY?

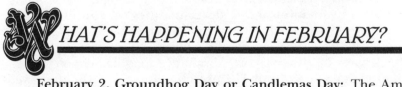

February 2, Groundhog Day or Candlemas Day: The American folk custom of foretelling the weather by observing the behavior of a groundhog dates back to the Christian feast day of Candlemas. Candlemas is an observance of the presentation of the infant Jesus in the temple, 40 days after his birth (a requirement of Jewish law in those times). In early Christian times, this feast day was celebrated by lighting many candles and by the consecration of all of the candles to be used in the coming church year. The behavior of certain animals on Candlemas was thought to be a reliable prediction of the weather to come. The German version of this folk belief was that the badger predicted the weather on Candlemas.

The transplanted Germans of the New World continued their observation of Candlemas as Groundhog Day. The groundhog, or woodchuck, is a pudgy, burrowing rodent indigenous to the northeastern United States and Canada. Although it hibernates in the winter, it is said to emerge from its burrow on Groundhog Day. If the day is sunny, the groundhog will see its shadow and return to its burrow for another six weeks of cold winter weather. If the day is overcast, the groundhog sees no shadow and remains out of its burrow. This is taken to be a sure sign that winter is almost over.

Nowhere in the United States is the original German observance celebrated with more hoopla than in Punxsutawney, Pennsylvania. On Groundhog Day, the entire town of Punxsutawney turns out to watch for Punxsutawney Phil, the town pet groundhog who lives in special quarters adjacent to the Punxsutawney Public Library. By February, Phil has been asleep for over four months in a deluxe burrow provided by the Punxsutawney Groundhog Club, a 101-year-old service club dedicated to keeping alive the fun and spirit of Groundhog Day. Punxsutawney Phil always makes his annual winter forecast from the top of Gobbler's Knob, a hill outside of town that's connected to Phil's winter burrow by a secret labyrinth of tunnels known only to Phil himself. After Phil's annual winter forecast, the Groundhog Club hosts a festive breakfast for all Groundhog Day celebrants. For more information about Punxsutawney's Groundhog Day Celebration, write to the Punxsutawney Groundhog Club, 123 South Gilpin Street, Punxsutawney, PA 15767.

February 12, Birthday of Abraham Lincoln: Schoolchildren learn to admire our sixteenth U.S. president as the one who preserved the Union and freed the slaves. What we don't often remember is that he became a great president despite considerable hardship and private suffering. The son of an illiterate Kentucky farmer, Lincoln received no more than a year's formal schooling throughout his entire life. Born into poverty and a hard farming life, he spent his early adulthood in numerous successive careers such as a hired fence maker (called a rail-splitter), a flatboatman on the Mississippi, a storekeeper, a postmaster, and a surveyor. It was not until he had already been elected to the Illinois State Assembly that he began to study law. Despite the fact that he suffered frequently from bouts of depression, he was known for his sense of humor. It's said that, to appease his law partner who objected to the clutter of his desk, he kept an envelope marked, "When you can't find it anywhere else, look into this."

February 14, St. Valentine's Day: St. Valentine had nothing at all to do with love and romance. This Christian martyr was arrested and killed on February 14, A.D. 269, for helping persecuted Christians. It was merely a coincidence that this date was the same as the pagan feast day of Juno, the goddess of women and marriage. The pagan holiday continues, but, since A.D. 269, in the name of a Christian.

February 22, Birthday of George Washington: The schoolchild's story of Washington's cutting down his father's cherry tree was the invention of eighteenth-century author Mason L. Weems. The Weems book, called *Life of Washington,* was actually one of the few books Abraham Lincoln could recall having owned as a child. No doubt Lincoln was inspired by the true exploits of Washington rather than the fictitious ones. Among the inspiring *facts* that we know about Washington is that he served for the duration of the Revolutionary War as commander-in-chief and steadfastly refused to receive any salary for his efforts. We know that his determination and strength of character made him a victor in a war in which his own troops were always underpaid, usually undersupplied, and sometimes at the edge of desertion. George Washington is the only president in our history to receive unanimous election to office. Of the 69 electoral votes, all 69 were cast in his name.

February 29, Leap Day also known as Bachelor's Day: This day, which comes only in years divisible by the number four, is really a day designed to keep the calendar in order. A year is counted as the time it takes the earth to travel around the sun, but the journey really takes 365 days and 6 hours instead of the neat 365 days we assign to a year. The result is that every four years, we have an extra 24 hours (4 × 6 hours) accumulated in the calendar. Leap Day takes care of the extra time and also, according to ancient folk practice, provides an outstanding opportunity for unwed maidens. Folk custom dating back to thirteenth-century Scotland gives any maiden of high or low estate the Leap Day privilege of proposing marriage to the unbetrothed bachelor of her choice. If the bachelor in question declines the honor, he must pay the disappointed lady a Bachelor's Day fine.

February Is Potato Lover's Month

The average American family of four throws away about 20 percent of the nutrients in the potatoes it eats—in the skins that are peeled away to make French fries, mashed potatoes, or potato salad, or are left on the plate after a baked potato is eaten. Over the course of a year, these discarded skins add up to the equivalent of the iron from 500 eggs, the protein of 60 steaks, and the vitamin C from almost 200 glasses of orange juice!

An average-sized, unadorned baked potato contains only 100 calories. Garnish it with a tablespoon of butter or margarine and you've just doubled the calorie count. To enjoy a baked potato as a healthy, low-calorie food, add a dollop of low-fat yogurt or cottage cheese. A tablespoon of either of these adds calcium and protein to your potato at a cost of less than 25 calories.

IN THE GARDEN

THE SEED GAME

February is seed-ordering and seed-starting time for many areas of the country. Yet, despite the lures of the shiny pictures in the seed catalogs, many gardeners wonder, "Why bother?" when it comes to starting from scratch. A roadside garden stand or a local hardware store supplies them with all the seedling selection they think necessary. But to those who start their own seeds, relying on such slim pickings is like using a paint-by-numbers kit instead of creativity and inspiration.

In starting your own seeds, you become a creator instead of a consumer, a player in the seed game instead of a spectator. A world of colors, shapes, textures, sizes, and tastes suddenly becomes yours to play with. As a gardener playing the seed game, you will find that you are free to try new things, free to imagine what *might* be done with your little patch of earth, free to fail at some things, free to figure out what went wrong, and free to succeed in a creation that is yours alone.

Like all real games, the outcome of the seed game is never certain until the event is over. The new pansy variety you accidentally planted in a hot, sunny spot thrives when you know it should wither; the lupines you've seen only in catalogs and never in your neighborhood, shine in a bed where you formerly settled for a ground cover; the new yellow tomato tastes great, but you wonder why you got only two healthy plants out of an entire seed packet; a packet of seeds you discarded appears weeks later in the far corner of your garden, sprouted and growing in a tangled mass.

If you'd like to join the seed game, you should know that the first rule is to relax and have fun. It's not at all mysterious or difficult to play. After you've mastered the fun part, we have more tips to pass on to you. The ideas that follow are sure to increase your score.

Starting Seeds Indoors

Read about your seeds first. Not all seeds are created equal. Some are notoriously difficult to start (even for experienced gardeners), and some are quite easy. Most fall somewhere in the middle. Reading the back of a seed packet does *not* give you a good idea of the difficulty a particular seed represents. Seed packet information is always brief and even misleading in some cases. Spend some time with a book on seed starting before you place your seed order. Two highly usable books that cover this subject are *The New Seed-Starters Handbook* by Nancy Bubel (Rodale Press, 1988) and *Park's*

Success With Seeds by Anne Reilly (George Park Seed Company, 1987).

Lighten up. The best light for starting seeds is sunlight. A sunny windowsill is usually a beginner's choice for seed starting. But if you choose to start your seeds on a windowsill, be prepared for the soil to overheat and dry up frequently due to the sun's heat. Be prepared also for plants that will lean over and grow leggy in one direction as they compete for the available light coming from one side. Unless you enjoy turning your seedlings twice a day and checking them constantly for overheating, a far better bet is to use homemade sunlight from fluorescent lights. By placing your seeds under a pair of flourescent lights (one warm light and one cool light), you have an excellent replica of sunlight without the worry of plants drying out in excessive heat or growing leggy while competing for one-sided light. You can also keep the lights on for 16 to 18 hours a day—an improvement over nature that has been proven to develop stronger seedlings. Keep in mind, too, that some seeds (although certainly not the majority) require *darkness* to begin germination. Keep these seeds in a dark closet and move them to your light bath just after they have begun to sprout.

Purchase or make sterile seed-starting soil mix. Most seeds are vulnerable to soil-borne fungi that can cause them to rot instead of sprout. Young seedlings are susceptible to damping-off (another soil-borne disease), which causes them to wither and die no matter how well you've cared for them. Avoid disappointment by using a starting mix that doesn't contain disease. Use either a commercial, sterile, bagged seed-starting mix, or make your own mix using equal parts milled sphagnum moss and vermiculite. Later, when your seedlings have developed true leaves and are ready for transplanting to larger pots or flats, you can use a mix containing finished compost, leaf mold, and garden soil to meet their need for more nutrients.

Control temperature and humidity. Most seeds will sprout in soil kept in the temperature range of 75° to 90°F. Keep in mind that we're talking about *soil* temperature, not air temperature. You may find that placing your seed flat near a radiator raises soil temperature well over 90°F. Or you may discover that you need a soil cable (a heating device available through garden supply catalogs) to maintain optimum temperature for flats you keep in your unheated basement.

Seeds also germinate best if they are kept in soil that is uniformly moist but not soggy. As you wait for your seedlings to appear, make sure the soil surface does not dry out and crust over. Using a houseplant mister or a recycled plastic spray bottle, apply a water mist to the soil daily. You can also maintain soil moisture in a dry room by placing your flats over an inch of stones resting in ½ inch of water. Any flat pan (such as a cookie sheet) will do.

Homemade Compost Thermometer

For about $10 you can make a compost thermometer that works as well as catalog models costing two or three times as much. Simply purchase an automobile heat gauge (the instrument that tells whether your engine is overheating) at a discount auto-supply store. Attach the heat-sensing thermistor part of the gauge to one end of a broomstick, anchor the wire along the length of the broomstick, and attach the gauge portion to the opposite end. Insert the thermistor end of the broomstick into your compost pile, and you're in business.

Seed-Starter's Guide

Seeds That Need Light to Germinate*

Alyssum
Begonia
Coleus
Columbine
Dill
Fuchsia
Gloxinia
Impatiens
Lettuce
Oriental poppy
Petunia
Salvia
Savory
Shasta daisy
Snapdragon
Strawflower
Yarrow

Seeds That Need Darkness to Germinate†

Bachelor's-button
Borage
Coriander
Delphinium
Fennel
Larkspur
Phlox

Poppy (except oriental varieties)
Statice
Sweet pea
Viola (including pansy)

Seeds That Require Soaking before Sowing

Asparagus
Lupine
Morning glory
Okra
Parsley
Parsnip
Sweet pea

Seeds That Need Cold Treatment to Germinate‡

Allium
Bleeding-heart
Columbine
Daylily
Iris
Lavender
Lily (some species)
Monkshood
Perennial phlox
Primula
Viola (including pansy)

*Seeds that need light to germinate should be sprinkled on the soil surface, misted with water, and exposed to sunlight or fluorescent light without a soil cover.

†If seeds are very fine (as in poppy or viola seeds), sprinkle them on the soil surface, mist the soil with water, and keep the damp flats in a dark closet until germination is evident. For larger seeds, simply make sure the seed is covered with soil to ensure darkness.

‡Cold treatment (called stratification) involves placing the moist, planted flats of seeds in a refrigerator or freezer for a period of time ranging from days to weeks. Seeds break dormancy when they are exposed to room temperature following stratification. The time and temperature of stratification changes with the variety of seed you plant.

Plant seeds at correct depth. With experience in handling seeds, you'll become more adept at judging what depth to plant each type of seed. The conventional gardener's wisdom is to plant seeds at a depth three times their size. In practice, most gardeners never plant seeds deeper than ½ inch. Beginners typically worry over how to plant extremely fine seeds such as carrot, begonia, or snapdragon seeds. An easy way to plant these seeds is to mix them with sand and then scatter the sand/seed mixture over the flat. Following this step, sprinkle a very fine layer of soil mix over the seed layer (unless your seeds require light to germinate) and moisten the soil with a plant mister.

Using these guidelines, you can substantially improve your score in the seed game. And to give you some real insider's tips, we've included a set of specific instructions for those quirky seeds that don't follow the germination norm.

ALMANAC GARDENING CALENDAR

Gardeners in the northernmost zones can do a lot more than sit by the window and wish for spring. It's time to study the seed catalogs and clean up seed-starting supplies; gardeners who take the time to do this now will lose fewer spring seedlings to damping-off. For warm-climate gardeners (Zones 5, 6, and 7), now's the time to plant out cool-season vegetables, such as spinach, cabbage, carrots, and potatoes.

Zone 1

To prevent damping-off, wash seed-starting containers and soak them for 15 minutes in a mixture of one part household bleach to three parts water. Set up grow lights anywhere that is warm enough for plant growth. Start lettuce, spinach and other greens, onions, and leeks indoors. Transplant container-variety tomatoes started in January and reduce night temperature to 50° to 55°F to encourage early flowering.

Favorite Gardener's Wisdom

Ashes scattered around fruit trees on Ash Wednesday will protect trees from insects for the entire year.

Maryland Folk Saying

For perfect spring crops, plant onions, lettuce, and peas on St. Valentine's Day.

North Carolina Folk Saying

Start seeds for petunias, geraniums, carnations, pansies, snapdragons, dahlias, and impatiens under lights or on a very bright windowsill. Also start seeds of perennials such as delphiniums, columbines, lupines, primroses, rudbeckias, and gaillardias. Start tuberous begonias by midmonth under lights or in a frost-free cold frame. Check berry plants and grapes to make sure a protective mulch remains on plants.

Zone 2

Start herbs such as chive, lavender, oregano, peppermint, marjoram, and thyme in 3-inch pots for early spring gifts or bazaar items. Start leeks and onions under lights to plant out early in the spring. Late in the month sow peppers, eggplants, celery, and brassicas under lights. Start seeds of container-variety tomatoes as well as petunias and begonias. Order rhubarb and asparagus roots for early spring planting. Continue harvesting crops wintered in the garden such as carrots and beets. Harvest parsnips before tops start to sprout or they'll be bitter. Cut branches of apple, peach, forsythia, and other spring-flowering woody plants for indoor forcing. Prune fruit trees (except peaches) and grapes this month. If daytime temperatures rise above 40°F for several consecutive days, apply dormant-oil spray to fruit trees. Check berry plants to maintain a winter mulch cover.

Zone 3

By mid- to late February, start brassicas, herbs, and leaf crops in flats. These will go into your cold frame in late March or early April. Toward the end of the month, remove mulch from garden areas where you intend to plant early crops, so the soil may warm up and dry out. Remove mulch from over-wintering spinach and set a cold frame over the patch. The spinach will quickly produce early greens. Late in the month start snapdragons, begonias, impatiens, and petunias indoors under lights. Check perennials for signs of heaving and press exposed crowns back into the soil. Cover with soil or mulch. Cut bagworm cases off evergreens to prevent feeding injury later, and remove and destroy insect egg cases found on fruit trees. Prune fruit trees, bushes, and grape vines. Hold off pruning peaches until just before budswell. If daytime temperatures rise above 40°F for several consecutive days, apply dormant-oil spray to fruit trees.

Zone 4

Early in the month, sow cole crops indoors; these crops can be set outdoors by midmonth in mild areas. Also start pots of basil, marjoram, oregano, and thyme. Later in the month, start seeds of tomatoes, peppers, and eggplants for setting out in about eight weeks. Work manure and compost into your garden as soon as a ball of soil crumbles easily in your hands. Plant new asparagus roots in deeply dug, well-composted beds. Toward the end of the month, begin sowing outdoors early vegetables such as peas, lettuce, spinach, onions, beets, and radishes. Harvest all overwintering root crops before the tops begin to sprout new growth. Start slow-growing annuals such as petunias, snapdragons, coleus, impatiens, and salvias indoors. Root cuttings of coleus, fuchsias, geraniums, and lantanas for spring bedding and container plants. If daytime temperatures rise above 40°F, apply dormant-oil spray to shrubs and trees to protect against scale. Prune deadwood from shade trees (except birches, elms, and maples) and from summer- and fall-blooming shrubs. Before dormancy is broken, prune fruits, nuts, and grapevines. Destroy any insect eggs you find, and place sticky bands on tree trunks to stop female cankerworms.

Zone 5

If hard frost is no longer likely, plant Irish potatoes, onions, and cabbage outside by midmonth. Also direct-seed spinach, beets, endive, salsify, chard, carrots, lettuce, peas, and radishes. Move brassicas and hardy herbs to the cold frame and water regularly with fish emulsion. Turn compost heap and add manure to rot for summer and fall use. Indoors, sow peppers, eggplants,

tender herbs, and early tomatoes. Set out new shrubs, vines, and trees. Propagate stem cuttings of ornamental shrubs by planting the cuttings in a partially shaded bed at about the time of the last frost. Prune and mulch summer- and fall-blooming shrubs, but wait to trim those that flower in the spring. Severely prune bush roses as soon as they show signs of growth. Right after last frost, set out pansies, dianthus, and other hardy annuals. Indoors start salvias, marigolds, strawflowers, and calendulas. Start new plants of impatiens and coleus from cuttings. Prune peaches, plums, nectarines, and apples around midmonth but before budswell. Follow up with dormant-oil spray. Clean strawberry beds of weeds and unwanted runners. Fertilize strawberries with compost, cottonseed meal, or rotted manure.

Zone 6

Direct-seed mustard, spinach, carrots, peas, collards, beets, turnips, leaf lettuce, radishes, brussels sprouts, and sorrel. Transplant or direct-seed all but the most cold-sensitive herbs. If you haven't already done so, put in onion sets, chives, shallots, garlic, and leeks. Plant asparagus roots, rhubarb, and horseradish. Pull back mulches and prepare soil for warm-season vegetables such as tomatoes, peppers, and eggplants. At midmonth begin direct-seeding beans, tomatoes, and corn. Plant vine crops after all danger of frost is past. Bed sweet potatoes in a cold frame or indoors to produce sprouts for April planting. At the end of the month plant buckwheat as a green manure on new garden areas. Fertilize ornamentals with compost, rock fertilizer, and bonemeal to stimulate vigorous root growth. Plant glads, calla lilies, dahlias, cannas, caladiums, ageratums, alyssum, sweet Williams, portulacas, salvias, marigolds, snapdragons, and petunias. Prune, fertilize, and mulch roses by midmonth. Plant new roses as well as bare-rooted shrubs and trees. Prune fruit and nut trees, vines, and bush fruits before budswell. Plant muscadines, figs, raspberries, and blackberries.

Zone 7

Early in the month, dig out all parsnips, leeks, beets, and carrots wintering in the ground. In the northern tier of this zone, continue to plant cool-weather crops such as carrots, beets, spinach, chard, radishes, broccoli, early cabbage, and Asian greens. In the southern tier, set out tomatoes, peppers, and eggplants. Also in the southern tier, begin planting blocks of corn and beans after the middle of the month. Plant onions from sets or seeds and plant red or white potatoes. Bed sweet potatoes and cover asparagus beds with 6 inches of manure to keep down weeds and make thick stalks next year. At midmonth start sowing beans, tomatoes, and corn outdoors. Early in the month, prune roses and manure all ornamentals except camellias, rhododendrons, and azaleas, which should be mulched with acidic peat, bark, or leaves. Plant glads, dahlias, cannas, tuberous begonias, sternbergias, colchicums, and amaryllises. Fertilize these with bonemeal and finished compost. Early in the month plant roses. Sow flats of petunias, alyssum, gloriosa daisies, coreopsis, and impatiens. Put in plants of petunias, salvias, pinks, snapdragons, four-o'clocks, verbenas, and wax begonias. Direct-seed California poppies, nasturtiums, cosmos, and forget-me-nots. This is the last month for transplanting trees, strawberries, cane crops, and grapes. In the southern tier, try growing strawberries as annuals. Set out these plants now, and till them under for warm-weather crops when berry production declines. Before budbreak, treat peaches with lime-sulfur spray to combat peach leaf curl. Treat orchards heavily with manure and rock phosphate to promote spring growth.

IN GOOD HEALTH

HOW HEART SMART ARE YOU?

February is National Heart Month. As North Americans, we're all accustomed to being inundated almost daily with information on heart disease. After all, it is the leading cause of death in the United States, outdistancing cancer by a ratio of more than 1.5 to 1. If you're in good health now, it's easy to assume that heart disease is someone else's problem and not something you need to know about. Nothing could be further from the truth. Armed with knowledge while you're still healthy, you can fight heart disease using the very best strategy—prevention. Do you have a healthy heart now? Count your lucky stars and resolve to keep it that way. For a quick course in heart disease prevention, take the "Heart Smart Quiz," and then, just for fun, test a friend or loved one. Heart disease prevention is for everyone.

Heart Smart Quiz

1. The three most important heart disease risk factors that you can do something about are high blood pressure, smoking, and elevated blood cholesterol.　T or F

2. A heart attack or stroke is often the first symptom of high blood pressure and/or elevated blood cholesterol.　T or F

3. People with high blood pressure are generally nervous and tense people.　T or F

4. A blood pressure of 140/90 or more is generally considered to be high.　T or F

5. High blood pressure is even more of a problem among blacks than it is among whites.　T or F

6. It is only a scientific theory that elevated blood cholesterol is related to heart disease.　T or F

7. Dietary cholesterol is found only in animal foods.　T or F

8. The most effective dietary way to lower the level of your blood cholesterol is to eat less cholesterol. T or F

9. A food product in your grocery store that is labeled "no cholesterol" is a safe choice for people with elevated cholesterol levels. T or F

10. Cigarette smoking by itself will increase your risk of heart attack. T or F

11. In addition to the large number of cancer and heart disease deaths that result from smoking, more than 90 percent of all emphysema deaths are due to smoking. T or F

12. People who quit smoking reduce their chances of developing heart disease.   T or F

13. Heart disease is the number two killer of women in the United States.   T or F

14. Physical inactivity is related to heart disease.   T or F

Answers to Heart Smart Quiz

1. *True.* Though there are other risk factors that you cannot change, such as family history and age, the three major risk factors that you can change are high blood pressure, smoking, and elevated blood cholesterol. Someone who has all three of these risk factors is about eight times more likely to develop heart disease than someone who has none of them.

2. *True.* A person with high blood pressure or elevated blood cholesterol may feel fine and look great; there are often no signs at all that might signal these conditions until a heart attack or stroke occurs. To find out whether you have elevated blood cholesterol or high blood pressure, you should be tested by a doctor, nurse, or other qualified health professional. The blood cholesterol test currently requires a laboratory analysis of a sample of your blood.

3. *False.* High blood pressure does not mean that a person is nervous or tense. It means that the blood flowing through your body is pressing against your artery walls too strongly. Calm and relaxed people can have high blood pressure.

4. *True.* The higher your blood pressure is, the higher your risk of developing heart disease or having a stroke. Blood pressure that is 140/90 or higher (either number) should be treated and controlled. If you have high blood pressure, follow your doctor's advice: Keep your weight down to normal. Decrease your consumption of sodium—not only table salt, but also foods with a high sodium content, such as some snack and overly processed foods. Remember to take all physician-prescribed blood pressure medication exactly as directed.

5. *True.* While high blood pressure affects more than 28 out of every 100 white adults, it affects more than 38 out of every 100 black adults. Also, high blood pressure is generally more severe among blacks than whites.

6. *False.* Scientific studies have shown that people with high blood cholesterol are more likely to develop heart disease than people with lower levels of blood cholesterol. People with a blood cholesterol level over 265 mg/dl (milligrams per deciliter of blood) may have four times

greater the risk of developing heart disease than those with a level of 190 mg/dl or lower. Scientific studies have also shown that people who reduce their elevated blood cholesterol reduce their risk of having a heart attack.

7. *True.* Dietary cholesterol is never found in foods from plants. All meat, poultry, fish, and butter fat contain cholesterol; the richest sources are liver, brain, kidney, and egg yolks.

8. *False.* Reducing the amount of cholesterol in your diet is clearly important; however, eating less saturated fat *along with* less cholesterol is the most effective dietary means of lowering your blood cholesterol levels. Saturated fats are found in meats, whole milk or cream dairy products, butter, and some cooking fats like shortening; this type of fat causes an elevation in blood cholesterol. To reduce your consumption of saturated fat, you should choose lean meats, poultry, or fish; trim excess fat off meats before cooking; broil, bake, or boil rather than fry; avoid butter and use skim milk and low-fat dairy products.

9. *False.* A product, such as a commercially prepared cake, may contain no cholesterol and still be high in saturated fats, which raise your blood cholesterol. Commercial bakery products containing coconut oil or heavily hydrogenated vegetable oil are high in saturated fats and will cause elevated cholesterol even though the products themselves contain no cholesterol. As you shop, be sure to check labels for a list of the amounts of saturated and polyunsaturated fat contained in the food product. Choose the product that contains more polyunsaturated fat (from safflower, sunflower, corn, or soybean oils) than saturated fat (from coconut, palm, or hydrogenated vegetable oils). Remember, too, that all fats are a rich source of calories. If you are overweight, it is desirable to consume fewer calories and less fat of all kinds.

10. *True.* Smoking is definitely a strong risk factor for heart disease. The heart disease death rate among smokers is 70 percent greater than that of nonsmokers. Heavy smokers are at even greater risk, and those smokers with elevated blood cholesterol or high blood pressure increase their chances of heart disease dramatically.

11. *True.* Emphysema, a lung disease that makes breathing difficult and often leads to death, would be almost eliminated if people did not smoke.

12. *True.* Absolutely. Smokers can and do reduce their risk of heart disease and early death when they quit smoking. In one major study, cigarette smokers who quit smoking reduced their risk of heart disease by more than 50 percent compared to the risk of those who continued to smoke.

13. *False.* It is the number one killer. Of the 750,000 Americans who die each year of heart disease, 350,000 of them are women.

14. *True.* People who are inactive tend to have more heart disease than people who exercise. Regular brisk and sustained exercise improves overall conditioning, helps to reduce blood pressure, aids in weight loss, and, in some people, helps reduce blood cholesterol. In addition, there are reports which suggest that smokers who exercise are more likely to give up smoking. As an added bonus, regular aerobic exercise can improve the way that you look and feel.

The "Heart Smart Quiz" is reprinted, by permission, from "Test Your Healthy Heart IQ," a publication of the National Heart, Lung, and Blood Institute.

"Select" Leaner Beef for a Healthier Heart

Thanks to the efforts of Public Voice for Food and Health Policy, a consumer organization in Washington, D.C., the lowest-fat cuts of beef are now labeled "select." Before this consumer watchdog organization got into the act, the cuts of beef lowest in fat had the unimaginative label, "good." To consumers this just doesn't have the appeal of the labels "prime" and "choice," which the U.S. Department of Agriculture attaches to fattier cuts of beef. Now you should, for your heart's sake, choose "select."

LOOK MA, NO CAVITIES!

February is National Children's Dental Health Month. Many of us remember the TV commercial featuring a cute kid with a big, white smile shouting joyfully after a dental checkup, "Look Ma, no cavities!"

It was a familiar advertising slogan that helped sell a popular fluoride-containing toothpaste. But it was more than that. It also marked the beginning of a new age in dentistry —a time when we began to understand what caused tooth decay and what we could do about it.

Fluoride, the Beginning of Preventive Dentistry

The connection between cavities and fluoride was actually first made way back in 1901 when a Colorado Springs dentist, Dr. Frederick McKay, noticed that something was staining his patients' teeth but also seemed to be making them stronger. Researchers soon figured out that this staining and the resistance to decay was due to the high concentration of naturally occurring fluoride in the city's drinking water. They also discovered that a much smaller amount of fluoride added to water would make teeth just as decay-resistant without staining them. Despite these early discoveries, it wasn't until the 1950s and 1960s that cities around the country began adding fluoride to their water. By the 1970s, the incidence of tooth decay in American schoolchildren had dropped by one-third.

Until the early 1970s researchers believed that fluoride's sole contribution to dental health was in strengthening children's teeth as they were developing. They now know that fluoride does more. It also speeds the regrowth of tooth enamel after it's been damaged by acids in the mouth, and it inhibits the chemical change that turns sugars remaining in the mouth after eating into decay-causing acids.

New Tools for Prevention

Fluoridation of drinking water and fluoride toothpastes are staple items in modern dentistry. But they're hardly the only innovations. Here's a rundown of some of the others.

Sealants for Children

In 1984 the National Institute of Dental Research in Bethesda, Maryland, advised that sealants be used on all children to prevent tooth decay. Sealants are clear or shaded plastic compounds, similar to some composites that are now used to fill cavities. They are painted on healthy back teeth to seal bacteria out and "starve" any bacteria that are already on those teeth. Not all dentists approve sealants, though. Perhaps future sealants will be more durable, but those used now soften and must be reapplied after a few years. Some of them also shrink when they harden, creating tiny pockets at the gumline that invite bacteria.

Calcium Phosphate Solutions

In the mid-1980s, American Dental Association (ADA) scientists developed a process that makes teeth more reactive to fluoride and therefore more resistant to cavities. They found that a calcium phosphate solution can bind fluoride to tooth enamel so that saliva has a harder time dissolving it. Teeth can be treated with this natural mineral solution simply by using a special toothpaste, mouthwash, or gel. The ADA is finishing up a three-year study so that it can get Food and Drug Administration approval for its widespread use.

Plaque Fighters

Plaque, the most dreaded of all dental bad guys, is the collective name given to the more than 300 different kinds of bacteria that populate even the cleanest mouth. Plaque is natural and unavoidable, and when kept in balance it does little harm. But when there's a population explosion, the friendly bacteria that make up a portion of this plaque are overwhelmed by their nastier cousins. The bad guys creep into crevices between teeth and gums and start infections that lead to gingivitis, a gum disease that hits about three-quarters of all American adults over the age of 35.

Brushing at least once in the morning and then again before bedtime for a minimum of 3 minutes each time, and flossing between teeth once a day, is the best way to keep mouth bacteria in check; in addition, there are now new products to help you control plaque. Toothpastes and mouthwashes that contain essential oils, pyrophosphates, baking soda, and peroxide have been shown in tests to live up to their plaque-fighting claim. But these products are not substitutes for brushing and flossing because they do not reach bacteria hiding under the gums.

New Electric Toothbrush

A new type of electric toothbrush may also help you keep that plaque in check. It's called InterPlak, and in one clinical study, this new instrument removed 98.2 percent of plaque from tooth surfaces, versus 48.6 percent for hand brushing. This new toothbrushing device may be of particular help to people who wear braces, because braces make thorough cleaning of the teeth extremely difficult.

How does InterPlak achieve such good results? It has two rows of bristle tufts that are positioned to follow the gum line. Each tuft of bristles rotates in the opposite direction from adjacent tufts and reverses direction 46 times a second. A study at Indiana University showed that this motion gives a thorough cleaning to tooth surfaces and even cleans between the teeth and below the gumline without damage to tooth surfaces. InterPlak is accepted by the American Dental Association. Acceptance by the ADA indicates that the association has reviewed the clinical trial reports of this product and is convinced that the claims of safety and effectiveness made by the product's manufacturer are essentially correct.

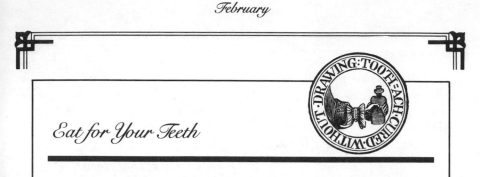

Eat for Your Teeth

There's no magic combination of nutrients that will give you strong, healthy teeth and gums, but most experts agree that a healthy, well-balanced diet helps protect your beautiful smile. What *can* affect the health of your mouth, however, are the sugars and carbohydrates that mouth bacteria convert to tooth-destroying acid. By avoiding sweets, you starve these bacterial colonies and save your teeth. That's why dentists warn against eating too many sweets. But there's more you should know. For instance:

All sugars are the same. The bacteria in your mouth don't discriminate between the refined sugar in a candy bar and the fructose in an orange. That doesn't mean you should give up the fruit that's part of a well-balanced diet. But if you brush and floss your teeth after a chocolate bar, brush and floss them after an orange, too.

Sticky foods cause trouble. Foods like raisins, dried fruits, and even honey stick to the teeth and may even be more harmful than refined sugars. Limit them and brush and floss after eating.

You should limit the amount and frequency of refined carbohydrates in your diet. Pay particular attention to frequency. If you munch on sugary foods all day, your mouth is under constant attack by acid. If you're going to eat sweets, it's better to eat them all at once and then brush your teeth.

You should beware the hidden sugar. It lurks in everything from ketchup to cough syrup. Be especially wary of foods you keep in your mouth for a long time, such as mints and cough drops. The sugar barrage can lead to cavities.

Walking Tip for February

If you find that snowy weather works against your walking schedule, plan to take your walks this month in a shopping mall or museum or even in a gymnasium or indoor tennis court. Any large enclosed space will do. Why not start or join a mall-walking club? You may find some like-minded walkers by contacting the manager of a local shopping mall and requesting space on its community bulletin board.

AT HOME

PREPARING YOUR HOME FOR RESALE

By the end of February, some homeowners begin looking forward to the coming spring season as a prime time to sell their home. If you plan to sell, early February is a good time to come up with a plan of action, because selling a home involves a lot more than putting up a "For Sale" sign and contacting a real estate agent. If you want to sell your home as quickly as possible at *your* price, you'll have to "dress your house for success," both inside and out.

Begin by taking a tour of your property, looking at it critically through the eyes of a prospective buyer. Make a list of repairs that need to be made. Also, look for opportunities to improve the intangible qualities of your house, such as its warmth and spaciousness.

If your home is in fairly good shape to begin with, making it look its best need not be costly or time-consuming. Here's a list of easy fix-up ideas from Valli Swerdlow, real estate consultant and author of the booklet, *Dress Your House for Success.* They will cost you little and help you a lot when it's time to

negotiate with a buyer. If you schedule these changes now, you can have your home in prime shape for the spring buying season.

Lawn and Garden

☞ Remove dead or ailing bushes; prune and water the rest to give them all a healthy look.

☞ Remove garden tools, hoses, toys, bicycles, garbage cans, pet excrement, and debris from the yard.

☞ Mow and rake your lawn regularly to give it a trim look.

☞ Remove distracting lawn objects, such as religious figurines, animal statues, and plastic flowers. But leave the lawn chairs, picnic table, and grill—they'll help prospective buyers to imagine themselves relaxing and entertaining on your property.

Siding

☞ Hose down dirty siding.

☞ Make sure that all painted surfaces are free of mold and mildew. Pay special attention to the southern exposure, under the eaves, and areas behind shrubs, which tend to weather and discolor faster than other areas.

☞ Repaint worn or peeling paint. Use light, neutral colors; they are the least likely to cause offense. If your house is small, painting it all a single color will make it look larger.

☞ Make sure your house number is clearly visible.

Windows

☞ Clean windows until they sparkle.

☞ Check that awnings and shutters are properly hung and that they have no holes, rips, or missing parts.

☞ Repair cracked panes and torn screens.

☞ For a neat appearance, keep window sashes, storm windows, and screens at the same position (preferably closed), especially in the front of the house.

☞ Window treatments should appear uniform from the exterior.

The backs of shades or the linings of drapes look best when they are all the same color, such as white or off-white.

☞ In the evening, turn on at least one light in each front room.

☞ Brightly colored lamps, huge ornate statues, multicolored plastic flower arrangements, and bowling trophies are all distractions that may prevent prospective buyers from seeing your home as a whole. Remove them.

Interior Walls

☞ Paint walls and moldings a neutral color, such as white or beige. If you choose to paper your walls, choose solid-colored wallpaper. Mini-prints and small geometrics are your next-best bet.

☞ Tie adjacent rooms together visually with color-coordinated accessories.

☞ Remove all political and religious pictures, posters, and emblems from your walls.

☞ Clean surfaces of fingerprints and dirt, especially around front doorways and entranceways, daily.

Fireplaces

☞ Remove and clean ashes from your fireplace when it is not in use.

☞ Check fireplace screens for holes and glass panes for cracks.

☞ During the cold winter months, set a crackling fire ablaze in your fireplace: Buyers will respond positively to the glow, the smell, and the sounds of the fire. Brighten up a nonworking fireplace with decorative fans of paper or brass.

Bathrooms

☞ Inspect tiled walls for missing pieces and loose grout.

☞ Update your wall hardware.

☞ If your old shower curtain is moldy, buy a new one.

☞ Check caulking around the tubs and sinks to be sure it's tight.

☞ Repair dripping faucets.

☞ Check for proper flushing of toilets, and make sure handles and seats are securely fastened. Keep toilet seats closed on open-house days.

☞ Display at least one new fluffy bath towel, fingertip towel, and washcloth in white or beige.

Kitchen

☞ Ventilate the kitchen to get rid of any cooking odors.

☞ Unclutter your kitchen by storing small appliances such as blenders, food processors, electric mixers, and coffee grinders in a cabinet. It's fine to leave the basics out, such as a toaster, coffeepot, and can opener.

☞ Clean all appliances—especially the oven.

More Tips from the Experts

A panel of real estate agents and home appraisers gathered together by *Practical Homeowner* magazine agreed that quality materials, products, and craftsmanship are important to home buyers today. "While family size is decreasing and houses could be getting smaller, the demand for quality remains," said appraiser Mary Jo Thomas of Fort Worth, Texas. "Quality materials and workmanship are important."

Realtor Judy Nice of Kirkland, Washington, agreed. "People buying homes today are more knowledgeable and sophisticated," she said. "They're looking to see that repairs and remodeling work have been done correctly. Prospective buyers don't hesitate to bring in experts for inspection."

On the other hand, the experts stressed that overimprovement is one of the biggest pitfalls to renovation. If you spend too much on your new kitchen or deck, you'll have more money invested in your home than others in your neighborhood are worth. The result is that you'll have trouble getting your price at the time of sale. "The rule of thumb," explained appraiser Elaine Kirsch of Pittsburgh, Pennsylvania, "is that someone will compensate you for up to 50 percent of your *overimprovement.*"

Even if it's not an overimprovement, the remodeling project that pays back 100 percent or more of its cost at resale is the exception, not the rule. So if you're planning to sell very soon, be conservative. Unless your home has some eyesore in need of remedy, you'll fare best financially by doing as little renovating as possible. "You get more money back out of a bucket of paint than anything else," said Edith Duncan, an appraiser in Florida. "Stick to things you can do inexpensively, especially if you can use your own labor. Make sure your yard is mowed and the house is clean, and clear out the clutter."

Did You Know? Curious Home Facts

☛ Your hot, not cold, water pipes may be the first ones to freeze in winter. Previously heated water, left to cool in supply pipes, has less air in it than cold water. Since air takes longer to freeze than water, the water with less air in it freezes first.

☛ Lightning can and often does strike twice in the same place. Lightning seeks the path of least resistance. And high buildings, trees, and metal towers are less resistant to electric current than is air.

☛ Portland cement doesn't come from a place named Portland. Portland cement is named for its color similarity to building stone naturally found on the Isle of Portland, off the coast of England.

☛ In early America, if there were two privies in a row, the one with the cut-out in the shape of a sun was for men, and the one with a crescent moon was for women.

☛ Dry rot is actually a misnomer for a type of wood rot that requires moisture to damage wood. If you find dry rot on your house exterior, your first job is to find out where the moisture is coming from.

☛ A septic system works through the efforts of millions of soil-dwelling bacteria. These bacteria, which break down liquid household wastes into plant-supporting nutrients, can be accidentally destroyed by paint thinners, pesticides, motor oil, and other foreign substances flushed down household drains.

Frost in the Attic

Condensation forms in an unheated attic when humidity migrating from warm living spaces meets cold surfaces in the attic. During the winter this condensation may even appear as frost. It's not a situation to ignore, because attic condensation can, over the years, rot wood and harm insulation. A simple solution is to provide more ventilation to your attic. If you have this problem now, make plans to add louvers or vents to your attic during the upcoming spring. In the meantime, open an attic window just a crack for the remainder of the heating season. You'll lose a small amount of household heat, but you'll save your attic from further damage.

Look Before You Leap

Consult a real estate agent or appraiser in your area *before* you make a costly home improvement. Ask what buyers in your home's price range are looking for. This type of research will enable you to make an informed decision on spending a large sum to improve your home. Even if your agent thinks your improvement is a wise investment, you may find that you cannot recoup 100 percent of the cost of the improvement when you sell your home. You should consider whether you are willing to forgo a complete compensation for your project at resale. You may decide that part of your payback for an improvement will come in the pleasure and convenience you enjoy while living in your remodeled home.

GET THE MOST FROM YOUR VCR

By 1990, every household with a television will have a VCR in it, according to the Electronics Industry Association. If you're part of one of the majority of households that already has a VCR, you'll find the following tips will help you get the most out of your equipment.

Buy the grade of tape that is appropriate for your use. Video stores usually carry several different grades of blank videotape. The standard grade of tape is appropriate for tapes that you use and tape over frequently. If you're only going to tape the evening news and reuse the tape another night for the same or other shows, then you don't need to spend extra for a higher grade of tape. High-grade tapes are worth the extra cost if you are taping something you plan to keep, such as your daughter's wedding or a concert by your favorite guitarist.

Use the lock-out tab to keep permanent tapes safe from loss. Every videotape has a special tab that, once removed, prevents any further recording on the tape.

Quick Tips for Little Problems

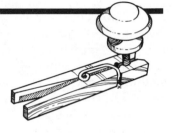

Painting Wooden Knobs

To paint a wooden drawer knob, insert a wood screw into the back of the knob, then clasp the screw near the head with a common clothespin. The clothespin will serve to hold the knob upright for painting and drying.

Save Your Thumb

The reason it hurts so much when you hit your thumb with a hammer is that your thumbnail is inflexible and has very little padding. If you get into the habit of holding nails between your middle and index fingers (with the palm of your hand up), you'll be in a lot less pain should your hammer miss the nail head.

Cork Aid for Wood Screws

When a screw won't tighten because the hole has worn and enlarged, cut some cork from a wine bottle and pack this into the screw hole (maybe using glue to hold the cork in place). The cork does an excellent job of holding the screw's threads.

Mixing Paint

You can mix paint quickly with a paddle mixer attachment for an electric drill. This method is a great time-saver, but it can be messy. To avoid splatter problems, place the paint can in a paper shopping bag while mixing. The splattered paint stays in the bag, and once mixing is complete, you can simply throw the bag away.

Freezer Checkup

Winter is the ideal time to check the operation of your freezer and to remove frost accumulation in manual-defrost models. You can wrap up your frozen food in towels or newspapers and store it temporarily in a cold porch or unheated garage. You can check your freezer temperature with an ordinary weather thermometer. The proper temperature for a freezer is 0°F, plus or minus two degrees. Freezers built into refrigerators may register a bit warmer.

Remove this tab immediately after you've taped something valuable. Later you won't accidentally tape something else over your original. If you should change your mind later and wish to reuse your permanent tape, simply cover the tab hole with adhesive tape and you can tape over your old recording.

Keep tapes in their dust jackets to keep your recordings in the best possible condition. Dirt and dust from the air can accumulate on the tape and get between the tape and the recorder heads. This can cause picture distortion and eventual damage to the heads.

Discard tapes after about 200 recording/playback cycles. Tapes used over and over again can shed some of their oxide coating and cause damage to the video head assembly.

YOUR FEBRUARY SHOPPER'S TIP

The best buys in produce this month are carrots, grapefruit, peas, and oranges. This February, warm hearts as well as your kitchen by baking a carrot and apple casserole, a tasty side dish loaded with vitamin A.

Baked Carrot and Apple Casserole

2 cups sliced carrots
5 apples, cut into ¼-inch slices
2 tablespoons whole wheat flour
4 tablespoons honey
3 tablespoons butter*
¾ cup orange juice

Preheat oven to 350°F. Steam carrots for 12 minutes. Put half the apples in a shallow 1-quart baking dish and cover them with half the carrots. Sprinkle 1 tablespoon of flour over carrots and apples; then drizzle 2 tablespoons of honey over flour. Dot with 1½ tablespoons of butter. Repeat layers. Pour orange juice over entire casserole and bake for 40 to 45 minutes. Serve hot.

6 servings

*The 3 tablespoons of butter in this recipe give the casserole a fat content of 27 percent—a figure within the American Heart Association target guidelines of 30 percent fat consumption for your overall diet. To further reduce the fat content of this dish and to totally eliminate the cholesterol, substitute 3 tablespoons of diet margarine for the butter. This gives the casserole a fat content of 17 percent and a cholesterol count of zero.

YOUR HOME MAINTENANCE CHECKLIST

☛ Vacuum the baseboard elements of an electric heating system monthly during heating season.

☛ Check your freezer for ice buildup on manual-defrost models and defrost when ice is ¼-inch thick.

☛ Check your freezer temperature with a household thermometer.

☛ Check and clean refrigerator.

Fire Drill

Home fire extinguishers are among those things we hang in a handy closet and hope we never have to use. Conveniently forgotten, we assume that they'll just be there for us when things go wrong. Instead of making that all-too-human assumption, form a habit of checking your fire extinguishers every six months. Check the indicator on the pressure gauge to be sure the extinguisher is charged. Be sure the lock pin is firmly in place and intact. Check the discharge nozzle to be sure it's clear, and check the extinguisher body for dents, scratches, and corrosion. *Do not test a fire extinguisher by discharging it. Loss of pressure will result.*

And while fire safety is on your mind, test your smoke alarms by holding a lit match or candle three inches away from each unit. To reduce alarm time during the test, blow into the unit to clear away smoke.

☞ Lubricate garbage disposal oil ports with a drop or two of 20-weight oil.

☞ Clean dust from exhaust hose of your clothes dryer.

☞ Check and clean humidifier.

☞ Check for moisture condensation in attic.

☞ Check your fire extinguishers.

☞ Test your smoke alarms with smoke source.

Dryer Duty

Excess lint buildup in the flexible exhaust pipe of a dryer reduces the efficiency of your appliance and can also become a fire hazard. To clean the exhaust pipe of an electric dryer, simply disconnect the electrical connection, pull the dryer away from the wall, detach the exhaust pipe from the machine, and shake or pull out excess lint. A vacuum cleaner is a handy way to clean the pipe thoroughly. If you have a gas dryer, *before you do anything, turn off the gas at the appliance shutoff valve.* If your gas dryer has a flexible connection (a movable connector between the gas line and your appliance) you can pull the dryer away from the wall and follow the cleaning instructions for electric dryers. If your dryer has an old rigid gas connection, you may not be able to move it away from the wall far enough to detach the exhaust pipe. You will have to rely on a service representative to detach the dryer so that the exhaust may be cleaned.

You may clean the ignition area of a gas dryer by simply removing the grille over the burner area and wiping away lint and dust. Many dryers have an ignition glow bar instead of a pilot light. Because the glow bar is brittle and easily damaged, be careful not to strike it with a vacuum attachment. After cleaning your gas dryer, return it to its normal position, and restore the gas supply at the appliance shutoff valve.

EVENTS AND FESTIVALS

St. Paul Winter Carnival
St. Paul, Minnesota

Early February. The nation's oldest (102 years) winter carnival features the King of the Winds and the Queen of the Snows presiding over speed skating, sleigh rides, hot-air balloon races, ice-sculpting contests, and fireworks. For the not-so-hearty, the carnival also features an indoor fun fair at the St. Paul Civic Center, with ethnic foods, live music, comedy acts, and sporting exhibits. Information: Winter Carnival, 600 NCL Tower, 445 Minnesota Street, St. Paul, MN 55101.

Snowflake Festival Winter Carnival
Lyndonville and Burke, Vermont

Early February. This week-long festival kicks off with a skiers' torchlight parade down Burke Mountain. During the week you'll have a chance to see championship skating exhibitions, snow-sculpture contests, daily ski races, and a dogsled race. As if that weren't enough, you can also go on a sleigh ride, fill up at an old-fashioned pancake breakfast, and dance at the Snowflake Carnival Ball. Festivities end with a final torchlight parade down Shonyo Hill. Information: Bruce James, Lyndon Area Chamber of Commerce, Box 886, Lyndonville, VT 05851.

Wild Game Feed
Kimball, Nebraska

First Saturday in February. How about bear pie or venison stew? If that's too tame, try squirrel pie, barbecued porcupine, breaded raccoon, or rattlesnake stew. Price of admission includes a trip to the salad bar. Information: Chamber of Commerce, 119 East Second Street, Kimball, NE 69145.

Mardi Gras
New Orleans, Louisiana

Early to mid-February (the two weeks preceding Lent). Probably America's oldest and most famous carnival, the Mardi Gras clearly dates back to ancient European carnivals held just prior to Lent (the annual Christian season of fasting and penitence). For two weeks during the festival, fantastic and colorful parades are held through the city of New Orleans, with the floats and costumes provided by private Mardi Gras clubs called "krewes." Those riding the floats toss collectible trinkets and emblems to the crowd. Parades held at night are illuminated by hand-held torches or *flambeaux*. Information: Greater New Orleans Tourist and Conventions Commission, 334 Royal Street, New Orleans, LA 70130.

Gasparilla Pirate Invasion
Tampa, Florida

First week in February. Gasparilla celebrates the life of the infamous pirate José Gaspar, who may have hidden out in Tampa Bay centuries ago. Held in conjuction with the Florida State Fair, the festivities begin with an invasion of 700 "pirates," who sail across Tampa Bay in a real pirate vessel to land at the city docks. Following the ceremonial "surrender" of the city, the pirates join in for the Gasparilla Day Parade. Gasparilla week in Tampa includes various private and public events and always concludes with a night parade in the Latin quarters of the city. Information: Gasparilla, P.O. Box 1514, Tampa, FL 33601.

Yuma Square and Round Dance Festival
Yuma, Arizona

Second weekend in February. Put your glad rags on for a dancing jamboree. The Yuma Dance Festival appeals to those dance enthusiasts who want to learn new patterns and calls while they stomp it all out with other cloggers and shufflers. This event features well-known callers for square and round dance styles as well as workshops on new dance patterns. Preregistration recommended. Information: Yuma Square and Round Dance Association, P.O. Box 4056, Yuma, AZ 85366–4056, or Yuma Chamber of Commerce, P.O. Box 230, Yuma, AZ 85366.

Gold Rush Days
Wickenburg, Arizona

Mid-February. On opening day of this celebration of the Wild West, the Gold Shirt Gang shoots up the town and hangs the mayor. What follows is a community-wide celebration featuring a three-day rodeo, a parade, a carnival, and gold panning (with visitors keeping any gold they find). An old-fashioned cowboy melodrama is acted out nightly, and visitors may conclude the festivities at the Cowboy Dance featuring country and western music. Information: Chamber of Commerce, Drawer CC, Wickenburg, AZ 85358.

Oregon Shakespeare Festival
Ashland, Oregon

Mid-February through October. This thespian extravaganza is a several-months-long annual festival held in three theaters featuring 11 different plays. Besides Shakespeare, the festival presents outstanding classic and modern plays. Visitors can attend backstage tours, actors' workshops, and lectures at an Exhibit Center. Closet thespians may even try on costumes and hold forth with their favorite lines on a real stage. Information: Oregon Shakespeare Festival, Box 158, Ashland, OR 97520.

Deadwood Winter Carnival
Deadwood, South Dakota

Third weekend in February. Enjoy a winter carnival for the ornery and the stout-hearted. Events include arm wrestling, a tug-of-war, log splitting, and the Ride and Slide Triathlon (cross-country skiing, mountain biking, downhill skiing). Information: Chamber of Commerce, 735 Main Street, Deadwood, SD 57732.

Maple Sugar Days
Terre Haute, Indiana

Last week in February through second week of March. Visit the Prairie Creek Park to watch maple trees tapped for syrup. This 106-acre county park contains over 1,500 sugar maples, all of which are tapped for the winter syrup collection. Visit the sugar cabin where the syrup is made and purchase the real thing. Information: Vigo County Park and Recreation Department, Court House Room 13, Terre Haute, IN 47807.

Almond Blossom Festival
Ripon, California

End of February through the beginning of March. Treat your senses to a three-day celebration of California's largest tree crop. Miss Almond Blossom presides over a festival featuring tours of almond groves and the almond processing plant, a needlework and baked goods sale, hobby show, art show, and antique show. Gourmands will want to taste the results of the annual almond bake-off as well as the smorgasbord, the ham breakfast, and the barbecue. Information: Chamber of Commerce, P.O. Box 327, Ripon, CA 96366.

MARCH

AH, MARCH! WE KNOW THOU ART
KIND-HEARTED, SPITE OF UGLY LOOKS
AND THREATS,
AND, OUT OF SIGHT, ART NURSING
APRIL'S VIOLETS.

Helen Hunt Jackson

WHAT'S HAPPENING IN MARCH?

March 6, Alamo Day: On this day in 1836, following a 13-day siege, some 3,000 Mexicans led by General Santa Anna slaughtered all of the inhabitants of the Alamo, a fort at San Antonio, Texas. Formerly a Franciscan mission, the fort had become a defense post for a garrison of Texans in revolt against the Mexican government. Killed in that legendary battle were two American folk heroes, Davy Crockett and James Bowie. Six weeks later when Sam Houston led Texans to victory over Mexico at the battle of San Jacinto, the battle cry was "Remember the Alamo!"

Early March, Purim: Also known as the Feast of Lots, the exact day of this Jewish celebration varies with the lunar cycle. Purim celebrates the deliverance from death of the Persian Jewish community by the intervention of the Jewish Queen Esther. Thought to have taken place during the fifth century B.C., the massacre of the Jews, who were subject to the Persians, was initiated by Haman, an aide to the Persian King Ahasuerus. Esther, the favorite wife in the King's harem, saved her people by revealing Haman's plot to annihilate the Jews. The word *purim* is derived from the ancient word *pur,* meaning lot or dice. Haman appointed the day of his planned pogrom by the throw of dice or lots. The Feast of Lots celebrates the overthrow of Haman's evil deeds.

March 16, Birthday of James Madison: In addition to serving as the fourth president of the United States, James Madison also wrote and sponsored the first ten amendments to the Constitution, our Bill of Rights. As the president who succeeded Jefferson, he presided over a lively Washington social life with the help of his beautiful and popular wife, Dolley. Later, during the War of 1812, he and Dolley were forced to flee the city while the British burned the Capitol, the president's home, and most of the public buildings.

March 17, St. Patrick's Day: Though the patron saint of Ireland, Patrick himself was English. As a bishop in the fifth century Christian church, Patrick left his home in the Severn Valley of England to bring Ireland into the Christian fold. The wearing of the shamrock commemorates Patrick's use of this plant to demonstrate the Trinity to his new converts.

Mid- to Late March, Passiontide: Passiontide is the last two weeks of Lent (a season of fasting and penitence). Passiontide culminates in the great Christian feast of Easter, a commemoration of Christ's resurrection from the dead. Because Easter is a movable feast in the Christian calendar, the dates of Lent and Passiontide also vary from year to year. Passiontide celebrates the last events in the life of Christ—his triumphal return to Jerusalem, his last meal with friends, his betrayal in the Garden of Gethsemane, and his death by crucifixion.

March 21, the Vernal Equinox: The vernal equinox is the first day of spring for the Northern Hemisphere. On this day the sun is directly over the equator so that night and day are equal in length all over the earth. In the coming spring months the sun moves toward the

Northern Hemisphere until it reaches its northernmost point on the globe, the Tropic of Cancer.

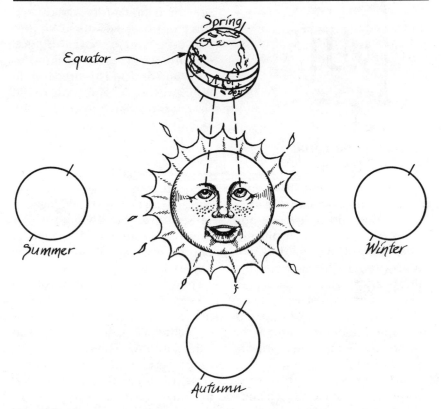

Vernal Equinox

Spring officially begins with the vernal equinox, the day on which the sun crosses over the equator and heads for the Northern Hemisphere.

March 23, Liberty Day: On this day in 1775, Patrick Henry, the famed Virginia orator and delegate to the Continental Congress, gave his memorable speech in favor of arming the Virginia militia for war with Britain. Every schoolchild learns the closing words of his address to the second Virginia revolutionary convention: "I know not what course others may take, but as for me, give me liberty or give me death!"

March Is National Peanut Month

Peanuts are not really nuts; they're members of the legume (bean) family and as such resemble soybeans or peas in their nutritive value. Curiously, peanuts don't grow on the plant in the same way that other beans do. As the peanut plant matures, the ends of its branches root into the earth and the peanuts are formed under the earth at this junction between rooted growing tips and earth.

The typical after-school snack of a peanut butter sandwich and a glass of milk is a sound nutritional choice for a growing child because of the protein in both foods and because the peanut butter is richer in B vitamins and iron than milk.

Adults may enjoy more creative uses for peanuts: as a crunchy and flavorful addition to vegetable casseroles, as a salad topping, or even as a soup topping. A traditional Georgia dish is cream of peanut soup. A simple and pleasant use for peanuts (dry-roasted and unsalted) is to add them to your rice. After you've cooked the rice, add about ¼ cup raw peanuts for every cup of rice. This simple addition gives a pleasant crunch and flavor to an otherwise ordinary rice side dish.

If you own a blender or a food processor, you can easily make your own fresh peanut butter. By making your own, you get a delicious spread with no added salt, sugar, or preservatives. Put 1½ cups of raw or roasted peanuts into your blender or processor (equipped with a metal blade), and process for 1 minute, turning the machine on and off for 10-second spurts. You should end up with a thick paste. Then add oil or boiling water, one tablespoon at a time, to smooth and thin out the butter. Just add a little of either at first, because the heat of the machine will release more oil in the peanuts. Turn the machine on and off again, in 30-second spurts this time, until the butter is smooth and spreadable. This should take about 5 minutes if you're using a blender and about 3 in a processor. For chunky peanut butter, add some whole nuts at the very end and process for 15 to 30 seconds more.

IN THE GARDEN

THE EARLY BIRD GETS THE FIRST TOMATO

March is a time of feverish activity for southern gardeners and of hopeful anticipation for northern ones. While southern gardeners may be setting out such warm-weather crops as cantaloupes and tomatoes or making a final seeding of lettuce and peas, gardeners in the mid-Atlantic region and Northeast may be gazing impatiently out the window at 6 inches of snow newly arrived after a 50°F day.

For cold-region gardeners, the best tonic for this annual fit of March impatience is *season extension,* a collection of techniques that allow gardening to begin before Nature says it's okay. Season extension techniques stretch the growing season on both ends, allowing for earlier spring sowing as well as postfrost harvesting. The crafty use of season extension may allow a northern gardener to sow his first lettuce in early March and a southern gardener to harvest the last of his lettuce in December. Whatever part of the gardening country is yours, you'll find a use for these tech-

niques that rely on optimum use of soil temperature instead of the whims of your local weather.

Soil Temperature: The Key to Early Yields

One gardener who has developed an elegant system for the optimum use of soil temperature is Jeff Ball, author of *Jeff Ball's 60-Minute Garden* (Rodale Press, 1985) and host of the gardening video series, *Yardening* (Kartes Video Communications, 1986). In *National Gardening* magazine, Jeff reports on his technique for extending the growing season by manipulating the soil temperature with row covers and various types of mulch:

The best time to take the garden's temperature is between 6:00 and 8:00 A.M., when it's lowest. If you're using a glass thermometer, remember to shake it down first, as you would a medical thermometer. Then place the thermometer or probe so it's measuring the temperature 4 to 6 inches below the surface.

In the top few inches temperature can vary considerably, but lower down it changes more slowly. Once the soil warms up to about 45°F, it's unlikely to drop again. Keep in mind that even though seeds are in the upper soil, they generally send roots down 5 to 6 inches before their leaves poke up through the surface, making the below-ground temperature the most important.

Thinking about gardening in terms of soil temperatures changed our perspective about planting schedules. Our growing season no longer begins on St. Patrick's Day, or some other calendar date. Instead we get started when the soil temperature in our garden reaches 45° to 50°F and stop not with the first frost, but when the soil temperature falls to 45°F again. We've also found ways to manage the soil temperature to get better results. The critical factor is mulch and knowing how it works. Our choice of mulch materials can raise or lower soil temperatures significantly. Clear plastic film mulches can raise soil temperatures as much as 12°F; black plastic pushes it up only 6°F. Putting a row cover over plastic-mulched soil can raise the temperature even more. Organic mulches, such as straw, have the opposite effect, insulating the soil from the sun, lowering the soil temperature as much as 18°F.

Anywhere from six to eight weeks before the last spring frost, while the ground is still frozen, we lay black plastic mulch over the garden beds and secure it with bricks or rocks. Then we rig clear plastic tunnels over the beds and let them begin to heat up.

When the soil thermometer indicates the temperature has reached 50°F (research shows that growth starts around 45°F, but I like to add in another 5°F as a safety factor), we begin sowing our earliest crops—peas, lettuce, and spinach. Because we've raised the soil temperature, we're able to get a head start of several weeks over other gardeners in our area.

The Three-Part System

To develop your own system of season extenders, you need to be familiar with three different types of simple garden products: soil thermometers, plastic mulches, and floating row covers. These simple products combine to make one powerful system for season extension.

Soil thermometers come in two versions: a glass-encased thermometer that resembles a candy thermometer and a metal-encased device that looks something like a meat thermometer. While they are not common items at a neighborhood variety store, they are frequently offered through garden supply catalogs (see resource list at the end of this article) and well-stocked hardware stores. Using this little tool, you know exactly where you are in your quest for optimum soil temperature.

Plastic mulches are simply sheets of polyethylene in pigmented form (black) and unpigmented form (clear). The material, easily available at garden supply stores, comes on bolts like cloth and is available in a number of thicknesses, with the price per square foot increasing as the material thickness increases. The usefulness of the material is related to thickness, because the thicker material may be used and reused for several garden seasons, while the thinner material tears and shreds easily enough to limit reuse. Black plastic tends to last longer than clear because clear plastic is damaged by the ultraviolet rays in sunlight. Although clear plastic transmits more heat to the soil than black plastic, you can raise your soil temperature with either of these plastics, particularly if you combine them with a row cover. Remember also that organic mulches don't aid in early spring planting. Organic mulches keep the soil cooler than normal (which makes them useful during the hot summer months), and your first job in preparing a bed for an early-season start is to remove last year's organic mulch.

Floating row covers may be of polyethlylene, polypropylene, or polyester. All are lightweight (light enough to be placed directly on the plants without causing damage), transmit sunlight, and allow water to pass through. They are common items in garden supply stores and mail-order garden catalogs and vary in price from about $.50 to $1.00 per square yard. The materials differ mainly in their ability to trap heat and in their durability. The most durable are spun-bonded polyester (Reemay) and microperforated polyethylene film (Visipore). Visipore also ranks near the top in heat retention. Other brand names to look for are Agronet, which provides moderate heat retention with good water penetration, and Argyl P17, which is ultraviolet stabilized.

Your Game Plan

Armed with your choice of season-extending products, you can come up with your own game plan to get a head start on your normal planting season. A typical start to your early-season planting may be to clear a row of your garden six weeks before your normal last frost date. Cover your row with black plastic and then rig a clear plastic tunnel over the works. Use your soil thermometer to monitor the temperature and plant your first peas or lettuce when the soil temperature rises to between 45° and 50°F. As the soil temperature continues to rise in your garden cloche, you can plant a succession of different crops. At some point you will want to remove the clear plastic tunnel and substitute a floating row cover to avoid overheating the young plants and to provide better air circulation. The floating row cover protects against unexpected frosts, retains moderate amounts of heat, and deters insects.

After you've harvested your spring crops from this row, you can

Optimum Soil and Air Temperatures

Crop	Soil Germination Temperature (°F)	Ideal Soil Temperature (°F)	Ideal Daytime Air Temperature (°F)
Beans	65–86	70–80	50–80
Beets	50–85	65–75	40–75
Broccoli	45–85	65–75	40–75
Cabbage	50–85	65–75	40–75
Carrots	60–80	65–75	45–75
Cauliflower	50–85	65–75	45–75
Celery	50–70	60–70	45–75
Chinese cabbage	40–85	60–70	45–75
Corn	55–85	75–85	50–95
Cucumbers	65–85	70–80	60–80
Eggplant	65–85	75–85	65–95
Kale	40–70	60–70	40–75
Kohlrabi	50–85	65–75	40–75
Leeks	40–75	65–75	45–85
Lettuce	40–80	65–75	45–75
Melons	65–85	70–80	60–80
Onions	50–85	65–75	45–85
Parsley	50–85	65–75	45–75
Peas	40–85	65–75	45–75
Peppers	65–85	70–80	65–80
Radishes	40–85	65–75	40–75
Spinach	40–85	60–70	40–75
Squash, summer	65–85	75–85	50–90
Squash, winter	65–85	75–85	50–90
Sweet potatoes	60–85	75–85	65–95
Swiss chard	35–70	60–70	40–75
Tomatoes	65–85	70–80	65–80

SOURCE: Reprinted from *Jeff Ball's 60-Minute Garden* © 1985 by Jeff Ball. Permission granted by Rodale Press, Inc.

easily pull up the old plants in order to plant a row of heat-loving crops. As summer progresses, you can add organic mulch over your original black plastic mulch to reduce soil temperature and keep water requirements minimal. In early fall you may elect to harvest and remove the last of your summer crops, pull back the organic mulch to expose the black plastic, and sow a fall crop on this same row. As the season gets cooler, add your floating row covers and continue harvesting your fall crop well past frost.

To help you become an early-bird gardener, we've included a table of optimum soil temperatures for common garden vegetables. Practiced use of soil temperatures can give you early summer tomatoes or late fall leaf lettuce. Either way, by managing soil temperature you can reap an abundant and tasty harvest.

Quotations by Jeff Ball were adapted from the article "Time and Temperature," with the permission of National Gardening, March 1988. National Gardening is the monthly publication of the National Gardening Association, 180 Flynn Avenue, Burlington, VT 05401.

Mail-Order Sources for Soil Thermometers

A. M. Leonard, Inc.
P.O. Box 816
Piqua, OH 45356

Gardener's Supply Co.
128 Intervale Road
Burlington, VT 05401

Smith & Hawken
25 Corte Madera
Mill Valley, CA 94941

SPRING LAWN CARE GUIDE

March is a great time to assess the current state of your lawn. If your little patch of green is not all you want it to be, here is a ten-step lawn renovation program that will give great results.

1. Clean it up. In the spring rake up leaves, old grass, and winter debris with a leaf rake. You can recycle the accumulated debris in your garden compost pile.

2. Give it a physical. As you're raking, look it over carefully for any signs of problems. Patches of moss indicate low fertility, poor drainage, or not enough sun. A patch of turf that comes up easily as you rake might mean your lawn has white grubs, the larvae of root-feeding beetles such as Japanese beetles or pill bugs.

3. Do a soil test. You can buy a soil-testing kit or you can send sam-

ples to your county extension agent. A soil test gives you information on the pH (lawn grasses need a pH between 6 and 7) and the availability of nitrogen, phosphorus, and potassium in your soil. You can plan your fertilizing needs more accurately with this information.

4. Aerate the soil. Rent an aerator, a machine which punches holes in your lawn (and the soil underneath) without disturbing it. You can also buy a manual areating fork through garden supply stores and catalogs. Aeration reduces thatch density and helps the soil hold and release plant nutrients.

5. Feed the soil so that the soil can feed the grass. Current research in turf management indicates that regular application of artificial fertilizers weakens grass by inducing shallow root development and by forcing heavy top growth without the deep root development needed to sustain it. Artificial fertilizers also acidify the soil and cause a decline of normal soil organisms. These soil microbes are vital to a healthy grass because they break down thatch and also aid in making nutrients available to the grass roots. Creating a healthy soil insures beautiful grass. Use only low-analysis, slow-acting natural fertilizers such as blood meal, dried poultry manure, and cottonseed meal, or commer-cial organic fertilizers (brands available include Fertrell, Erth-Rite, and Ringer's Lawn Restore).

6. Mow it right. Keep creeping and velvet bent grasses at about ½ inch high. Colonial bent grass, annual bluegrass, and Bermuda and zoysia grasses should be cut to ½ to 1 inch high. Buffalo grass, red fescue, centipede grass, carpet grass, Kentucky bluegrass, perennial ryegrass, and meadow (fine) fescue are best kept at 1 to 2 inches. Bahia, tall fescue, and St. Augustine grass should be kept 1½ to 3 inches high. Mow often enough so that you're only cutting off one-third of the grass height at a time. Mow higher and less often in summer to encourage deeper root growth and drought tolerance. And mow ½ to 1 inch higher in shady areas, because more leaf surface ensures adequate photosynthesis in shade.

7. Thatch the lawn. Early fall is the best time to pull out the layer of matted organic material near the soil surface. If it's allowed to get too thick, it will harbor insects and diseases. If your lawn's thatch layer is very thick, you may wish to rent a thatching machine rather than do it by hand. As the health of your soil increases, you will find that thatch buildup becomes less of a problem because healthy soil sup-

ports microbes that break down and decompose the grass clippings.

8. Water intelligently. Water heavily every 7 to 10 days, which means leaving your sprinkler in one spot for two to four hours. Avoid frequent shallow watering, which encourages shallow root growth and decreased drought tolerance.

9. Reseed bare spots. An easy way to do this is to mix a bushel of topsoil with 5 pounds of organic fertilizer and 1 pound of grass seed. Spread this mixture over the bare area, rake lightly, and cover with straw or wet burlap. Keep the area damp for three weeks to allow the grass to sprout.

10. Control weeds. If you've followed the previous nine steps, you should not have to do much about Step 10. Weeds are seldom a problem in a healthy lawn because lawn grasses crowd them out. The ones that do grow through should be dug up, making sure you get their roots. Loosen the bare soil with a garden fork, then reseed these spots as in Step 9. If you have a lot of crabgrass, try covering those parts of your lawn that have the problem with a tarp or black plastic sheet for two weeks. This may bleach out the lawn grass, but it won't kill it. The crabgrass is less shade tolerant and will be killed.

Garden Lore

Plant your peas by St. Patrick's Day.
Pennsylvania German Folk Saying

Prune roses and plant potatoes on St. Patrick's Day.
Irish Folk Saying

Plant peas when apple blossoms are out.
Kentucky Folk Saying

ALMANAC GARDENING CALENDAR

If you've procrastinated in ordering your seeds, get your order in this month as soon as possible. Gardeners in even the coldest zones can start summer vegetables indoors in March, and gardeners in the middle zones can begin outdoor gardening by planting out cool-weather crops, such as peas, spinach, and brassicas. Gardeners in the Deep South can plant warm-weather crops this month, including tomatoes, watermelon, and corn.

Zone 1

Move February-started tomatoes, onions, leeks, lettuce, spinach, and other greens to a frost-free cold frame or a cool south window by midmonth. Fertilize lightly every two weeks with manure tea or fish emulsion. At midmonth, start eggplants and peppers indoors at 75° to 85°F. As soon as the seed leaves are fully expanded, transplant to larger pots and place in the cold frame or near a bright window with grow lights. Lower the temperature to 60° to 65°F. In the third to fourth weeks, start main-crop tomatoes. Divide old rhubarb plants and enrich their soil with compost or aged manure.

Every two weeks, lightly fertilize all seedlings started in February, perennials and annuals. By midmonth start indoors seeds of asters, stocks, calendulas, zinnias, marigolds, and quick-flowering dahlias. As seeds germinate, move the flats to a frost-free cold frame or a cool, sunny window. Divide established perennials and replant in soil enriched with aged manure and bonemeal. Prune tree and bush fruits by removing winter-damaged and diseased wood first. As you prune, look for overwintering insects, and weeds within 3 feet of the trunk. Fertilize with manure and bonemeal. To control scale, aphids, and mites, apply dormant-oil spray before buds open. Toward the end of the month, remove dead strawberry leaves and older plants from crowded beds.

Zone 2

Make one or more additional sowings of tomatoes, peppers, and eggplants. Pepper and eggplant seeds require 72° to 75°F both day and night for germination. At midmonth, sow lettuce outdoors. Start melons in pots indoors. Make sure the lawn mower is tuned up and the blade sharpened. Spread wood ashes or lime on the lawn if the soil tests acid. Most lawn grasses like a pH of 6 to 7. Rake leaves from hedges and add to the compost pile. Turn the compost pile over now and then to help spring rains soak into the materials and hasten decomposition. To avoid damage from late March or April freezes, don't uncover roses until warm weather sets in. After uncovering the plants, cut blackened canes back to live tissue.

Start tuberous begonias indoors now in a mix of peat moss, leaf mold, and garden loam. Water lightly until sprouting starts. To start tubers overwintered in pots, scrape off the upper 2 inches of soil, replace with fresh mix and water. Remove leaves and debris gradually from tulips and daffodils to let sunlight stretch the stems. Prune peach trees. Feed trees, shrubs, and perennials. To make a good all-purpose fertilizer, mix two parts each of bonemeal and dried blood with one part each of cottonseed meal, phosphate rock, and greensand. If your mail-order fruit or nut trees arrive and you can't plant immediately, place moist sphagnum moss around the roots or heel them in the ground. Do *not* set them in buckets of water—this cuts off oxygen from the roots. Have a supply of Bt (*Bacillus thuringiensis*) on hand to fight tent caterpillars or gypsy moths.

Zone 3

Early in the month, apply rock fertilizers as recommended by last fall's soil test and turn under cover crops and winter mulches. Until shortly before planting, leave the soil in clods to reduce erosion and enhance drying. Work up beds for cool-weather crops now so the soil will have settled by planting time. During the first break in the weather, plant peas, radishes, early potatoes, fava beans, onions, garlic, lettuce, turnips, spinach, and the cole crops. All will need the frost protection of cloches, floating row covers, or a loose mulch. Start planting roots of asparagus, horseradish, and rhubarb. About midmonth start tomatoes, peppers, eggplants, and annual herbs like basil in flats indoors. They'll be ready for transplanting in 6 to 8 weeks, about the time of the last killing frost. Inspect aspara-

gus beds to make sure the mulch is loose and thick enough to protect the earliest shoots from frost. If the winter has been dry, water deeply. When the soil is workable, direct-seed sweet peas as early in the month as possible. In mid- to late March, start flats of annuals such as marigolds, nasturtiums, strawflowers, bachelor's-buttons, and zinnias indoors.

Late in the month, begin removing mulch from perennial beds. Work in fertilizer—rock powders, rotted manure, or compost—among the plants, being careful not to damage tender shoots. Remove dead, misshapen, and weak branches from spring-flowering shrubs. Delay heavier pruning until after bloom. If you delayed pruning your fruit and nut trees in February, do so early in March. Prune peaches at budswell. After pruning, on a day above 40°F, spray trees with dormant oil. Remove and destroy tent caterpillar eggs (which look like old chewing gum). Fruit trees, vines, and bushes prefer their largest feeding of the year during March. Spread well-rotted manure or compost and rock fertilizers under the plants out to the drip line. Remove mulch from the strawberry patch an inch or so per week until the plants are thoroughly hardened to cold nights. Plant new fruit trees as weather permits. Water deeply, mulch heavily, and stake to prevent wind damage.

Zone 4

Harden cole plants in cold frames, but wait until the worst cold is past to set them out. Sprout sweet potatoes by laying them lengthwise on 3 inches of soil, covering them with an inch of sand and keeping them warm and moist. Each will send up several slips for May planting. By midmonth, sow hardy herbs such as chervil, chives, and dill as well as carrots, mustard, onions, parsnips, and potatoes. Dig remaining horseradish roots and replant 3-inch cuttings, barely covering them with soil. In the warmer western regions, start cantaloupes, cucumbers, and squashes in pots late in the month for setting out in a few weeks. Plant corn and beans when the soil reaches 60°F. For a longer asparagus harvest, remove the mulch from half of your established beds to start early growth. Thin annuals sown indoors last month and keep them at 50° to 60°F to prevent thin, straggly growth. If they've rooted, pot up cuttings of fuchsias, geraniums and other plants taken in February.

Sow sweet peas outdoors when the soil is workable, and plant bareroot trees, shrubs, roses, and perennials. Cut newly planted deciduous hedges to about 6 inches to stimulate branching. Dig old chrysanthemums, discard their worn-out centers and replant vigorous shoots from the edge of the clump. Side-dress peonies with bonemeal and aged manure or compost. Continue removing mulch from bulbs and perennials as new growth appears. Gradually remove soil mulches around tender roses, but wait until budswell to prune the canes. Keep all new fruit and nut plantings well watered during dry periods. Set out new strawberry plants, and gradually remove mulch from established beds. Don't fertilize until after harvest.

Zone 5

In the eastern half of the zone, make final spring sowings of beets, carrots, lettuce, garden peas, fast-maturing spinach, radishes, and rutabagas early in the month. Set out seedlings of broccoli, cauliflower, and kohlrabi. Be prepared to spray Bt (*Bacillus thuringiensis*) on all brassicas if green cabbageworms appear. Plant Irish potatoes around the time of the last frost, and keep them covered with a thick mulch. Late in the month, begin planting bush beans, early corn, and cucumbers. Farther west, it's time to start planting all warm-weather crops: cantaloupes, lima beans, eggplants, summer squash, cucumbers, early-bearing tomatoes, and watermelons. Keep plastic milk jug cloches on hand to protect tender plants from sudden harsh weather. Asparagus crowns may be planted this month throughout the zone. Put in sweet potatoes when the weather begins to warm. Harden off tomatoes, peppers, and eggplants to be set out next month. Enrich planting sites for summer flowers with compost, manure, or a balanced, slow-release natural fertilizer. Set out cold-hardy bedding plants, such as alyssum, daisies, phlox, and chrysanthemums.

Dig and divide chrysanthemums, Shasta daisies, and phlox. Plant gladiolus bulbs and dahlia tubers after the last frost, and harden off flats of marigolds, zinnias, and other warm-weather annuals. Top-dress lilies, peonies, and other summer bloomers with compost. Apply compost and fresh mulch to roses, especially around climbers and other roses that bloom only once a year. Also fertilize and mulch clematis, jasmine, and other ornamental vines. Mulch strawberries with pine straw or chopped leaves. Before grapes and berries blossom, fertilize them with rotted manure or compost mixed with cottonseed meal. Fertilize fruit and nut trees as soon as they leaf out, and irrigate pecans if the weather is unusually dry. Remove mulch from around figs after the last hard freeze. To reduce insect damage in orchards, clean the orchard floor *before* pests emerge by mowing all weeds and grasses and lightly cultivating beneath trees to a depth of 2 to 3 inches. Use Bt (*Bacillus thuringiensis*) sprays to control caterpillars. In northern areas, protect fruit blossoms during late frosts by spraying the trees lightly with water. A thin coating of ice will form over the flowers and prevent freeze damage.

Zone 6

Keep cloches handy to protect seedlings from unpredictable late-season frosts. If warm temperatures prevail at midmonth, plant squash to get a crop before the squash vine borer appears. Plant herbs, cucumbers, more lettuce, lima beans, mustard greens, and snap beans. Plant sweet corn in blocks at 2-week intervals. Set out tomato, pepper, and eggplant transplants after all danger of frost has passed. Plant asparagus crowns. Cool-weather crops that can still be seeded are peas, chard, lettuce, carrots, and beets. Side-dress vegetables already in the garden with compost. Thin fall-planted onions to 4-inch spacing. Mow remaining green manure crops and till them in.

Spread compost around roses, shrubs, trees, and lawns. Feed delphiniums, clematis, and wisterias. Transplants of alyssum, daisies, verbenas, asters, dianthus, phlox, pentstemons, lobelia, chrysanthemums, petunias, and geraniums can be set out early in the month. Sow seeds of morning glories, globe amaranth, and gloriosa daisies. Set out impatiens and zinnias at the end of the month. Leave mulch around fruit trees that need a long dormancy. If a fruit tree is in bloom and a frost hits, try spraying the flowers and branches with a fine mist of water to prevent serious bud loss. Spray fruit trees with liquid seaweed at 10-day intervals throughout the growing season. As trees begin to show active growth, apply compost around trunks. Plant grapes, dewberries, blackberries, strawberries, and raspberries, and cut back established dewberries and blackberries.

Zone 7

Because hot weather will soon arrive, plant only fast-maturing cool-weather vegetables like radishes, spinach, mustard, and turnips. Continue to plant carrots, beets, chard, bolt-resistant asian greens, early cabbage, and kohlrabi, all of which can take some heat. Mulching will help these crops come through. In the warmer tier of the zone—southern Louisiana, Florida, Texas, and the interior valleys of California—plant heat-tolerant fruits and vegetables such as cantaloupes, okra, green onions, tomatoes, sweet potatoes, and watermelons.

In the cooler tier of the zone, wait until the soil has warmed up before planting field peas and lima beans. Throughout the month, plant blocks of sweet corn and green beans. When danger of frost has passed, set out tomatoes, peppers, eggplants, and sweet potatoes. Turn under the last of the green manure crops started in fall.

Cover your compost pile with plastic to keep it from drying out in the heat. Fall-started compost should be usable by April. Start a second compost heap beside the first. Root begonia tubers (round side down) in leaf mold for later transplanting. Start caladiums in containers in a protected spot. Continue to plant glads, dahlias, and bedding annuals. Divide daylilies, hostas, chrysanthemums, marguerites, and Shasta daisies. Early in the month, prune summer-blooming shrubs like hibiscus and crape myrtle to encourage new flowering wood. Prune azaleas, rhododendrons and camellias after bloom. This late in spring, purchase only balled-and-burlapped trees. Plant new citrus and avocados. Wait to prune frost-damaged citrus and avocado trees until late April. Water trees frequently during March, especially along the Gulf, where it can sometimes be dry at this time of year. Compost or rotted manure applied now will feed the trees and hold in moisture, especially on sandy soil. Keep weeds down in the berry patch and orchard by cutting or tilling them under before their seed heads mature.

IN GOOD HEALTH

IMPROVE YOUR DIET WITH JUST TWO SIMPLE CHANGES

March is National Nutrition Month. When the topic of nutrition comes up, you're probably like most folks—well aware that your own diet could be improved, and a little overwhelmed with all the nutrition advice you've read or heard about. You may recall hearing advice like: "Cut down on the red meats . . . eat more fresh fruits and vegetables . . . increase your intake of complex carbohydrates . . . reduce high-cholesterol foods . . . get more calcium and eat foods high in omega-3 fatty acids." If all that sounds like a major dietary overhaul that you're just not ready to make, don't despair. You can make just two changes in your diet that would improve it dramatically: Eat more fiber and eat less fat. Why should you emphasize these two changes? Let's start with fiber.

Fiber Facts

Repeated studies have shown fiber to contribute a whole range of health benefits. Here's the evidence:

☞ Certain kinds of dietary fiber, primarily lignin, pectin and gum, have been shown to reduce levels of blood cholesterol. High blood cholesterol is a primary risk factor for heart disease.

☞ High-fiber diets aid in preventing obesity. People with high-fiber diets are seldom fat because fiber fills you up without adding calories. And since fibrous foods take longer to chew, they slow you down at the table.

☞ Fiber, especially from whole grains, can stop constipation. It can also prevent diverticulosis, a painful inflammation of pouches in the walls of the large intestine. High-fiber diets have also been used successfully to treat irritable bowel syndrome.

☞ High-fiber diets reduce the incidence of colon cancer, which is the second most common form of cancer in the United States. Colon cancer is thought to be triggered by carcinogens in the digestive tract. Just how fiber helps is not clear. It may reduce the bacteria that interact with stomach acids to form carcinogens, or it may help flush out carcinogens before the body absorbs them. What is clear is that fiber helps prevent colon cancer, and stomach and bowel cancer as well.

☞ High-fiber diets promote steady blood sugar levels. Fiber seems to slow the release of sugar in the blood, thereby preventing a sudden, enormous demand for insulin, the hormone that guides sugar molecules to the cells to be burned for food. High fiber intake prevents wide swings in insulin requirements (a bonus to diabetics) and helps to prevent the light-headedness and mood swings that can accompany sudden drops in blood sugar.

Fat Facts

Too much fat can do our bodies serious harm, and that's why we should cut down the amount we eat. Here's why:

☞ The evidence is very strong that too much fat can be carcinogenic. To one degree or another, fat has been implicated in cancers of the breast, uterus, prostate, colon, pancreas, and ovaries. Several dietary studies have shown that animals fed sparsely are less likely to develop tumors than those fed sumptuously. Much of the evidence is indirect, based on comparisons of fat consumption patterns and cancer rates. But the facts are compelling.

☞ Saturated fats, such as those fats in meats and dairy foods, stimulate your body to produce more cholesterol which, in excess, may clog arteries and restrict the blood supply to the heart or brain, causing a heart attack or a stroke.

☞ Fat consumption can make you fat. And obesity increases one's risk of heart disease, diabetes, cancer, and other health problems.

A High-Fiber Diet: It's Easier Than You Think

Because fiber comes in many different forms, it's a lot easier than you might think to increase your fiber intake. There are at least five different types of fiber, and high-fiber foods range all over the ball park, from wheat bran cereal to blueberries to carrots. The fibers *cellulose* and *hemicellulose* increase food bulk in the intestinal tract; they prevent constipation and are thought to reduce the incidence of cancer of the bowel. These fibers are found most abundantly in fruits, vegetables, bran, beans, and whole grains. The water-soluble fibers *pectin* and *gum* both reduce blood cholesterol levels. You can easily get pectin from apples, citrus fruits, grapes, and berries. The best sources for gum are oat bran and dried beans. *Lignin*, another type of fiber found in vegetables, fruits, and whole grains, binds itself with cholesterol and bile acids and effectively prevents cholesterol absorption into the bloodstream. You'll find plenty of lignin in such diverse foods as bran, whole grain cereals,

Fiber Content of Food

Food	Serving Size	Dietary Fiber (grams)
All-Bran cereal	½ cup	12.6
Lima beans (cooked)	½ cup	8.3
Peanuts	3 oz.	8.0
Peas (canned)	½ cup	6.7
Shredded Wheat	2 large biscuits	5.6
Corn (fresh)	1 medium ear	5.2
Raspberries	½ cup	4.6
Bran muffin	1 medium	4.2
Apple	1 medium	4.0
Pear	1 medium	4.0
Potato (baked)	1 medium	3.9
Broccoli (cooked)	½ cup	3.8
Banana	1 medium	3.0
Spaghetti (uncooked)	3 oz.	3.0
Prunes (dried)	2 medium	2.4
Rice, brown (cooked)	½ cup	2.4
Rye crackers	3 wafers	2.3
Beets (cooked)	½ cup	2.1
Carrot (raw)	1 medium	1.8
Strawberries	½ cup	1.6
Whole wheat bread	1 slice	1.3
Celery (raw)	1 stalk	1.1

strawberries, peas, and pears.

Most Americans don't eat enough fiber. The U.S. Department of Agriculture estimates Americans consume about 12 to 15 grams of fiber per day, about half of what's needed for good health. The National Cancer Institute (NCI), a division of the National Institutes of Health in Bethesda, Maryland, recommends eating foods that provide 25 to 35 grams of dietary fiber a day. It's really very easy to reach the NCI daily dietary fiber goal. For instance, eating a cup of bran cereal, an apple, a potato, and ½ cup of spinach in one day will provide about 37 grams.

Tips for Reaching Your Fiber Goal

A simple rule of thumb to increase your fiber intake is to "think plants." The best sources of fiber are all in one of three food categories: fruits, vegetables, and grains. And these are all products of living plants. You don't have to be a vegetarian to get plenty of fiber, but the more you steer your diet toward traditional vegetarian fare, the greater your fiber intake will be. The following tips will help you include more fiber in your diet:

☞ Eat a variety of fiber-rich foods. You need fiber from fresh fruits and vegetables as well as whole grains.

☞ Include unprocessed foods in your diet. Getting fiber from a natural cereal is more nutritionally sound than sprinkling bran on top of a hot fudge sundae.

☞ Drink plenty of liquids. Without enough fluids, fiber can cause digestive discomfort.

Targeting Your Fat Consumption

The American Heart Association suggests eating no more than 30 percent of your calories in fat. But what does a diet of 30 percent fat look like in the real world of steak au poivre and créme caramel?

"Asking the average person the percent of fat in his diet is like asking him the number of liters of air he breathes a day," says Diane Drabinsky, a registered dietitian at the Rodale Food Center. "Most people simply don't know where to begin in making an assessment like that."

So here's a start. The target in the illustration shows high-fat foods at its outer edges and lower-fat foods toward its center. The percentage noted within each ring of the target indicates the proportion of total calories that are from fat for the foods listed in that ring. If your buying habits favor the outer-limits foods, you can assume your diet approaches the outer limits of fat content. If your buying hovers toward the center, you can trust you're in territory that provides a healthier lifestyle.

What about all those foods that don't appear on the target? If your food has a nutritional label, you can figure its fat content for yourself. Nutritional labels don't give fat percentages directly, but they do give enough information for you to calculate it yourself.

Here's how: Take the number of grams of fat contained in one serving according to the product's

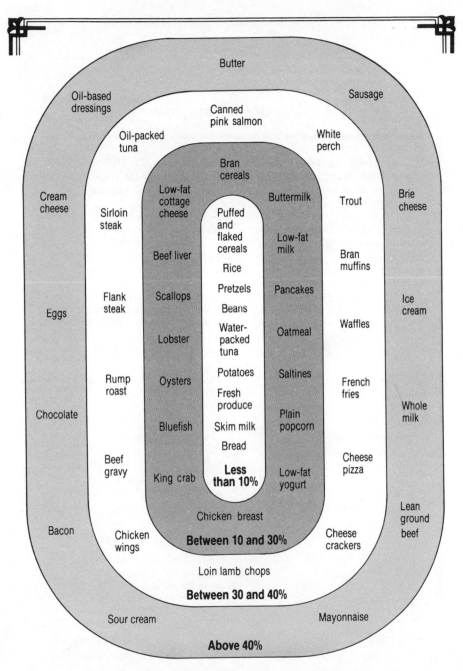

Stay on target for healthy eating. The percentages within the target indicate the proportion of total calories that are from fat. Fill your shopping cart with foods from the center and first inner ring of the target.

If You Can't Eliminate, Then Trade Off Fats

Since most of us eat too much fat "hidden" in meats, dairy foods, vegetable oils, and processed foods, we'd be far better off to eliminate whatever fats we can consciously avoid. Second best to eliminating them is to balance high-fat foods with other foods that are low in fat.

The "trade-offs" in the table here show approximately how much fat is in some typical foods. Use these trade-off equivalents to help you lower your fat consumption. For example, if you prefer whole milk over skim, you can moderate the amount of fat you eat by eliminating from your meals two teaspoons of fat for every cup of whole milk you drink. An easy way to do that is to eliminate some of the added fat in your diet, such as margarine. A pat of margarine is usually equal to 3 teaspoons of margarine, or 3 teaspoons of fat. If you choose to drink whole milk over skim, you should now put one-third of a pat of margarine on your morning toast, instead of a whole pat.

Fat Trade-Offs

1 cup whole milk	=	1 cup skim milk + 2 tsp fat
1 cup 2% low-fat milk	=	1 cup skim milk + 1 tsp fat
1 cup plain low-fat yogurt	=	1 cup skim milk + 1 tsp fat
1½ oz. natural cheese	=	1 cup skim milk + 3 tsp fat
2 oz. process American cheese	=	1 cup skim milk + 4 tsp fat
½ cup ice cream	=	⅓ cup skim milk + 2 tsp fat + 3 tsp sugar
2 oz. bologna	=	1 oz. lean meat, fish, or poultry + 3 tsp fat
2 tbsp peanut butter	=	1 oz. lean meat, fish, or poultry + 3 tsp fat
¼ cup seeds	=	1 oz. lean meat, fish, or poultry + 4 tsp fat
⅓ cup nuts	=	1 oz. lean meat, fish, or poultry + 5 tsp fat

You can also trade off according to food preparation method. For example:

18 potato chips	=	1 medium boiled potato + 3 tsp fat
10 french fries	=	1 medium boiled potato + 2 tsp fat

SOURCE: U.S. Department of Agriculture.

label, and multiply by nine (the number of calories in a single gram of fat). Now divide the result by the total number of calories in the serving and you've got the percentage of fat calories in the food.

As an example, calculate the fat content of a serving of whole milk. One cup (8 ounces) of whole milk contains 8 grams of fat. Multiply 8 grams by 9 calories per gram and you get 72 calories. Now divide 72 by 150 (the total number of calories in 1 cup of whole milk) and you get 0.48—48 percent of the total calories in a cup of milk are from fat.

So why is whole milk advertised as only 4 percent fat? The 4 percent fat advertised for milk is a percentage by weight, not a percentage by calories. Confusion arises when you think in terms of weight, not calories. The 30 percent fat recommendation of the American Heart Association is a calorie percentage. As a graphic example, if your plate contains 1,000 calories' worth of food, only 300 of those calories should be accounted for by fat. (Obviously only adults who engage in heavy physical labor would eat 1,000 calories at a single meal, but the 30 percent fat figure still holds, no matter how low or high your daily calorie intake.)

TIPS FOR CHOOSING A DOCTOR

Finding the doctor or other health professional who best suits your needs may take time and effort. A good place to start is with friends and relatives who may recommend someone they use. Other possible sources of referrals are teaching hospitals, medical schools, dental schools, other health professionals, local chapters of professional societies, or local consumer groups. For information about a specific health professional's education, specialty, and qualifications, simply call his or her office and ask questions. Questions you might want answered include: From which school did the health professional graduate? Is the person certified to practice by the appropriate licensing board in your state? Does the person belong to any professional organizations? Has he or she completed a residency or other graduate medical training that confers special expertise? You can also check your library for professional membership directories such as the American Medical Association Directory and the Directory of Medical Specialists. The yellow pages section of your phone directory also lists health professionals by specialties.

When you have collected a list of candidates, call their offices to get information about what is particularly important to you. For example, you might ask:

☞ How much will services cost and when are payments due?

☞ Is it possible to arrange a special payment schedule to fit my budget?

☞ Does the professional accept the type of insurance that I carry? Does he or she accept Medicare or Medicaid assignments? If so, for what services?

☞ Does the professional employ or recommend the use of other health professionals, such as physician's assistants or nurse practitioners?

☞ In the case of a doctor, is another physician on call when the doctor is unavailable?

Answers to these questions should help you narrow your choices. During your initial visit, you can decide whether or not this particular health provider is for you by asking yourself the following questions.

☞ Is the service prompt and efficient?

☞ Does the professional give a thorough examination, based on your experience?

☞ Does he or she make you feel at ease and respond thoughtfully to your questions?

☞ Are diagnoses, test results, treatments, and prescribed medications explained clearly and simply?

☞ Are fees and payment schedules clearly disclosed before treatment is given?

☞ Does the professional suggest ways to keep costs down?

☞ Is the office clean and well-equipped?

Do not be reluctant to go elsewhere if the professional does not meet your needs or expectations. You have a right to be as satisfied with health care services as you expect to be with other services you buy.

"Tips for Choosing a Doctor" is adapted from "Healthy Questions," by the American Association of Retired Persons in cooperation with the Federal Trade Commission. Used by permission.

Walking Tip for March

DMS, delayed-onset muscle soreness, occurs when you fail to condition your body gradually to endure greater stress and strain. For walkers this usually means sore calf muscles, but it can also affect arms, hips, or buttocks. To avoid pain from your walking workouts, start slowly and gradually add minutes, miles, and speed. If you experience DMS, take one day of rest and then do a shorter, lighter workout with a day of rest in between sessions. If the pain is in your shin, you probably have tendinitis rather than DMS. According to Dr. Robert Willix, Jr., a sports medicine physician at the Willix Health Institute, this usually responds to aspirin taken every four hours for two days.

AT HOME

WILL YOUR NEXT HOUSE COME FROM A FACTORY?

With March comes the opening of what real estate agents know as the annual spring buying season. It's the season in which many homeowners begin to look for a new home, frequently with the goal of completing a move over the summer while the kids are out of school. For new retirees, it's a popular time to sell a home because it's just easier to relocate if you don't have to wade through a snow storm to get a moving van loaded. If you're going house hunting this spring you might want to consider the possibility of owning a *new* home, one built just for you on your own property.

More and more home buyers are considering a brand-new home because prefabricated housing has become a viable and sometimes less-costly alternative to a custom-built home. "But what do they look like?" you ask. The answer is that they look like almost anything you can imagine. From New England saltbox to California chic, almost every size and style you could want comes as a manufactured home. Passive solar homes, log homes, post-and-beam homes, and even geodesic domes all tumble out of the many catalogs available from the kit-home manufacturers. There are hundreds of companies making these houses today, and you can buy a kit to build anything from a one-car garage to a luxurious six-bedroom house. Why should you be interested in prefabricated houses? Here are some of the reasons:

☞ Flexibility of design. Most of today's prefabs come in sophisticated designs that enable buyers to select the number of bedrooms, bathrooms, or decks as well as the size of kitchen, dining room, and living room. Some Japanese firms invite their home buyers to sit in front of a computer terminal and customize their houses themselves. The customer walks out of the showroom with actual floor plans and cost sheets. American home buyers may soon have this option also.

☞ Quality. The best manufactured homes have top-quality construction because craftsmanship and materials can be much more carefully controlled in a factory than at a building site.

☞ Energy efficiency. Several of them, particularly Scandinavian-manufactured houses, are built of panels that have the insulation and vapor barrier already in place when they arrive at the site. The Scandinavian houses use a super-dense mineral wool batt that will not settle in the stud cavity. They also use a thicker, high-strength vapor barrier that has proven to be more stable than the polymer sheet barriers used in the United States. All this makes the Scandinavian prefabs the most energy efficient of any housing in the world, and about twice as energy efficient as the average American home.

☞ Faster on-site construction. Because so much of the work is done at the factory, there is less work to do at the house site. The result is that the buyer can move into his new home sooner than with conventional construction. One importer of Swedish panelized houses, SvenskaHus/USA, claims that construction time at the site, including all interior finish work, is only 650 man-hours—about one-third the time an American crew would spend building a comparable, nonpanelized house.

What Does It Cost?

If you're more handy than the average person, and if you're knowledgeable about home construction, you can order a precut or panelized house as a kit (see "How Prefabricated Is It?" for the different kinds of factory-built houses) and do much of the site preparation and finish work yourself. This will save you money and is a good way to save considerable labor costs without taking on the entire house-building job yourself. If you plan to do this, be prepared to sacrifice enormous amounts of time to this project. As a part-time job (after hours from your regular job), site preparation alone can easily take a whole summer. In any event, you will need to hire a professional for parts of the job that are simply too difficult (such as drilling a well or installing a septic field on a rural property).

Another option is to hire a contractor to prepare the site and put up the house for you. If you choose this route, don't expect a factory-built house to save much money over a custom-built one. The kit you select from a catalog may at first appear to be inexpensive when you compare it to the selling price of the new houses in the development down the road. But it isn't such a bargain when you find that the foundation, erection, and finish work done by a contractor will result in a finished house price of two to four times the cost of the kit itself. And this doesn't include the cost of your lot.

Some Shopping Tips

Don Best, author of "Factory-Built Houses" (*Practical Homeowner,* September 1987), points out that shopping for a prefab house is very different from shopping for a site-built house. Here are a few tips from him to keep in mind:

☞ Begin your search with firms that are within a few hundred miles of your building site—beyond that point transportation costs escalate and service becomes difficult.

☞ Take the time to shop around.

Compare the homes, costs, warranties, and shipping charges of several different companies. Most firms charge a few dollars for their brochures, but this small investment is insignificant compared to the money you can save by comparison shopping.

☞ Unless you're skilled enough to handle construction yourself, you'll need a good local builder to oversee the foundation work, mounting and assembly, and some of the finishing. In fact, having a good builder is more important with a factory-built house than it is with a stick-built job because there's a lot less margin for error. Lack of experience or poor communications between your builder and the factory could leave you with a house that doesn't sit squarely on its foundation.

☞ The company that builds your house will probably specify the limits of its responsibility for unsatisfactory work—the remainder will rest with your builder. You may want to ask the manufacturer to recommend local builders who have experience with factory-built homes. This is especially important if you're buying a log house or post-and-beam home because many contractors have no experience with such designs. Panelized homes, on the other hand, are very popular now, and many contractors are quite familiar with them.

☞ As long as you're working with a professional builder and licensed subcontractors, lending institutions don't normally make any distinction between factory-built and stick-built houses. As with conventional house construction, they usually set up a payment schedule based on the amount of work completed and verified by a building inspector. Because so much of a manufactured house is built in the factory before it ever reaches the site, you may find yourself having to lay out lots of cash before the materials arrive and you receive a payment from your bank.

If you're going to build the house yourself and you don't have a track record in the building trades, your banker is probably going to be tight-fisted with the terms of the loan. Expect frequent visits to the site to check your progress. The reason for this is that self-builders tend to underestimate the amount of time and work involved in building a house. If local financing is a problem, you may be able to get a loan from the manufacturer. Once your house is completed, you can refinance it through the bank and repay your loan to the company.

A complete listing of prefab home manufacturers, including firms that sell to home buyers and those that sell only to builders, is available from Home Manufacturers Councils of the National Association of Home Builders of the U.S., 15th and M Street NW, Washington, DC 20005. Specify what type of house you're interested in: precut, panelized, modular, or log home.

HOW PREFABRICATED IS IT?

Before you can be an informed shopper, you need to know the different terms applied to prefabricated homes. The glossary here should provide you with all the information necessary to understand the differences between the many types of homes available.

Kit Home

House "kits" are generally either precut or panelized homes sold directly to homeowners or developers. Typically, a kit-home company will supply the house shell, including structural supports, sheathing in the form of stressed-skin panels (a structural wall panel made of insulating foam with drywall on one side and plywood or flakeboard on the other) or more traditional finish material, and connectors. In addition, some include prepanelized interior walls, plumbing fixtures, and other components.

With a kit home, the consumer is usually responsible for preparing the foundation and completing, or arranging to have completed, all electrical, plumbing, and heating work. Erection costs also are the responsibility of the buyer.

Manufactured Home

This is not a consistently used term. Some use the word "manufactured" to denote all of the various homes described in this lexicon. Others mean something more specific. The mobile home is called a "manufactured home" by its trade association, the Manufactured Housing Institute. However, some manufacturers of factory houses other than mobile homes do not accept the mobile home as a "manufactured" house at all.

Mobile Home

This type of home has an integral chassis for highway shipment. If a home is placed directly on a flatbed truck, it is a modular home, not a mobile home.

Modular Home

The "modular" is a three-dimensional house, 95 percent complete when it comes off the assembly line. It is shipped in one, two, or more sections for placement on a foundation at the building site. There, it is hooked up to electrical, water, and other utility lines.

Panelized Home

Panelized means that the complete walls of a house are factory-made in large sections, or panels, usually 8 feet high and up to 40 feet long. Sometimes the doors and windows are factory-installed in the panels; other times these are installed at the site. The wall panels are designed to be erected immediately after delivery.

Precut Home

A precut house contains wood framing members that are precut in a factory to the correct lengths, but delivered to the building site unassembled. It is the type of prefabricated house that is least completed in the factory.

Prefabricated Home

This is a generic term for all forms of factory-made houses. If a house uses factory prefabricated components, such as roof trusses, but is otherwise site-fabricated, the house may also be called "field prefabricated."

Stick-Built Home

The stick-built home is primarily site-fabricated in the traditional platform, balloon, or post-and-beam method. Today, even the stick-built house inevitably contains some elements of prefabrication, such as prehung windows and doors or roof trusses.

Glossary terms reprinted from a glossary by Donald Prowler as part of the article "Factory-Built Houses," Practical Homeowner, September, 1987.

Purple for Pounds Off

If you plan to do some interior painting during the coming spring months, remember that you can use color to your advantage in your home. Knowing which hues stimulate, excite, depress, soothe, and tranquilize can help you create a positive, nurturing home environment. According to Richard Wurtman, Ph.D., professor of endocrinology and metabolism at the Massachusetts Institute of Technology, "Color, which is a form of light, is the most important environmental input after food in controlling body function." The suggestions here may provide you with some ideas for your next repainting job, but before you pull out the paint charts, keep in mind that each person has his own particular way of reacting to color.

☞ Use blue in an area where you frequently perform a routine or monotonous task such as ironing or homework. Cool hues (blues and greens) make time seem to pass faster.

☞ Use light blue or gray in an area where you need to feel calm and efficient, such as a study or home office.

☞ Use primary colors (red, blue, yellow) in areas where you want to feel stimulated and full of energy and self-esteem. This might be appropriate for a nursery, a child's room, the family room, or the kitchen.

☞ Use pale blue to keep flies away. Since flies avoid pale blue, it's a good choice for painting barn stalls and porch ceilings and walls.

☞ Use purple to discourage overeating. Cool shades of purple suppress appetite, slow muscular response and induce a tranquilizing effect. How about adding touches of purple to your dining room or breakfast nook?

YOUR MARCH SHOPPER'S TIP

The best buys in produce this month are broccoli, cabbage, carrots, grapefruit, and spinach. This colorful, easy salad celebrates the coming of spring and provides a tasty dish for your first harvest of garden peas.

Equinox Salad

2 cups spinach leaves
8 red radishes, thinly sliced
4 scallions, cut into julienne strips
½ cup peas
½ cup coarsely shredded daikon
   radishes
¼ cup fresh mushrooms
1 tablespoon olive oil
2 teaspoons balsamic vinegar
½ teaspoon Dijon mustard
   pinch of freshly grated nutmeg

In a large bowl, combine spinach, red radishes, scallions, peas, daikon radishes, and mushrooms. In a small bowl, whisk together oil, vinegar, mustard, and nutmeg. Pour dressing over vegetables and toss well.

4 servings

YOUR HOME MAINTENANCE CHECKLIST

☞ Check and clean the sump pump.

☞ Check and clean the dehumidifier.

☞ Check and clean the washing machine.

☞ Clean filter in the range hood.

☞ Test your smoke alarms with a smoke source (see February for directions).

Wet Basement Tune-Up

If you're among the millions of folks who must make the best of a damp or leaky basement, you can spare yourself from an unexpected deluge or from mildew damage by performing a regular maintenance check on your sump pump and basement dehumidifier.

To check a sump pump: Inspect the screen for debris or dirt and clean if necessary. Check the switch operation by submerging the pump into a bucket of water or by pouring two buckets of water into the pit. The float on the pump should rise as water accumulates.

To maintain your dehumidifier: Remove the cover and clean the coils. Check the drain hole and unclog it if necessary. Lubricate the motor shaft and oil ports with a few drops of 20-weight oil.

Keeping the Washer Happy

To keep your washing machine in peak operating condition, periodically remove and wash the water filters in the inlet hoses at the back of the machine. To do this, first close the water faucets, pull the machine away from the wall, and disconnect the hoses. Have a tub ready to catch the runoff. Remove the fine mesh screen filters located just inside the machine and on the other end of the hoses. Remove and wash the screens thoroughly and replace.

Clean out the lint filter. This is often located beneath the top panel, which you'll have to pry up from the front or unscrew from the back, depending upon your model. After the first time, it's easy.

EVENTS AND FESTIVALS

Chalo Nitka
Moore Haven, Florida

First full weekend in March. Fishermen will especially enjoy this three-day celebration of Lake Okeechobee bass fishing and of the Seminole people, who were the first native Floridians. Chalo Nitka, which means day of the big bass in the Seminole language, features a bass fishing contest with awards given for catching the largest bass and for catching one of the specially tagged bass introduced into the lake for the occasion. The Chalo Nitka Queen and the Seminole Princess reign over a parade and celebration at the Chalo Nitka grounds. Information: Glades County Chamber of Commerce, Box 490, Moore Haven, FL 33471.

Carnival Miami
Miami, Florida

Early March. Celebrate Florida's Hispanic culture at the nation's largest Hispanic festival. Festivities include Latin entertainment and dance contests held at the Orange Bowl, as well as the Paseo Parade held in Miami's Latin quarter. Carnival Miami includes the Calle Ocho Festival, a street celebration in Miami's Latin quarter that features Latin theme floats and costumes as well as street vendors offering a wide variety of traditional Latin food. Information: Greater Miami Convention and Visitors Bureau, 4770 Biscayne Boulevard, Miami, FL 33137, or Calle Ocho Festival, Kiwanis Club, 970 Southwest First Street, Miami, FL 33130.

Snowfest
North Lake Tahoe, Nevada
and Truckee, California

Early March. This extensive ten-day festival celebrates life in the high Sierra with over 150 events for participants of every age, taste, and interest. The festival offers ski races for all levels of ability from casual recreational to professional. Choose from an imaginative selection of daily events including a wild game and fish cookoff, a barbecue, fireworks, parades, a street dance, a concert of country and western music, an ice cream-eating contest, and softball and golf tournaments on skis. Information: Festivals at Tahoe, P.O. Box 7590, Tahoe City, CA 95730.

St. Patrick's Day Parade
New York, New York

March 17. Always held on this day come rain, shine, or snow (unless March 17 falls on a Sunday). New York's St. Patrick's Day Parade is the largest nonmilitary, non-professional parade in the entire United States, with bands and brigades marching for 6 hours along Fifth Avenue from 44th to 86th Street. Information: St. Patrick's Day Parade, New York Convention and Visitor's Bureau, 2 Columbus Circle, New York, NY 10019.

Natchez Spring Pilgrimage
Natchez, Mississippi

Mid-March through mid-April. Celebrate the Old South during this month-long festival that includes tours of 30 antebellum homes and a Confederate Pageant at City Auditorium. Enjoy a performance of *Southern Exposure,* a comedy about the oddities and quirks of southerners, given nightly at the Natchez Playhouse. Information: Natchez Pilgrimage, Tourist Headquarters, P.O. Box 347, Natchez, MS 39121.

Jonquil Festival
Washington, Arkansas

Mid-March. Enjoy a spring weekend festival in the Old Washington Historic State Park. The entire town of Washington is contained within this state park, which was established to preserve the Greek-revival style, pre-Civil war buildings of Washington and its surrounding area. During the Jonquil Festival visitors enjoy a sea of jonquils, thousands of them, planted over the last twenty years in the town of Washington and all over the park. Information: Old Washington State Historic Park, P.O. Box 98, Washington, AR 71862.

Storytelling Weekend
Greenup, Kentucky

Mid-March. Find a weekend of joyful entertainment at Greenbo Lake State Resort Park as Kentucky storytellers dazzle you with their vivid tales and olios (storytelling language for a hodgepodge of rhyme and story). Members of a professional storytellers' guild, International EARS, provide day-long workshops in the art of storytelling. During the evening sessions, the professionals pull out the stops by giving their best tales for an appreciative audience. Information: Greenbo Lake State Resort Park, HC 60 Box 562, Greenup, KY 41144.

Great American Turkey Call-Off
Montgomery, Alabama

Mid-March. This one-day, one-of-a-kind event held at the Montgomery Civic Center features callers of wild turkeys in the junior, amateur, and professional divisions. Professional and amateur turkey callers from as far away as Arkansas and New York compete for the right to go on to the National Turkey Calling Championships held later in the week in Mobile, Alabama. Spectators welcome. Plenty of fun for everyone. For nightowls, there's an owling contest. Information: Montgomery Parks and Recreation Department, 1010 Forest Avenue, Montgomery, AL 36106.

Southeastern Livestock Exposition
& World Championship Rodeo
Montgomery, Alabama

Mid-March. Sponsored by the Alabama Cattlemen's Association and held at the Garrett Coliseum, this rodeo features performances by members of the Professional Rodeo Circuit Association as well as a championship steer show and a registered quarter horse show. Information: Southeastern Livestock Expo and Rodeo, Cattlemen's Building, 600 Adams Avenue, Montgomery, AL 36104.

APRIL

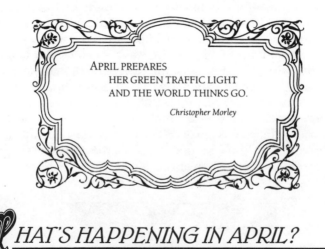

APRIL PREPARES
HER GREEN TRAFFIC LIGHT
AND THE WORLD THINKS GO.

Christopher Morley

WHAT'S HAPPENING IN APRIL?

April 1, April Fools' Day: The observance of April Fools' Day probably began in France on the first day of April in 1564. France officially adopted the Gregorian calendar in 1564 and in that year changed its New Year's Day observance from April 1 to January 1 as required by the new calendar. Some resisted the new calendar by continuing to observe the new year as they had always done, by celebrating throughout the last week of March until April 1. Proponents of the new calendar ridiculed these conservatives by sending them invitations to nonexistent parties and giving them silly gifts.

April 13, Birthday of Thomas Jefferson: The genius of our third president of the United States is reflected in the remark made about him by President John F. Kennedy. On beginning a speech to a room full of Nobel Laureates gathered at the White House for a ceremonial dinner, Kennedy remarked that the room contained a gathering of the greatest geniuses ever in one place "except when Thomas Jefferson dined alone." As chairman of the Declaration Committee of the Second Continental Congress, he authored the Declaration of Independence. As a president twice elected to office, he initiated the Louisiana Purchase, the purchase of the western half of the Mississippi River Basin from France. This single act of foresight and good sense became the greatest land bargain in our history. Its 828,000 square miles (purchased at a cost of less than 3¢ per acre) more than doubled the size of the United States and moved our country for the first time into the realm of a world power. Jefferson was not only a statesman of genius and foresight, he was also an expert violinist, an accomplished singer and dancer, an expert horseman, and an avid gardener and farmer. He died on the fiftieth anniversary of the Declaration of Independence, July 4, 1826, and was buried at Monticello, his Virginia home, under a stone marked with an epitaph he composed himself: "Here was buried Thomas Jefferson, author of the Declaration of American Independence, of the statute of Virginia for religious freedom, and father of the University of Virginia."

April 15, Anniversary of the Sinking of the *Titanic:* On the night of April 14, 1912, the "unsinkable" luxury liner, *Titanic,* on its maiden voyage from Southampton, England, to New York, struck an iceberg in the ocean off the coast of Newfoundland. After its near-midnight collision, the liner sank at 2:27 A.M. on the morning of April 15. Of the 2,224 passengers, 1,513 went down with the ship. Tragically, the luxury liner *The Californian,* which was less than 20 miles away, did not receive the *Titanic's* distress calls because that ship's radio operator was asleep. The survivors were rescued by the liner *Carpathia,* which reached the scene of the wreck 20 minutes after the ship went down. In July 1986, a joint French-American expedition, led by Dr. Robert Ballard, a marine geologist from the Woods Hole Oceanographic Institute, descended to the deck of the ship in a submersible craft and explored the interior of the wreck via a guided robot.

April 22, National Arbor Day: Due to the efforts of Sterling Morton, an editor of the Nebraska City *News* and an avid horticulturist, the state of Nebraska set aside the first official holiday for planting trees—April 10, 1872. Although April 22 is National Arbor Day, many states celebrate Arbor Day on other dates because April 22 is not the best date to plant trees in all gardening zones of the United States.

You can plan an Arbor Day of historic proportions for yourself or for your neighborhood. The American Forestry Association, the national citizens' organization for trees and forests, published a book in 1976, *Famous and Historic Trees.* The book contains over 250 descriptive entries on trees or groves of trees that are of national historic significance. Using the research from this book as a starting point, the American Forestry Association began growing seedlings from the seeds of some of these still-vital historic trees. For a price list of these special historic seedlings, or for more information on the book *Famous and Historic Trees,* write to: Famous and Historic Trees, The American Forestry Association, P.O. Box 2000, Washington, DC 20013.

Late March to Mid-April, Easter: Easter is a movable feast established by the early Christian church in A.D. 325 as the first Sunday after the first full moon on or after the vernal equinox (March 20). Many other holidays in the Christian year are determined by the date of Easter, among them Lent and Passiontide. Easter is the most joyous feast in the Christian world because it celebrates the culmination of the life of Christ, his resurrection from the dead.

Late March to Mid-April, Passover: The Jewish feast of Pesach (or Passover) commemorates events in the Book of Exodus in which God "passed over" the homes of the Israelites while inflicting death on the first-born sons of their oppressors, the Egyptians. Jews celebrate this sign of God's divine favor toward them by worshipping at a synagogue and performing a Seder (a meal during which the events of the exodus from Egypt are narrated) in their homes. During this eight-day holiday, they refrain from eating foods containing leavening agents, in remembrance of the fact that the Israelites fled Egypt in such haste that they had no time to allow their bread to rise.

Third Monday in April, Patriots' Day: This holiday, celebrated most faithfully in New England, commemorates the first armed conflict of the American Revolution. On April 19, 1775, a brave group of only 77 Minutemen, hastily summoned to the village green by Paul Revere's legendary night ride, attempted to fight off a contingent of redcoats, sent by British General Thomas Gage to seize a cache of arms hidden in the village of Concord, Massachusetts. The event was movingly commemorated some 70 years later by the poet Ralph Waldo Emerson:

> BY THE RUDE BRIDGE THAT ARCHED THE FLOOD,
> THEIR FLAG TO APRIL'S BREEZE UNFURLED
> HERE ONCE THE EMBATTLED FARMERS STOOD
> AND FIRED THE SHOT HEARD ROUND THE WORLD.
>
> *from "Concord Hymn"*

April 27, Birthday of Ulysses S. Grant: This eighteenth president of the United States presided over two terms marked by corruption and scandal totally unworthy of his real character and Civil War achievements. Before the Civil War, Grant was a 39-year-old washed-out West Point graduate who had been forced to resign his army commission to avoid a court-martial for habitual drunkenness. He had failed at several business ventures, including real estate and farming, and had gone to work in his father's leather goods store as a clerk. At the outbreak of the war, he volunteered and was granted command of a group of Illinois volunteers. From this obscure post he rose to the rank of lieutenant general over the entire Union Army. His ascent into prominence was marked by courage and dogged resourcefulness in every battle he led. After the battle of Shiloh, in which Grant snatched victory from the open jaws of defeat (but at the cost of 13,000 Union lives), there was a public outcry over his "lack of precaution" and the terrible loss of human life. Responding to political pressure to remove Grant from command, President Lincoln is said to have replied, "I can't spare this man; he fights."

The Second Week in April Is National Gardening Week

On April 18, 1986, President Ronald Reagan signed a presidential proclamation naming the second full week in April as National Gardening Week. The National Garden Bureau is a nonprofit organization that supplies ideas and information for the celebration of National Gardening Week.

Your favorite club or charity may sponsor a National Gardening Week activity in your community. An activity, such as a seed sale, can be a great fund-raiser that generates money for your group and also encourages gardening in your home town. Classroom teachers can use the National Garden Bureau as a source for information about a poster contest that involves children in gardening.

Individuals, schools, and clubs may all write to the National Garden Bureau for an individualized packet of suggestions for ways to celebrate National Gardening Week. To receive a free packet of information, write to: National Garden Bureau, 1311 Butterfield Road, Suite 310, Downers Grove, IL 60515.

The National Garden Bureau also provides free pamphlets on the flower of the year and the vegetable of the year. To receive these pamphlets, send a stamped, self-addressed, business-sized envelope to the address above. To receive both pamphlets, stamp your envelope with two first-class stamps. For just one pamphlet, use one first-class stamp.

IN THE GARDEN

AN INTRODUCTION TO HEIRLOOM SEEDS

This April as you harvest your cool-weather crops, why not add a little garden history to your summer garden plans by including an heirloom variety? A variety is usually called an heirloom if its seeds result from random open pollination or from self-pollination (in contrast to the controlled cross-pollination between two specific plants needed to produce hybrids), and if it was generally available for purchase before the advent of commercial hybridization of seeds (the early 1940s). A pleasing bonus from heirloom seeds is that the seeds of this year's plant will all spring "true" and may be used to start the very same plant next year. Once you've planted an heirloom variety of vegetable or flower, you have a supply of seeds for that plant forever, or at least for as many seasons as you care to harvest, dry, and store the seeds.

If you are interested in an old variety of vegetable or flower, you may begin to search for it through the commonly available commercial seed catalogs. If you resort to this tactic, you'll soon discover that commercial seed catalogs primarily carry seeds for hybrid plants, many of them patented and most of them bred for specific characteristics, such as plant size and shape (bush beans) or early crop production (early bearing tomatoes). But the price for all this convenience is that many grand old varieties, plants grown by your grandmother or great-aunt Mary, are no longer available through commercial seed houses. The reasons are primarily economic. Seed companies, like other businesses, cannot afford to stock an infinite variety of merchandise, and it is easier to sell a new variety with proven characteristics than to sell an old one whose performance is not quite so predictable. Also, since most hybrid varieties do not make seeds that faithfully reproduce the original plant for the next growing season, the consumer must return to the seed company each year for a resupply of his favorite hybrids. That certainly makes money for the seed companies, even if it does nothing to foster the independence of the gardener.

Still, the thoughtful gardener might reflect on the fact that many old varieties of vegetables, flowers, trees, and shrubs may eventually be lost to us if no one takes the trouble to preserve their seeds. Fortunately, gardeners are by tradition a sharing and thoughtful group. They love to share information, cuttings, formulas, seeds, and advice. In this tradition of sharing, seed exchanges flourish as a source for heirloom and unusual varieties no longer available through large commercial seed houses. As an adventure in garden history and as a great way to plant something truly unusual, why not take advantage of a seed exchange this garden season? You may discover that you prefer the heirloom 'Moon & Stars' watermelon to the contemporary 'Sugar Baby', or that the tastiest bean soup you ever made comes from heirloom 'Adventist' dry bush beans.

If you decide to try a seed exchange, you should know how they work. Some exchanges are simply old-fashioned seed swaps conducted through the mail. Members of a group or subscribers to a publication typically advertise some unusual seed they'd like to give away or trade for something else. These simple swap exchanges are usually sponsored by gardening magazines and newsletters. Other seed exchanges operate somewhat like a club with membership dues (usually a very nominal fee). For your membership fee, you receive an annual catalog listing all of the seeds that members are offering to exchange. As a member of this type of seed exchange you are expected to save seeds yourself in order to exchange them with other members.

In addition to seed exchanges, a number of small seed companies, some of them nonprofit corporations or foundations, also offer heirloom seeds through mail-order catalogs. Most of these companies specialize in seeds native to a given geographic area, with particular emphasis on preserving old varieties currently being dropped from the large commercial seed catalogs. In most cases, you pay a nominal fee to receive an initial catalog and then receive succeeding catalogs free after you have ordered from the first one.

To get you started in the neighborly world of seed swapping, we've provided a descriptive list of some well-known seed exchanges. If you like to write letters to other gardeners, like to hear folklore and garden tips from others, and like to try a little variety in your garden each year, a seed exchange is a great place to start. If you can't find what you're looking for through a seed exchange, we've provided a list of alternative sources, including companies that sell heirloom seeds.

Seed Exchanges

The requirements for belonging to each exchange vary. Be sure you would like to participate by offering seeds or cuttings for exchange yourself. Some, but not all, exchanges require this for full membership privileges.

American Horticultural Society
7931 E. Boulevard Drive
Alexandria, VA 22308

For an annual dues of $30, members of the American Horticultural Society receive a subscription for the monthly publication *American Horticulturist*. In addition, members receive an annual seed exchange catalog, which is mailed each January. The exchange of seeds through the catalog is available to members only, and only members may list seeds for exchange in the catalog. The seed exchange catalog includes hybrid varieties donated by commercial seed companies as well as open-pollinated, heirloom varieties offered by members. You do not have to participate in the seed exchange in order to join the society.

Gardeners Share
P.O. Box 243
Columbus, IN 47202

For $15 you can purchase a one-year subscription to a bimonthly newsletter called *Gardeners Share*. Devoted exclusively to gardeners' lively interest in swapping information and plants, this newsletter also features short articles on such diverse topics as seed-saving techniques, hardy native azaleas, and plants that attract bees to orchards. Many of the articles feature a little-known source for unusual plants and gardening supplies. Subscribers may offer to give away or swap seeds, bulbs, or cuttings through the newsletter's "Trading List."

National Gardening Association
180 Flynn Avenue
Burlington, VT 05401

National Gardening magazine publishes "Seed Swap" pages, which give members of the National Gardening Association an opportunity to trade seeds with one another each month. In addition, the magazine features a monthly column called "Seed Search." This column focuses on rare and hard-to-find seeds. Members send their requests for unusual seeds to the Seed Search Service of the National Gardening Association. The association makes every attempt to locate a source for the seed and then publishes requests for those varieties that the search service is unable to locate. Mem-

bers who own the requested seed or who know of a source for it are then free to write to the person who is searching for it. You may join the National Gardening Association for a membership fee of $18 per year. Membership includes access to the seed swap and seed search programs as well as a subscription to the monthly publication *National Gardening*.

The North American Fruit
Explorers
c/o Jill Vorbeck
Route 1, Box 94
Chapin, IL 62628

For the modest membership fee of $11 ($15 in Canada), you can receive *Pomona*, the quarterly report of the North American Fruit Explorers. Published for the fruit-growing hobbiest with only a few trees as well as the enthusiastic professional grower, this publication reports to its members on all of the latest developments in the area of fruit growing. Members get a chance to buy scions and budwood from new varieties before they are commercially available in nurseries. In *Pomona* you can read of a new breed of peach tree developed in Montana and hardy to -45°F, or of English walnut trees that bear 2 years after planting instead of the usual 15 years. As a service to its members, *Pomona* features a regular swap column in which members exchange seeds, grafting wood, scions, and budwood for fruit trees. Members may also use the swap column to search for rare fruit varieties by asking other members to write if they know of a source.

Seed Savers Exchange
Rural Route 3
Box 239
Decorah, IA 52101

Seed Exchange director Kent Whealy, one of the modern pioneers in preserving this country's large and varied seed bank, has established an astonishing list of gardeners who want to exchange endangered and heirloom seeds. When you become a member of the Seed Savers Exchange you'll receive three publications: the *Winter Yearbook,* which lists over 770 members and the *more than 5,000* rare varieties of fruit and vegetable seeds they have to offer, and the *Spring* and *Harvest Editions,* which give current information on seed saving and preserving genetic heritage through seeds. Annual membership dues are $15. You may obtain free information about the seed exchange simply by writing to the address shown and including a business-sized, stamped, self-addressed envelope for reply.

Other Sources for Heirloom Seeds

These companies offer seeds through mail-order purchase. Some of them are nonprofit corporations and foundations that utilize their profits from seeds for seed research and preservation programs, and some of them are simply small companies that cater to the gardener's desire for heirloom varieties.

Abundant Life Seed Foundation
P.O. Box 772
Port Townsend, WA 98368

Abundant Life is a nonprofit corporation dedicated to propagating and preserving seeds and plants of the native and naturalized flora indigenous to the North Pacific Rim (the coastal area from Alaska through northern California). Membership dues are a minimum of $5, with members being asked to donate additional tax-deductible funds in any amount to the foundation. Members receive an annual seed catalog and book list as well as several newsletters. The catalog, which costs $1 for nonmembers, lists over 600 varieties of seeds, many of which are not commercially available, and includes seeds for vegetables, flowers, herbs, shrubs, and trees.

Garden City Seeds
Box 297
Victor, MT 59875

Garden City Seeds specializes in open-pollinated varieties suited for the harsh growing conditions of the northern Rocky Mountain plains areas: short growing seasons, cold nights, and cold soil. You may purchase their catalog listing over

300 vegetables, flowers, and herbs by sending $2 to the address shown above. The company offers more than 20 varieties of heirloom vegetables, and almost all of the varieties offered in the catalog are open-pollinated.

Johnny's Selected Seeds
Box 305, Foss Hill Road
Albion, ME 04910

Johnny's Selected Seeds offers over 400 varieties of vegetables, flowers, and herbs, all selected for adaptability to the cold-climate gardening typical of New England. Of the varieties of seed offered, about 150 are designated as heirloom varieties, and about 100 varieties are actually produced at the company's Albion research farm. You may obtain a free catalog by writing to the address shown.

Native Seeds/ SEARCH
2509 N. Campbell Avenue #325
Tucson, AZ 85719

This nonprofit organization has a large selection of native crop seed stocks from the Greater Southwest. Almost all of the varieties offered are traditional crops grown by native American Indians, and more than half of the seeds offered are produced by Indians who trade, sell, or give them to Native Seeds. The catalog offers detailed descriptions and cultivation requirements

of over 200 varieties of grains, vegetables, and herbs. Choices include truly novel plants, such as blue corn and Devil's Claw (a vegetable resembling okra), as well as traditional grains, such as amaranth. For a membership fee of $10, you receive a quarterly newsletter and two issues of the seed catalog from Native Seeds. Members also receive a 10 percent discount on all seed orders and catalog gift items. If you are not a member of the organization, you may also order a single copy of the seed catalog by sending $1 to the address shown.

Seeds Blüm
Idaho City Stage
Boise, ID 83706

Seeds Blüm produces an extensive catalog full of gardening and seed-saving tips, gardening folklore, and reviews of gardening books. In addition to a wealth of gardening information, the catalog lists over 1,000 varieties of flowers and vegetables, all open-pollinated and available for purchase. Over half of the listings are for heirloom varieties grown more than 65 years ago. As a service to its customers, Seeds Blüm offers a "Seedfind" service. Using a form supplied in the catalog, you can request a search for any variety of seed, and the company will locate a source for you (if it's available) free of charge. You may order your first catalog by sending $3 to the address shown above. After your first order, you will receive an annual catalog free of charge.

Southern Exposure Seed Exchange
P.O. Box 158
North Garden, VA 22959

Southern Exposure is a small company specializing in seeds of varieties especially adapted to the mid-Atlantic region and the South. If you deal with hot, humid summers in your garden, you'll find something here to interest you. Southern Exposure offers over 350 varieties of vegetables and herbs, and heirloom varieties are marked for easy location in the catalog. In addition to offering old and unusual varieties, Southern Exposure also offers a gift certificate to any customer who supplies the company with a sample of heirloom seeds. Special attention is given to seeds passed down through many family generations. The company grows these seeds collected from

their customers in order to offer them to others through the catalog. You may receive your initial catalog by sending $3 to the address above. Following your initial order, all subsequent catalogs will be sent free of charge.

If All Else Fails

If you have trouble locating a seed variety, you may find one of these resources helpful. Using any one of these four resources, you should be able to locate many other companies, foundations, and even private individuals offering rare and unusual seeds and cuttings.

L.H. Bailey Hortorium
Bailey Nursery and Seed Catalog Collection
467 Mann Library Building
Cornell University
Ithaca, NY 14853

This prestigious hortorium boasts a seed catalog collection of over 128,000 volumes spanning time from the late 1800s to the present. The hortorium currently receives over 700 nursery catalogs, and conducts ongoing research into the availability of plants throughout the United States. As a service to the public, the hortorium will locate a source of seeds or plants for you for the modest fee of $2 per plant. Their sources include large and small commercial seed companies as well as nonprofit seed banks, exchanges, and foundations. If you can't find what you're looking for in a seed exchange or company we've mentioned, this is a good alternative.

Gardening by Mail
Tusker Press, 1987
P.O. Box 1338
Sebastopol, CA 95473
　　In this 336-page softcover book by Barbara J. Barton, you will find over 2,000 mail-order sources for specific plants and seeds, garden supplies, societies, libraries, magazines, and gardening books. The book is available for $16 plus $2.50 postage and handling ($3.50 for California and foreign orders), and is a treasury of hard-to-find sources of information (such as horticultural libraries) as well as seeds and plants.

The Mail-Order Gardener
Harper & Row Publishers, 1988
Downsville Pike
Route 3, Box 20-B
Hagerstown, MD 21740
　　This 287-page softcover book by Hal Morgan offers a directory of more than 1,500 mail-order sources for seeds, tools, and garden accessories. Although this book is directed more toward the mainstream con-sumer than *Gardening by Mail*, you still might find it useful if you'd like to find some unusual tool or garden furnishing in addition to sources for unusual seeds. The list price for paperback is $12.95 plus $1.50 for fourth-class shipping and handling.

Seed and Nursery Directory
Rural Advancement Fund
P.O. Box 1029
Pittsboro, NC 27312
　　The Rural Advancement Fund is a nonprofit organization founded in 1937 to further the cause of the family farm and a just, ecologically sound agricultural system. A major activity of this group is the promotion of crop diversity and the preservation of old varieties of fruits, grains, and vegetables. The organization publishes a directory of sources for traditional vegetables, fruits, nuts, herbs, and other native American plants. Included in the directory is a list of small, family-owned seed companies; fruit, nut, and berry nurseries that sell old varieties; organizations that promote the conservation of old varieties; sources for wildflower plants and seeds; and other useful information on heirloom plants. For a copy of the directory, send $3 to the address shown.

Weather Lore

Gardeners have always been interested in the age-old sayings of weather lore. Some of these folk sayings are outrageously false, some partly true, and some amazingly accurate. In any event, weather lore forms a link between us and the gardeners of the past, a sort of indelible shared experience that charms and cajoles us into seeing our own gardening as part of a valuable human experience throughout history.

EVERYBODY TALKS ABOUT THE WEATHER
BUT NOBODY DOES ANYTHING ABOUT IT.
Mark Twain

IF THE SUN IN RED SHOULD SET,
THE NEXT DAY WILL SURELY BE WET.
IF THE SUN SHOULD SET IN GRAY,
THE NEXT WILL BE A RAINY DAY.
American Folk Saying

IF CANDLEMAS BE FAIR AND CLEAR,
TWO WINTERS WILL YOU HAVE THIS YEAR.
Pennsylvania Dutch Saying

CLEAR MOON,
FROST SOON.
American Folk Saying

PALE MOON DOTH RAIN
RED MOON DOTH BLOW,
WHITE MOON DOTH NEITHER RAIN NOR SNOW.
EVERY WIND HAS ITS WEATHER.
Sir Francis Bacon

A COW WITH ITS TAIL TO THE WEST
MAKES WEATHER THE BEST.
A COW WITH ITS TAIL TO THE EAST
MAKES WEATHER THE LEAST.
American Folk Saying

ALL CLOUDS BRING NOT RAIN.
American Folk Saying

ALMANAC GARDENING CALENDAR

With northern zone gardeners gearing up for spring and southern zone gardeners preparing for summer, April is probably the busiest month for all gardeners everywhere. Upper zone gardeners hope to see a pansy in bud by the end of the month; gardeners in Zones 4 and 5 can look forward to harvesting cool-season crops and the beginning of rose-blooming season; folks in Zones 6 and 7 can work on the summer garden in earnest by planting more hot-weather crops and harvesting the first tomatoes and cucumbers.

Zone 1

In the first week, dig and refrigerate remaining carrots, parsnips, and beets stored in the ground. Spread manure or compost in the garden and till the soil as soon as it is dry enough to work. Remove mulch from overwintering spinach and lettuce, but replace mulch if night temperatures fall below 20°F. Begin planting outdoors peas, lettuce, onions (transplants, sets, or seeds), beets, chard, spinach, radishes, turnips, shallots, chives, and parsley. For early harvests, warm the soil by erecting plastic tunnels or portable cold frames. By the last two weeks, begin planting carrots and parsnips. In the first three weeks, start cole crops indoors for planting outside in May. As soon as the plants are up, move them to a cold frame that is left open during the day, or take them outside on days when the temperature is above 40°F. At midmonth move seedlings started in February and March (tomatoes, peppers, and eggplants) into a cold frame.

In early April, remove the mulch from overwintering pansies, roses, and other tender ornamentals. Fertilize roses and perennials with rotted manure or compost. Harden off pansies and dianthus grown indoors so they can be planted out after midmonth. Direct-seed sweet peas, alyssum, and Shasta daisies. There is still time to start asters, calendulas, stocks, marigolds, and zinnias indoors. As soon as seeds have germinated, move the flats to a frost-free cold frame, a cool, sunny window, or a window with grow lights.

Plant young fruit trees and bushes as soon as they arrive. Clear and mulch a 3-foot circle around each tree. Water weekly if there is little rain. Cover strawberry beds when frost threatens. Frost won't kill the leaves but will destroy blossoms, reducing yield. Put aged manure and peat moss around blueberries.

Zone 2

Sow cole crops indoors now so that the plants will be nice and blocky at transplanting time. Start celery plants about eight weeks before you plan to set them out. Peas and onion sets can be sown outdoors in cold, wet soil. Place tallest seedlings of tomatoes, peppers, and eggplants (sown indoors in February and March) in the cold frame to harden off. It will slow their growth and make them bushier. Cover cold frames at night in case temperature drops to 25°F or so. Be sure to vent the frames a crack on hot, sunny days.

Early in the month sow ageratums indoors to have flowers in late May and early June. Seedlings transplant better if sown now. Sow annual asters and impatiens indoors now for early summer flowers. In late April remove mulch from roses. Loosen up bare spots in the lawn and scatter grass seed over them. Rake debris from your peony bed to cut down on Botrytis blight. Plant ferns outdoors in a shady spot. Lady, sword, cinnamon, and maidenhair ferns are all hardy in Zone 2. There's still time to prune peach, apple, and cherry trees. Thin the canopy so that sunlight can enter. Don't paint pruning wounds. If you're an inexperienced pruner, consult your extension service or a book on pruning before trying it.

Zone 3

Early in the month, gradually harden off transplants of cool-weather crops, such as cabbage, broccoli, kohlrabi, and cauliflower, for planting into the garden by midmonth. Keep cloches handy to guard against killing frosts.

In early April, sow outdoors more peas, spinach, turnips, lettuce, radishes, carrots, and beets. Set out onion sets and potatoes at the beginning of April and make succession plantings of these crops in mid- and late April. In the second half of the month, start watermelon, cantaloupe, and summer squash seeds indoors for transplanting outside in May. If April has been warm, begin hardening off tomatoes, peppers, and eggplants at the end of the month. Your asparagus bed should move into full production during April. Beds more than two years old can be picked daily by snapping off 6- to 8-inch spears just below the ground. New beds should also be planted now so they'll be established by the time hot weather arrives. Prepare planting areas for warm-weather crops by the end of the month. Turn under winter mulches, cover crops, and rock fertilizers, leaving the soil rough to reduce erosion.

Gradually remove winter mulches from perennials and roses. Leave soil exposed to warming sun, and prune roses to remove winter-killed wood. Side-dress peonies and delphiniums with wood ashes, compost, and bonemeal. Pinch peonies to one bud per stalk if you want larger blooms. Get new perennials, shrubs, trees, and ground covers into the ground as soon as they arrive. Plant in large holes or well-prepared beds, then mulch and water frequently until they're established. Seed bare patches in the lawn as soon as soil can be worked. Hold off fertilizing the lawn until after the first mowing.

Work compost and rock fertilizers into annual flower beds at the beginning of the month. Toward the end of the month, sow outdoors annuals that germinate well in cool soil, such as cornflowers, baby's-breath, phlox, strawflowers, and poppies. Prune lilacs, forsythias, and dogwoods after petal drop. Late in the month, start hardening off bedding plants started indoors during February and March. Reduce water and keep protected until plants have adjusted to outdoor conditions. Plant new fruit trees, bushes, and vines as soon as the soil can be worked. Mulch, stake if necessary, and water frequently until they're established.

If spring has been warm, fruit bloom may begin during April. Just as budswell begins, prune winter-killed and unproductive wood from peaches and nectarines. Fertilize bushes, vines, and trees by spreading a generous layer of compost or aged manure in a ring around each. Work an extra helping of bonemeal into the soil around grapevines. Remove winter trunk protectors from fruit trees and check around the soil line for holes and gummy sawdust, which are signs of borers. Kill borers with a stiff wire. Apply a fresh ring of Tanglefoot to the trunks of trees and vines. Treat bark cracks caused by winter weather with tree wound dressing. Prevent this injury next year by painting trunks and large branches with white latex paint in fall.

Zone 4

Outdoors make succession plantings of lettuce, radishes, beets, turnips and other fast-maturing crops. Plant seedlings of cole plants, but keep frost protection nearby. Begin mounding earth or compost 5 or 6 inches deep over asparagus to cool soil and increase spear size. In warmer areas, set out tomatoes, peppers, and eggplants sown indoors during February. Eggplants need a daytime temperature of 70°F. Be ready to cover plants if frost occurs. In the rest of the zone, plant cucurbits in peat pots for setting out next month. Watch for aphids and other pests—handpicking or spraying with a jet of soapy water now will reduce the size of later generations.

Sow hardy annuals outdoors as early as possible. As buds swell, prune roses by removing all injured wood and weak canes. Prune early blooming shrubs within a week or two after flowering. Scratch in manure and bonemeal around perennials. Thin out aggressive plants like bee balm, yarrow, and the larger artemisias. Divide other perennials by discarding woody centers and replanting outer parts. Begin pinching the tips of taller varieties of chrysanthemums after every 4 inches of growth until midsummer. Dig and divide iris clumps and check rhizomes for signs of rot or borers; discard unhealthy plants. Search out borers in the stem and trunk bases of dogwoods, rhododendrons, mountain ashes, and lilacs by inserting wires in grub holes. Watch for oystershell scale on lilacs and willows, cutting out heavy infestations. As warm weather settles in, sow tender annuals and harden bedding plants. Sprout dahlia and begonia tubers indoors in peat moss. Plant cannas and glads outdoors. Feed all ornamentals generous helpings of aged compost or manure.

Cut black and purple raspberries to about 30 inches when they begin to leaf out. Remove blossoms of new strawberry plants now; everbearers can be allowed to flower in July for a fall crop. Renew mulches, and water all new fruit plantings in dry weather. They need an inch of water a week. Cut off fire blight-infected pear twigs along with 4 inches of healthy growth using sterile clippers.

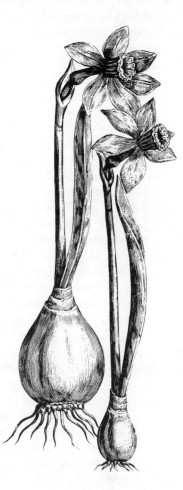

Zone 5

Plant outdoors warm-season vegetables such as beans, corn, squash, melons, and cucumbers. Thin and begin mulching when the plants are two weeks old. Also thin lettuce and other spring greens. If aphids are a problem, spray the leaves with cool, soapy water. Continue to treat cabbage, broccoli, and other brassicas with Bt (*Bacillus thuringiensis*) to control cabbageworms. Harden off early tomato and pepper seedlings and set them out. Direct-seed dill, basil, mint, and other herbs. Top-dress bulb onions with compost, or fertilize with manure tea. Thoroughly water peas when each flush of blossoms appears. Move eggplants to the garden late in the month, and begin planting okra, watermelons, field peas, sweet potatoes, pumpkins, and peanuts. Keep Irish potatoes planted in March well mulched, and carefully handpick potato-beetle larvae as soon as they appear. Plant buckwheat or clover where cover crops are needed. Spring grass clippings are extra rich in nitrogen— use them as mulch on short-season crops.

Begin setting out warm-weather bedding plants. By midmonth, the soil should be warm enough to direct-seed marigolds, zinnias, touch-me-nots, four-o'clocks, and sunflowers. Morning glories self- seed so well they can become a pest, so be careful where you plant them. Set out glads just after the first of the month, followed by dahlias at midmonth and caladiums after warm weather sets in. Dig and divide chrysanthemums. Leave the foliage of daffodils and other spring- flowering bulbs in place until it turns brown. Top-dress azaleas and camellias with leaf mold or compost. After the flowers fade on forsythia, quince, and other spring-flowering shrubs, prune the plants.

Closely mow lawns that have have been overplanted with rye. Late in the month, feed zoysia and Bermuda lawns with compost or a slow-release organic fertilizer to stimulate new growth and earthworm activity. Continue to plant raspberries, blackberries, and boysenberries as soon as the plants arrive. Fertilize and mulch established berry plantings, grapes, figs, and gooseberries. When strawberries begin to blossom, give the plants a booster feeding of manure tea to help prolong production and cover the beds with bird netting. Starting this month, thin the fruits of plums, peaches, nectarines, apples, and pears until they are 4 to 6 inches apart. Add the picked fruit and other ground debris to the compost heap. Also thin bunch grapes on vines that are three to five years old, leaving only the three best bunches on each vine. Keep the sod around fruit trees mowed. Spray leaf-eating worms with Bt.

Zone 6

Begin planting black-eyed peas, squash, melons, cucumbers, and corn to get a harvest before insects are a problem. At the end of the month, plant okra, peanuts, sweet potatoes, and Malabar and New Zealand spinach. Be careful not to over-crowd seedlings. Don't mulch until the soil has warmed up. Before planting, work in compost or de-cayed manure to supply the nutrients and hold the water plants need to produce maximum yields. Plant oregano, mint, marjoram, coriander, and basil from seeds or cuttings. You may also direct-seed anise, fennel, catnip, borage, and sage, but yarrow, comfrey, summer savory, and salad burnet do better if transplanted.

Plant cosmos, sunflowers, stocks, foxgloves, petunias, verbenas, pansies, and nasturtiums. Marigolds are important in the garden, but be sure to also include zinnias, gaillardias, morning glories, and periwinkle for varied color. Also plant irises, glads, and dahlias in sunny spots with good drainage. In shady areas, caladiums, impatiens, coleus, hostas, and violets do well. Prune climbing roses and other spring-flowering shrubs after they've

bloomed. Apply compost to azaleas and camellias when they finish blooming. Pinch dead blooms from perennials, and root cuttings of chrysanthemums, discarding the old, woody clumps. In areas where summer evenings are cool, plant begonia tubers and poppies.

Now that fruit has set, top-dress fruit and nut trees, grapes, figs, and berries with compost and moderate amounts of nitrogen- and phosphorus-rich fertilizers. Fish emulsion, chicken manure, cotton-seed meal, and blood meal are good sources of nitrogen, and bonemeal and rock phosphate will provide needed phosphorus. Apply bird netting before fruit ripens. Do not fertilize newly planted fruit and nut trees, but water them regularly and apply a thick mulch. To get large-sized fruits, thin a crop when fruit is still smaller than a Ping-Pong ball. Keep grapes and muscadines vigorous by deep watering and periodic foliar feeding with liquid seaweed. Worms on grapes and muscadines can easily be controlled with Bt (*Bacillus thuringiensis*).

Zone 7

The soil should be warm enough throughout the zone to plant sweet potato slips, soybeans, lima beans, southern peas, and okra. Start chayote, or mirliton, outdoors by midmonth, and plant three to make sure that there will be female and male plants. In southern Florida, Texas, Louisiana, and the interior desert valleys of California, plant beets, lettuce, turnips, and mustard for the last time until fall. In this hot tier also plant sweet corn, green beans, collards, cucumbers, tomatoes, peppers, and eggplants before the middle of the month. Continue planting watermelons, squashes, pumpkins, sweet potatoes, and green onions throughout the month. In the cooler tier of the zone, plant warm-weather vegetables, and continue planting fast-maturing cool-weather crops, such as kohlrabi, beets, lettuce, turnips, radishes, carrots, and potatoes, throughout the month. Start planting hot-weather spinach substitutes, such as New Zealand spinach and chard. Plant blocks of bush beans and sweet corn throughout the month.

As the weather heats up, keep your crops growing vigorously by side-dressing with fertilizers or watering with manure tea. Make sure drip lines, soaker hoses, sprinklers or irrigation trenches are in place before plants get too large. Mulch the garden to conserve water. Plan watering systems and lay mulches around ornamentals to bring them through the hot season. Caladiums

can be planted out in the warm tier of the zone. In cooler areas, start them in pots. Houseplants can be moved outside for greening up. First place them in shade, then move them gradually into filtered light.

Prune to shape azaleas, camellias, and rhododendrons after they have finished blooming. Azalea trimmings and softwood cuttings of many other shrubs and perennials can easily be rooted in sand and peat moss. Start replacing winter flowers like calendulas and pansies with heat-tolerant annuals like ageratums, petunias, four-o'clocks, marigolds, and salvias.

To keep down aphids and thrips in orchards, spray the first invaders with jets of water early in the morning. If the problem gets worse, use soap sprays or a botanical insecticide such as rotenone or pyrethrum. Remove tent caterpillar nests from pecan or fruit trees with a stick. Fertilize strawberries with compost early in the month and mulch before the leaves become dense and the berries form. By midmonth, when the strawberries begin to turn red, protect the fruit from birds by laying down netting. The cheapest netting is nylon net purchased from a fabric shop. Brown, black, or dark green seem to foil the birds best. Install watering systems before the weather heats up.

Planting Lore

Farmers and gardeners of old didn't have the six o'clock news to give them the five-day forecast. They relied on a treasury of folk sayings and their own personal experience to decide when to cut the hay and when to plant the potatoes. The old way is still a good one. It doesn't need a plug and a TV screen to help you along, and it connects you to an earlier, simpler time when the cycles of nature were inextricably bound into the workaday lives of everyone. Some of the most helpful (and puzzling) lore relates to an activity everybody did—planting:

For planting corn, beans, and peas: "One for the rook, one for the crow, one to rot, and one to grow."

For planting parsley, a plant thought to be linked to the devil: "Plant parsley only on Good Friday, for only on that day is the devil without power. Planting parsley on any other day puts your life in danger."

For planting by the moon, which was thought to have the power to draw things out of the earth: "Sow seed when the moon is waxing [growing larger]. Sow root crops when the moon is waning."

For planting peas: "Plant peas on St. Patrick's Day for the blessing of the saint himself on your entire garden."

For planting corn: "Plant corn when oak leaves are as big a squirrels' ears."

For planting beans: "Plant your beans when the elm leaves are as big as a penny."

IN GOOD HEALTH

THE FIRST WEEK OF APRIL IS KNOW YOUR CHOLESTEROL WEEK

How do I know if I have it?

If "it" is poison ivy, a broken leg, or incontinence, that's a question you probably won't need to ask. At the very least, you'll know that something is very wrong—enough to propel you to the doctor, if necessary.

But heart disease is different. Too much cholesterol in your blood works insidiously over decades, depositing layers of plaque that narrow arteries, slowing blood flow to a trickle and ending in a heart attack that could be fatal. All this without so much as a hint of trouble beforehand, in many cases.

That's why having your cholesterol level checked is so important. It's like taking a peek inside your arteries, like a sneak preview that gives you the chance to avoid a bad movie. And you can. Doctors have found that reducing a high cholesterol level reduces the risk of heart attack.

So how do you go about checking out your cholesterol? The best place to start is at your doctor's office. The next time you're there, simply ask to have your cholesterol tested. Or call to make an appointment to have it done.

It's best to do it at a time in your life when your diet is not changing a lot and you're not gaining or losing weight—what's called a steady state. "People say, 'Oh, I'm gonna get my cholesterol measured,' and start changing their diet to the way they think they should eat," says John W. Farquhar, M.D., director of the Stanford Center for Research in Disease Prevention at Stanford University. "It's better to see what it is on your usual diet, then if you want to experiment, you can change and see what happens."

The test consists of having a small tube of blood drawn from your arm—about 10 cc, or ⅓ ounce —not exactly the stuff horror films are made of. It's not usually painful, either. The blood can be drawn right in the doctor's office, although some physicians may send you to a laboratory to have it done.

If you're testing only for total cholesterol, the blood can be drawn on the spot. But if your doctor decides to test for triglycerides as well, you'll be instructed to fast before having the test. That means nothing to eat after dinner (about 6:00 P.M.) the night before the test. No chips during your favorite TV show. No ice cream during the 11 o'clock news. No real hardship.

Schedule the test for first thing the following morning, and your fast will be over in short order.

Once the sample reaches the lab, a technician spins the tube of blood in a centrifuge to separate the cells from the serum. The cells end up in the bottom of the tube, with the serum on top, kind of like sediment resting at the bottom of a lake. A small sample of the serum is removed and a machine does the actual test. Depending on how busy the lab is, your doctor could have the results the next day.

Cholesterol Guidelines

Desirable Blood Cholesterol	Borderline-High Blood Cholesterol	High Blood Cholesterol
Less than 200 mg/dl	200 to 239 mg/dl	240 mg/dl and above

SOURCE: "So You Have High Blood Cholesterol . . ." National Institutes of Health Publication No. 87-2922, September, 1987.

NOTE: The table refers to total blood cholesterol. These categories apply to anyone 20 years of age or older.

What It All Means

The first thing to know about your cholesterol measurement is that you should take it with a grain of salt. "It's best not to think of it as a magical number that really is your number," says Dr. Farquhar. For one thing, your cholesterol level varies. "People know that there's variability in body weight, they know blood pressure bounces around, and they need to be told that cholesterol bounces around, too."

There's also variability at the laboratory. "Some of the variation is technical. There are different methods for measuring total cholesterol that give slightly different results," says John C. LaRosa, M.D., director of the Lipid Research Clinic at George Washington University School of Medicine and Health Sciences. "And there's probably some variation within laboratories, too." For those reasons, and because there can be an occasional fluke, Dr. LaRosa recommends that you have at least two cholesterol measurements done within two weeks. Dr. Farquhar recommends having it done three times and taking the average.

What's a safe cholesterol level? A panel of experts met in 1984 to decide that question, among others. That "consensus development panel," set up by the National Institutes of Health, issued a chart listing the risks of various cholesterol levels in people of various ages. It's so detailed that it's a little unwieldy. But it's probably safe to generalize that a cholesterol measurement over 200 milligrams per deciliter may be cause for concern. "Ideally, it should be 180 or below," says Dr. Farquhar.

Another question you might have is whether to have your levels of triglycerides and HDL cholesterol (high-density lipoprotein—the protective kind) checked while you're at it. There's no definitive answer yet, but that aspect of cholesterol testing is being considered as part of the work of an expert panel on detection, evaluation, and treatment of high blood cholesterol. In the meantime, most doctors recommend using total cholesterol as a screening test, then checking further if the level is elevated.

"You're not going to get agreement on whether all of the tests ought to be done on everyone," says Dr. LaRosa. "But there's reasonable agreement that a total cholesterol point somewhere around 200 ought to be a trigger for separating people who probably don't need any more attention (provided there is no family history of heart disease) and people who need a triglyceride and HDL test. If there is a family history of heart disease, you probably ought to measure triglycerides and HDL anyway." Some doctors measure triglycerides and/or HDL cholesterol as a matter of course.

Hold the HDL?

One argument for holding off on HDL testing is that it has even more problems with accuracy than the total cholesterol test. In addition, it adds considerable expense. While a measurement of total cholesterol averages about $25, a full "cardiovascular profile" may cost $60 or more. Check with your insurer about coverage.

If you do have your HDL tested, the lab can then also calculate the level of LDL cholesterol (low-density lipoprotein—the dangerous kind). Basically, the more HDL, the better, and the less LDL, the better. An HDL below 40 or 50 is cause for concern; so is an LDL over 160.

But it's not cut-and-dried. Various genetic and environmental factors can influence these levels. Here's where the interpretation of the results gets pretty complicated—a good argument for doing all of this through your doctor.

Some doctors rely on the ratio between total cholesterol and HDL as an indication of risk. The ratio is attained by dividing the total cholesterol number by the HDL number. The lower the ratio, the better—that means that there's more HDL compared to LDL. A ratio below 3.5 would be considered ideal, and a ratio of 4.0 to 5.0 indicates about average risk. But there are situations where the ratio method doesn't work. One of those situations is when the total cholesterol level is in the upper 200s. If a person has a total cholesterol of 280, for example, and an HDL of 80, his ratio would be 3.5, which sounds pretty good, right? "I'd still worry about that person," says Dr. LaRosa. "The HDL is high, but the LDL is also very high. I'm not too reassured by high HDL in the presence of high LDL." Dr. Farquhar agrees, "If the LDL is high, I want to see it down. I don't want to trust the protection of HDL."

The first step in lowering a high cholesterol level is a change in diet. "Regardless of your cholesterol level, you should change your diet toward the prudent diet," says Dr. Farquhar. "If the test indicates moderate or high risk, you should start pursuing it more vigorously."

Dr. LaRosa agrees. "Everybody should be tried on a diet first," he says. "Most doctors would agree that the American Heart Association (AHA) diet is appropriate. It's actually a series of diets that starts by lowering cholesterol and saturated-fat content and increasingly lowering those components more and more as the 'phase' of the diet is increased." Your local AHA can provide you with the details.

Time to Change

Just don't expect immediate changes. "It takes time to get your mind made up, learn new habits of eating, change your palate preference around, get used to it, practice it, and feel comfortable with it," says Dr. Farquhar. "Let's say that takes you two to three months. Once you've made the change, it takes only a week to ten days on that particular diet to affect your cholesterol level. Then you can go back and have your cholesterol checked two or three more times. If it hasn't gone down enough, then go into a more advanced nutritional-change program. Try that for three months. See if it works. If it still doesn't work, consider medications under your doctor's careful guidance."

If your doctor advises exercise and weight loss, you'll need even more patience. Those can take even longer to accomplish than changing the nature of your diet. "After you reach the weight you think you'll be able to maintain, stay there for a couple of weeks and get into a steady state before you get your cholesterol done again," says Dr. Farquhar.

If your cholesterol level is normal, keeping track of it is a much simpler affair. "Assuming that your cholesterol level is normal, the AHA has somewhat arbitrarily decided on checking it once every five years," says Dr. LaRosa. "But that's assuming that there's no major change in health, weight, diet, or exercise patterns." If you're very concerned, you may want to have it checked every year.

The age at which to begin testing is another subject of intense debate. "I think all adults should have a cholesterol measurement done," says Dr. LaRosa. "Whether or not to screen all children is still debatable. Children with a strong family history of coronary disease should be tested. And I think it's very practical to say that children who go to a pediatrician for any reason should have a cholesterol test. But most people agree that in children under the age of two, it's not worth being concerned about."

APRIL IS NATIONAL CANCER CONTROL MONTH

The American Cancer Society recommends that for early detection of cancer, people 20-40 years of age have a cancer-related checkup every three years, and people over 40 have a checkup every year. And the Committee on Diet, Nutrition, and Cancer of the National Research Council advises you to take these dietary steps to lower your cancer risk:

☞ Reduce your intake of both saturated and unsaturated fats. High fat intake is associated with an increased incidence of breast and colon cancer. The average American gets about 40 percent of his or her total calories from fats; this should be reduced to 30 percent.

☞ Include fruits, vegetables, and whole-grain cereals in your daily diet, especially citrus fruits, cabbage-family vegetables, and fruits and vegetables rich in beta-carotene (yellow and orange ones). Populations that frequently consume these foods have been found to have reduced incidence of cancer.

☞ Minimize the intake of salt-cured, pickled, and smoked foods. Populations that frequently consume salt-cured or smoked foods have been found to have a greater incidence of cancer of the stomach and esophagus.

☞ Drink alcoholic beverages in moderation, if at all. Excessive drinking, particularly when combined with cigarette smoking, has been associated with an increased risk of cancer of the upper gastrointestinal and respiratory tracts.

Dietary guidelines above adapted from the 1982 report, Diet, Nutrition, and Cancer, *by the Committee on Diet, Nutrition, and Cancer, a committee of scientists appointed by the National Research Council. The National Research Council is part of the National Academy of Sciences in Washington, D.C. Copies of the report are available for $19.95 (shipping included) from National Academy Press, 2101 Constitution Avenue NW, Washington, DC 20418.*

THE THIRD WEEK OF APRIL IS NATIONAL CONSUMER'S WEEK

The cost of medical care concerns all of us because we are all consumers. We all depend on medical care for wellness services (such as prenatal exams and child inoculations) as well as for care of acute or chronic illness. The rate of increase in medical care costs has consistently been higher than the overall inflation rate in the United States. In 1986, the cost of medical care rose 7.7 percent. During that same year the Consumer Price Index rose only 1.1 percent. In other words, the cost of medical care increased seven times faster than the rate of general inflation.

It pays to shop for medical care just as you would shop for other services. Remember that doctors have signs asking people to pay at the time of their visit. Hospitals post notices about minimum fees for use of their emergency room. No matter how helpful or necessary a medical service may be, money is always exchanged for the service rendered. Make your medical decisions with as much care as you make any other major money-spending decision. You may not be able to do anything about the outrageous pace of inflation in medical care costs, but you certainly can do your part to reduce its impact on your own pocketbook. Here are some tips that can save you money in medical care costs:

☞ Use a medical specialist only if it's truly necessary. Specialists cost more. Be certain that your problem requires the care of a specialist; sometimes a general practitioner is just as qualified and capable of doing the procedure.

☞ Avoid unnecessary lab tests. Five billion lab tests are performed each year. That's more than 20 per person.

Are *all* these tests necessary? Probably not. That's why you should always question the need for lab work, especially if you've already had the same test done for you recently. Ask your doctor whether the test results will affect his or her choice of treatment. If the answer is no, and you'll be getting the same therapy anyway, why pay good money for what may be a needless test? Many simple, inexpensive lab tests are considered standard. Among these are: blood and urine tests for diabetes, stool blood tests for colon cancer, and bacterial culture for strep throat.

☞ Get a second opinion for surgery. Don't be embarrassed or feel that you may insult your doctor if you seek another opinion. If you have any doubts about a particular course of therapy, a second opinion is well worth the money. By preventing unneeded procedures and identifying alternative treatment, second opinions can actually result in higher-quality care. And many insurance companies now require that you get a second opinion for some kinds of surgery. To save some money on the second opinion ask your doctor to send copies of your medical records, x-rays, and lab tests to the second opinion doctor so that you don't pay for duplicate tests.

☞ Get a third or fourth opinion if the first two don't agree. A thorough investigation on your part removes any lingering doubts you may have about a treatment course, and you may save money by discovering a simpler way to cope with your problem.

☞ Use non-M.D. health providers for routine care of uncomplicated health problems. Examples of health providers who can take care of simple problems (and who are trained to refer you to a physician if your problem is truly serious) are: optometrists, podiatrists, psychologists, audiologists, and nurse practitioners.

☞ Check doctors' fees in advance of a visit. There are variations in basic fees and lab charges. If you are considering two physicians who are both board certified in a specialty, it makes sense to first try the one who has the lower fee.

☞ Seek telephone advice from your doctor when possible. Most doctors are happy to answer simple questions and provide advice over the phone for uncomplicated problems, drug reactions, or a chronic problem they've already evaluated. Most doctors are also willing to authorize a refill of a prescription over the phone if, in their professional judgment, it's warranted. Telephone advice saves time (yours and the doctor's) and money (just yours).

☞ Request that your doctor accept Medicare payments on assignment. This means that the doctor will accept the assigned fee Medicare allows for his service and that you will not be required to pay more than your copayment. If your doctor refuses this request, find another doctor.

☞ Say "No" to any treatment, test, or procedure that you do not understand. Keep asking questions until you get a satisfactory answer.

Cost-saving tips above adapted from 150 Ways to Lower Your Medical Costs by Charles B. Inlander, published by the People's Medical Society, 1987.

IF THE SHOE FITS, WEAR IT

If your feet don't hurt, consider yourself an exception. In a 1984 survey by the Gallup organization, 73 percent of the people polled said their feet hurt. Some causes of sore feet require the attention of a doctor or a podiatrist, but frequently a trip to one of these specialists may be avoided by a simple preventive tactic: buying shoes that fit properly. The following tips, developed by *Prevention* magazine for walkers, should help you get the best shoe for avoiding foot problems. Keep these tips in mind when you purchase all types of shoes, especially walking shoes.

Don't be "small-minded." The most common mistake people make is buying shoes that are too small. Foot size changes with age, weight gain or loss, and changes in exercise patterns. Never assume that just because you've "always worn a size 8," that's the size that fits you best. (You wouldn't expect your prom dress to fit you forever, would you?) In fact, proper fitting is often as simple as buying a shoe one half-size larger than usual.

Judge a shoe by its fit, not its size. Keep in mind, too, that not every size-8 shoe is created equal. The fit will vary considerably with style and features, even within the same brand. Always have both feet measured and use that size as a starting point. Then concentrate on fit. Forget the size. Ask yourself: How does it feel?

Fit your "Bigfoot." Your feet are probably slightly different in size. Make sure you fit the larger foot. It's better to add a half-insole to the front of the shoe of the smaller foot than to cram the larger foot into a too-small size.

Give your toes some space. Pay some attention to the shape of the toe of your prospective shoes. The wider and higher the toe box, the more comfort for your foot. Don't be afraid of extra space between the tips of your toes and the end of the shoe. If you press on the toe of the shoe and hit nothing but air space, don't worry. It does not mean the shoe is too big. You need that extra room during the motion of walking.

If the shoe "just fits," don't buy it. Many people think that if a new shoe feels roomy, it's too big. Maybe that's because some styles cut for fashion, such as pumps, flats, or loafers, will fall off if they're not tight. But a walking shoe should have sufficient room to allow for adequate space when your foot flexes. Shoes that are too small will restrict the normal exercising of the muscles and tendons, causing pain and cramping. Keep in mind that your foot can swell to a whole

size larger when you walk, and that you'll be wearing socks to soak up perspiration. Take your socks along with you when you purchase new walking shoes.

Become well-heeled. Contrary to popular belief, a new pair of shoes shouldn't hug your heels. In fact, there should be room enough to slide a pencil between your heel and back of the shoe to guarantee proper fit. Instead, many people test the shoe's heel fit by contracting their feet and pulling up. If their heels slip out, they think the shoe is too big. They buy a smaller size and end up with blisters (which are generally caused by tight shoes, not loose ones.) The fact of the matter is that the heel of a shoe really doesn't begin to fit until after the shoe has been flexed repeatedly. Over time, the shoe heel will "cup," or turn in at the top, and begin to conform to the curve of your heel.

Don't assume that tight shoes will "break in." Discard that idea with your Band-Aids and corn plasters. The only thing you're breaking in with a too-small shoe is your foot. As we already noted, your feet swell in response to walking, and that will make that already-tight shoe become unbearable as the day goes on. Shoes can get a little bit wider with use, but that can be controlled by adjusting the laces. A correctly fitted shoe should feel great right from the start.

Pride goeth before a sore foot. Lots of people, especially women, feel uncomfortable about large shoe sizes. They tend to blush and become embarrassed when they have to tell someone their shoe size. Don't allow this kind of misplaced vanity to keep you from taking a larger shoe size. Remember pain in your feet will show up as agony on your face, the part of you the world really focuses on.

Go to a pro for a perfect fit. Find a shoe store where you can get the assistance of an experienced shoe fitter. If you have any special problems with your feet, find a store with a shoe fitter who is a member of the Professional Shoe Fitters Society or the Prescription Footwear Association. Consult your yellow pages and look for stores with nationally recognized, high-quality shoes. Yellow pages sometimes even list a professional fitting service. When you do find a good fitter, be flexible and open to new suggestions. Your feet deserve the best advice you can get.

Walking Tip for April

Don't let April showers keep you inside. Don some weatherproof gear, put on your walking shoes and recapture that joy you felt as a child hopping over puddles. For the greatest comfort, you'll find that lightweight raingear made with ripstop nylon allows you more mobility than the traditional rubberized, heavy raincoat. The main obstacle to complete enjoyment of a rainy walk is wet feet. When you return home, get out of those wet shoes as soon as possible. Dry your feet thoroughly (especially between toes and around nails) to prevent any foot fungus (a cause of athlete's foot) from taking hold. Moisture on your feet has the same effect as a sprinkler on a lawn. Something will grow, but the question is, is it something you want. To rescue your soggy shoes, be sure to dry them properly. If your walking shoes are canvas or nylon, you can simply tumble dry them. If your shoes are of leather or other nonwashable material, fill them loosely with paper towels or crumpled newspaper and set them in a warm place to dry. Don't put them on or near a radiator. Direct heat to leather shoes can cause them to shrink and distort beyond rescue.

AT HOME

RAINY DAY TUNE-UP

April showers may put you in mind of May flowers or they may bring on the unpleasant realization that your gutters don't work. If the sound of rain is not music to your ears, maybe a simple gutter and downspout inspection tour will reveal what's causing your mildewing housepaint or your leaky basement. Gutters and downspouts are simply a system for getting water off your roof and away from your house where, left to follow its own path, it can wreak major damage. Water that cascades over the side of clogged gutters wears away the exterior paint, stains the siding, or fosters mildew. It can also seep into the sills and frames of windows and doors, causing them to rot. Properly functioning gutters also direct water away from the basement and foundation of a home and thus serve as a first-line defense against a leaky basement.

Gutter Maintenance

All downspouts should be equipped with a cage strainer to trap leaves, tree seeds, and catkins. At the end of the fall leaf season and at the end of spring (when gutters may be clogged with white oak catkins and winged seeds from maple and ash trees), you should clean each of these strainers. This simple precaution prevents downspouts from becoming clogged with debris, a situation that causes the gutter to fill and overflow with water just as a sink with a clogged drain will overflow.

Some manufacturers offer plastic or metal screens that clip over the top of the entire gutter. Reports on the usefulness of these devices vary. If your roof is overhung with large deciduous trees, you may find that the screens become easily coated with leaves so that water running off a steep roof partially cascades over the leaf layer and directly onto the ground. If your roof pitch is not particularly steep and if your roof area is not subject to an annual heavy leaf fall, you may find these screens helpful in keeping your gutters debris free. In any case, the traditional downspout cage strainer is the best device for keeping your downspouts clear.

Your first job in gutter maintenance is to remove the collected debris from the gutters with a small garden trowel. Shovel the debris into a bucket beginning at the downspout end of the gutter, working away from the downspout and toward the stop end. If you work toward the downspout end, you risk shoving more debris down the downspout. After cleaning the gutters, move on to inspect the downspouts.

If you have neglected to install downspout strainers or if you haven't regularly cleaned the strainers, you may find your downspouts clogged with debris. In this case, gently tapping on the downspout with a screwdriver handle or rubber mallet may loosen the debris. Follow this procedure with a stream of water from a hose directed up or down the spout. This will usually loosen and wash out the plug of debris. For severely clogged gutters, you may have to resort to a plumber's snake (also called a trap-and-drain auger). This inexpensive device is simply a metal cable sheathed in a metal coil with a handle on one end. By inserting the snake through the downspout from the top and rotating it as you insert it, you can usually dislodge any blockage.

Following downspout maintenance, you should inspect gutters for holes and splits. If your gutters are of galvanized steel, you may repair cracks and small holes with ordinary asphalt cement. A larger deteriorated area in a steel gutter can be kept functional for a while by sandwiching two layers of heavy-duty aluminum foil between three layers of asphalt cement over the rusted section. Avoid buiding up the patch too high because it may interfere with the downhill flow of water toward the downspout. For repairing small holes or leaking joints in aluminum and vinyl gutters, use a fiberglass repair kit (sold in auto supply stores for auto body repair).

If you choose to replace a damaged section of gutter, never mix dissimilar metals—steel with aluminum or copper, for example. Placing dissimilar metals in direct contact results in corrosion at the points of contact between the two pieces. In attaching a replacement piece to existing gutter, the upstream piece should overlap the downstream piece by 5 inches so that water is running away from the new joint. Cut the first 5 inches of top rim off the upstream piece so that it will slide snugly into the downstream piece. Sandwich a layer of silicone rubber caulk between the two pieces at each of the two joints to further seal the seams from water incursion. Finally, drill two holes 3 inches apart in the front wall of the overlapping gutter sections. Insert short sheet metal screws into each hole, making sure that the screws are steel for steel gutters and aluminum for aluminum gutters.

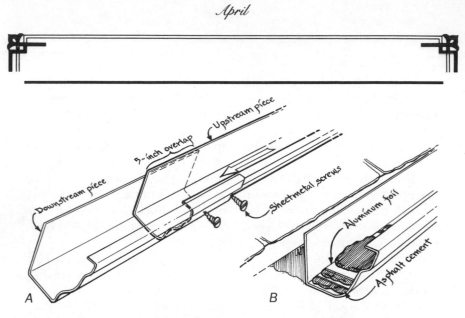

(A) In replacing a damaged section of gutter, the upstream piece should overlap the downstream piece by 5 inches so that water runs away from the new joint. Sandwich a layer of silicone caulk between the two pieces at both joints. Drill two holes on the front and secure the repair piece with two sheet metal screws.
(B) Repair small holes in galvanized steel gutters by applying two layers of aluminum foil sandwiched between three layers of asphalt cement.

Gutter Replacement

If you choose to replace failing old gutters, you have many options, each with an advantage and a different price. You can save money by installing a gutter system yourself, but be aware that it's an up-and-down-ladders job that requires patience and care; in addition, you won't be able to judge how good a job you've done until the next rainstorm.

In planning your installation keep these four points in mind:

1. You will need a downspout for every 30 linear feet of gutter or a downspout for every 400 square feet of room area.

2. You should slope your gutters downhill toward the downspout ½ inch for every 10 feet of gutter.

3. For very long gutter sections, pitch the gutters so that they're higher in the middle and slope both ways toward downspouts at opposite ends. Also take care that they pitch *away* from roof valleys and *toward* corners.

4. You need to space hangers 24 to 32 inches apart. You should have at least three hangers per individual section.

In selecting a new gutter system, three materials are suitable for a do-it-yourself job: vinyl, aluminum, and galvanized steel. Two other gutter materials, wood and copper, cause too many difficulties for the average do-it-yourself project. Wood gutters are commonly made of cedar and require an experienced installer to do the job properly. They are not as expensive as copper and typically last 10 to 15 years. Copper is the most expensive type of gutter material and is difficult to install because all joints must be soldered together. Although the cost is high, a copper installation has a long life expectancy—typically about 50 years.

Vinyl Gutters

Vinyl gutters are made of polyvinyl chloride (PVC), a soft, semirigid plastic material. Vinyl gutters have been treated with plasticizers to prevent brittleness and ultraviolet stabilizers to prevent damage of the plastic by the sun's ultraviolet light. PVC systems are the most expensive of all gutter systems with the exception of copper. But they are the easiest for the do-it-yourselfer to install, and they last up to 60 years. They glue or snap together and are lightweight enough to be carried easily up a ladder. They also need no paint but can be painted if you wish to match a particular color of roofing or siding. Because PVC is a plastic, it is not subject to rot, rust, corrosion, or

denting. If you plan to keep your home for a long while and want to end gutter replacement forever, vinyl is a good choice.

Aluminum Gutters

Aluminum gutters are lighter than galvanized steel and come in a variety of precut lengths to fit almost any project. They're available unfinished, plastic-clad, and enameled. Their cost is moderate compared to vinyl or copper, and they typically last 15 to 20 years. If you are considering aluminum gutters, you should also get an estimate for having an on-site contractor form and install your gutters. An on-site aluminum installer forms your gutters using a truck-mounted forming machine. The advantage to this type of installation is that your gutters will have absolutely no seams except at the downspout junction. This simple construction detail completely eliminates later maintenance problems in which the gutter begins to leak at the joint between two pieces. Aluminum's main advantage is that it is corrosion resistant, but it may be dented by a heavy weight, such as a wooden ladder, placed against it.

Galvanized Steel Gutters

This is the lowest-priced gutter material. You may buy it pre-enameled, or you may paint it yourself after it has weathered in the bare state for at least a year. The best tactic is to keep these gutters painted because they are prone to rust. You can expect about a 20-year life span from galvanized steel gutters. Another thing to remember about steel gutters is that they are heavier than vinyl or aluminum. Because of their weight, they must be supported by strap hangers, which reach under the first row of

roofing shingles and attach directly to the roof sheathing. If your current roofing system is cedar shake, slate, or tile, you wiil probably find it too difficult to install these hangers. If you have an asphalt shingle roof, you still must deal with the job of lifting the lower run of shingles in order to nail the strap hanger to the roof.

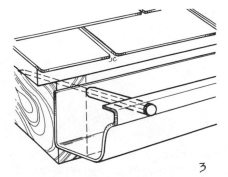

1

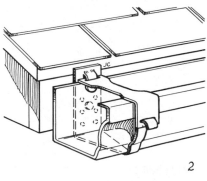

2

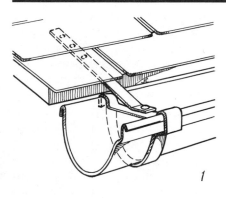

3

Gutter sections are supported in three ways, depending on the weight and type of gutter, the roof edge, and the projected gutter load. 1) Strap hangers must be nailed to the roof sheathing under the first row of shingles. 2) Fascia brackets snap around gutters and nail into the fascia board. 3) Spike-and-ferrule sets support the gutter through a spike nailed into the rafter end.

Choosing a Hanger

In addition to the strap hanger used for steel gutters, you may choose from two other types of gutter hanger systems—a spike-and-ferrule system and a fascia bracket system. The spike-and-ferrule system is probably the simplest to install, but it is not as strong as the fascia bracket or strap hanger systems. You can use spikes and ferrules alone to support aluminum or vinyl gutters, but you will have a sturdier support if you use spikes and ferrules as additional support for a fascia bracket system. If you live in an area subject to heavy ice and snow loads, a simple spike-and-ferrule system is usually inadequate to keep your gutters from sagging.

SPRING DECK-BUILDING HINTS

The hint of spring in the air invariably conjures up images of the barbecue grill, the lounge chair, the lazy Saturday, the tall, cool drink after the grass has been mowed, and maybe a new deck as the setting for all these summer pleasures. If a new deck is on your agenda this summer, the following building tips are for you:

☞ Take advantage of your yard's natural characteristics. Don't cut down a big tree if it's in the way—deck around it. Just leave enough room in the framing for sway and growth.

☞ Use concrete footings that extend at least 2 feet underground or 6 inches below the frost line, whichever is deeper. Anchor posts to the footings with metal connectors embedded in the concrete footings before they dry.

☞ Protect your deck against moisture. Build it with corrosion-resistant nails and connectors. The ground under the deck should slope away from the house, or else you must provide for drainage. Protect the ledger (the section attached to the house that holds up the deck's joists) with aluminum flashing, or put several washers on the bolts between the ledger and the house (they'll create a space that will let water drain away.)

☞ Build with redwood if you can afford it. It ages gracefully and resists rot and insects without chemical treatment. For decks on or near the East Coast, cedar is cheaper than redwood and is also rot-resistant. Pressure-treated wood is most economical and lasts longest. For in-ground posts, wood that's been treated with at least 0.40 pounds of pressure per cubic foot is your best choice.

☛ To properly season the deck's wood, wait at least two months before applying any sealer, stain, or paint. If you use a sealer, reapply it every two to five years.

YOUR APRIL SHOPPER'S TIP

Artichokes, asparagus, avocados, rhubarb, and spinach are most plentiful and therefore a better buy this month. This month's recipe uses your spring asparagus crop. For best results, prepare the recipe immediately after harvesting your asparagus. If you must wait a day or so after harvesting, store your fresh asparagus in the refrigerator. Stand it upright in a tall 2-quart pitcher with the stem ends standing in about 2 inches of water. Loosely cover the top of the pitcher with a plastic bag. Asparagus kept this way will remain fresh tasting for several days. The chili oil used in this recipe is available in specialty food stores. The rice vinegar, low-sodium soy sauce, and gingerroot are found in the oriental foods section of supermarkets.

Asparagus with Chinese Vinaigrette

1⅓ pounds fresh asparagus
1 tablespoon rice vinegar
1 teaspoon low-sodium soy sauce
1 teaspoon sesame oil
1 clove garlic, minced
¼ teaspoon minced gingerroot
   dash of chili oil

Peel asparagus, starting an inch below where tip area ends. Snap off tough ends. Arrange spears on a flat plate in a starburst pattern, with tender tips in the center. Cover plate with vented plastic wrap. Microwave on high for 3 to 4 minutes, depending upon thickness of spears.

In a small bowl, mix remaining ingredients. Pour over asparagus. Chill for 30 minutes.

4 servings

YOUR HOME MAINTENANCE CHECKLIST

☛ Check and clean the oil burner.

☛ Check and clean the oil furnace.

☛ Oil the circulating pump of a hot water heating system with 20-weight oil at oil ports.

☛ Check and clean the heat pump.

☛ Check and clean the wood stove.

Put Your Heating System to Bed

With warmer weather in sight, remember to give your heating system those little attentions it needs to ensure perfect performance on that first nippy fall morning that now seems so far away. If you've been having trouble with your heating plant, April is a perfect month to get some professional attention for it. You won't have to wait long to get some professional advice, because heating and plumbing repair services are not overwhelmed with broken air conditioners yet, and most folks will let their furnace troubles slide until next winter. If your heating plant worked fine over the winter, here's what you can do to keep it that way. What follows are general instructions for heating system maintenance. Be sure to check the manufacturer's recommendations for your particular system before performing these maintenance routines.

For an oil burner: At the end of the heating season clean or replace the nozzle. Remove any crusty deposits from the tip of the nozzle and be sure the ignition electrodes on either side are at least ¼ inch from the oil spray. Have a professional tune up and check the efficiency of the ignition system, the oil/air mix of the burner, and the filter in the supply hose leading from the supply tank. Keep the supply tank filled with oil to prevent water condensation inside the tank, which could corrode it and cause leaks.

For an oil furnace: Remove the breeching (the stovepipe that connects the furnace to the chimney) and scrub it with a wire brush; then vacuum away loose debris. Check the barometric damper (the "swinging door" in the breeching). Clean the pivots with a wire brush and oil them with one drop of 20-weight oil. Clean the flue pipe damper and oil damper bearings. Remove the stack controller (which is in the upper part of the furnace or in the exhaust breeching) and clean it with a soft brush.

For a heat pump: Clean or replace the filter, which is usually located in the furnace. Remove debris around the compressor, which is in the outdoor cabinet, and trim any nearby shrubbery. Flush the evaporator drain line.

For a wood stove: Wait for at least three days after the last fire (to allow ashes sufficient time to cool), shovel out the ashes and vacuum inside. Then scrape the interior with a wire brush, getting to all nooks and crannies, and vacuum again. Check for cracks in the firebox and repair with stove cement as necessary. Wash and rinse the exterior. Let dry and repaint with high-temperature stove paint if necessary. Some stoves have finishes that should not be painted. Check the manufacturer's literature before painting. If you use a woodstove as your primary source of winter heat, *have your chimney cleaned over the summer.* An annual chimney cleaning is a necessity for the safe operation of a woodstove heating system. If the stove has a blower, vacuum the blower, clean or replace its filters, and oil the motor.

EVENTS AND FESTIVALS

Peter's Hollow Easter Egg Fight
Elizabethton, Tennessee

Easter Sunday. Enjoy some Easter Sunday egg-citement in Elizabethton as participants from near and far "knock eggs" to see whose hens lay the hardest eggs. Anyone can enter this contest, which began in 1823, but beware—don't show up with turkey, duck, goose, or guinea eggs. Only chicken eggs are allowed. A person holds an egg in the palm of his hand with the tip (small end) facing up. The challenger, holding his egg with the tip between his thumb and two forefingers, begins to tap the first egg with his own. If the tip end of the first egg breaks, the egg is turned and the fight begins again with the large end facing up. If both ends break, the egg is given to the challenger. The contest continues until there is only one contestant and his unbroken egg left. The winner must return the following year and bring a trophy to replace the one that he has won. Southern hospitality guarantees a good time for all, so gather up your eggs, come on down, and take a crack at it. Information: Elizabethton-Carter County Chamber of Commerce, P.O. Box 190, 19-E By-Pass, Elizabethton, TN 37643.

West Virginia Dance Festival
Charleston, West Virginia

Early to mid-April. Whether you're a dancing student or an ardent fan of dance performance, you'll find a dance event to satisfy your every wish here. Students may choose from a variety of dance workshops taught by a team of professional instructors. Dance aficionados may attend one of the many performances offered in ballet, jazz, or modern dance. Information: Director of Information Services, Department of Culture and History, Cultural Center, Capitol Complex, Charleston, WV 25305.

Senior Spring Frolic
Racine, Wisconsin

Mid-April. Senior citizens strut their stuff at an elaborate "senior prom." Over a thousand happy "hoofers" attend this event to prove that they still have what it takes to have fun. Held at the Lakefront Festival Hall and featuring a live band playing music from the 1930s and 1940s, this annual gala is the highlight of the social season for Racine-area senior citizens, many of whom attend in full formal attire. Admission is free, and refreshments are included. Information: Bill Pugh, 200 Dodge Street, Racine, WI 53402.

Eighty-Niner Day Celebration
Guthrie, Oklahoma

Mid-April. Get a taste of pioneer life in this historically restored town. The celebration features an "Old West" gunfight, a chuckwagon feed with frontier food, a professional rodeo, arts and crafts, a carnival, and Oklahoma's largest parade of bands, floats, and round-up clubs from every corner of the state. Information: Guthrie Chamber of Commerce, P.O. Box 995, Guthrie, OK 73044.

Polk County Ramp Tramp
Benton, Tennessee

Third week in April. Fight back your tears as Benton, Tennessee, pays tribute to the ramp, a wild and pungent onionlike plant that grows only in the Appalachian Mountains. Enjoy plenty of bluegrass music and down-home Southern cooking as celebrators from throughout the United States fill up with cornbread, fried potatoes, streaked meat (bacon), and, of course, lots of dishes prepared with ramps. Information: William Don Ledford, P.O. Box 189, Benton, TN 37307.

Old Settler Days
Sumner, Illinois

Late April. Join over 45,000 visitors at the Red Hills State Park who will come to re-create the hearty lifestyle of early pioneers. Enjoy the performance of traditional American Indian dances and visit displays depicting the history and culture of a number of Indian tribes. Other highlights include puppet shows, folk singing, storytelling, and traditional games such as "Needle in the Haystack," egg-tossing, and pie-eating contests. Authentically costumed craftspersons demonstrate the skills prairie pioneers needed for survival, including blacksmithing, tin-smithing, barrel making, and basket weaving. Grab a free ride in a horse-drawn wagon across the festival grounds to find some old-time pioneer vittles like ham and beans, buffalo burgers, apple fritters, and homemade root beer and ice cream. Information: Jim Fulgenzi, Conservation Dept., 524 South Second Street, Springfield, IL 62701.

Cape May Tulip Festival
Cape May, New Jersey

Last weekend in April. The Cape May community proudly celebrates its strong Dutch heritage with special tours of local historical sites and lectures on the Dutch influence in New Jersey. Enjoy the magnificent tulip displays and the authentic Dutch costumes and folk dancing provided by members of the Dutch community. Information: Cape May Chamber of Commerce, P.O. Box 109, Cape May, NJ 08204.

Arbor Day Celebration
Nebraska City, Nebraska

Last weekend in April. Celebrate America's tree-planting holiday in the city where Arbor Day originated. During the celebration you may tour Arbor Lodge, the 52-room mansion and home of the founder of Arbor Day, the late J. Sterling Morton. During the house tour you may admire the authentic Victorian and Empire furnishings as well as the surrounding 65-acre arboretum, which boasts over 250 varieties of trees scattered among colorful flower beds and an immense rose garden. Town activities include a barbecue prepared for over 1,000 hungry celebrators, a flea market, a crafts fair, a horseshoe tournament, environmental awareness games, a kiddie walking parade, and an official Arbor Day Parade. Information: Chamber of Commerce, 806 First Avenue, Nebraska City, NE 68410.

Sheep Shearing Day/Barbecue
Harrison, Maine

Last Saturday in April. Come on out to the Chardia Farm for a wild and woolly day of fun! You are invited to see first-hand the entire wool-making process beginning with a team of shearers and sheep in need of a haircut. Watch spinners turn the wool into yarn, and browse through a shop in the barn to find plenty of wool sweaters, toys, slippers, and other clothing. A lamb barbecue, hay rides, and, weather permitting, hot-air balloon rides are also included in this free event. Information: Chardia Farm, Rural Route 1, Box 1533, Maple Ridge Road, Harrison, ME 04040.

MAY

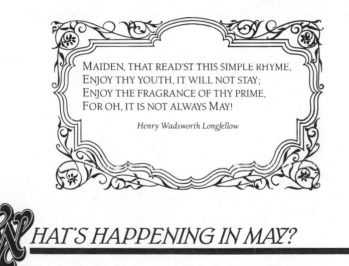

MAIDEN, THAT READ'ST THIS SIMPLE RHYME,
ENJOY THY YOUTH, IT WILL NOT STAY;
ENJOY THE FRAGRANCE OF THY PRIME,
FOR OH, IT IS NOT ALWAYS MAY!

Henry Wadsworth Longfellow

WHAT'S HAPPENING IN MAY?

May 1, May Day and Law Day: Old observances of May 1 included the crowning of the May queen and the dancing of young girls around a Maypole. Since 1958, the United States has observed May 1 as Law Day. The purpose of this day, sponsored by the American Bar Association, is to remind Americans of the freedoms they enjoy under the U.S. Constitution and to foster respect for law and understanding of its essential place in American life.

May 8, VE Day and Birthday of Harry Truman: By wonderful coincidence the Allies received the unconditional surrender of Germany on President Harry Truman's birthday. Despite this first step toward the official end of World War II, the war continued in the Pacific until the surrender of Japan on August 14. Truman, who had succeeded to the office of president upon the death of Franklin D. Roosevelt just 26 days before VE Day, was known for his plain talking and lack of pretense. Affectionately known as "Give 'em hell Harry," Truman was fond of plain-spoken political aphorisms. Commenting on the pressures a president must withstand to lead effectively, Truman advised, "If you can't stand the heat, get out of the kitchen."

May 12, Limerick Day: The limerick, a type of humorous poetry that dates from the early eighteenth century, was perfected by the British poet, Edward Lear, who was born on this day in 1812. It's easy to celebrate Limerick Day. Simply compose a silly poem and read it to someone. If poetry is not your strong point, here are some samples to get you started:

> HOW PLEASANT TO KNOW MR. LEAR!
> WHO HAS WRITTEN SUCH VOLUMES OF STUFF!
> SOME THINK HIM ILL-TEMPERED AND QUEER!
> BUT A FEW THINK HIM PLEASANT ENOUGH.
>
> *Edward Lear*

> THERE WAS AN OLD MAN OF PERU
> WHO DREAMT HE WAS EATING HIS SHOE
> HE WOKE IN THE NIGHT
> IN A TERRIBLE FRIGHT
> AND FOUND IT WAS PERFECTLY TRUE.
>
> *Anonymous*

> THERE WAS A YOUNG LADY OF LYNN
> WHO WAS SO UNCOMMONLY THIN
> THAT WHEN SHE ESSAYED
> TO DRINK LEMONADE
> SHE SLIPPED THROUGH THE STRAW AND FELL IN.
>
> *Anonymous*

May 20, Anniversary of the First Transatlantic Solo Flight: On May 20, 1927 at 7:52 A.M., 25-year-old Charles Lindbergh ("Lucky Lindy") took off alone from Roosevelt Field, Long Island, New York, in a Ryan monoplane called *The Spirit of St. Louis*. He landed at the LeBourget airfield in Paris at 5:25 P.M. (New York time) on May 21, and claimed the $25,000 prize offered by New Yorker Raymond Orteig for the first nonstop flight from New York to Paris. For his historic

3,600-mile flight, the daring and inspired Lindbergh carried five sandwiches and a quart of water but no parachute or flight radio. *The Spirit of St. Louis* hangs on permanent display in the Milestones of Flight Gallery at the National Air and Space Museum (part of the Smithsonian Institution in Washington, D.C.). Visitors to the museum who climb to the second floor mezzanine can look right into Lucky Lindy's cockpit and get a sense of what it must have been like to face a vast and empty ocean in a fragile, 27-foot-long, single-engine plane.

Second Sunday in May, Mother's Day: Anna Jarvis chose May 9 as a day to remember mothers because it was the anniversary of her own mother's death, and she established the carnation as the flower of the day because it was her mother's favorite. Anna Jarvis organized the first Mother's Day in her hometown of Grafton, West Virginia, in 1908, and then spent the next six years campaigning for a national day. In 1914 President Woodrow Wilson made the day an official U.S. holiday.

GOD COULD NOT BE EVERYWHERE, AND SO HE MADE MOTHERS.

Yiddish Saying

Monday Closest to May 24, Victoria Day: This Canadian holiday has been observed since 1903 and actually began as a celebration of Queen Victoria's birthday. Known in other British Commonwealth countries as Empire Day, Canadians celebrate Victoria Day as a national day of recognition of the British Empire and as a day on which to educate children about their heritage as members of the British Commonwealth.

Early to Mid-May, the Feast of Pentecost: Pentecost (also known as Whitsunday) is a movable feast in the Christian year and is celebrated on the seventh Sunday after Easter. The celebration of Pentecost is a commemoration of an event described in the New Testament Book of Acts in which the apostles were visited by the Holy Spirit in the form of tongues of fire. Because Pentecost became a favored day for baptism in the early Christian church, it became known as Whitsunday for the white garments worn by the baptismal candidates.

May 29, Birthday of John F. Kennedy: John Kennedy, the thirty-fifth president of the United States was, at the age of 43, the youngest man ever elected president and the first Roman Catholic. Kennedy was assassinated on November 22, 1963, while riding in an open car in a Dallas, Texas, parade. Kennedy came from a wealthy Boston family of nine children distinguished by its outstanding public service. His father, Joseph Kennedy, served as head of the Securities and Exchange Commission and as U.S. ambassador to Great Britain; his brother Joseph Jr., was killed in a plane crash while serving in England during World War II; his brother Robert served as U.S. Attorney General during John's presidency and was assassinated in 1968 while campaigning for the Democratic presidential nomination; his youngest brother Edward has served as senator from Massachusetts for 26 years; and his sister, Eunice Kennedy Shriver, is the founder of Special Olympics International, an organization which benefits physically and mentally challenged children and adults.

Last Monday in May, Memorial Day: This "day of prayer for permanent peace," as it is described in a Congressional request in 1948, is also known as decoration day, for it is the day we annually decorate the graves of those who have died fighting for our country. In 1971 Congress passed a bill declaring the last Monday in May as the official observance of Memorial Day. Americans now think of Memorial Day as the unofficial start of summer. Summer really begins with the summer solstice on June 21.

May or Early June, Shavuot: Also called the Feast of Weeks, Jews celebrate Shavuot 50 days after Passover. In Old Testament times, it was a holiday to mark the end of the grain harvest season and was called the Feast of Weeks because it was celebrated seven weeks after Passover. In modern times, Shavuot has become a celebration of Moses' receiving the Torah from God on Mt. Sinai, an event recorded in the Book of Exodus.

May Is Better Sleep Month

What you do—or don't do—from dawn to dusk has an enormous impact on how well you'll rest from midnight to morning. The best time to get a head start on a good night's rest is long before you get into bed. For insomniacs everywhere, the Better Sleep Council, an association of bedding manufacturers, has some hints for a deep and restful sleep.

Keep regular hours. The best way to ensure perfect nights is to stick to a regular schedule. If you sleep late one morning and rise before dawn the next, you can come down with a homebound version of jet lag. To keep your biological clock in sync, get up at the same time, regardless of how much or how little you've slept. Try to stick close to your usual sleep schedule on weekends and holidays as well as workdays. If you stay up late on Friday and Saturday nights and sleep late the following mornings, you may give yourself a recurring case of "Sunday-night insomnia."

Exercise regularly. Exercise enhances sleep by burning off the tensions that accumulate during the day, allowing both the body and mind to relax. While the fit seem to sleep better than the flabby, you don't have to exercise to exhaustion.

A 20- to 30-minute walk, jog, swim, or bicycle ride at least three days a week—the minimum for cardiovascular benefits—should be your goal. And the ideal exercise time is late afternoon or early evening, when your workout can help you shift gears from daytime pressures to evening pleasures.

Stay away from stimulants. North Americans drink 400 million cups of coffee a day, and get extra doses of caffeine in tea, cola drinks, and chocolate. Some people seem sensitive to even small amounts; others build up a tolerance. If you're a coffee lover, have your last cup of the day no later than 6 to 8 hours before your bedtime. Its stimulating effects will peak 2 to 4 hours later, although they'll linger for several hours more. Caffeine isn't the only dietary sleep-robber. Some medications can also disrupt your nights. If you're taking any prescription or over-the-counter drugs, ask your doctor whether they can affect your sleep.

Don't smoke. Nicotine is an even stronger stimulant than caffeine. According to several studies, heavy smokers take longer to fall asleep, wake more often and spend less time in REM (rapid-eye-movement sleep, the stage associated with dreaming) and NREM (non-rapid-eye-movement sleep, the stage of deepest rest) sleep. Because nicotine withdrawal can start 2 to 3 hours after the last smoke, smokers may wake in the night craving a cigarette.

Drink only in moderation. Alcohol suppresses REM sleep. After the effects of alcohol wear off, you experience a big surge in REM sleep with its normal accompaniment of dreams. This abnormal surge of dream sleep intrudes into the NREM stages, which you need for deepest rest. This alcohol-induced displacement of REM causes you to sleep in fragments and wake often in the early morning hours. Alcohol at bedtime may make you fall asleep initially, but you'll find it harder to stay asleep as REM sleep takes over during the night.

Go for quality, not quantity. Six hours of good, solid sleep can make you feel more rested than 8 hours of light or disturbed sleep. Limiting the time you spend in bed to what you need, and no more, deepens sleep; allowing yourself to doze on and off for many hours leads to lighter, more fragmented sleep. Don't feel you have to log 8 hours every night. If 5 hours are enough to recharge your battery, consider yourself lucky. You're not an insomniac—just a naturally short sleeper.

If you're having problems sleeping at night, don't nap. By one wit's definition, a nap is "any rest episode up to 20 minutes in duration involving unconsciousness but not pajamas." Although some people are natural nappers—Napoleon, Thomas Edison, and Winston Churchill all indulged—most people find that napping makes insomnia worse. Frequency of napping usually increases with age; virtually everyone over 80 naps often. But unless you're in the over-60 age group, it's best to fight the urge to nap by taking a 10-minute time-out for meditation or relaxation exercises.

Set aside a worry or planning time early in the evening. Instead of lying in bed thinking of what you should have done during the day or have to do the next day, try to deal with such distractions before getting into bed. Make a to-do list so that you can forget about reminding yourself of things to do while you're trying to fall asleep.

Don't go to bed stuffed or starved. A big meal late at night forces your digestive system to work overtime. While you may feel drowsy initially, you'll probably toss and turn through the night. Avoid items (such as peanuts and beans) that can cause gas, and stay away from high-fat items because they take longer to digest.

Develop a sleep ritual. Your sleep ritual can be as simple or as elaborate as you choose. It might start with some gentle stretches to release knots of tension in your muscles, or with a warm bath. Maybe you like to listen to some quiet music or curl up with a book. Whatever you choose, be sure to do the same things every evening until they become cues for your body to settle down for the night. Use your bedroom for sleep and sex only. Don't watch TV, do your tax returns, or catch up on office paperwork in bed.

These tips should help with most insomnia problems. Unfortunately, some folks suffer from severe sleep problems that ruin their lives. These can run the gamut from terrible insomnia lasting for years to falling asleep at totally inappropriate times (narcolepsy). If you have a long-standing sleep problem, you can receive medical treatment from doctors who specialize in the treatment of sleep disorders. For the name and address of the sleep disorders clinic nearest you, contact the Association of Sleep Disorders Centers, 604 Second Street SW, Rochester, MN 55932.

Other Sleep Tips

If you've been catching your 40 winks on the same mattress for over ten years, you probably should perform a bed check. The Better Sleep Council estimates that a good-quality bedding set should last eight to ten years before its support qual-ity begins to deteriorate. Most of us tend to get accustomed to our old mattress and box spring—like a favorite pair of running shoes—and don't recognize that they've gradually lost comfort and support over the years. In particular, a mattress that sags allows your body to sag and forces your muscles to work during the night to straighten your spine. Instead of feeling rested in the morning, you may arise feeling as if you spent the night in the ring with Mike Tyson. If you find yourself crawling out of a hole every time you get out of bed, shop for a mattress and keep the following tips in mind:

☞ Mattresses and box springs are engineered to perform as a unit to provide support. The box spring acts as a giant shock absorber and bears about 40 percent of the nightly wear and tear on your mattress. If you put a new mattress on an old box spring, the mattress will not feel as good as it did in the store nor will it last as long as it should.

☞ You will be able to choose from three different types of bedding systems: the conventional steel spring systems, foam-based systems, and flotation systems (waterbeds). All of these systems have been vastly improved in both comfort and durability within the last 15 years.

☞ Shop for bedding when you are comfortable, relaxed, and unhurried so that you can concentrate on finding what feels right for you. Wear comfortable clothes (slacks are ideal) and shoes that you can remove easily for lying down.

☞ If you sleep with a partner, take your partner with you. Both of you should make the buying decision.

☞ Grab a pillow, lie down on each mattress you are considering, and stay there. Give yourself plenty of time. Roll over and lie on your side. Your hips and shoulders should be comfortable. Try the mattress with your partner. Both of you should feel that there is enough room to be comfortable. If you've always used a double bed, consider moving up one size to a queen-sized mattress. A standard double bed gives two adults proportionally about the same room as an infant in a crib. Tall adults in particular may find they rest more comfortably on a larger mattress.

☞ Get the complete story on every mattress you are considering. The salesperson should be able to tell you the mechanical differences between each of the models he sells. As a starting point, any steel spring mattress should have more than 300 total coils in a double-bed size and more than 375 total coils in a queen size. If you're choosing a foam mattress, the foam should have a minimum density of 2.0; the higher the density number, the better the foam. If you're choosing a waterbed, the mattress vinyl should be a minimum of 20 mils thick, and all seams should be lap seams. The highest standard for waterbeds is called the California standard, and you can ask if the mattress meets this standard even if you don't live in California. A good strategy is to decide which mattress best meets your needs and then comparison shop for the best price on the model you've chosen.

Tips for Better Sleep Month adapted from "A to Zzzzz Guide to Better Sleep," by the Better Sleep Council, a nonprofit association of bedding manufacturers. You can order your own free copy of this booklet by writing to the Better Sleep Council, P.O. Box 13, Washington, DC 20044.

IN THE GARDEN

YOUR WILDLIFE GARDEN

A garden can have as many purposes as there are gardeners. For many of us, the primary purpose of a garden is to provide food and the satisfaction that comes from growing that food without heavy reliance on pesticides and synthetic fertilizers. It's a way of having food that connects us to the earth and connects us also to that unique virtue called patience. The only shortcuts we take are the ones that flow with the forces of nature, and the craft and perseverance we use in dealing with pests and diseases make the rewards of good food even sweeter.

But there are reasons other than food for a garden. In May we discover that a garden connects us to the earth by the simple enjoyment of its beauty. A flower garden accomplishes this purpose; so does a collection of flowering shrubs, a grove of pine trees, an expanse of cool lawn, or a path to a favorite bird-watching spot.

For those of us whose gardens are a spiritual connection to the beauty of Earth, nothing adds more pleasure than an assortment of wildlife to watch. Wildlife gardening, however, is different than gardening for food or showy flowers. The goal of a wildlife gardener is to use plants in a way that both benefits animals and pleases the eye of the gardener. It is impossible to achieve a wildlife garden all at once, unless you happen to inherit one or you live in a remote unspoiled part of the world. But if you have the patience, over time you can create a haven for yourself and for wildlife. Here are some tips:

☞ For the best variety of birds, butterflies, and small animals in your garden, provide food, shelter, and water suitable for each species. Each of these essentials can take many forms. Food can come in the form of nectar-bearing *Buddleia* flowers for butterflies and hummingbirds or acorns for squirrels. Shelter can be dense evergreens, shrubs for birds, or a rotting, hollow tree left in your yard as a home for a raccoon family. Water might be a traditional birdbath or, better yet, a shallow, ground-level dish to make water available to small mammals as well as birds.

☞ Bird feeders attract primarily seed-eating or omnivorous birds, so supplement the feeder with plantings designed to feed a wide variety of your flying friends. Examples of plants that attract birds are given in the table "Best Plants for Bees, Birds, and Butterflies" on page 145.

☞ Provide dense cover around the edges of your property and near bird feeders and watering sites. The cover gives birds and small animals the shelter they need before they'll venture into the open. Shelter around a feeder or water source also provides birds and small animals with a resting place in which to enjoy the food you provide. An easy way to create year-round shelter is to plant evergreens around the border of your property or leave an edge of your property unmowed and overgrown. Placing feeders near large shrubs or vines or even near a woodpile provides birds with the resting place and cover they need. Leaving shrubs such as forsythia untrimmed and in a natural shape provides another source of cover. Avoid trimming shrubs into tight geometric shapes because birds can't hide in them easily.

☞ Provide water in winter as well as summer. Keep your birdbath full at the height of summer drought season and during the deep freeze of winter. To help keep water from freezing in the winter: use any handy object to elevate the water bowl off the ground; place the water source on the south side of your property where the sun will melt ice most quickly; or install an aquarium or birdbath heater, which can be purchased from a pet shop or garden center. Do *not* add alcohol or auto antifreeze to birdbath water. It kills birds.

☞ Keep your pesticide use to an absolute minimum. Better yet, don't use it at all. Even the botanical pesticide rotenone, which is biodegradable, is toxic to bees, birds, and butterflies at the time it is applied. If your neighbor sprays pesticide, be sure to locate your bird feeder and water source in a spot sheltered from any spray drift. Birds

die from pesticide-contaminated water.

☞ Encourage diversity of plant life by installing a variety of plants. Encouraging diversity includes allowing some part of your property to revert to a natural state, weeds and all. Some of these "weeds" such as goldenrod (which does *not* cause hayfever) provide nectar for bees and butterflies, seeds for birds, and shelter for ground-nesting birds such as quail and bobwhite. If leaving weeds and brambles in a small portion of your yard seems like a big hurdle to you, devote a corner of your property to a real wildflower garden, one that you don't mow after you've planted the wildflowers. Encouraging diversity may mean leaving a dying tree in place as a source of insect food for woodpeckers or it may mean allowing some of those "volunteer" maples and cedars to thrive in your ground cover bed. Remember, neatness doesn't count in a wildlife garden. For your plant selections, choose a wide variety of shrubs for berries as well as flowers; mix deciduous shrubs and trees with evergreen types. In choosing trees and shrubs, select nut and seed-bearing types, such as sweet gum and beech; flowering types, such as mimosa or lilac; and fruiting types, such as crabapple and elderberry.

☞ Maintain a healthy soil. Soil is the basis of all life. In a healthy soil you find plenty of worms, small insects, insect eggs, and larvae—food for the birds you want to attract. Healthy soil is the life-giver to the wide variety of plants you need to grow. Healthy soil is not an end product in the sense that once you've got it, it's yours forever. Healthy soil requires your constant vigilance and care through the regular incorpo-

(continued on page 148)

Best Plants for Bees, Birds, and Butterflies

Bees	Birds	Humming-birds	Butterflies
Wildflowers	*Flowers and Vines**	*Garden Flowers*	*Wildflowers*
Aster	Bittersweet	Bee balm	Aster
Catnip	California poppy	Lobelia	Black-eyed Susan
Dandelion	Calendula	Cleome	Daisy
Goldenrod	Cornflower	Columbine	Dogbane
Milkweed	Cosmos	Delphinium	Goldenrod
Purple loosestrife	Goldenrod	Four-o'clock	Ironweed
Red clover	Sunflower	Honeysuckle	Milkweed
White clover	Virginia creeper	Impatiens	Queen-Anne's-lace
Violet	Wild grape	Petunia	Vetch
Wild strawberry	Zinnia	Trumpet vine	Yarrow
Garden Flowers	*Shrubs and Trees*		*Garden Flowers*
Balsam	Barberry		Bee balm
Cleome	Bush honeysuckle		Coneflower
Lantana	Chokecherry		Cosmos
Lily	Crabapple		Daylily
Marigold	Dogwood		Foxglove
Peony	Elderberry		Gaillardia
Rosemary	Holly		Phlox
Sage	Mulberry		Verbena
Sedum	Pyracantha		Yarrow
Snapdragon	Sweet gum		Zinnia

*Birds consume the seed heads of unpicked, spent flowers or the berries that follow some flowers.

Keeping Critters Out

Even dedicated wildlife gardeners may have parts of a garden that are off-limits to visiting wildlife. If you enjoy birds and furry critters, but not what they do to your garden or orchard, try some of these tricks:

☞ Keep birds out of your fruit trees by tying transparent dropcloths between each pair of trees. Hang the plastic sheets from the tree branches by long pieces of twine tied to each corner of the dropcloth. The sheets flap in the wind and disrupt birds' normal pattern of flying.

Trap

Chicken wire fence

Garden fence

Path of armadillo or other small animal

☞ To catch a groundhog, skunk, opossum, or armadillo (an armored mammal that is a pest to gardeners along the Gulf Coast and throughout Texas) that invades a fenced garden, stake up a 20-foot length of chicken wire at a 30-degree angle to your fence (on the inside of the garden). Place a live-animal trap at the point where the chicken wire meets the fence. The fence and the chicken wire form a chute that directs the wandering animal toward the trap. It's not necessary to bait the trap. Wandering groundhogs, armadillos, and opossums will run into the fence and head back toward the chicken wire. They will normally follow the path of least resistance, wandering back and forth between the fence and the chicken wire until they enter the trap. It's up to you to take the animal you've trapped to the nearest county or state park. Hope it's not a skunk.

☛ To discourage deer from jumping into a fenced garden, lay 6-foot-high woven-wire fence flat on the ground around the entire perimeter of your enclosed garden. Deer don't want to get their hooves caught in the ground fence, so they won't approach close enough to make that final jump into your lettuce.

☛ To get rid of moles, treat your lawn with *Bacillus popilliae* powder (also called milky spore disease and available commercially as a product called Grub Attack, Japidemic, or simply milky spore disease). Milky spore disease attacks and kills ground-dwelling grubs, the real food the moles crave. It may take at least one complete growing cycle to completely rid your lawn of grubs, but once the grubs are gone, the moles move on to dine elsewhere. The beneficial effects of a single milky spore treatment last about 15 years.

☛ To keep raccoons from sampling your ripe corn, cover each ripening ear with a large plastic container (such as a milk jug, a bleach bottle). Hang the jugs especially over ripe ears at the perimeter of the patch. As you pick the corn simply move the jug to the next ripening ear. The sound of the jugs bumping and the ghostly appearance they make at night keeps raccoons guessing and out of your corn. This trick works best on a small, garden-sized plot of corn.

☛ To protect a fairly large stand of corn from raccoons and birds, try taping each ear with one-inch-wide nylon-filament tape (the kind used to wrap packages for mailing). First circle the tape around the top of the ear, below where the kernels are unfilled, then loop the tape around the stalk before wrapping it one full turn around the base of the ear. The tape forms a tough loop that prevents raccoons and birds from opening the husk to get to the corn. If you're able to get a good buy on the tape, the cost per ear for this preventive treatment can be as low as 4¢ per ear of corn. You can tape about 60 ears of corn in one hour.

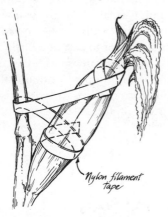

Nylon filament tape

Milky spore disease is available through catalogs from all of the following suppliers:

Necessary Trading Company
6211 Salem Avenue, Box 305
New Castle, VA 24127

Ringer Corporation
9959 Valley View Road
Eden Prairie, MN 55344

Peaceful Valley Farm Supply
11173 Peaceful Valley Road
Nevada City, CA 95959

ration of compost and other natural soil amendments and through respectful treatment. Treating soil respectfully means preventing erosion, not compacting it when it's wet and cold, and avoiding any other form of soil abuse, such as pesticide and herbicide application.

☞ Tolerate a little inconvenience. The mole that's tunneling around the edge of your petunia bed is performing a valuable service by eating ground-dwelling grubs that grow into voracious Japanese beetles. In addition, that mole, as well as the squirrel that regularly patrols your bird feeder, may become the evening meal of the owl you sometimes hear calling at sunrise. It's always better to outwit a pesky animal than to dispense with it entirely. Life is interdependent, and those folks who can live with the greatest variety of life forms are the best wildlife gardeners.

ALMANAC GARDENING CALENDAR

Gardeners in the northernmost zones can still plant cool-weather crops such as peas, spinach, and lettuce. Gardeners in the warmest zones can begin harvesting tomatoes, cucumbers, and other warm-weather crops. In the warm zones, it's time to remove old, spent, cool-season crops, which can act as havens for pests that later attack other garden plants.

Zone 1

Until midmonth, continue planting more lettuce, onions, spinach, beets, chard, carrots, parsnips, radishes, turnips, shallots, chives, and parsley if you need them. During the first two weeks, start squash, cucumbers, melons, okra, and fennel indoors at 70° to 80°F. After germination, move them to a frost-free cold frame. By midmonth, start to harden off tomatoes, eggplants, and peppers by exposing them gradually to full sun and wind so they will be ready to plant by the first week of June. Transplant cabbage, broccoli, and cauliflower to the garden in midmonth. Plant corn and potatoes in mid- to late May and beans at the end of the month.

Plant out delphiniums, peonies, lupines, columbines, bleeding-hearts, irises, and primroses by midmonth. Direct-seed asters, balsams, clarkias, stocks, marigolds, sunflowers, and zinnias. Be prepared to cover the seedlings if frosty weather occurs. After midmonth, plant glads and dahlias, sprinkling bonemeal or compost in the planting hole if the soil is poor. Plant out hardened-off calendulas, asters, and stocks that were started in March. By mid-May, start to harden tender annuals started in March or April so they can be planted outdoors in June. All month, plant evergreen and deciduous trees and shrubs. Plant roses during the first two weeks. Water all newly planted ornamentals regularly. Prune grapevines before midmonth. In northern sections and high altitudes be ready with tarps or blankets to protect strawberries from late frost. Apply mulch around fruit trees and around bramble fruits. Renew sticky ant barriers around fruit tree trunks. Always apply Tanglefoot to paper bands, never directly to the bark.

Zone 2

Plant cool-weather vegetables such as peas, beets, carrots, chard, lettuce, radishes, leeks, shallots, and onions. Set out cole-crop transplants by midmonth. Wait until Memorial Day to set out tomatoes, peppers, and eggplants. Keep frost protection handy. If you plan to grow sweet potatoes, put down black plastic to warm the soil. Divide and plant cannas about midmonth. Pinch tips of leggy annuals started indoors in March and April before setting them out near the end of the month. Divide chrysanthemums and other perennials in early May before growth is too far advanced. Stake delphiniums and other tall peren-

nials before the heavy flower heads pull the stems to the ground. To get the biggest flowers, pinch all but the central bud from peony stalks.

Tie bags containing one or two handfuls of sand to vertical branches of young apple and pear trees to widen crotch angles and encourage earlier fruiting. Spread nitrogen-rich fertilizers or manure mixed with wood chips or sawdust around fruit trees. Check for borer holes under resinous bubbles on peach and apricot trees. Kill the pests by probing the holes with a stiff wire. Clear a 3-foot area around fruit trees in lawns to reduce competition from grass and to prevent mower injury. Cut out suckers and water sprouts on trunks. Remove apple and pear branches that have been wilted and blackened by fire blight. Cut at least 4 inches into healthy tissue to make certain the disease is excised. Sterilize loppers or saw by dipping them in household bleach or alcohol before making each cut. Remove blossoms on newly planted strawberries and mulch young plants with straw.

Zone 3

Thin and harvest radishes, spinach, lettuce, carrots, beets, and scallions as needed. Cultivate these crops at least once a week to keep the soil loose, and mulch only after the plants are well established. Mulch cabbage, broccoli, cauliflower, and peas now to keep the soil moist and cool. Feed with weak manure tea or compost tea. Early in the month, make first sowings of bush and pole beans, Swiss chard, New Zealand spinach, and herbs. Make succession plantings of beets and carrots. At midmonth, direct-seed corn, lima beans, cucumbers, cantaloupes, pumpkins, pole beans, squash, and zucchini. Harden off seedlings of tomatoes, peppers, squash, melons, eggplants, and herbs before transplanting them into prepared beds in mid- to late May. By the end of the month, asparagus harvest should be tapering off. Stop picking when spears are smaller than a pencil. After harvest, fertilize beds and mulch heavily.

After the last frost, sow annuals such as snapdragons, four-o'clocks, asters, zinnias, marigolds, daisies, and bachelor's-buttons. As the soil warms and dries, set out glads, dahlias, cannas, nasturtiums, and petunias. As the first shoots appear in perennial beds, side-dress with compost, a balanced granular organic fertilizer, or well-rotted manure. Divide Shasta daisies and chrysanthemums at first signs of growth. As blossoms fade, prune mock orange, forsythias, lilacs, and other early flowering shrubs. To induce bushiness, pinch back chrysanthemums. If you want extra-large blooms on peonies, remove all buds except the terminal one. Hand-pick early-emerging pests, such as tent caterpillars and bagworms, to avoid costlier treatment later. Apply Bt (*Bacillus thuringiensis*) if infestations are heavy. Check lilacs for scale and scrape off now before it spreads.

In the orchard, remove suckers and misshapen or damaged fruit as they appear, but do not thin fruits until after the spring drop. Renew mulch around trees, canes, and bushes after the soil has warmed. If the spring has been dry, water trees to ensure good fruit set. Begin monitoring for pests and diseases and treat them early. After the blossoms have fallen, spray fruit trees with summer oil solution to reduce insect problems. To increase raspberry production cut back canes to 30 inches. In the strawberry patch, remove blossoms from plants set out earlier in the spring. Cover early strawberries with netting. In established beds, remove any plants showing signs of disease. Mulch with pine needles or straw to conserve moisture and to keep developing fruit off the ground. Feed all fruits with manure tea or compost tea.

Zone 4

Set out tomatoes, eggplants, and peppers. Transplant or direct-seed okra, cucumbers, melons, and squash. Make succession sowings of bush beans and corn. Sweet potato slips can be planted in sandy soil by midmonth, or when nighttime temperatures are no cooler than

60°F. Lay them horizontally under 2 or 3 inches of soil, with only their top nodes aboveground. Set out plants of basil, marjoram, and other tender herbs, or keep them in pots in a sunny place near your kitchen door. Stop harvesting asparagus when the plants begin sending up spears thinner than a pencil. Mulch the garden to conserve moisture and keep down weeds.

Set out tender bulbs like dahlias and tuberous begonias early in the month. Tuberoses and glads can be planted every ten days to two weeks for the next six weeks for a succession of blooms. Thin annuals sown last month and set out bedding plants. Pinch out one-third to one-half of each transplant's central stem for more blooms over a longer period. Pick off old blooms of perennials, but leave their foliage and that of spring bulbs to store energy for next year's display. Trim lilacs and other early flowering shrubs after blossoms fade, cutting the oldest wood to 10 to 15 inches from the ground. Prune out tea rose suckers that sprout below their bud grafts. Give azaleas their post-bloom feeding of cottonseed meal.

Continue removing blossoms of new strawberry plants. Mulch established beds with fresh straw, and cover with netting to protect the ripening fruit from birds. Renew orchard and vineyard mulches. Apply collars of corrugated cardboard to apple trees to trap codling moth larvae; they'll spin their cocoons there during the summer and can be burned in September. Check lower trunks of peach trees for ooze containing sawdust from borers; destroy by probing holes with a thin wire. Deep-soak all fruit trees during dry spells and remove suckers as soon as they develop.

Zone 5

Replace spent cool-weather crops with drought-resistant vegetables such as southern peas, peppers, watermelon, okra, and peanuts. Set out sweet potato slips and keep them watered for at least a week. Plant midseason corn and sunflowers where they can shade rows of parsley and snap beans. Blanch heads of cauliflower and broccoli as soon as they begin to form, and continue to apply Bt (*Bacillus thuringiensis*) as necessary to control loopers. Continue to water lettuce and carrots until harvest. Water onions to increase bulb size. In areas where rainfall is sufficient to permit summer cover-cropping, plant buckwheat, soybeans, or amaranth as summer green manures. Keep potato plants mulched until the tubers are fully mature. Reserve your best mulch material for the tomato patch, and tuck it in as soon as the cages or stakes are in place. Mulch space-grabbing crops like corn and melons with grass clippings over newspaper.

Among the destructive insects

that emerge this month are Colorado potato beetles, squash bugs, and Mexican bean beetles. Handpick them often—as much to prevent future generations as to keep them from eating your plants. Discourage squash vine borers by mounding loose soil over the base of all bush-type squash (the most susceptible kind). If Mexican bean beetle larvae damage more than one-fourth of bean foliage, treat with rotenone.

Clean debris from chrysanthemum beds, and begin pinching the plants to encourage bushy growth. Also pinch impatiens and other long-season flowers that have begun to bloom. Direct-seed warm-weather annuals such as marigolds, salvias, nasturtiums, and zinnias. Continue to set out dahlias and glads for late-summer bloom. Set out container-grown shrubs and keep them watered until they show signs of new growth. Fertilize crape myrtle and althea bushes with cottonseed meal. Also fertilize lawn grasses (except centipede) with cottonseed meal or another slow-release organic fertilizer.

When the strawberry harvest ends, pull out older plants and allow remaining plants to rest for a few weeks before fertilizing and watering. Give blackberries, blueberries, and raspberries a booster feeding of fish emulsion or other fertilizer when they are in bloom. Fertilize muscadines, bunch grapes, and young fruit trees with cottonseed meal or compost. Mulch all 2- and 3-year-old trees, and make sure they never run short of water. Bearing fruit trees need plenty of calcium. On acid soils, top-dress inside the drip line with rock phosphate or dolomitic limestone. Use gypsum on alkaline or neutral soils. If calcium deficiency is severe and needs to be corrected quickly, use a liquid seaweed/fish emulsion foliar spray. Remember that trees growing in grass need more fertilizer than those that are mulched—enough for both the tree and the sod. Remove tree fruit that appears abnormal or is heavily infested with insects, and clear the orchard floor of rotting debris. Watch for colonies of leaf-eating worms on grapes and fruit and nut trees, and treat with Bt (*Bacillus thuringiensis*) if necessary.

Zone 6

Cool-weather crops that have stopped producing should be removed before they begin breeding insects and disease. Cool-weather legumes should be turned under. Continue to plant sweet potato slips throughout the month. Corn can still be planted using two-week intervals to space the harvest over a longer period. Continue to plant peppers, bush beans, field peas, lima beans, snap beans, squash, cucumbers, mustard greens, okra, pumpkins, watermelons, and New Zealand spinach. Control worms on tomatoes, cucumbers, and leafy vegetables with Bt (*Bacillus thuringiensis*). Spider mites can also be a problem at this time of year, especially on tomatoes. Spraying the undersides of leaves with insecticidal soap or a hard stream of water helps keep them in check. Keep soil around tomatoes evenly moist to prevent blossom end rot. Minimize foliar diseases by watering early in the day or by installing drip systems. Remember to sketch your spring garden so you can plan crop rotations for fall.

Landscape plants grown in containers are easily established this month. Mulch with leaves, straw, or compost to help the new transplants root. Leave foliage on spring bulbs until it dies back. Plants in bloom benefit from light feedings and spraying with a foliar application of seaweed extract. For summer and fall color, plant dahlias, amaranth, celosias, marigolds, cosmos, periwinkles, zinnias, portulacas, copper plants, coleus, sunflowers, chrysanthemums, torenias, hollyhocks, and salvias.

Apples and pears should be thinned to two fruits per cluster, and peaches should be thinned to 4 to 6 inches apart. Discard or compost any fallen fruit and leaves. Apply finished compost around trees to help mulch and feed them during the summer, but don't let compost touch the trunks. Don't harvest blackberries until they're completely ripe—soft and very sweet. When harvest is complete, remove any rambling canes and those that bore fruit. Mulch strawberries to keep fruit from touching the ground. Continue to apply seaweed foliar sprays to all fruits, nuts, and berries.

Zone 7

Dig Irish potatoes when the tops have died back. Yellowing foliage on onions, garlic, and shallots means that the bulbs are maturing. To produce long-keeping bulbs, stop watering the plants even if this means digging a trench around the bed to divert water. After the tops die, let the bulbs cure in the sun for about a month before storing them. Continue planting peanuts, okra, soybeans, southern peas, limas, and sweet potatoes. In the warmer parts of the West, also plant blocks of sweet corn and bush beans. On the

West Coast, where gardens are bathed by summer fog, plant cool-weather crops like lettuce, Asian greens, cabbages, beets, carrots, broccoli, and Irish potatoes. In the cool coastal region from San Luis Obispo to Washington state, plant brussels sprouts now to have them mature in time to be sweetened by fall frosts. Cage tomatoes, peppers, and eggplants to keep branches in bounds and to prevent the plants from falling over when the fruit becomes heavy. To get large water-melons, thin them to two or three fist-size fruits per plant. Thin cantaloupes and other melons to four or five per plant. Summer heat cooks organic matter out of the soil. Side-dress crops with manure, and mulch all vegetables to conserve moisture and increase yields. Mulch-ing will help prevent blossom drop on tomatoes.

In the West, where tuberous begonias grow well, transplant the tubers from starter pots to the garden or into hanging baskets. Throughout the zone, early May is a good time to plant many other bulb-type plants, including amaryl-lises, caladiums, callas, cannas, dahlias, glads, tigridias, tuberoses, and watsonias. Some, like amaryl-lises, are relatively carefree and come back year after year. Early in the month, continue to plant heat-resistant annuals.

Excessive fruit drop from cit-rus trees usually indicates too much water in heavy soils or too little water in sandy soils. Citrus needs lots of water, but good drainage. Citrus also needs regular and ample feeding. Give small trees two buckets of manure tea every three weeks throughout the summer, and give mature trees four to six buckets every three weeks. After the normal spring fruit drop, thin peaches and nec-tarines to 4 to 5 inches apart, plums and apricots 3 to 4 inches apart, and apples 5 inches apart. If the trees still seem overloaded after thinning, support the branches with stout poles and boards. Mulch the trees to conserve moisture and pre-vent summer fruit drop. Thin grapes to get good air circulation, leaving only as many clusters as your fam-ily will eat.

IN GOOD HEALTH

MAY IS NATIONAL SIGHT-SAVING MONTH

Now that summer is around the corner, you're probably looking forward to the lazy days at the beach or pool, the games of tennis after work, or the extra round of golf you can get in each week. Before you get on with the summer fun, keep the following eye care tips in mind. They could mean all the difference to maintaining healthy eyes.

☞ Wear sunglasses in bright sunlight. The long-term effects of the sun's ultraviolet rays are not yet known, so opthalmologists agree that it's a good idea to wear sunglasses when outdoors during the day. Choose quality sunglasses that screen out 90 to 95 percent of the ultraviolet light.

☞ Don't apply suntan or sunscreen products to your eyelids or around your eyes. These products can cause conjunctivitis (inflammation of the lining of the eyelids) and keratitis (inflammation of the cornea). If the chemicals accidentally get into the eye, irrigate with an eyewash.

☞ Wear goggles when swimming in chlorinated pools. Pool disinfectants, such as chlorine, may cause chemical conjunctivitis. For swimmers who wear glasses, it's possible to have goggles made with prescription lenses.

☞ Don't wear contact lenses in a pool, lake, or hot tub. Soft contact lens wearers are susceptible to a corneal infection caused by acanthamoeba, a parasite found in water. Routine levels of chlorination in pools and hot tubs do not kill this organism, which can cause a serious, extremely painful corneal infection resulting in partial or total blindness.

☞ Wear protective eyewear when operating lawn mowers and weed trimmers. Small stones, twigs and other debris can be caught up in mower or trimmer blades and then propelled out with great force. These objects may strike the eye and cause serious injuries. Wear goggles when operating such equipment, and always be certain to turn off a mower engine before emptying the clippings. Those not operating the mower or trimmer, including playing children, should stay away from the area being trimmed.

☞ Wear protective goggles or face guards when playing sports. This safety tip applies to all sports in all seasons. Balls, bats, and racquets can severely injure the eye upon impact. If a player is struck, apply crushed ice immediately, and if there is pain, swelling, discoloration, impaired or double vision, see an ophthalmologist immediately.

Eye Emergencies

In the United States, more than one million people a year suffer eye injuries. According to John B. Jeffers, M.D., director of Emergency Services at Wills Eye Hospital in Philadelphia, knowing what to do in the event of an eye emergency can prevent permanent damage. To familiarize yourself with eye emergency care, check over these tips, but be aware that this information is for first aid only. Dr. Jeffers

Eye Exam Schedule

If you don't wear glasses or have any other health problems that affect your eyes, you may wonder how frequently you should have your eyes examined. The American Academy of Ophthalmology recommends that persons who have a family history of eye disease or who have diabetes mellitus or hypertension (two diseases that can cause eye damage) have regular periodic eye exams, with the frequency of the exam dependent upon the severity of the health problem. Those who have no symptoms and who are at low risk for hereditary eye disease should follow these recommendations.

☞ Infants born in families with a history of congenital eye disease should be examined by an ophthalmologist soon after birth.

☞ All children between the ages of three and four should be examined by a general practitioner or a pediatrician for visual acuity, eye alignment, and evidence of eye disease.

☞ All school-age children should have a regular eye screening (such as eye tests provided by a school nurse, a public health department, or a volunteer organization) every two years. The screening should be for visual acuity and for eye alignment.

☞ Individuals from the age of puberty to age 40 should have occasional eye examinations to detect asymptomatic eye disease.

☞ At age 40, everyone should have an examination for presbyopia, a loss of elasticity in the eye lens that occurs with aging and causes difficulty in focusing at short distances.

☞ Individuals aged 40 and older should have a regular ophthalmologic evaluation every two to five years, because the frequency of significant eye disease increases after the age of 40.

cautions, "Don't underestimate the severity of an eye injury. Severe trauma can cause permanent damage resulting in decreased vision, blindness, or loss of an eye. See an ophthalmologist immediately after administering first aid."

Chemical Burns: Chemical splashes to the eye should immediately be flushed with water or any nonirritating liquid (even milk) continuously and gently for at least 30 minutes. Hold your head under a shower, water fountain, or garden hose (a clean container may also be used), keeping the eye open as widely as possible and tilting your head to prevent contamination of the uninjured eye. Do *not* patch the injured eye.

Blows to the Eye: Apply ice or a cold compress immediately to reduce pain and swelling. Crushed ice in a small plastic bag placed gently over the injured area works better than ice cubes. Avoid blowing your nose since there could be a fractured bone. If discoloration occurs or there is blurred or double vision, see an ophthalmologist immediately.

Cuts or Punctures of the Eye or Lid: Patch the eye lightly and see an ophthalmologist immediately. If an object is stuck in the eye, *do not try to remove it or wash it out.* Never apply pressure. Protect the eye with something hard, such as sunglasses, or the bottom of a milk carton, cut and taped over the injured area. Seek medical help immediately.

Foreign Particle in the Eye: Do not rub the eye. Pull the upper lid down over the lower lid, allowing it to push the speck from the eye. If natural tearing doesn't flush out the particle, use a squeeze bottle eye irrigating solution to help dislodge it. Do not use an eye cup because they harbor infectious organisms. If the particle doesn't wash out, keep the eye closed and see an ophthalmologist immediately.

MAY IS NATIONAL ARTHRITIS MONTH

Nowhere is the adage, "Use it or lose it" more appropriate than in dealing with arthritis. The old school of thought held that no activity was good for inflamed joints, and rest was almost always the first prescription. Now, there is ample medical evidence, through controlled studies of sedentary patients versus active ones, to merit the recommendation of exercise for almost every arthritic. The primary rule-of-thumb is that the exercise must be appropriate for the age, disease stage, and general condition of the patient. It's never too late to start an exercise program, even if you have a long history of arthritis. The trick is to enter a program designed to make the best of the joint mobility you still have and to prevent further loss of joint function. Arthritis is one disease where the willpower of the patient has an enormous effect on the outcome of the disease. Those who are willing to endure the discomfort caused by moving afflicted joints will enjoy the benefits of increased mobility and continuing function of those joints. If you have arthritis and would like to begin an exercise program keep the following tips in mind.

☞ Ask your doctor or physical therapist for some range-of-motion exercises specifically suited for the joints affected by arthritis.

☞ Ask your doctor to refer you to an occupational therapist if your arthritis impairs your ability to function in your own household. Occupational therapists are trained to help people keep functioning in the everyday world despite a crippling handicap. Occupational therapists help patients by teaching them how to use adaptive devices (such as a gripper to lift cans from a shelf) and how to alter their daily routines to fit comfortably around a handicap. There are a great many devices available that enable a disabled person to function in an everyday environment, and an occupational therapist can help you figure out which aids will work for you.

☞ If you begin an exercise program, maintain a proper pace. Begin at a comfortable level and gradually increase the number of repetitions to avoid unnecessary pain. Use slow and steady rhythms, relax your muscles for about 10 to 15 seconds between repetitions and breathe deeply and rhythmically as you exercise. Never hold your breath.

☞ Balance your exercise with periods of rest and relaxation. The discomfort of arthritis can cause you to tire more easily than a normal person would. You'll need to pay special attention to your rest needs. This doesn't mean that you must get more sleep, but you may need to schedule periods of relaxation exercises or meditation into your day. Most physicians recommend 10 to 12 hours of rest for every 24-hour period, with the 12 hours being divided between sleep and daytime rest periods.

☞ Plan to exercise twice a day for the rest of your life unless you experience severe pain, in which case see your doctor. This must be a high priority in your life and you shouldn't skip your exercises simply because you're too busy. If you find skipping a few days unavoidable, start again at a slightly lower level.

☞ Plan your twice-daily routines when you are in the least pain and when you are not too tired. If you're taking medication for pain or inflammation, plan your range-of-motion exercises for the time when the drugs are having the greatest effect. Even if you experience slight pain, you should do the range-of-motion exercises to keep your joint mobility.

☞ Avoid exercise programs that strain joints. Among the types of exercise unsuitable for arthritics are jogging, running, weight lifting, and, for those with arthritis of the knees or hips, bicycling and tennis. You may be able to ride a stationary bike, however, because you can adjust the tension to put minimum strain on your joints.

☞ Always exercise in warm conditions. Wear warm clothing and avoid chills. If you swim or exercise in a pool, the water temperature should be 83° to 88°F.

Water Exercise

If you've never been an exerciser or you're just in too much pain to start an exercise program, you should check with your local YMCA for pool exercise classes given especially for arthritis sufferers. The YMCA and the Arthritis Foundation have jointly developed an aquatic exercise program. Called the Arthritis/YMCA Aquatic Program, this supervised exercise routine is safe and helpful for every type of arthritis. Many people disabled with arthritis have found that they obtain relief from a regular pool workout designed especially for arthritics. Water lifts 90 percent of your body weight, making it possible for you to move your joints with considerably less pain than normal.

In addition you may be interested in reading a helpful book called *Pain-Free Arthritis* by Dvera Berson. Berson is a 76-year-old Brooklyn native whose career in the New York fashion industry was brought to a screeching halt when she developed crippling arthritis at the age of 54. While visiting with a friend in Florida, she discovered that she could move with a little less pain when she stood in a swim-

ming pool. Upon returning home to Brooklyn, she joined a health club and began to go to the pool daily. Through nine months of patient effort, Berson developed a series of water exercises which enabled her to lead a pain-free life despite her arthritis. Her book, which has sold over 90,000 copies, describes the exercise program that helped Berson regain her mobility. The reader is advised that arthritis is at present an incurable degenerative disease but that it is possible to reduce the amount of pain it causes through water exercise. The program requires that the exercises be done five times a week in the beginning. Berson cautions that the program may not work for everyone and that no water exercise program should be started without the advice of a physician or physical therapist. To order your copy of *Pain-Free Arthritis*, send $16.95 (includes shipping) to S & J Books, Box 31 Gravesend Station, Brooklyn, NY 11223.

The Arthritis Foundation endorses water exercise as a valuable tool in the treatment of arthritis. In addition, the Arthritis Foundation publishes helpful booklets on self-help for arthritics, such as "Exercise and Your Arthritis." To get your copy of this publication, to find out about your local Arthritis/YMCA Aquatics Program, or to find out about other self-help courses that are offered by the Arthritis Foundation, contact your local chapter of the Arthritis Foundation. The national office of the Arthritis Foundation will help you locate a chapter in your area if you send a stamped, self-addressed envelope to this address: Arthritis Foundation, Chapter Operations, 1314 Spring Street NW, Atlanta, GA 30309.

MAY IS NATIONAL HIGH BLOOD PRESSURE MONTH

High blood pressure is a silent disease. It produces no pain, no fatigue, and no other overt symptoms. It is a sneaky killer because its victims have no warning of its work until they suffer from the effects of years of untreated high blood pressure—heart attack, stroke, kidney disease, or eye damage. If you're one of the many people who suffer from "a little high blood pressure," you should know that your blood pressure reading may be a lot more than a little problem.

Blood Pressure Guidelines

There are now clear medical guidelines for what is an unacceptable blood pressure reading from *The Complete Guide to Living with High Blood Pressure* by Michael K. Rees, M.D.:

Certain guideline numbers have in fact been established. It is now known that any person 40 years old or less who has systolic blood pressure of 140 millimeters of mercury or greater or a diastolic blood pressure of 90 millimeters of mercury or greater has high blood pressure and requires treatment. (Remember that unless the numbers are very high, two out of three readings should be abnormal on two different days to establish that abnormality in fact exists.) Obviously, any numbers greater than 140 or greater than 90 make the need for treatment even more urgent. If a person is over 40 years of age, the numbers are raised to 160 for systolic blood pressure and 95 for diastolic blood pressure. Notice that only one of the two numbers that measures blood pressure has to be elevated to define high blood pressure. If either number is elevated, treatment is required.

Blood Pressure Health Tips

If you have hypertension, or a tendency toward it, there's a good deal that you can do to keep it in check. The American Heart Association offers this checklist:

☞ Know what your blood pressure is. Have it checked regularly by your doctor. You may want to get a home monitor, too, so that you can check it yourself on a regular basis. Never let just one reading determine whether you have high blood pressure or not. A 1987 random sample of 3,000 people showed that hypertension is overestimated by as much as 30 percent when the diagnosis is based on one reading as compared with three readings done at separate times.

☞ Discuss with your doctor what your weight should be and keep it at that level or below.

☞ Watch your salt intake. Avoid salty foods and don't add salt to foods.

☞ Eat foods low in fat and cholesterol. Read labels and choose carefully when you dine out.

☞ Don't smoke cigarettes.

☞ Restrict the amount of alcohol you drink. Choose wine spritzers, juice or seltzer over something stronger.

☞ Take your blood pressure medication just as it's prescribed. Don't run out of pills for even one day. Work the prescription refills into your schedule as you would any other important task.

☞ Keep appointments with your doctor so that your progress can be monitored regularly.

☞ Follow your doctor's advice about exercise and stick to a routine you've worked out together.

☞ Make sure your parents, siblings, and children have their blood pressure checked, too, since hypertension tends to run in families.

Quotation on blood pressure guidelines from The Complete Guide to Living with High Blood Pressure, Revised Edition, *by Michael K. Rees, M.D., © 1980, 1988. Reprinted by permission of the publisher, Prentice Hall Press, New York, N.Y.*

Walking Tip for May

Now that warm weather is in the works, you'll find that you're more comfortable in shorts and a tee shirt for your walks. That can present a problem for walkers with generous thighs who find their inner thigh area becoming chapped from the friction of walking. If you have this problem, stick to your more comfortable shorts but treat your inner thigh area to a layer of petroleum jelly before you walk. You'll avoid the rash and irritation of chapped legs, and you can maintain your walking schedule even on the hottest days.

AT HOME

CHOOSE PAINT LIKE A PRO

May is fix-up time, and one of the most popular fix-up jobs is a fresh coat of exterior paint. Painting your home is a relatively easy do-it-yourself project and also one of the most cost-effective fix-up projects for making a home ready for resale. A person who paints his home's exterior near the time of resale can, according to *Practical Homeowner* magazine, recoup over ten times the cost of supplies for the job.

May is also an ideal time to paint the exterior of a house because you have plenty of warm weather ahead to help your paint job cure rapidly. Rapid drying and curing prevents surface flaws caused by dust, pollen, and insects becoming imbedded in the surface of the wet paint.

Understanding how different types of exterior paint work will help

you select the most appropriate paint for your project. The two main types of exterior house paint available are alkyd paint (often called oil-based paint) and latex paint (sometimes called water-based paint). These two types of paint differ in many respects.

Alkyd versus Latex: What's the Difference?

The primary difference between alkyd and latex paints—and the difference most vital to painters (especially do-it-yourselfers)—is that latex paint uses water as the fluid component and alkyd paint uses a non-water-soluble, organic solvent. In addition to the annoying odor associated with the evaporating organic solvents, another inconvenience of alkyd paints is that the clean-up of brushes and equipment must all be done with solvents such as paint thinner or turpentine. Many homeowners quite reasonably find that keeping cans of organic solvent at home to help with paint clean-up is an objectionable and somewhat hazardous practice that is best avoided. Organic solvents are definitely a fire hazard; some are poisonous to people, animals, and aquatic life, and are, at least at some levels of exposure, associated with increased risk of cancer and brain damage. Several Scandinavian studies of groups of tradesmen painters have found evidence of brain damage in those who worked with solvent-based paints for many years. While the exposure of a person who paints his house every seven years can't compare with the exposure of a person who paints every day, the really conservative person might ask himself why he would want to voluntarily expose himself at all to organic solvents.

Another major difference between latex and alkyd paint is in the type of film the paint forms when it dries. An alkyd paint forms a film by reaction of its binder (a resin component of the paint) with oxygen. This reaction with oxygen continues for a very long time (years,

in fact) after the paint is applied. As the film reacts continuously with oxygen in the air it becomes harder and more impervious to water as time goes by. This might seem like an advantage, but as alkyd paint becomes harder and more impervious to water, it also becomes far more brittle than latex paint. The greater brittleness causes it to crack as it ages, especially if the paint covers wood that moves or expands and contracts with the seasons. Latex paint does not become harder and more brittle with age because it doesn't react with anything in the atmosphere. The film formed by latex paint stays flexible and somewhat porous for water vapor passage through the film. If you are

Characteristics of Latex and Alkyd Paints

Paint Type	Cleanup Agents	Water Resistance	Type of Film Formed
Latex	Water	Breathable, allows water vapor in and out of wood	Soft, remains pliable with age
Alkyd	Mineral spirits Turpentine Paint thinner	Impervious to water	Hard, becomes brittle with age

painting over wood, especially new wood, the greater breathability and flexibility of latex paint is a real advantage. Wood is almost like a living thing in that it is constantly expanding and contracting and taking up or giving off water. A latex paint allows the wood to go through its normal water exchange cycles, and because the latex film is flexible and allows for the passage of water vapor, it moves with the wood and doesn't crack.

Paint Questions and Answers

In choosing the best exterior paint for the job, many factors besides the ones discussed above come into play. There are many different exterior jobs because there are many different types of materials on the exterior of houses. If you paint your home's exterior, you may have to deal with such diverse surfaces as aluminum window frames, a brick foundation wall, a steel front door, galvanized steel gutters, and wooden or aluminum siding.

What's the best paint to apply over new exterior wood? With new wood or wood products, many experts feel that the best combination is an alkyd-based primer followed by a latex exterior paint. The alkyd-based primer acts as the best

available sealer for the new wood, and the latex finish paint acts as the most flexible and durable final coat for allowing the wood to breathe.

What's the best paint to apply over old exterior wood previously painted with alkyd or oil-based paint? The traditional, conservative principle of painting wood emphasized that "like should cover like." With this in mind, a traditionalist would only paint an old alkyd-covered surface with another alkyd paint. However, if you want to repaint old alkyd-covered exterior wood with a new coat of latex, you'll find that the exterior latex works just fine. Exterior paint is subject to extreme weathering conditions, and these act to roughen a smooth alkyd surface just as sandpaper would do. Good-quality exterior latex paint will adhere in a perfectly acceptable manner to an old, weathered, exterior alkyd-covered surface.

Why are some latex paints more expensive than others? Just as in all basic shopping decisions, you get what you pay for in latex paint. Most higher-priced exterior latex paints use acrylic as the plastic binder. In addition, in the more expensive latex paint, you get a higher concentration of binder and pigment in the water. More binder and pigment per brush stroke gives the most complete coverage per brush stroke. This advantage becomes the most important if you are trying to cover old color "A" with new color "B." With the higher-priced paint you are more likely to get complete one-coat coverage (you don't have to do a second coat to hide the old color). For the higher cost per gallon, you should have to buy less paint to complete the job and, more important, spend less time doing the job because you only need one coat of paint. If your old color "A" is very different from new color "B," you may need two coats of a high-quality paint but would likely need three coats of a low-quality paint.

How do I know how much paint to buy? Read the label on the paint you are considering. Most labels give the theoretical square-foot coverage of a gallon of paint. The theoretical coverage, however, may have nothing to do with the actual coverage on your house. If you try to cover a dark color with a light one, you may find that you must use two coats, even if you buy high-quality paint. If you are painting a porous surface, such as stucco, you may find that the surface absorbs so much of the paint that you need two coats to get the coverage you want.

A simple approach is to buy a quart of the paint you are considering and paint a measured square footage area in an inconspicuous place. You'll see how well the paint you've selected covers your old paint, you'll discover whether or not you need two coats, and you'll get to see whether you really like the color before you buy 25 gallons of it. When you know for sure how many coats of paint you need to get good coverage, you'll be able to calculate how much paint to buy.

How do I decide which type of brush to buy? Just as with paint, read labels. If you are buying brushes for an important job like painting your whole house, buy the very best brushes you can afford. A general rule of thumb is: Buy natural hair (hog bristle or ox hair) brushes for alkyd paints, and buy synthetic brushes (nylon or polyester) for latex paints. Whichever type of suitable brush you buy, remember that the higher-priced brush always gives better results because it holds more paint than a cheap brush, has tapered or splayed ends to eliminate brush marks, holds a smooth, solid shape under the pressure of applying paint, and does not shed bristles onto the painted surface.

What are the ideal weather conditions for applying exterior paint? You should never apply exterior latex when there is a chance of the temperature going below 50°F within a few hours after you finish. If the temperature dips below this cutoff point, the film formed by the paint will have many microscopic defects. You won't be able to see these defects because they are so small, but the paint will not weather well or last as long as it should. If temperatures should dip near freezing following the application of latex paint, the water solvent can actually freeze on the surface of the paint, and you will have a real mess on your hands. For alkyd paints, temperatures following application don't have much effect on the paint except that drying will take longer as temperatures decrease. A prolonged drying time affects the quality of the paint job because dust and insects collect on the surface of the wet paint and mar the surface. The primary weather consideration with alkyd paints is that they should never be applied over wood that is damp or wet because they simply won't adhere well.

What's the best paint for aluminum siding, aluminum gutters, or galvanized steel gutters? You can use either alkyd or latex over these substrates, but latex probably gives the best long-term results because the paint film is flexible. It won't crack as the metal expands and contracts with outside temperature changes. The primary consideration in painting over old factory-painted aluminum siding is to remove the old chalky pigment on the surface of the aluminum. If loose chalk is not removed, it interferes with the adhesion of new paint. Scrub aluminum siding with a solution of TSP (tri-sodium phosphate) and water before any repainting job. New galvanized steel or aluminum gutters should be left bare for about a year before they receive their first coat of paint. Weathering causes the surface of the metal to roughen and thus form a better surface for paint adhesion.

What's the best paint for unpainted cinder block, brick, concrete, or stucco? Latex is recommended for each of these applications because all of these surfaces are highly alkaline (as opposed to acid), particularly when fresh, and the alkali attacks and breaks down the binder in alkyd paint. Latex binders are unaffected by an alkaline substrate.

The Way It Was:
Life in Late Eighteenth-Century America

As you turn on your coffee maker, pop a casserole into the microwave, and settle down for an evening with a favorite movie on the VCR, it's interesting to remember that for millions of early Americans, life as we live it today would have been beyond imagination. For our ancestors of 200 years ago, even having a pair of shoes that fit properly was a feat beyond the technology of the time. For a quick time trip, try to imagine some of these facts of life for eighteenth-century Americans:

☞ Ninety-five percent of all Americans lived on farms or in towns of less than 2,500 people—all within 90 miles of the Atlantic Ocean, with the exception of American Indians.

☞ Half the women could write their own names and about two-thirds of the men were literate.

☞ Cincinatti was known as the "Metropolis of the Northwest Territory" with a population of a whopping 750.

☞ Most women married at 23 or 24 and most men at 26.

☞ There were no right and left shoes; all were straight. Each person alternated his or her shoes from right foot to left foot daily so that they wore evenly.

☞ Only the ruffles on a man's shirt showed because the rest of the shirt was considered an undergarment. Indeed, the long shirttails, which were wrapped between the legs, took the place of today's undershorts.

☞ About a third of New England women were pregnant on their wedding day. They could expect to become pregnant every two or three years thereafter, having five to ten pregnancies in their lifetimes. But because many young children died of disease or infection, a mother could expect to have three to eight surviving children.

☞ Between 1780 and 1820, the number of colleges in the United States grew from 9 to over 70; most of them were sponsored by churches.

Facts courtesy of the Smithsonian's National Museum of American History, "After the Revolution" exhibit.

HOTLINES: WHOM TO CALL WHEN NO ONE ELSE WILL HELP

What do you do when you think your well may be contaminated by the leaky underground gas tank at the service station down the road, or when you've signed a contract to buy a set of encyclopedias and decide the next day that you really can't afford the payments, or when your new refrigerator has been "repaired" by three different servicemen in the last month and still doesn't work right? You look for a hotline, a place you can call to get a sympathetic hearing and more than that, a place that will give you the information to solve your problem.

We've included hotlines known to be of value to homeowners. If you can't find the help you need here, a call or visit to your local library should do the trick. Most libraries stock directories of hotlines and toll-free numbers.

Chemical Referral Center
1-800-262-8200

This hotline sponsored by the Chemical Manufacturers Association maintains a data bank listing over 250,000 chemicals made by 130 different companies. The center provides information to people who encounter an unfamiliar chemical at home or at work; the information provided includes the name of the manufacturer and the name of a qualified expert on the chemical in question. Questions do *not* have to be emergencies; any inquiry is answered.

Federal Deposit Insurance Corporation Consumer Hotline
1-800-424-5488

Use this hotline to make any complaint or ask any question about FDIC-insured banking procedures. The staff at this hotline is prepared to give you complete information about the Truth-In-Lending Act, the Equal Credit Opportunity Act, the Fair Credit Reporting Act, and other consumer protection laws related to banking.

Federal Tax Information
1-800-424-1040

The IRS staff answers this hotline. You can get information on tax laws, IRS procedures, and your own personal account. Use this number if the IRS claims you owe money, if you cannot obtain a W-2 form from your employer, or if you have any other unresolved problem with the IRS.

Federal Trade Commission
(202) 326-3175

The Federal Trade Commission enforces federal laws that protect consumers in many credit and loan transactions. Call this number and ask for a Duty Officer to discuss your particular credit card or loan difficulty. The Duty Officer can send you free information describing your rights under the federal laws relating to credit ratings, credit cards, and loans, such as the Truth-In-Lending Act, the Fair Credit Reporting Act, the Fair Credit Billing Act, the Fair Debt Collection Practices Act, and the Equal Credit Opportunity Act.

In addition, if you have a problem involving a purchase on credit with a time-payment contract, you can call the local branch of your state Attorney General's office. Most states have laws that allow a person to cancel a time-payment contract within three business days of the contract signing. Also, if you feel you have been a victim of fraudulent or deceptive business practices, the Consumer Protection Division of your state Attorney General's office can help you file a complaint.

Insurance Information Institute
1-800-221-4954

The staff of this hotline can answer any question you may have about the purchase of auto, home, or tenants insurance. They can tell you how to comparison shop for policies, what kind of coverage is available, and when to update your coverage.

Interstate Commerce Commission
(202) 275-0860

This is the court of last resort if you have an unresolved complaint against a moving company that transported your household goods. Moving companies that transport goods across state lines are all regulated by the ICC, and the staff here is usually influential in getting your complaint adjusted as long as your case has merit.

Meat and Poultry Hotline
1-800-535-4555

This hotline is a service of the U.S. Department of Agriculture. The home economists who answer this line give information on proper food storage and answer any questions related to meat or poultry. You may also call this line to report bad meat or poultry purchased in your local market.

National Appropriate Technology Assistance Service
1-800-428-2525
1-800-428-1718 (in Montana)

Funded by the U.S. Department of Energy, this hotline is a government public service to encourage private citizens and businesses to conserve energy. Because the staff here has access to the latest scientific data on energy conservation, they can help you decide how to insulate your attic or what type of furnace you should buy, or they can help you develop a marketing plan for an energy-related product.

National Pesticide Information Clearinghouse
1-800-858-7378

This clearinghouse is a service of the Environmental Protection Agency (EPA) and Texas Tech University Health Sciences Center. It provides 24-hour-a-day information on the health effects, safe handling, and disposal of pesticides, insecticides, herbicides, and fungicides.

Public Information Center of the Environmental Protection Agency
(202) 382-2080

The staff at this hotline will answer questions about the activities of the EPA and refer you to other EPA officials if your problem involves EPA jurisdiction. If you have a problem with groundwater contamination, your very first step is to call your own state Department of Environmental Resources. Most states handle the initial investigation of groundwater contamination through a state environmental resources department. While the EPA does not have jurisdiction over local groundwater issues, the Public Information Center of the EPA can provide you with a number of free publications that deal with air and groundwater pollution.

U.S. Consumer Product Safety Commission Hotline
1-800-638-2772

Call this line, operated by the U.S. Consumer Product Safety Commission, to report a product-related injury, file a complaint about a hazardous product, or get product recall or safety information.

Appliance Hotlines

If you can't find a part for your ten-year-old dishwasher or you're not able to get satisfactory repair service for your stove, these manufacturers' hotlines are here to help.

Admiral
1-800-447-8371

Carrier
1-800-227-7437

General Electric
1-800-626-2000

Hamilton Beach
1-800-334-2785

Kelvinator
1-800-323-7773

Tappan
1-800-537-5530

Whirlpool
1-800-253-1301

White-Westinghouse
1-800-245-0600

Preserving Clothes Naturally

May is the time to put away your winter woolens. Here's how to do a professional job of storing your winter wardrobe:

☞ Before you store it, clean it. Food stains and body oils attract insects such as moths and carpet beetles, whose larvae will enjoy a summer-long feast on your clothes. Also, professional cleaning removes any insect eggs that may be already hidden in your clothes. If you wash clothes before storage, do not use fabric softeners or starches since they attract silverfish and carpet beetles.

☞ Once clothes are clean, store them in a closed chest or sealed container, such as a cardboard box with all seams taped. Do not store garments sealed in a polyethylene bag (such as a dry-cleaning bag) because these bags sometimes change the dyes in clothes. Use polyethylene only as a shoulder cover to prevent dust from settling on the tops of hung clothes. Sealed vinyl or nylon bags do not allow for exchange of air and moisture, may cause mildew, and are particularly bad for fine woolens, silks, or other natural fibers. For natural fibers the best clothing bags for storage are made of unbleached muslin or sheeting. Vinyl bags *are* acceptable for storing synthetics or for short-term storage of frequently used items.

☞ Cedar chips do not kill moth larvae. It is the volatile oil in the heartwood of cedar that kills moth larvae; the smell of cedar does not repel them. An effective cedar chest or closet must be lined with at least ¾-inch-thick cedar heartwood and must close tightly enough to keep the cedar oil from evaporating out of the chamber.

☞ Mothballs and crystals do kill the egg, larvae, and adult stages of moths, if you use enough of the product, and if your storage container is airtight. As noted earlier, storing natural fibers in airtight conditions reduces the life of the garment, so you will have to compromise on storage of natural fibers if you choose to place them in mothballs. You will need a pound of balls or crystals for every 100 cubic feet of sealed space. For sealed boxes, distribute the mothballs throughout the layers of clothes, but do not allow the product to touch the clothing directly because it may leave a stain. Place two layers of acid-free paper between each layer of clothing with mothballs sandwiched between the layers of paper. After filling the box, seal all seams with tape.

☞ The U.S. Department of Agriculture has tested herbal moth repellents and has found that many of these remedies are ineffective against moth larvae. These herbals do have a place, however, in displacing the objectionable odor of mothballs on clothing. Common herbs for clothing storage include anise, cloves, caraway, cinnamon, rose petals, lavender, thyme, and bay leaves.

YOUR MAY SHOPPER'S TIP

The best buys in produce this month are artichokes, avocados, pineapples, rhubarb, and tomatoes. For a refreshing but quick avocado dish, try this citrus and avocado salad.

Citrus-Avocado Toss

2 ripe avocados
2 grapefruits
4 to 6 cups torn leaf lettuce or escarole
1 small red onion
½ cup vinaigrette salad dressing

Thinly slice red onion. Cut grapefruits in half and remove each individual section from rind. Toss lettuce or escarole with grapefruit sections and onion slices. If early preparation is desired, this part of the salad may be refrigerated for a few hours in a closed plastic bag or sealed container. Just before serving, peel and slice avocados and toss with greens, grapefruit, and onion. Pour vinaigrette dressing over all and toss lightly just before serving.

4 servings

YOUR HOME MAINTENANCE CHECKLIST

☞ Check and clean whole-house fan.

☞ Check and clean air conditioner.

☞ Replace storm windows with screens.

☞ Check for roof leaks and weak or missing flashing before spring rains come.

☞ Remove abandoned wasp and bee nests around house.

☞ Remove barbeque and outdoor furniture from storage.

☞ Paint or touch up home exteriors and trim.

☞ Tune up lawn mower and sharpen blades.

☞ Check and clean gutters and downspouts.

Summer Cooling System Tune-Up

To make sure you're ready for the first hot day, check your home's cooling system early in the month.

If you have a central air conditioner: It's a good idea to turn it on for a day before the cooling season gets in full swing. The coolant sometimes leaks out of an air conditioning unit over the course of several years; unfortunately you won't know this has happened until the first 90-degree week, when all the air conditioning repair services are swamped with repair calls for nonfunctioning units. If you try your unit out early in the season before you really need it, you can discover whether or not your air conditioner has retained its cooling capacity. Before you turn on your central air conditioner, clean or replace the filter, which is usually located in the furnace. Remove debris around the compressor, which is in the outdoor cabinet, and trim any nearby shrubbery. Flush the evaporator drain line.

If you have a window air conditioner: Remove the entire unit and clean it. Vacuum dust from the condenser and evaporator. Wipe dirt and grime from the compressor, tubing, motor, and blades with soap and water. Clean leaves and debris from the outside. Straighten any bent metal fins. Scrape off any rust, reprime and paint. Vacuum the outer cabinet.

If you have a whole-house fan: Dislodge leaves and debris from the louvers and pivots. Clean the fan blades. Lubricate the motor and pulley bearings with a drop of oil on each pivot and oil port. Check the drive belt and replace it if the sides are glazed, smooth, and slippery. Check the tension; it should deflect ½ inch when pressed in the middle. Replace the belt if necessary.

EVENTS AND FESTIVALS

International Children's Festival
Vancouver, Washington

May. Children of all ages will be dazzled by this four-day festival featuring performers from around the world. Circus tents hold a melting pot of excitement, including jugglers, singers, puppeteers, and clowns. Included also are demonstrations of traditional children's activities such as kite-making and top-spinning. Information: Tears of Joy Theater, 1109 East 5th Street, Vancouver, WA 98661, Attn. Festival Director.

Busch Gardens
Storytelling Festival
Williamsburg, Virginia

May. Storytellers from around the United States convene under a big tent in the German section of Busch Gardens to spin tales for both children and adults. Variety is the rule of thumb in this five-day event, with ghost stories, folklore, comedy, family stories, mime artists, and celebrity storytellers on the bill. Information: Storytelling Festival, Busch Gardens, The Old Country, P.O. Drawer F-C, Williamsburg, VA 23187.

Great River Days Festival
Aberdeen, Mississippi

Early May. Surprise! Did you expect this festival to take place along the banks of the Ole Mississippi? Actually, this event is a celebration on the new Tennessee-Tombigbee Waterway, which was recently completed by the Army Corps of Engineers and which connects the Tennessee River in northernmost Mississippi with the Alabama port of Mobile on the Gulf of Mexico. You'll enjoy a variety of river-inspired entertainment, a fishing tournament, arts and crafts displays, candlelight walking tours of the city, and a fantastic fireworks show over the waterway. Information: Aberdeen Chamber of Commerce, P.O. Box 727, Aberdeen, MS 39730.

Kentucky Derby Festival
Louisville, Kentucky

First week in May. Often called "the most exciting two minutes in sports," the Kentucky Derby has been a Louisville tradition since 1874. Preceding the race, the Kentucky Derby Festival produces ten days of festivities, including a hot-air balloon race, an Ohio River steamboat race between the "Delta Queen" and the "Belle of Louisville," and the Pegasus Parade in downtown Louisville. Chow wagons provide Kentucky specialties such as burgoo (a wild game and vegetable stew), and spectators who attend the race can sit

back and enjoy the traditional Derby mint julep as "the Run for the Roses" commences. Information: Kentucky Derby Festival, Inc., 137 West Muhammed Ali Boulevard, Louisville, KY 40202.

Calaveras County Fair
and Jumping Frog Jubilee
Angels Camp, California

Third full weekend in May. This nationally recognized county fair includes a rodeo, country and western music, a junior livestock exhibition, and all the usual county fair prizes for quilts, baked goods, jelly, and pickles. In addition, the 42,000 fair visitors get a ringside seat at three days of frog jumping. Frogs from all over the United States (toads need not apply) compete for the grand prize of $500 (to the owner not the frog). Any frog that beats the world record jump (set in 1986) of 21 feet, 5¾ inches wins $1,500. Mark Twain celebrated Calaveras County's Jumping Frog Jubilee in a famous short story, and things have never been the same since then. Over 3,000 contestants bring frogs to the annual race, and Calaveras County even sponsors a Rent-A-Frog program for folks who can't find a frog to bring to the fairgrounds. For $3 you can rent a frog—and you *can* claim the prize money if your rented frog wins the race. Frog lovers, please note: No rented frog is allowed to jump more than twice a day, and all rental frogs are returned unscathed to the marshes of Calaveras County. Information: 39th District Agricultural Association, Box 96, Angels Camp, CA 95222.

International Chicken Flying Meet
Columbus, Ohio

Third Saturday in May. Do chickens really fly? Come to this contest to see for yourself. Since Bob Evans Farms began this contest in 1971, people from throughout the country either bring or borrow a chicken to participate in this world class chicken fly-off. Chickens are placed in a mailbox "starting gate" on a launching pad 10 feet off the ground. At 1:00 P.M. sharp, the mailbox doors are thrown open, and the chicken that flies the farthest takes the prize. A flight director oversees the contest and makes sure that the race is conducted according to the bylaws of the International Chicken Flying Association, bylaws that include rules on completely humane treatment of the "athletes." The world's chicken flying record, set in 1979 by a 15-ounce West Virginia bantam named "Lola B.," is 302 feet, 8 inches, and any chicken that breaks this record takes home a $1,000 prize. Information: International Chicken Flying Meet, Carol Haas, Chief Squawker, Bob Evans Farms, 3776 High Street, Columbus, OH 43207.

Lewis and Clark Rendezvous
St. Charles, Missouri

Third weekend in May. The town of St. Charles, the oldest town in Missouri, reverts to 1804 for this festival. The highlight of this celebration is an authentic re-enactment of the beginning of the Lewis and Clark expedition. In May, 1804 Lewis and Clark, two officers in the U.S. Army, left St. Charles with 32 soldiers and 10 civilians, all packed into three small boats for their celebrated exploration of the Louisiana Purchase. The town continues to celebrate that landmark event with a bona fide history festival. During festival days you can enjoy homemade ice cream and a hodgepodge of traditional foods, such as buffalo burgers, catfish, elk, funnel cakes, apple butter, and sassafras tea, all cooked over an open flame in honor of this pre-electricity period of history. You can linger in a crafts demonstration from the 1804 period, including rug weaving, broom making, wood carving, soap making, and blacksmithing—all demonstrated by authentically costumed craftspersons. Or you can sign up for the landmark preservation tour of St. Charles homes dating from the 1790s to the 1920s. Part of the festivities includes an old-time fiddle contest and a grand parade, which ends with the re-enactment of a court-martial that first took place during the Lewis and Clark encampment in 1804. Information: Department of Tourism, Box 745, St. Charles, MO 63320.

Dragonboat Races
Oquawka, Illinois

Memorial Day weekend. A tradition that began over 2,000 years ago in China comes to Illinois over the Memorial Day weekend as Taiwanese dragonboats are raced on the Mississippi. Since these 40-foot boats require at least 25 people on a team—22 to serve as paddlers, 1 as a coxswain, 1 as a flagcatcher, and 1 as the pacesetter—there is ample opportunity for rowing enthusiasts to participate. Each participant receives a medallion, and those who place first, second, or third receive a handcarved paddle. Over 35 additional events are part of this festive weekend, including a street dance, bathtub race, musical entertainment, arts and crafts fair, and a flea market. Information: Henderson County Tourism Council, Box 278, Oquawka, IL 61469.

Memorial Day Polar Bear Swim
Nome, Alaska

Memorial Day. The Bering Sea beckons with a typical water temperature of 35°F or less when Nomites gather, ice permitting, to welcome summer with a brief but refreshing dip in the water. Submersion of the entire body earns a participant blue lips and an honorary membership in the Polar Bear Club. Information: Nome Convention and Visitors Bureau, P.O. Box 251, Nome, AK 99762.

JUNE

IT IS THE MONTH OF JUNE,
THE MONTH OF LEAVES AND ROSES,
WHEN PLEASANT SIGHTS SALUTE THE EYES
AND PLEASANT SCENTS THE NOSES.

Nathaniel Parker Willis

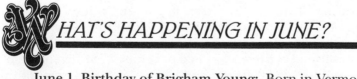

WHAT'S HAPPENING IN JUNE?

June 1, Birthday of Brigham Young: Born in Vermont in 1801, Brigham Young was the 46-year-old successor to Joseph Smith (the founder of the Mormon Church) when he led the first band of pilgrims into the Salt Lake Valley of Utah on July 24, 1847 (now commemorated as a state holiday in Utah). The Mormons, who practiced polygamy and communal ownership of property, had been continually harassed and finally driven from a succession of states— from New York, Ohio, Missouri, and Illinois (where Joseph Smith was murdered). As the final haven for the beseiged Mormons, Utah is the only state outside of the original thirteen colonies that served as "the promised land" for a religious group. At his death in 1877, Brigham Young was survived by 17 wives and 47 children.

June 3, Birthday of Jefferson Davis: The first and only president of the Confederate States of America, Jefferson Davis, whose father had fought in the Revolutionary War, began his political career as U.S. representative and then senator from Mississippi. He was personally opposed to the secession of the South, and after Mississippi seceded from the Union, he made a moving farewell speech on the Senate floor in which he pleaded eloquently for peace. Elected to the office of Confederate President by the confederate convention in Montgomery, his first official act as president was to send a peace envoy to Abraham Lincoln, who turned the Southern emissaries away. Following the Civil War he was imprisoned at Ft. Monroe, Virginia, from 1865 to 1867. He was never brought to trial, but was deprived of all rights of citizenship for the remainder of his life. Throughout the Civil War, he kept all of his old friends in the North, and when he died in New Orleans at the age of 81, he was accorded the greatest funeral the South had ever known.

June 6, Anniversary of D Day: The Normandy Beach names Omaha, Utah, Gold, Juno, and Sword should stir up memories for those who remember the unbearable and yet thrilling tension surrounding this momentous day during World War II. Led by General Dwight Eisenhower, commander of the combined forces of the United States and Great Britain, the Allies became the first invading army to cross the English Channel since 1688. Beginning with an invading force of 176,000 men on the night of June 5-6, 1944, the Allies fought and moved with fierce determination to control a beachhead only 7 miles long. By the end of a week they had penetrated 5 to 15 miles into France, had deployed 326,000 men, and had begun the summer-long campaign that was crowned with the liberation of Paris on August 25.

June 14, Flag Day: This national day to honor the Stars and Stripes was first proclaimed by President Roosevelt in 1941 and has been observed as a day to honor our flag ever since that date. The first real flag day was on June 14, 1777. On that day, John Adams introduced a resolution to the Continental Congress meeting in Philadelphia: "Resolved, that the flag of the thirteen United States shall be thirteen stripes, alternate red and white; that the union be thirteen stars, white on a blue field, representing a new constellation." Betsy Ross, a Philadelphia upholsterer, made the first flag in the early summer of 1777 at the request of George Washington and two other members of the Continental Congress, who called on her in her Arch Street Shop. Today, visitors to Philadelphia's Independence National Park can visit the modest little shop where Betsy lived and carried on her trade as upholsterer and flag maker.

The Pledge of Allegiance, which is usually part of every Flag Day ceremony and which is learned by every public schoolchild in the United States, is a fairly recent invention. The original version of the Pledge of Allegiance was written by Francis Bellamy, an associate editor of a Boston children's magazine called the *Youth's Companion*. It became part of public school daily ritual around 1892 in response to a plea from President Benjamin Harrison for patriotic observances in honor of the 400th anniversary of Columbus's discovery of America. It was not until 1942 that Congress included the Pledge of Allegiance in our national flag code. Congress added the phrase "under God" to the pledge in 1954.

June 14, Birthday of Harriet Beecher Stowe: Described by President Lincoln as "the little woman who wrote the book that made this great war," Harriet Beecher Stowe, a Connecticut clergyman's daughter, wrote and published in 1852 the renowned antislavery tale *Uncle Tom's Cabin*. The book sprang into unprecedented popularity and was translated into at least 23 languages. It so fueled northern outrage against slavery, that the characters in the story became a part of our national consciousness. Who has not heard of a compliant Black described as an "Uncle Tom," or a cruel, inhumane person described as a "Simon Legree"?

Third Sunday in June, Father's Day: The first Father's Day was celebrated on June 19, 1910. It was a local celebration in Spokane, Washington, led by Sonora Smart Dodd, whose father had raised six children after their mother died in childbirth. But it wasn't actually until 1972 that President Richard Nixon signed a congressional bill that officially established Father's Day as a national holiday. The spirit of the day is summed up with a quote from Angelo Patri: "This fathering is a man's second chance at living."

June 21, the Summer Solstice: In the Northern Hemisphere, this is the beginning of summer. In the Southern Hemisphere, it's the beginning of winter. The sun on this day is at the Tropic of Cancer, its northernmost point over the earth. At the North Pole today, daylight lasts for 24 hours. For the rest of the inhabitants of the Northern Hemisphere, daylight is at its maximum length. For the rest of the summer, the hours of daylight slowly decline as we head toward the fall equinox.

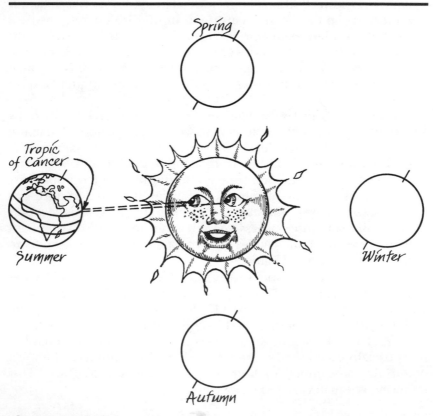

Summer Solstice

Summer officially begins on the day the sun reaches the Tropic of Cancer. The Tropic of Cancer is the northernmost latitude reached by the sun in its annual journey across the globe.

June Is National Dairy Month

Dairy foods are a vital part of any healthy diet because they are the very best sources of calcium you can get (with turnip greens and canned sardines also near the top of the list). If you're one of the many adults who doesn't drink milk, you should make a special effort to consume dairy products in some other form. If your avoidance of milk is due to a lactase deficiency (many adults lack the enzyme lactase, needed to digest the milk sugar lactose), you may find that you can eat unpasteurized yogurt because not only is it low in lactose, it also contains the lactase enzyme. Pasteurized yogurt does not have the lactase enzyme but is still low in lactose. You may also add the lactase enzyme (available in tablet form) to milk 18 to 20 hours before drinking it.

As an adult, you may wonder—why all the fuss about milk? The simple answer is that milk and milk products provide the highest concentration of calcium available in the American diet. Two-thirds of all American adults consume less than the Recommended Dietary Allowance (800 milligrams of calcium daily) and are at significant risk of developing osteoporosis with age. Calcium deficiency in adults is much more common than iron deficiency because calcium is one element that adults need to consume in *increasing* amounts with age. There is strong scientific evidence that adults need 1,000 milligrams of calcium daily (the current U.S. Recommended Daily Allowance) and that this need increases to 1,500 milligrams as they enter their fifties, sixties, and beyond.

Why Calcium Needs Increase with Age

☞ Older adults lose the ability to adjust to a reduced calcium intake. Young, healthy adults adjust to a low-calcium diet by absorbing a greater proportion of dietary calcium that passes through the gut. The ability to make that adaptive change to increase calcium absorption as a response to calcium deficiency decreases with age.

☞ Aging skin does not make vitamin D as efficiently as young skin. Even adequate exposure to sunlight sometimes does not maintain sufficient vitamin D in elderly people.

☞ Aging kidneys lose their ability to convert vitamin D in sufficient quantities to maintain calcium absorption at optimum levels.

☞ Women lose estrogen with age, and the loss of this hormone makes bones much more vulnerable to calcium deficiency.

☞ Older adults typically experience more chronic health problems and take more drugs on a daily basis. Many prescription and over-the-counter drugs interfere with calcium absorption or cause calcium excretion in the urine, including thyroid hormones, corticosteroids, aluminum-containing antacids, and certain antibiotics, such as tetracycline.

It's Easier Than You Think

If you would like to keep your calcium intake within the 1,000 to 1,500 milligram per day range, you'll find that it's a lot easier than you think. You don't have to resign yourself to fighting calories because there are plenty of low-fat dairy products that will give you the calcium you need without the fat you don't need. Consider the following dairy facts:

☞ Skim milk (at 86 calories per cup) has a higher concentration of calcium (301 milligrams per cup) than whole milk (150 calories and 290 milligrams of calcium per cup).

☞ Low-fat milk is not as low-fat as you might think. It usually contains 2 percent fat, and whole milk contains 3 percent. The percentage,

High Calcium Foods

Food	Serving Size	Calcium (in milligrams)	Calories
Ricotta cheese	1 cup	670	340
Evaporated milk, canned	1 cup	637	345
Plain low-fat yogurt	1 cup	415	113
Sardines, canned whole, with bones, drained	3 oz.	372	220
Fruited yogurt	1 cup	345	240
Skim milk	1 cup	301	86
2% low-fat milk	1 cup	298	145
Whole milk	1 cup	290	150
Buttermilk	1 cup	283	89
Swiss cheese	1 oz.	273	107
Turnip greens	1 cup	266	30
Spinach	1 cup	232	48

by the way, is the percentage by weight. A cup of low-fat milk contains a little over 5 grams of fat. Since a gram of fat contains 9 calories, a cup of low-fat milk contains about 45 calories in fat. If you're a normal, calorie-conscious adult, stick to skim milk.

☞ Buttermilk does *not* contain butter. Buttermilk is cultured skim milk. It has the lowest calorie count per cup of any milk. For an easy, nutritious, low-fat breakfast drink try whirling in a blender a cup of cold buttermilk, a few frozen whole strawberries, a banana, two or three ice cubes, and a tablespoon of honey.

☞ You can reduce the saturated fat content of casseroles and baked goods by substituting any one of the following for each cup of whole milk that your recipe calls for:

> ½ cup evaporated skim milk plus ½ cup water plus 2 teaspoons vegetable oil;
> ½ cup skim milk plus ½ cup plain low-fat yogurt;
> 1 cup reconstituted nonfat dry milk powder plus 2 teaspoons vegetable oil

☞ In casseroles and baked good recipes that call for cream, you can substitute a cup of condensed skim milk for every cup of cream. Your dish will contain more calcium than the same dish made with cream, and the calories and fat will be considerably reduced.

☞ To keep your calcium needs in mind, you should concentrate on the foods that provide the greatest amount of calcium per serving. Check the list here for your best calcium bets, and note that you can consume more than 1,000 milligrams of calcium by simply drinking three glasses of skim milk and eating one serving of a high-calcium food, such as sardines, turnip greens, or yogurt.

IN THE GARDEN

PEST CONTROL PRIMER

June brings the beginning of summer and the end of the spring grace period. Spring gardeners may have to contend with unseasonable cold or newly sprouted weeds, but the fight for survival against insects is usually reserved for the hot season. Summer brings dry spells, hot weather, and bugs. Many may be "good" bugs, but it's the pests that take all the fun out of a garden and challenge the wits of even the most dedicated organic gardener. They test our patience, our ingenuity, and our commitment to keeping a natural garden. Unfortunately, there is no single all-bug solution for organic gardeners. What's good for the cutworm doesn't work for the wireworm, and a beleagered gardener may begin to feel that his garden has turned into a scene from a science fiction movie, complete with giant, gape-jawed, radiation-mutated insects devouring the first tomato, the best of the beans, and maybe the dog as it ambles innocently through the garden gate.

Before the bug-bashing season gets in full swing, take heart. Good pest control is really a matter of knowledge and management. You can conquer your bug nightmares with a reasoned, multistep approach aimed at nipping problems early, before they reach the "throw-in-the-towel" or "bring-in-the-pesticides" stage. This summer, plan your defense early by consulting the battle plan below.

Know your bugs. Most bugs in your garden are neutral (like Switzerland) or even beneficial. The number one rule in your defense plan is to know your enemies. Get a good "Wanted" poster or mug shot of the most common pests in your area. You need photos or drawings of all stages of each insect's life from egg through larvae, pupae, nymph, and adult forms. *Rodale's Color Handbook of Garden Insects* (Rodale Press, 1979) is an excellent guide for you to study; in addition, check your bookstores or library

for color field guides to insects—the more detailed the better.

Care for your soil. A healthy soil makes plants more resistant to insect attacks. Incorporate as much compost and humus as you can manage over a garden season. Add only slow-release natural amendments, such as blood meal, cottonseed meal, greensand, ground limestone, and wood ashes. Don't abuse your soil by adding quick-acting synthetic fertilizers because these destroy the natural balance of soil organisms. Avoid cultivating or walking on cold or wet soil; it drives out air and destroys the soil structure. Plant cover crops on bare garden areas to control erosion and increase fertility.

Avoid large plantings of pest-prone crops. In many parts of the country, potatoes, eggplant, cabbage and other cole crops, strawberries, and apples can be very difficult to manage, especially on a large scale, without pesticides. Plant small amounts of these. If you keep your plantings small, you can protect some of these crops with row covers without undue expense. Also focus on easier crops such as peas, carrots, beans, rhubarb, and blueberries.

Grow a wide variety but a small amount of many crops. Since insects generally have favorite crops, they'll do more damage to one type of vegetable than another. If you have many types of vegetables or fruit, the loss of one crop won't seriously dent your harvest.

Rotate your garden plantings. Avoid planting the same vegetable in the same spot year after year. Aside from giving your vegetables a change of scenery, this has the advantage of confusing the bugs. They can't find the kitchen early in the season. By the time the Colorado potato beetles discover where you've moved the potatoes, you may have already made off with half of the harvest. Crop rotation really puts a dent in the activities of bugs that lay eggs in soil or that overwinter in garden debris.

Plant resistant varieties. Careful breeding has given us varieties that are more resistant to specific insects and diseases than others. Scan your seed catalogs for these "superplants." It's worth spending a few extra cents for the seeds to get a bug- or disease-resistant variety.

Plant early. As a rule, vegetables that are started early will be bigger and stronger and better able to withstand insects. If you're starting your own seedlings indoors, acclimatize them to the outdoors (harden them off) carefully before planting them out in the garden. Plant them outdoors on an overcast day and water them regularly but gently at the start.

Attract beneficial insects to your garden. Plant as wide an array of flowers, shrubs, and trees in your garden as possible. Try to plan it so that there's something in flower at all times. Ladybugs, praying mantises, tiny wasps, predatory mites, and other "good" bugs need plenty of food to live on, and the more flowering plants you have for them, the more likely they'll be to enter your garden and then stick around.

Fertilize conscientiously during heavy insect attack. Extra nutrients from manure or seaweed tea or fish emulsion will help plants under stress and enable them to regrow damaged tissue more quickly.

Keep the garden clean. A tidy garden is a healthy garden. Weeds can harbor viruses, and they compete with vegetables for sun, nutrients, and water. Remove infected leaves, stems, and plants promptly and burn or bury them so that they don't spread insects or disease. Plant parts remaining after harvest should also be removed from the garden and composted so that insects don't have an opportunity to build up on crop residue and re-infest another area of the garden. Such good sanitation can limit problems with European corn borers in corn, imported cabbageworm, cabbage looper and diamondback moth on cabbage and broccoli, and Mexican bean beetles and mites on beans.

Get rid of pests as soon as you can. When you notice pests (be sure that they are indeed pests), handpick adults as soon as possible and destroy their eggs. For some pests, handpicking means actually removing the insects with your gloved fingers and dropping them into a can of water mixed with a few drops of detergent. For others it means setting traps and cleaning them out daily. For earwigs use rolled up newspaper or short lengths of bamboo. For slugs set out shallow dishes of beer or lay boards on the ground. For cucumber beetles use wilted squash leaves.

When the infestation has gotten out of hand, use natural spray or dust. Sometimes the only way to save a crop is to resort to a plant-derived insecticide like rotenone, pyrethrum; or nicotine. Use natural insecticides sparingly and carefully because they will destroy good bugs as well as the pests, and even though they're made from plants, they aren't good for people. Many soft-bodied insects can be killed with a dusting of diatomaceous earth (DT). Tiny crystals in DT puncture the skin of such insects and cause them to dehydrate. DT doesn't harm people, but it will kill soft-bodied beneficial insects like ladybug larvae.

PEST CONTROL ALTERNATIVES

Commenting in *Panoscope* (an international journal on sustaina-ble development), Dr. David Pimentel of the Department of Entomology at Cornell University, Ithaca, New York, opines that insects are now destroying 13 percent of U.S. crop production despite the fact that insecticide use in this country has increased over tenfold within the past 35 years. Pimentel believes that crop losses have almost doubled, rising from 7 to 13 percent, despite this tenfold increase in pesticide use. Among the list of causes for this pesticide failure, Pimentel cites (1) the destruction of natural enemies of pests by "broad spectrum" insecticides, (2) the effects of weed killers, which can make crops more susceptible to attack, (3) a reduction in crop rotation, and (4) an increase in the use of monocultures. (Editor's note: Monoculture is an agricultural practice that relies on one crop or land use to turn a profit. It is the opposite of diversity.)

Dedicated organic gardeners already know what is now being amply demonstrated by agricultural research in universities such as Cornell. Pesticides and herbicides frequently do more harm than good; diversity is a good defense against being overrun by a single pest; and crop rotation solves a lot of problems by preventing the buildup of pests in a specific location.

But even the most conscientious practice of crop diversification and rotation sometimes fails to protect your garden from the ravages of hungry insects. When this happens, you don't have to stand by helplessly watching the destruction of your prime produce. You have at your disposal a whole arsenal of pest-control strategies that get rid of the marauders without poisoning your soil and air. Some of these controls, such as row covers and hand picking of insects, are completely benign. Other controls, such as botanical pesticides, should be used with restraint and care because they have the potential to harm beneficial insects as well as pests. Included in your arsenal of natural pest controls are the following:

Bacillus Thuringiensis

The common name for this helpful bacteria is Bt. Widely available in garden centers and through mail-order catalogs, Bt is a bacterium that causes the larvae of certain pests to sicken and die. While harmful to nearly 200 pests, Bt causes no damage to plants, wildlife, beneficial insects, pets, or people. You can buy Bt under a variety of commercial names: Dipel, Thuricide, Safer Caterpillar Killer, Reuter's Caterpillar Attack, and others.

Bacillus Popilliae

The common name for this bacterial control is milky spore disease. The bacteria are applied to the soil where the grub stage of an insect dwells. Once ingested by the grub, the bacteria cause sickness and death. The result is one less grub to mature into an adult pest. This biological control is harmless to pets, people, and beneficial insects. It also causes no contamination to groundwater (an important consideration for people who live near streams or who have domestic wells).

Traps and Barriers

You can also beat pests by utilizing their need for food, water, and reproduction. Beetle traps, such as Bag-A-Bug and Blitz-A-Beetle, rely both on food bait and pheromones (substances that insects secrete to attract mating partners) as a means of drawing insects into inescapable bags or chambers. Other traps rely on insect-attracting colors coupled with a sticky mixture, such as Tanglefoot or Stickem, that prevents escape. Barriers include the many types of spun polyester row covers, such as Reemay, Agronet, and Agryl, which allow rain and sunlight to reach the plants while providing a barrier against pest invasion. Another simple barrier is a paper collar around seedlings to prevent cutworm attack.

Diatomaceous Earth

A powder made of the microscopic-sized fossils of prehistoric plankton or algae (called diatoms), this control works by piercing the

(continued on page 190)

Pest Control Alternatives

Insect Pest	Target	Chemical Control	Natural Control
Aphid	Most vegetables and ornamentals	Malathion, Orthene	Insecticidal soap; predators
Colorado potato beetle	Eggplants, peppers, potatoes, tomatoes	Malathion, Sevin	Handpicking; removing eggs from plants; row covers; heavy mulching; rotenone as a last resort
Flea beetle	Most vegetables, especially cole crops, eggplants, radishes, turnips	Malathion, Sevin	Lime; diatomaceous earth; row covers; rotenone as a last resort
Japanese beetle	Lawns, fruit trees, and many ornamentals	Malathion, Sevin	Beetle traps; *Bacillus popilliae* (milky spore disease) for larvae; rotenone as a last resort
Mexican bean beetle	Beans	Malathion, Sevin	Handpicking; row covers; rotenone and pyrethrum dust as a last resort
Squash bug	Cucumbers, pumpkins, squash	Malathion, Sevin	Handpicking; row covers; clean cultivation; rotenone as a last resort
Cabbage looper	Beans, broccoli, cabbage, cauliflower, celery, kale, lettuce, parsley, peas, potatoes, radishes, tomatoes	Malathion, Orthene, Sevin	Handpicking; Bt for serious infestations

Insect Pest	Target	Chemical Control	Natural Control
Corn earworm	Beans, corn, peas, peppers, potatoes, squash, tomatoes	Malathion, Orthene, Sevin	Half a dropper of mineral oil applied to corn silk; Bt for infestation of other vegetables
Cutworm	Most vegetables, particularly when young	Diazinon	Paper collars around seedlings and transplants; diatomaceous earth
European corn borer	Beans, corn, peppers, potatoes, spinach, Swiss chard, tomatoes	Sevin	Alter planting dates; handpick; split plant stalks below entrance holes and remove borer
Imported cabbageworm	Brussels sprouts, cabbage, cauliflower, kohlrabi, mustard, radishes, turnips	Malathion, Orthene, Sevin	Row covers; hand-picking; Bt
Squash vine borer	Cucumbers, pumpkins, squash	Sevin	Alter planting dates; slit plant stem, remove borer and cover damaged stalk with dirt; Bt injected into stems may help
Tomato hornworm	Eggplants, peppers, potatoes, tomatoes	Malathion, Orthene, Sevin	Handpick; if larva has papery cocoons on its back, natural parasite has already doomed it, so do not kill
Leaf miner	Beans, beets, cabbage, lettuce, peppers, potatoes, rutabaga, spinach, Swiss chard, turnips	Diazinon, Orthene	Row covers; remove and destroy infested leaves

soft bodies of some types of crawling insects, larvae, and slugs. Even though diatomaceous earth looks totally innocuous to us, diatoms are razor-sharp particles that cause numerous tiny cuts in the body of an insect that comes in contact with it. You can sprinkle diatomaceous earth on the leaves of plants or distribute it in a protective circle around the base of a plant (to kill cutworms before they cut off your seedlings). Although diatomaceous earth is nontoxic and can be applied without gloves, you should apply it using a dust mask to avoid inhaling the particles.

Botanicals

These are pesticides made from the extracts of plants. Common botanicals are rotenone (from the Malaysian derris plant), pyrethrum (from an African chrysanthemum), sabadilla dust (from seeds of the lily family), and ryania (from the South American ryania shrub). These controls should be used only as a last resort because even though they are derived from plants, their long-term effects on the environment have not been well documented. Some of these pesticides seem to cause no harm to pets or people, but at the time of application (before they have begun to degrade to other chemicals) they are quite toxic to fish, to birds, and to beneficial insects. If you do choose

to use botanicals, do so with the same restraint and care you would use for synthetic pesticides. Wear protective clothing, wear a face mask and gloves, and avoid introducing any of the pesticide directly into streams or drainage systems.

Before selecting any pest-control strategy, your first job is to find out exactly what pest you're dealing with. Select the method most specific to the pest. If you must resort to botanical pesticides, check the label to be sure that the product you buy has not been "beefed up" with additional synthetic pesticides. By following this policy, you avoid a shotgun approach that damages beneficial insects as well as the pests, and you get the results you want without unnecessary damage to the environment.

ALMANAC GARDENING CALENDAR

Gardeners from as far north as Zone 3 down to Zone 7 can all pick roses this month. The gardeners in the Deep South are blessed with a long rose season, with as many as seven bloom cycles from spring through fall. Northern gardeners must be content with two or three bloom cycles, with the first

Houseplant Vacations

This summer, send your houseplants on a tour of the great outdoors. They'll return home at the end of summer lush and green and rejuvenated. To ensure your houseplants the perfect outdoor season, keep these tips in mind.

☞ Before moving your houseplants outdoors for the summer, take each plant outside briefly on a sunny day just to check for signs of pests. Strong sunlight makes it easier to spot signs of pests such as mealybugs, aphids, scale, and spider mites. Use appropriate control measures to get your plants in good shape before the summer begins.

☞ Check each plant to be sure it is not pot-bound. Simply slide a blunt table knife around the inside edge of each pot. If the roots have reached the edge of the pot, you will feel a slight resistance in the knife, and you will be able to tap the pot lightly and then lift the plant from the pot in one piece with roots intact. Repot overgrown plants in a larger pot.

☞ Most foliage houseplants are related to wild understory plants—plants that thrive in the dappled light shade of other, taller, wild plants. They flourish in an outdoor location that allows them plenty of diffuse, indirect light. Avoid south-facing, exposed locations except for those plants that have high light requirements, such as hibiscus, geraniums, oleanders, cacti, and other succulents.

☞ Water outdoor houseplants daily; because summer heat drives moisture out of clay pots and causes rapid dehydration of soil, keep a saucer full of water under clay pots to insure adequate water. You can also prevent clay pots from overheating by burying them up to the rim in your garden.

☞ In order to keep slugs, pill bugs, and other pests out of a buried pot, slip a nylon stocking over the bottom of each pot. You can then sink the pot into the ground without fear of intruders entering through the bottom drainage hole. Also, this simple trick prevents plant roots from growing through the drainage hole into the ground over the summer.

☞ Every other week, feed houseplants with fish emulsion or manure tea. The warmth and light outdoors encourages rapid growth, which you can support with your biweekly feedings.

☞ To avoid bringing outdoor pests into your house, check each plant for insects before you bring it in.

☞ Bring plants back to their indoor spots before the arrival of fall has forced them to adapt to cooler temperatures. Plants exposed to the cool outdoor temperatures of fall (even 55° to 60°F) may experience shock and decline when they are brought into a warm house.

cycle beginning in late May to mid-June. During June, the month of weddings, graduations, and anniversaries, roses can be part of the celebration nearly everywhere on the gardening map.

Zone 1

In the first two weeks, set out hardened tomato, pepper, eggplant, okra, squash, cucumber, melon, basil, and fennel plants. For faster yields, cover plants on nights when temperatures fall below 50°F, or grow them in plastic tunnels. Open the tunnels on sunny days. Direct-seed later crops of squash, cucumber, basil, and fennel. Do not place soil-cooling mulch such as straw around heat-loving plants. Between the first and third weeks, plant out late broccoli, cauliflower, and cabbage. Sow fall carrots, and thin, weed, and mulch early carrots. Hill or mulch potatoes. Thin corn. To correct nutrient problems, fertilize with quick-acting fish emulsion or manure tea. All month long, thin, weed, feed, and mulch early planted annuals such as sweet peas, alyssum, asters, candytufts, portulacas, and nasturtiums. Pick off dead blossoms so plants will continue to flower. Weed, mulch, and deadhead perennials. In the first week, plant glads and dahlias if you haven't already done so, and put out annual bedding plants.

Check fruit trees and berries for nutrient deficiencies; correct with fish emulsion, manure tea, or other quick-acting organic fertilizer. Weed around all fruits. Thin apples and peaches to 6 to 8 inches apart, apricots to 2 to 3 inches apart, and plums to 4 to 6 inches apart. Spread sawdust or peat moss around blueberries to make the soil more acidic. Tie grapes and brambles to trellises. Remove blossoms from newly planted strawberries. In the first week, weed and mulch bearing strawberries and thin grape clusters. Cover strawberries with netting to prevent bird damage.

Zone 2

Plant tomatoes, peppers, and eggplants. If you live in a frost pocket, early June frost sometimes nips tomatoes. If that happens often, plant early varieties under hot caps or gallon milk jugs. Set out pepper plants 18 inches apart. Early June is the time to make a first sowing of bush beans. Sow seeds 1 inch apart, and make a planting every two or three weeks until mid- or late July. Lima beans are trickier to grow. The soil must be warm with ample moisture or the buds will drop. Put in onion sets and sweet onion plants, set 2 inches apart. Early June is a good time to make another sowing of edible-podded peas. Make the first sowing of corn by mid-June.

Plant early, midseason, and late varieties for successive crops.

Check tips of rose canes for aphids; a soap spray or tobacco tea (cigar or cigarette stubs soaked in water) keeps them in check. Pinch chrysanthemums after each 4 inches of growth. Stop pinching on July 4. Finish planting gladiolus corms. For conversation pieces, grow yellow calla lilies and miniature glads (acidantheras) in pots. Sow portulacas in hot, dry spots where few other things grow. Don't let transplants of zinnias, petunias, cockscombs, and other flowers dry out. Dry soil stunts growth, a condition from which the plants might not recover.

You can still prune out dead branches of any fruit or nut tree. Trim out deadwood and branches that crisscross or rub against each other. Check newly planted trees or shrubs for wire labels. Remove them before they girdle the branches or trunk. Mulch nut trees with a 3-inch-thick layer of sawdust or wood chips. Side-dress with high-nitrogen fertilizer such as cottonseed meal, compost, or rotted manure.

Zone 3

Early in the month, plant okra, southern peas, and sweet potatoes. Around midmonth, sow late corn, late bush beans, and a second crop of lima beans. Toward the end of the month, try a final planting of summer squash. As tomatoes begin to sprawl, train them to a stake or a cage. Start training early, since it is best not to move a vine once it has set fruit. As the weather settles into the 70° to 80°F range, tomatoes, peppers, eggplants, and squash will bloom. Foliar-feed with manure, seaweed, or compost tea to reduce blossom drop. In this same temperature range, also set out celery in well-worked beds.

Resist the temptation to mulch heat-loving crops until after the soil has dried and warmed sufficiently. Mulching too early can slow growth. When melons begin to vine, feed with manure or compost tea. Remove rhubarb seed stalks as they appear. Tie up cauliflower leaves to blanch heads. Throughout the month replace harvested crops with succession plantings of carrots, cucumbers, and late tomatoes. As always, keep an eye open for pests. If ignored, populations of squash bugs, Mexican bean beetles, and cabbageworms will explode during June.

Sow annuals outdoors as early in June as possible. Set out bedding plants and put in tuberous begonias, cannas, dahlias, and glads early in the month. Add bonemeal to new planting beds. Feed spring-flowering shrubs just after bloom. Apply a combination of compost and rock fertilizers or bonemeal, then mulch. Acid-loving ornamentals such as rhododendrons, camellias, and azaleas prefer cottonseed meal covered with a mulch of oak leaves or pine needles. Many shrubs and perennials are best propagated during June. To propagate azaleas, forsythias, roses, and viburnums by layering, simply bend the tips of supple branches to the ground. Hold them in place with a U-shaped wire, soil, or rocks until roots form. Keep roses heavily mulched. Water chrysanthemums frequently and keep mulched until they're established. After iris and lily blooms die back, lift and divide tubers. Prune spent blooms from lilacs before seedpods form. If you haven't sown perennials such as delphiniums, columbines, and primulas yet, do so in flats or cold frames early in the month. The most tender bedding plants, such as petunias, heliotropes, portulacas, and nasturtiums, can be set out from early to mid-June.

Keep strawberries picked, mulched, and watered. Mark the exceptional producers for propagation, and remove plants showing signs of rust or powdery mildew. Thinning grape clusters may prevent black rot later in the season. Replenish mulches around fruits. Use acid mulches on brambles, blueberries, and strawberries. If the month is dry, water new stock weekly to encourage root growth. After the spring fruit drop, thin apples, pears, and peaches to 6 inches apart and plums and apricots to 4 to 6 inches apart. Feed the orchard with tea made from seaweed, fish emulsion, and manure or compost. The nutrients in this mixture will encourage well-developed fruits. Keep an eye open for pests, especially Japanese beetles. Treat as necessary to prevent pest population explosions later in the season.

Zone 4

Plant warm-weather crops like muskmelons, okra, field peas, and lima beans early this month. Make succession sowings of sweet corn and bush beans. Keep soil moist until the seedlings are up, then apply a thick mulch. Pull early crops when harvests dwindle to make way for flowers or other vegetables. Remove suckers from tomato leaf axils once a week to keep plants from spreading out. When cauliflower heads grow about 4 inches wide, begin blanching by tying leaves around them. Dig fall-planted garlic bulbs when their tops yellow and fall over. Spread them in a single layer in a sheltered place, to dry for a couple of weeks. Hose away aphids and handpick tomato hornworms, cabbage loopers, and squash bugs; destroy squash borers with a pointed wire after slitting stems with a sharp knife, or inject stems with Bt (*Bacillus thuringiensis*).

Mulch ornamentals, giving top priority to rhododendrons and azaleas and new plantings. Provide deep soakings in dry weather. Feed all chrysanthemums and continue to pinch tall varieties after each 4 inches of growth. Feed bulb beds and peony plants, and provide ample water to peonies throughout the summer for best bloom next year. Remove yellowing leaves from spring bulbs and spent flowers from annuals and perennials. Leave the lower parts of delphinium bloom stems until the leaves have withered and new shoots have begun to grow from the ground. After tea roses pass peak bloom, cut flower stems to the axil of the nearest five-parted leaf and feed the plants manure tea. Remove enough old, darkened canes of climbing roses to make way for new shoots, and cut all blooming canes of ramblers to the ground. Feed roses every two or three weeks until late summer.

Top vigorous black and purple raspberry canes to increase branching; thin to three or four canes to a hill. After the strawberry harvest, thin out old, woody plants by hand or with a tiller, then dig in aged manure or compost around the rest and mulch thickly. Keep beds watered through the summer. At midmonth, begin hanging sticky red decoys in apple trees to trap maggots; renew them every few weeks. Pick up and compost fallen fruits to discourage pests and diseases. If there's still a heavy crop after the June drop, thin peaches and apples to 6 to 8 inches apart and plums to 4 to 6 inches apart. Use netting to protect developing cherries and blueberries from marauding birds.

Zone 5

Early in the month, plant another round of snap beans, squash, cucumbers, and midseason corn. Fill vacant garden space with okra, peanuts, field peas, and sweet potatoes. Late in the month, plant pumpkins for fall harvest. If space is limited, plant pumpkins or watermelons around the edge of the corn patch and allow the vines to run between the rows. To protect summer crops from drought, mound up soil over the plants' root zones, and cover with a thick mulch. Be especially diligent about watering plants when they are blossoming. Feed summer crops using foliar sprays of fish emulsion or fish emulsion mixed with kelp, to increase plant vigor and reduce insect damage. Mound soil over the bases of squash, cantaloupe, and cucumber vines to discourage squash vine borers. Treat severe infestations of Mexican bean beetle larvae with rotenone and use sabadilla dust to control squash bugs, harlequins, and other shield bugs.

Fill vacant space in flower beds with caladiums, dahlias, or chrysanthemums. As you work in the beds, remove dead foliage from tulips and daffodils and stake up tall lilies and dahlias if needed. Pinch back annual flowers after the first big flush of blossoms fades. Mulch long-season annuals, roses, and shrubs. Make additional sowings of sun-loving annuals, such as marigolds, zinnias, and celosias. Plant impatiens or coleus in sheltered or shaded places. Water crape myrtle, hydrangeas, and other late-blooming shrubs. Apply liquid fertilizer to young ornamental trees and bushes, especially those surrounded by grass. This is a good time to propagate mondo grass, ivies, and other ground covers that grow in moist shade. Thoroughly water any shrubs or trees set out this spring; heat stress can be more devastating than winter injury to plants that lack well-developed root systems.

When the strawberry harvest ends, move bird netting from the strawberry bed to the grape arbor. Fertilize bearing grapes with cottonseed meal, fish emulsion, or manure tea. Apply Bt (*Bacillus thuringiensis*) to grapes if leaf rollers or other leaf-eating worms appear. Water blackberries, raspberries, and blueberries to increase fruit size and stimulate new growth. Mow closely around berries that are not heavily mulched. Fruit and nut trees do their best growing in early summer. Remove weeds and grasses from under trees, apply fertilizer, and water deeply.

Zone 6

Harvest every two days to encourage your vegetables to keep producing a bumper crop. Leaving vegetables on the vine signals the plant that seed formation is under way and it can stop production. In spite of the heat, you can still plant tomatoes. You can also plant New Zealand spinach, okra, sweet potatoes, bush beans, and bush limas early in the month. Sow corn at ten-day intervals. Plant blackeyed peas, malabar spinach, cucumbers, pumpkins, and squash for the fall garden. When temperatures get above 90°F, many peppers stop setting fruit. Mulch, water, and a weekly foliar spray of seaweed will help get peppers and other vegetables through to fall. Potatoes planted in February will start to mature this month. Cut off dead foliage and allow the potatoes that will be stored to cure in the ground for up to a week. Remember to save the golf ball-sized potatoes for planting in the fall garden.

Heat-tolerant annuals and perennials can keep the garden colorful all summer. Colorful vines include thunbergias (also good for a ground cover) and morning glories. Mexican sunflowers make an impressive background plant. Nicotianas, zinnias, marigolds, heliotropes, coreopsis, gaillardias, and salvias add excellent color to flower beds. Also try lisianthus, or prairie gentian, which blooms all summer if spent flowers are removed. Astilbes, azaleas, rhododendrons, and camellias must never dry out, so water deeply and mulch. Prune wisteria and climbing roses that have finished blooming. Dig and store dormant bulbs. Divide irises and replant in soil enriched with compost and rock phosphate. Pinch dead blooms off annuals to keep flowers coming.

Thin heavy fruit loads on trees and grapevines to improve fruit quality and prevent breaking limbs. Water trees deeply and mulch heavily to prevent fruit drop later in the summer. To keep borers and other insects from attacking trees, remove about 2 inches of soil from around the base and wrap masking tape or tree tape around the trunk from just below the soil surface to 6 inches above ground. Rub Tanglefoot on the tape so insects can't crawl up. The tape will break and fall away as the tree grows. Flood nut trees periodically to be sure nuts fill out. Don't make heavy applications of nitrogen fertilizers on pears because lush growth often leads to fire blight. Remove suckers from below the graft on fruit trees. Cut out dewberry and blackberry canes that produced this year.

Zone 7

In the inland West and along the Gulf and Atlantic coasts, summer heat inhibits germination of many seeds and causes most vegetable crops to decline. Heavily mulch all plants you want to carry through the summer. Tomatoes, eggplants, and peppers will often hold their blossoms and keep producing through the heat if the soil is kept cool. In the hottest part of the zone, okra and sweet potato sets can be planted. If frost is more than four months away, try planting bush or even pole limas. If you stop gardening between June and August, cover the garden with compost, wood chips, manure, or any other organic material. Water occasionally to keep it damp and decomposing, or cover with black plastic. The soil will be in fine tilth and high fertility by August. In the cooler parts of the East, continue to plant tomatoes, eggplants, peppers, pole beans, okra, corn, soybeans, sweet potatoes, limas, and field peas. To improve germination of late-planted carrots and parsley, support a sheet of plywood about 1 inch above the seedbed to shade and cool the soil. Remove it as soon as the first seeds germinate. On the foggy West Coast, plant cool-weather crops like carrots, lettuce, parsley, cabbages, and beets. Along the northern Pacific Coast to the Washington border, you can even plant Irish potatoes.

Prune early blooming shrubs like lilacs, mock oranges, fuchsias, spireas, and rhododendrons. Prune to control wisteria, coral vine, clematis, Confederate jasmine, climbing fig, honeysuckle, and English and Algerian ivies. Pinch spent flower heads on annuals to keep new ones coming, and pinch tips of chrysanthemums to keep them low and bushy. As soon as bearded irises finish blooming, divide and replant them. Roses can produce five to seven bloom cycles in this zone if properly maintained. Give them adequate food and water to bring them through the summer heat. Water in the early morning to avoid mildew and black spot. In sandy soils, mulch to retain moisture. Try planting some out-of-the-ordinary perennials. Manaos beauty, a blue thistlelike flower, has few problems; lisianthus, or prairie gentian, produces blue, white, and pink flowers during the hottest months; Mexican evening primrose is drought-resistant and gives pink flowers with yellow centers.

Continue to water and feed citrus about every two weeks. In the sandy soils of Florida, more frequent watering may be necessary. In the West, a soil basin can be built around citrus trees to contain the water. To avoid shallow root development, don't mulch citrus in heavy soils. Check the depth of soil moisture daily and keep a record to get an idea of how often to water your trees. Small fruit size and fruit that does not taste sweet are most often a result of underwatering and low soil fertility. Avocados, guavas, mangoes, and papayas are also heavy feeders and drinkers; for these, mulches are recommended.

IN GOOD HEALTH

HEALTHY ALTERNATIVES TO EATING OUT ON THE ROAD

Summer is the time when many of us are trying to get from here to there in a hurry. The cabin we rented for a week in June is a whole day's drive away, or maybe the visit to Cousin Joe's place is down 800 miles and four hamburger stops of highway. When you're trying to get somewhere for vacation, getting there usually seems more important than what you eat on the way. But by thinking ahead, you can save money on your pit stops and arrive at your destination with your good health still intact.

Eating on the Run

Try these tips for eating out on the road. They save time (spent in line at a fast-food stop or at a table waiting to be served), they save money (by giving you fresh, wholesome food at grocery store prices),

they keep you in the good health you need to enjoy your vacation (by avoiding the grease and salt overload of typical fast food).

Eat Light

Sitting all day in a car is tiring, but it actually requires fewer calories than your normal activities. Loading up with food during a day's driving can make you pretty uncomfortable when you and your over-

---

Three Squares for the Road

Breakfast	Lunch	Dinner
Bagels spread with yogurt cheese and topped with raisins or fruit conserve English muffins, topped with cottage cheese and smoked, sliced turkey Apple-honey-oatmeal muffins Fruit compote Taco shells filled with sliced bananas or strawberries and topped with vanilla yogurt Pita pockets stuffed with sliced avocado and sprouts	Rice cakes or pita pockets with quick fillings Pear crunch salad Vegetable or fruit kabobs Tomatoes stuffed with tuna or chicken salad Assorted raw vegetables with cottage-cheddar cheese dip Cold carrot soup with whole wheat crackers	Vegetable marinade Chicken-tomato-pasta salad Fettuccine and vegetable salad Beef-bean-noodle casserole Cream of broccoli soup Pita pockets stuffed with shredded lettuce-peas-cheese salad

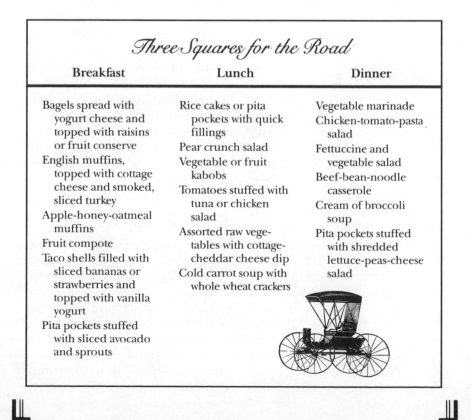

loaded stomach finally find that motel bed.

Use Simple Equipment

Invest in some simple equipment before your trip. Most of these items will already be in your home; if not, pick them up the week before your planned departure: a roomy ice chest; several large-size blocks of "blue ice"; disposable plates and bowls, cups, and eating utensils; a picnic hamper or large box to store your supplies; an inexpensive or disposable table cover for your roadside picnic table; a kitchen utility knife and a serving spoon.

Plan Ahead

Plan your menu from items that require little preparation to use, such as cheese, yogurt, fresh fruits and vegetables, cereals, marinated pasta salads, and whole grain muffins and breads; shop for the items you need several days before your trip. Store your "blue ice" in your freezer or stock up on ice cubes to fill your ice chest on the day of the trip. Several days before your trip prepare your travel meals and store everything in appropriate containers in your refrigerator. For menu items, select from this list of easy take-along foods. By mixing and matching according to your taste you can easily prepare three take-along meals in two to three hours.

JUNE STRESS ALERT

Most people think of December as the most stressful month of the year, but some social science research indicates that the real zinger for stress in most people's lives is June. June seems to be the peak month for a wide assortment of life changes including weddings, graduations, beginning new jobs, vacations, divorces, selling homes, moving, or remodeling houses. And for working parents, suddenly school's out, and everyone in the family must fit into a whole new round of adjustments.

Stress Escape Hatches

As you move into the changes June always brings, check out your stress coping strategies. Are you keeping your commitments to your health by maintaining your normal exercise schedule as much as possible despite the demands on your time? And are you scheduling some time out for yourself to practice other stress-reducing strategies such as yoga, meditation, listening to quiet music, or relaxation exercises? In addition, you have many other practical options for making a peak stress time more manageable for yourself.

Get Some Help

Get an extra pair of hands to help when your workload is just too overwhelming. If you and your spouse both work full time and must arrange your daughter's wedding, an anniversary party for your parents, or a bon voyage send-off for your sister, don't play the brave soldier and do it all alone. Now is the time to get some help. If you think you can't afford to hire professional help for a large party or celebration, hire the teenager who lives on your street to serve and wash dishes for a party or to clean your house before the guests arrive. Offer to pay your neighbor for a tray of beautiful hors d'oeuvres. Now is the time to buy professional help if you can afford it and to ask for help from relatives and friends in your time of need.

Take a Vacation

Get away from it all for at least a short time. Even if you're overwhelmed with the details of some big life change, take some time out, preferably with your spouse or a friend. Go to the mountains or the ocean for a one-day outing. Go out to dinner or to the movies or to a concert in the park. For your time out select any activity that requires no work or preparation on your part and that completely takes your mind off what's going on in your life right now.

Keep a "To-Do" List

Make a "to-do" list, and check and revise your list every evening several hours before you go to bed. Then forget about the task facing you until tomorrow. By making a list, you avoid garden-variety insomnia caused by worrying over details while you try to fall asleep.

Live within Your Means

Be realistic in your expectations. If your budget for your parents' anniversary party only allows for ten guests, then invite the ten and don't waste time on guilt about the people you must leave out. Forcing yourself to do more than you can afford will only cause you a great deal of anxiety and spoil whatever enjoyment you could be getting from this celebration. Watch out for thoughts that begin with "I should," "I ought to," or "I feel obligated to." Thoughts begun in this way usually end with unrealistic expectations that you place on yourself or on others.

Be Happy

If the change in your life right now is an unhappy one, minimize the damage by adjusting your mental attitude as much as you can. Don't indulge in thoughts that begin with "If only ": "If only I were rich," "If only I had married someone else," "If only I had been more careful," and so forth. "If only" thoughts don't change your situation, and they prevent you from using your energy to cope with your problem.

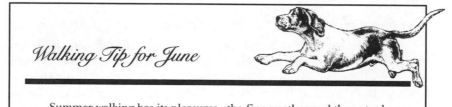

Walking Tip for June

Summer walking has its pleasures—the fine weather and the extra hours of light available for walking—and its hazards, such as loose dogs. In the summer, more folks seem to leave their dogs unattended and unleashed. Nothing spoils a walk more than being frightened by an unruly dog. A good preventive measure for any walker is to carry a walking stick. A walking stick in this case need not be a cane or other stick to lean on as you walk. In fact, for most people a 2-foot long section of broom handle works nicely. You can grasp it in either hand, it has a smooth and comfortable surface, and its short length will not interfere with your stride. If a menacing dog comes toward you, simply stop in your tracks, face the dog, hold up your stick, and shout, "No!" Most dogs know exactly what that word means, and most will be startled into hesitation so that you can be on your way. Remember, also, that dogs consider direct eye contact a threat. Never stare an aggressive dog in the eye. Focus your gaze on its tail or back.

AT HOME

SENSIBLE ADVICE ABOUT HOME SECURITY BEFORE YOU GO ON VACATION

June begins the annual summer vacation season, a time to shed worries, relax, and have fun. The last thing you need as a welcome home reception is a forced entry and burglary of your home while you are away. Unfortunately, residential burglary is America's fastest-growing crime—it's jumped 19 percent in five years. In 1987 you were three times more likely to be a burglary victim than you were in 1977. The FBI estimated there were 5 million residential burglaries in 1987. Statistics show that they're on the rise in medium-size cities and in suburban and rural areas of both the southern and western regions of the United States, but not in large cities, which are now actually a bit safer than they used to be.

According to the Insurance Information Institute, nine out of ten household burglaries are preventable. If you live in a high-crime neighborhood or have many valuables, an electronic security system may be what you need. But if you're like most people, a few simple and much less expensive approaches to home protection may be all that you need.

The Easiest Things First

You can lower your risk of becoming a burglary victim without buying a single deadbolt. Simply use the locks you have and be more security conscious in your personal habits and in your response to strangers.

☞ Never tell unidentified telephone callers when you won't be home.

☞ Ask for identification from utility and delivery people you don't know.

☞ Don't put your address on your key ring.

☞ Don't leave house keys with your car in a commercial parking lot.

☞ Don't leave a door unlocked while you're out, even for 5 minutes.

☞ Put a "Beware of Dog" sign or a fake security alarm sticker in a conspicuous window.

☞ If you hide a spare key outside, put it far from the door and not in any of the predictable spots (like under the mat, a large rock, or the potted geranium).

☞ Trim shrubs that grow close to windows, or plant sharp, spiky bushes such as cactus or holly there to discourage lurking.

☞ Start (or join) a Neighborhood Watch. Your police department can help organize this group.

Inexpensive Security Devices

A few small purchases can give you additional security without resorting to high-tech security devices. Try some of these commonsense approaches.

Light Protection

Get a few timers and use them when you're away to turn your lights, radio, and TV on and off. Use exterior lights at night, whether you're at home or not. They should illuminate all entrances and be hard to reach so that a would-be thief can't disconnect them or unscrew the bulbs. If you'd prefer not to have your exterior ablaze with light, you may be interested in an infrared detector that turns lights on only when someone comes in range.

Door Security

Put deadbolt locks on your doors; these locks have long bolts that resist both crowbars and credit cards. Install double-cylinder deadbolts on side and back doors and on doors that contain glazing. Since a key is needed to open these locks from either the outside or the inside, breaking the door glass won't do an intruder any good—he still needs a key. For a front door a single-cylinder deadbolt is probably sufficient so long as there is no glass within reaching distance of the knob. Having one door in your house with a single-cylinder deadbolt is a good idea in case of a fire; you need one door that you can open quickly without finding a key.

Window Protection

Buy special locks to secure double-hung windows. Don't rely on the locks that come with the windows; they're so weak that intruders can easily break them. If you don't want to invest in window locks, you can secure double-hung windows with a drill and a box of double-headed nails. Simply drill downward-pointing holes through the sashes and stick a duplex (double-headed) nail in. The nail will pin the window shut, but it will be easy to pull out when you want to open the window.

Secure basement windows as well as living area windows because even though they appear small, a burglar can squeeze through most of them. Also, they are often in inconspicuous places, shielded by shrubbery. Spot-weld a horizontal metal bar across the middle of each window, so even if the window is pushed in, the bar will make the opening too narrow to crawl through.

And Finally, Electronic Systems

In response to the greater number of burglaries nationwide, and because of our increasing knowledge and fascination with electronic gadgets and gimmicks, electronic home security systems are popular consumer products. In 1987 they guarded 1 in 11 American homes, and experts predict that by 1990, one house in every five will have them. Not long ago, a panel of convicted burglars in Washington, DC, agreed that alarm systems are the most effective crime deterrent available to homeowners. That's a pretty good endorsement.

Professionally installed systems start at around $1,800. Most people don't want to pay that much, so they opt for the self-installed systems. Just about every retail electronics store and many mail-order catalogs sell them now. David Petraglia, author of *The Complete Watchdog's Guide to Installing Your Own Home*

How to Have a Worry-Free Vacation

Summer is a busy time for burglars. When you leave for vacation, don't leave your home to thieves. The best vacation protection is a house sitter. If you can't find someone to stay in your house, don't advertise your absence. Eliminate the telltale signs that you're away:

☞ Never announce vacation plans in a public place or in want ads.

☞ Cancel all predictable deliveries; have a neighbor collect unexpected ones that reveal no one is home.

☞ Arrange to have your grass cut.

☞ Put cash, jewelry, and important papers in a safe-deposit box.

☞ Ask a trustworthy neighbor to watch your place, but ask him or her not to tell others that you're away. Explain your security system and leave your vacation phone number.

☞ Tell police when you're leaving and when you'll arrive back home.

☞ Secure all windows, doors, and other possible entry points.

☞ Don't leave lights on continuously—a sure sign to burglars. Use timers to turn lights on and off as you would normally use them. Vary times slightly from day to day. Also put the television and radio—at normal volume—on timers.

☞ Put empty trash cans in the basement or garage.

☞ Lock up tools and ladders that a thief could steal—or use to break in.

☞ Use an appliance timer to run your air conditioner (fan only) periodically.

☞ Turn down the bell so a burglar can't hear a phone ring unanswered.

☞ Leave some shades and drapes slightly open or in their usual position to keep the house from looking closed up.

☞ Close the door on an empty garage.

☞ If you leave a car at home, park it in your driveway.

☞ If you take your car, arrange to a have a neighbor park his or her second car in your driveway.

☞ If you leave your car at the airport, remove mail or other documents that show your address.

Burglar Alarm (Prentice-Hall, 1984), makes two good recommendations about putting in your own security system: Get commercial-grade equipment, and conceal all the wiring in your system (if you're installing a hand-wired system).

Recently, there's been a flood of low-cost, low-quality security devices—the kinds of things you might find on the shelves of a department store. Avoid these products. Go to an alarm wholesaler or a consumer electronics store such as Radio Shack and ask for their best residential security components. The cost will be slightly higher, but the equipment will be significantly more reliable.

Instead of running wires along the molding next to your doors and windows, thread them through the cavities inside your walls. This technique makes the system harder to install, but it has two advantages: Your home will look better, and the wiring will be protected from a burglar's efforts to tamper with it. Petraglia's book includes detailed instructions for maneuvering wires into your walls without destroying either the walls or your patience.

You also have the option of buying one of the wireless systems. These use transmitter sensors at every door and window; they signal the control panel via radio waves. Wireless systems are more expensive, but they're easier to install and you don't have to worry about whether the wires show.

WOOD-BORING INSECTS

June marks the beginning of summer fix-up and repair time as well as the midpoint for the traditional spring/summer house buying and moving season. It also marks the time when many people make the unfortunate discovery that they have some very hungry but uninvited guests—termites. Most home mortgages are granted with the proviso that the home be certified termite-free, and many would-be sellers find that their house sale won't go as planned because of termites. Other homeowners discover, sometimes while completing an outdoor painting job, that there's a reason the last two steps on the back porch feel like punk wood. Even though wood-boring insects are active all year-round, we seem to detect their unwanted presence most often during the summer.

If you've made the dismaying discovery that you've got some wood-boring bugs in your house, you should be aware that you've got more options than calling the first name in the phone book under "Exterminating." The more thoroughly you examine those options, the more likely you'll get a pest eradication job that doesn't make you or your cat or your great-aunt Sally, who sleeps in an apartment in the basement, sick from the effects of lingering toxins.

Time Is on Your Side

The first rule in termitology is: "Don't panic." It takes many, many years for termites to do major structural damage to a house, the one exception being Formosan termites, voracious little pests that currently are common only in Florida. The termites common to most of the United States (a species entomologists call *Reticulitermes hesperus*) just don't eat that fast. Before you treat your whole foundation with commercially applied termiticides, take the time to educate yourself on alternative methods of termite eradication and exclusion. If your house falls within the realm of fairly recent infestation, it certainly will not fall down while you delay treatment for a few weeks in order to examine your options.

The commercial extermination industry is being revolutionized by innovative, nontoxic ways to deal with wood-eating pests. Among the new techniques available for eradication of carpenter ants, for example, is the use of portable heaters that deliver intense heat to the nesting site of these pests. Since most insects can live in only a very narrow temperature range, this simple, nontoxic approach really works. An alternative method of termite eradication involves sealing off infested foundation areas with a special grade of sand that is impossible for termites to crawl through. Since the termites must leave the building to seek water, this method of eradication is also notably successful.

Where to Go for More Information

You can go to one good source to get information on all the latest low-toxicity methods of eradicating wood pests. The Bio-Integral Resource Center (BIRC), a nonprofit corporation devoted to publishing information on low-toxicity pest management, has just compiled all of the best information currently available on eradication of wood pests. Write to BIRC and ask for their new book, *Least Toxic Pest Management: Termites, Carpenter Ants and Bees, Wood Boring Beetles, and Wood Decay.* Send $10 plus $1 for postage and handling to: BIRC, P.O. Box 7414, Berkeley, CA 94707.

Household Firsts in History

If you were the first on your block to own a VCR, a cordless telephone, or a microwave, you can appreciate the feeling of pride and excitement that comes with being the first to own a recent innovation. But imagine yourself as the first on your street to install one of those newfangled indoor toilets. No doubt you'd be just as proud of that and just as eager to show it off to your friends. Imagine what life was like before each of these household innovations.

1750s—Wealthy Americans had the first indoor toilets, but they were nothing more than a chair with a hole in it and a chamber pot placed strategically underneath. Indoor toilets with running water made their debut in the 1820s. In 1825 President John Quincy Adams had the first White House toilet installed.

1790—Thomas Saint of St. Sepulchre, England, patented the first sewing machine. The first one to be marketed was designed by Barthelemy Thimmonier in Amplepuis, France, but his fledgling enterprize was thwarted by angry tailors who saw it as a threat to their livelihood.

1800—Philadelphia boasted the country's first municipal water and sewer system; Boston was next in 1823.

1830s—A few homes had the first built-in bathubs; they were wooden boxes lined with lead. Most were plain rectangular boxes. There were fancier ones, too, in shapes that accommodated the contours of the hips and even some that rocked like a baby's cradle. Before this time few people took many baths at all.

1876—Melville R. Bissell patented the carpet sweeper, precursor to today's vacuum cleaner.

1889—The first dishwasher was designed by Mrs. W. A. Cockran in Shelbyville, Indiana.

1897—The first electric washing machine was introduced.

1901—The first vacuum cleaner was produced by Hubert Cecil Booth in London. Because so few people then had electricity in their homes, the vacuum cleaner got its start as part of a housecleaning service. A horse-drawn van carrying the cumbersome gas- or electric-powered vacuum cleaner pulled up to the curb and long hoses that were attached to it were dragged into the house to clean rugs, floors, and furniture. The first portable vacuum cleaner was developed in San Francisco in 1905 by Chapman & Skinner.

1913—The first electric refrigerator for home use was marketed in Chicago under the name Domelre. Electrolux patented the first gas refrigerator in 1926.

1955—Tappan Stove Company patented the first electric kitchen range.

YOUR JUNE SHOPPER'S TIP

The best buys in produce this month are beets, cherries, peas, snow peas, and spinach. For a super-quick salad course, try this oriental-style snow pea salad.

Nutty Snow Peas

4 cups snow peas
1 cup hickory nuts or pecans
2 tablespoons low-sodium soy sauce
2 tablespoons olive oil

Combine peas and nuts. Sprinkle with soy sauce and oil. Mix thoroughly and serve.

4 servings

YOUR HOME MAINTENANCE CHECKLIST

☞ Drain and check the operation of your hot water heater using the instructions found in January.

☞ Clean the filters on your room air conditioning unit. Change the filters of your whole-house air conditioner.

☞ Wash out the water container of your basement or room dehumidifier with mild soap and water to prevent the growth of mold and mildew; do this monthly during use.

EVENTS AND FESTIVALS

Red Cloud Indian Art Show
Pine Ridge, South Dakota

Second Sunday in June through mid-August. As a celebration of Native American art, this show includes examples of almost every field of the visual arts. A highly regarded career launch for Native American artists, the Red Cloud show features over 300 works in oils, pastels, mixed media, sculpture, and graphics from over 30 American Indian tribes. The exhibition is juried, and over $7,000 in prize money awaits the top entrants. The Red Cloud Heritage Center is also open to visitors during the exhibition and houses a fantastic permanent collection of Native American art that provides visitors with informative insights into Indian tribal life. Information: H. Jane Nauman, Box 232, Custer, SD 57730.

American Indian
Strawberry Festival
Exeter, Rhode Island

Second Sunday in June. Did you know that the strawberry is the symbol of friendship among American Indians? This event celebrates that symbolic meaning, and the day serves as a time for people to fill themselves with strawberries and goodwill. Indians in tribal ceremonial costumes tell legends, demonstrate crafts, and perform traditional dances such as the Strawberry Friendship Dance. Included, of course, are lots of strawberry dishes. Anyone for strawberry cornbread? Information: Tomaquag Memorial Indian Museum, Summit Road, Exeter, RI 02822.

International Freedom Festival
Detroit, Michigan,
and Windsor, Ontario

Mid-June through July 4. The International Freedom Festival is an expansive joint celebration of freedom and friendship between the United States and Canada. The dates of the festival span United States Independence Day as well as Canada Day, the July 1 holiday that commemorates the 1867 creation of the Dominion of Canada. With two independence holidays to celebrate, it should come as no surprise that the Freedom Festival Fireworks is the largest fireworks display in North America. It features blazing pyrotechnics shipped in from China and Japan. During this two-week celebration you can choose from over 100 events, including jazz, classical, gospel, or pop music concerts; a bed race; a 6-kilometer run; a science circus at the Ontario Science Center; a dart tournament; parades; boating and water events; and appropriately enough, a New U.S. Citizens' Swearing-In Ceremony. Information: International Freedom Festival, 100 Renaissance Center, Suite 1760, Detroit, MI 48243.

National Hollerin' Contest
Spivey's Corner, North Carolina

Third Saturday in June. Loud enough to reach a distance of several miles, hollerin' preceded the telephone as the primary form of communication between southern farmers. Distress hollers signifying a need for help, wake-up hollers ensuring that neighbors weren't oversleeping, and work hollers sung during field and livestock work were all a part of farm life. The National Hollerin' Contest began as a way to save the almost-extinct art of hollerin'. Judges look for hollers that emulate farmers of the past. Loudness is not necessary to win the hollerin' contest, but style and technique are very important to claim a prize. Trophies are awarded for first, second, and third places, and people may enter the contest free of charge. Information: Mr. Ermon Godwin, P.O. Box 332, Spivey's Corner, NC 28334.

Minnesota Carp Festival
Coon Rapids, Minnesota

Mid-June. King Carpio and Queen Cyprinus preside over a sea of carp-related activities at this grand celebration of the *cyprinus carpio*—or carp fish. Sunday begins with a carp fishing contest, and samples of the catch are available throughout the day. Try some of the tasty carp cakes, carp soup, and various ethnic carp dishes. Games for kids, including pin the barbell on the carp and a beanbag toss into big wooden carp mouths, educational programs on carp and the Mississippi River, lots of music, and an art fair combine to make it a great family event. The purchase of a carp kite or jewelry made out of carp bones could make this a carptivating day for all. Information: Coon Rapids Dam Regional Park, 9750 Egret Boulevard, Coon Rapids, MN 55433.

Reno Rodeo
Reno, Nevada

Third week in June. "The wildest, richest rodeo in the West" boasts over $300,000 in prize money for those who are sturdy enough to participate in this saddle-splitting contest. Events scheduled include saddle bronc riding, barrel racing, calf roping, bareback riding, bull fighting, team roping, a wild horse race, and a businessmen's steer-decorating contest in which local businessmen tie a ribbon on a steer's tail. A western arts and crafts show and the Western States Drill Competition are also part of this rodeo. Information: Reno Rodeo Association, P.O. Box 12335, Reno, NV 89510.

Woodchoppers' Jamboree and Rodeo Encampment, Wyoming

Third weekend in June. Watch out for falling trees at the Wyoming Woodchoppers' Jamboree as lots of "wood-be Paul Bunyans" participate in Wyoming's largest timber carnival. Lumberjack contests, such as log-splitting, ax throwing, tree felling, and "hot rod chain saws" are just a part of the weekend's events. For those who wouldn't know an axe from an adz, a genuine western rodeo, parades, evening street dances, and a barbecue all promise ample fun and diversion. Information: Rawlins-Carbon County Chamber of Commerce, P.O. Box 1331, Rawlins, WY 82301.

Watermelon Thump
Luling, Texas

Last weekend in June. Watermelon mania hits Luling, Texas, for three days in June. The crowning of the Watermelon Thump Queen kicks off the festival on Thursday evening, with champion melon judging taking place the following morning. The Champion Melon Award goes to the local farmer who submits the heaviest melon of the Black Diamond variety. Past winning melons have averaged 65 pounds and are auctioned off to the public on Saturday afternoon. In 1983, the champion melon fetched a Thump record price of $3,500.00. If you are long-winded, you can enter the seed-spitting contests held throughout the weekend, with the Championship Spit-Off taking place on Saturday afternoon. The record spit of 65 feet, 4 inches, set in 1980 by John Wilkinson of Austin, Texas, is listed in the *Guinness Book of World Records*. The Thump Watermelon Eating Contest, Thump Car Rally, Old Fiddler's Contest, a giant parade, nightly street dances, and the Thump Golf Tournament are all part of the weekend's agenda. Information: Luling Watermelon Thump Association, Box 710, Luling, TX 78648.

JULY

THE SUMMER LOOKS OUT
FROM HER BRAZEN TOWER,
THROUGH THE FLASHING BARS OF JULY.

Francis Thompson

WHAT'S HAPPENING IN JULY?

July 1, Dominion Day: The national holiday of Canada, also known as Canada Day, commemorates the confederation of Upper and Lower Canada, Nova Scotia, and New Brunswick into the independent Dominion of Canada on July 1, 1867. Canadian independence from Great Britain and the unification of the colonies into one country was proposed by the Canadian colonies themselves and agreed to by Great Britain. The British parliamentary act recognizing Canadian independence originally titled the new country as the Kingdom of Canada, but Lord Derby, Queen Victoria's Colonial Secretary, thought that the Canadian "Yankees" would be offended by the mention of the word "kingdom." He suggested the tactful change of "kingdom" to "dominion."

July 4, Independence Day: Although we celebrate July 4 as our nation's birthday, July 2 or July 8 could also easily serve as our official date of birth. Our July 4 celebration commemorates the day on which the Declaration of Independence was officially adopted by the Second Continental Congress, but the Congress actually voted for independence on July 2, and the general public did not hear of the Declaration of Independence until July 8. On July 2, the Second Continental Congress adopted a resolution offered by Richard Henry Lee of Virginia: "Resolved, That these United Colonies are, and of right ought to be, free and independent States, that they are absolved from all allegiance to the British Crown, and that all political connection between them and the State of Great Britain is, and ought to be, totally dissolved."

When the actual Declaration of Independence (composed primarily by Thomas Jefferson with suggestions from four fellow committee members) was presented to the Second Continental Congress on July 4, only John Hancock (president of the Congress) and Charles Thomson (secretary) actually signed the document. The rest of the members of the Continental Congress added their signatures on August 2.

July 6, Birthday of John Paul Jones: Our most colorful and best remembered naval hero of the American Revolution was actually named John Paul and was the son of a gardener who labored on a baronial estate in Scotland. At the age of 12 he was apprenticed as a cabin boy on a merchant ship bound for Virginia. He spent his adventurous and wild youth at sea, during which time he even had a few scrapes with the law and was charged with murdering a mutinous crewman on a ship. Following the murder charge he fled to Virginia and changed his name to John Paul Jones. Upon becoming acquainted with a member of the Continental Congress, he received a commission as a senior lieutenant in the new Continental navy. During the Revolution he commanded a number of different ships, and developed a well-earned reputation for bravery and quick thinking in the heat of battle. His most famous battle took place off the coast of Scarborough, England on the night of September 23, 1779. Jones, as captain of the *Bonhomme Richard* (named in honor of Benjamin Franklin and *Poor Richard's Almanack*), engaged the British ship *Serapis*. For 3½ bloody hours the two ships battled yardarm to yardarm until the *Serapis* caught fire and struck her colors in surrender. It was one of the most bloody and well-fought battles in the history of naval warfare, and it was in the heat of this battle that the courageous John Paul Jones called out his famous taunt to the captain of the *Serapis:* "I have not yet begun to fight!"

July 11, Birthday of John Quincy Adams: John Quincy Adams, our sixth president, is the only president in our history whose father also was president (John Adams was our second president). Elected to the presidency in 1825, his single term of office was marked by a period of peace and prosperity. Following his presidency, he served the final 17 years of his life as a Massachusetts congressman and devoted the close of his political career to fighting the expansion of slavery.

July 20, Anniversary of Man's First Landing on the Moon: On July 20, 1969, Neil Armstrong, followed by Edwin Aldrin, Jr., descended from the lunar module *Eagle* and became the first man to set foot on the moon. Millions of Americans will remember with pride the first words spoken by Armstrong as he first stepped on the lunar surface: "That's one small step for man, one giant leap for mankind." During the time Armstrong and Aldrin spent on the moon, they collected soil and rock samples, took innumerable photographs, and deployed scientific instruments. After a stay of 21 hours and 37 minutes, the *Eagle* blasted off from the lunar surface and rejoined the spaceship *Columbia,* piloted by Michael Collins, for the return trip to Earth. Following that first moon visit, called Apollo 11, the United States launched six more Apollo excursions and was successful in all but one of them; those who are inclined toward superstition will doubtless remember that only Apollo 13 experienced several major equipment failures while in lunar orbit and returned to earth without landing men on the moon. The sixth and last human visit to the moon was aboard Apollo 17, launched on December 7, 1972.

Any Hot Day in July or August, Dog Day: An ancient term for the hottest days of summer, "Dog Days" actually stems from an old belief that the heat of the sun was increased in the summer by the heat of Sirius, the "dog star" and the brightest of the fixed stars. By the sixteenth century, rabies in dogs was thought to originate in the dog days of summer, the heat of the sun being thought to drive dogs mad.

July Is National Peach Month

If you're not growing your own, you're missing out on how good a peach can be. Tree-ripened peaches are infinitely sweeter and smoother-textured than supermarket peaches, which are picked green because ripe peaches bruise too easily for shipment. Even gardeners with limited space can enjoy homegrown peaches because the trees come in sizes right down to a genetic dwarf size that can be grown in a patio tub. 'Bonanza' and 'Stark Sensation' are two such dwarf varieties. If you'd like to plant a peach tree this fall, here are some tips to get you started:

If you have limited space, buy only one tree. Peach trees are self-fruitful. Unlike other fruit trees, such as apples, which need at least two trees of different varieties to set fruit, peach tree blossoms are self-pollinating. You'll get plenty of fruit from one tree.

Select a peach variety and root-stock suitable for your climate zone. Peaches are graft products; roots of one plant (chosen for some characteristic such as disease resistance or dwarfing of growth) are grafted onto the top of another plant. Sometimes the rootstock is not even the same species of plant as the top—plum roots may be grafted onto peach tops. Northern gardeners should be sure to select a peach variety that is cold-hardy for their zone. Southern gardeners should be sure to select a variety with a short chill requirement (the total number of hours at 32° to 45°F that a tree requires to break dormancy). Your best option is to ask your local state agricultural extension agent for the names of varieties that produce best in your area and the names of rootstocks that survive best in your area; then select the tree that combines the peach variety and root-stock recommended by your extension agent.

Avoid planting a peach tree in any area of your property susceptible to late spring frosts. Peach blossoms are extremely susceptible to frost damage, and flowers touched by frost will almost never bear fruit.

Plant your peach tree in an area with very good drainage. Soggy soil causes accumulation of cyanide (a poison) around the tree roots and almost certain decline and eventual death of the tree. If your drainage is marginal, delay planting your tree for a year in order to condition your soil better. Add large amounts of compost and builder's sand to a depth of at least 2 feet and in an area of at least 3 square feet. This change in soil profile may give you sufficient drainage to plant your tree the following season.

Be careful not to plant your tree too deeply. Peach trees have shallow root systems and should be positioned so that the upper roots are only an inch or two below the soil surface.

IN THE GARDEN

PICKING AT PRIME TIME

In July the growing season is near its peak for northern gardeners, who can now enjoy the summer bounty of tomatoes, cucumbers, and beans. Meanwhile, it's time for southern gardeners to pick the last of these warm-season crops before the heat finally destroys them. For all gardening regions there's something in July to pick and enjoy from the garden.

Nothing beats the pleasure of picking homegrown garden vegetables at the peak of goodness, whether it be a tomato, a cabbage, or a carrot. For vegetables, picking at the prime time means that you get not only the very best taste but also optimum nutrients in every bite. Some vegetables reach their prime when they are young and immature (corn or beans, for

example). If these early primers are left to mature on the plant, they become tough and starchy. Other vegetables need to hang around for a while (tomatoes and peppers). Leaving some vegetables on the plant until they are quite mature (or, in some cases, until the first light frost) gives you the best bite for your buck. To know when to "say when," keep these guidelines in mind.

Beets

Pick and eat the nutrient-rich tops almost anytime. You can combine young, tender beet tops with lettuce for a colorful salad, and you can cook larger, mature beet greens just as you would spinach. The roots taste best when they are harvested on the small side—between 1½ and 2½ inches in diameter. Large beets frequently become woody and fibrous unless they have been supplied with generous amounts of water during hot weather. Beets become sweeter after they have been exposed to cold weather. Your sweetest and most satisfying harvest will probably be the harvest after the first light frost.

If you must store beets in your refrigerator, remove the greens and leave about 1 inch of stem on each root. The 1-inch stem prevents bleeding from the root and slows deterioration. Beet roots shrivel more easily when they are stored with tops intact because the leaves draw moisture from the roots.

Broccoli

Harvest broccoli when the heads have tight green buds. Those little buds are really developing flowers, and the taste peaks when the flowers are at the immature bud stage. Delaying harvest for even a few days after the tight bud stage leaves time for the buds to elongate and loosen from the stalk. While you can still eat broccoli at this more mature stage, it tastes a bit more cabbagey and has a less pleasing texture. If you delay past the middle bud-elongation stage, your broccoli stalks may begin to flower and become poor fare indeed.

Broccoli tastes best when matured and harvested in cool weather with cool nights. Mature broccoli is frost resistant and improves in flavor after a light touch of frost. For a fall crop, set out vigorous seedlings seven to ten weeks before the average first-frost date for your area.

Cabbage

Cabbage, like other members of the cole family, develops a sweet, mild flavor if it matures in cool weather. Late-maturing varieties designed to be picked after a frost generally have the highest sugar

contents. For northern gardeners, late-maturing varieties should be set out near the end of June or in early July. For southern and West Coast areas that have mild winters, late varieties of cabbage can be set out in the late fall or early winter for a spring harvest. Cabbage heads are edible as soon as they become firm. Northern gardeners can leave heads in the garden through light frosts but not through a hard freeze. Warm-climate gardeners should be sure to harvest winter-season cabbage before spring heat arrives, because warm temperatures cause mature heads to split.

Carrots

Carrots increase in sweetness until they have reached maturity, but they don't lose sweetness if harvest is delayed after maturity. The smartest strategy is to note the maturity date on the seed packet and pull a carrot a few days before that time to discover whether your planting is on schedule. An easy way to tell which carrots are largest is to remember that the darker the foliage, the larger the root. After your crop has reached maturity, you can leave the roots in the ground and harvest them throughout the winter as you need them, if you take care to prevent the carrots from freezing. To keep the carrot bed unfrozen, simply cover it with 12 inches of mulch before hard freeze sets in.

If you decide to harvest your entire crop at one time and store it in your root cellar or refrigerator, cut off the tops and leave the harvested carrots out in the sun for a few hours to kill the root hairs and make the plants go dormant. Don't wash carrots before storing them because moisture encourages the root to break dormancy. Instead, give them a good scrubbing just before you use them.

Corn

Harvest corn ears about 18 days after the silk appears, when it looks dried and brown. Another simple test for ripeness is to peel back a small portion of husk, check for plump kernels, and puncture one with your fingernail. Ripe corn gives a milky-white liquid. If the liquid is clear, wait a day or two longer.

Standard sweet corn varieties begin converting sugar to starch as soon as the ear is picked. This characteristic produced the old gardener's rule of thumb that corn should be picked only after you've got the water boiling in the kitchen. The more modern supersweet varieties have a genetic alteration that blocks the conversion of sugar to starch. These varieties remain sweet for several days after harvest. However, all the supersweet varieties turn as starchy as field corn if they are pollinated by standard sweet corn, and standard sweet corn suffers the same fate if it is pollinated by supersweets. It's best not to grow the two varieties together unless your varieties mature at least two weeks apart or grow at least 250 feet apart.

Cucumbers

The mildest flavor and crunchiest texture comes from bright green, immature fruit that measures 6 to 7 inches long and 1½ to 2 inches in diameter. Harvest often to encourage greater productivity. A single ripe fruit left on the vine will stop production of more fruit. Leave a bit of stem on each fruit to minimize water loss during storage. Cucumber vines that have set fruit need at least an inch of water a week to produce a pleasing fruit. Because the cucumber fruit is itself 90 to 95 percent water, too little water during fruiting produces misshapen, bitter, or tasteless cucumbers.

Green Beans

Harvest standard garden snap beans when the pods are fully developed but before the seeds begin to swell. Pods containing swelled seeds are tough, lacking in flavor, and woody. Harvest the fillet-type green beans when the pods reach one-eighth inch in diameter, regardless of the length of the pods. Beans are generally ready to pick about a week after the first blossoms appear. Keep your vines well picked to encourage extended production.

Lettuce

Harvest the outer leaves of loose-leaf lettuce as soon as the plant has five or six mature leaves. You can continue to harvest the outer leaves of leaf types until heat takes its toll on the plant. Harvest heading lettuces by cutting the head off at its base as soon as the center feels firm. Lettuce tastes best when the plant is young and has not been subjected to heat, because heat exposure usually causes lettuce to develop a bitter flavor. Harvest leaves and heads very early in the morning while the leaves are filled with water. As the day warms up, the leaves become more dehydrated and less flavorful.

To store leaf lettuce for a few days, lay the leaves on a length of damp paper toweling, roll the leaves and paper up in a loose roll, and store in your refrigerator in a closed plastic bag. Store head lettuce in a closed container to prevent dehydration. Since lettuce flavor declines with storage, your best bet is to plant small quantities of lettuce every week during your growing season. By using staggered plantings, you have on hand only as much lettuce as you can use daily.

Spinach

Spinach is ready to harvest six to eight weeks after planting. The notion that spinach bolts because of heat is only partially true. The hormonal change that causes bolting is really brought on by longer daylight hours. The longest days of the summer season come very early in the summer—right after the last frost in the northernmost regions of the United States. The best strategy for getting a good spring crop is to plant as early as possible so that your plants are well into production before the longest days arrive. You can begin harvesting the outer leaves of the plant as soon as it has six leaves 7 to 8 inches long. As with other leaf crops, such as lettuce, spinach leaves taste best when they are harvested early in the day while the plants are turgid with water.

Summer Squashes

Harvest zucchini and other summer squashes before they are 7 inches long. The legendary baseball bat-sized zucchini may make a great conversation piece, but it will be almost totally lacking in flavor and filled with large seeds. Harvest scalloped or pattypan types before they are 2 to 3 inches in diameter. All summer squashes should be picked while the rind is tender enough to be pierced easily with a fingernail. You can store fresh summer squash for a few days by placing them unwrapped in the vegetable bin of the refrigerator. They will keep best without losing moisture if you leave an inch of stem on the fruit.

Sweet Peppers

Sweet peppers increase in sweetness and vitamin C content as they ripen. But peppers also tend to drop flowers and stop setting fruit as summer heat sets in, particularly if the plant already has a few fruit ripening. The best strategy is to pick the early fruit while it is relatively small and green. This tends to force the plant to keep flowering and setting fruit during the hottest part of the summer. You can leave this later-maturing fruit on the plant until it turns yellow or red to get the best flavor and vitamin content.

Tomatoes

Tomatoes taste best when they are left on the vine until they are fully red. Vine-ripened tomatoes have one-third more vitamin C than those ripened indoors, but they will stop ripening on the vine when night temperatures consistently drop to 55°F.

You can prolong your tomato harvest by picking green tomatoes when frost is imminent. The green fruit will continue to ripen indoors if left out in daylight at room temperature. If you have a large harvest of end-of-season green tomatoes that you cannot use all at once, delay ripening of part of the harvest by wrapping each tomato in newspaper and storing in a cool dark place such as a cellar or unheated attic. Once a week bring a few into your kitchen to redden. Another clever way to extend your tomato harvest well past frost is to pull up the entire tomato plant and hang it from the ceiling of your garage, shed, or barn. The tomatoes will continue to ripen on the vine long after the leaves have wilted and dropped from the plant.

T.L.C.: Tender Loving Conditioning for Beautiful Cut Flowers

With midsummer in full swing, you may find yourself with the unaccustomed luxury of having plenty of flowers for cutting. For the greatest satisfaction in your cut flowers and the longest-lasting bouquets, try some of these tips:

Carry a bucket of lukewarm water with you into the garden. Placing your blooms in a basket or garden trug may seem romantic, but it is the worst way to treat your flowers. The most important trick for getting the most from cut flowers is to immerse the stems immediately in lukewarm water.

Cut flowers early in the morning or late in the evening. At midday flowers have low turgidity (water content) and less stored starches for energy.

Always cut stems cleanly with a sharp knife or a pair of pruners. Cut stems at an angle to expose the greatest number of water-carrying cells.

Except for chrysanthemums (which take up water through leaves as well as stems), remove all leaves from the part of the stem that will be below water. Leaves left in the water quickly begin to grow bacteria, which clog the plant stems and prevent water uptake.

Choose newly opened flowers or those that are still partially in bud. Mature garden flowers fade quickly.

Once you've filled your bucket with flowers, leave them to soak five or six hours (or overnight) in a cool, dark place. This final step before placing the flowers in a vase or arrangement is called conditioning. Professional florists always condition flowers before arranging them because they know that it helps to make flowers last.

Before you add your flowers to the vase water, add a few drops of chlorine bleach to the water. Bleach reduces the number of bacteria in the water and does no harm to the flowers. If you choose to add some nourishment to feed the flowers while they are in the vase, don't add table sugar because it encourages bacteria. Use a professional floral preservative, which is sold in packets in florist shops and garden centers.

Some flowers require a little extra help to prolong vase life. Flowers that exude a milky sap from the stem, such as poppies, should have the cut end dipped in boiling water for about 30 seconds. Take care to shield the bloom from the steam of the boiling water. Flowers from bulbs, corms, and tubers (such as glads and dahlias), should be conditioned in cold instead of lukewarm water. Some foliage plants used in arrangements, such as ferns and ivies, keep better if the entire stem, leaves and all, is conditioned in cold water before being placed in a vase.

ALMANAC GARDENING CALENDAR

Water becomes the prime concern for all gardeners this month. Those in the northernmost zones can continue to pick cool-weather crops, as long as they take care to keep them watered and mulched. Gardeners in the middle zones should find their hot-weather crops at peak production by this month. Gardeners in the southernmost zones will find that warm-weather crops die off this month, and it's time to get ready for fall planting.

Zone 1

Mulch cool-weather vegetables such as peas, cole crops, onions, leeks, beets, and chard. Mulch lowers soil temperature and helps conserve moisture. Tie up trellised vegetables such as peas and cucumbers. Harvest early onions. Dig new potatoes as soon as the plants start to flower. Pick peas every other day when they begin producing in early July. Check for insect pests as you water. Spray with Bt (*Bacillus thuringiensis*) to control cabbageworms on brassicas. If you have high summer temperatures, use shaded areas such as the north side of the house or garage to grow a summer crop of lettuce, radishes, and beets. Plant by midmonth for harvest in late August. Plant fall crops of cauliflower, broccoli, cabbage, spinach, beets, kohlrabi, kale, collards, and lettuce by midmonth. New crops will need to be watered more frequently than established plants if the weather is very dry. Thin and weed new plantings to speed growth.

In early July, plant seeds of such perennials and biennials as pansies, sweet Williams, carnations, gaillardias, foxgloves, delphiniums, and Canterbury bells in a nursery bed for bloom next summer. Keep the bed moist until the seeds have germinated. The young plants will need more water than established plants. Renew the mulch around roses and perennials; remove dead flowers to encourage longer flowering. Stake taller plants such as Shasta daisies, Maltese crosses, and glads. Dig up and divide three- to five-year-old beds of irises, cutting back the leaves. Weed and enrich the soil with bonemeal and compost before replacing the divisions. During the last two weeks of July, divide and renew older primrose beds.

If the month is dry, regularly water all fruit. Watch for signs of deer damage. Cover strawberry beds and small cherry trees with nets to keep birds out. When everbearing strawberries have produced their first crop, feed lightly with a quick-acting organic fertilizer. Also feed June bearers and remove older, less productive plants from the beds.

Destroy plants with small, hard berries and leaves—they may be diseased. Remove and destroy raspberry plants that produce crumbly berries despite good soil, good pollination, regular watering, and no exposure to herbicides. They probably have a virus, which can spread to other plants.

Zone 2

July is the driest month, so give plant roots a good soaking, and mulch with grass clippings, compost, sawdust, wood chips, or shredded bark. July is also whitefly season. Trap the pests with pieces of yellow cardboard coated with a sticky material such as Tanglefoot or #90 motor oil. Handpick Colorado potato beetles and the yellow egg masses and adults of Mexican bean beetles. Sow onion seeds now for scallions in fall. Those you don't eat will carry over winter for spring munching. Sow lettuce and endive in late July for continuous fall harvest. Thin endive to 10 inches apart. Pull spent peas and sow a heat-resistant type for fall harvest. Direct-seed kale and set out transplants of cabbage, brussels sprouts, broccoli, and cauliflower. Keep tomatoes off the ground by staking or trellising to prevent rodent and slug damage. Pick summer squash daily whether you can use it or not. Overgrown squash shortens the picking season. Water annuals and perennials by soaking them slowly. Avoid flooding—it compacts the soil. Fertilize flowers with manure tea. Trim back leggy petunias. To fight powdery mildew on zinnias and phlox, dust with sulfur on a cool day. Dig and divide irises. To reduce moisture loss, trim foliage to a 3- or 4-inch fan. Look for and cut out rotted or borer-infested rhizomes. Replant shallowly, allowing the top of the rhizome to stick out. Water well until the roots take hold.

Renew your strawberry bed. In early July, apply Tacky Trap or Tanglefoot to the bases of trunks and lower branches of peach and plum trees to trap egg-laying moths of borers. Cut off gum boils on peach and plum trunks, and stab borers with wire poked into tunnels. Trim off or pull out suckers arising from the base of grapevines and peach, apple, and pear trees. Clean up and destroy all fruit left from the June fruit drop. Remove raspberry canes with droopy tips, a sure sign of cane-borer damage. After the bramble harvest, cut out all old canes, and weaker new ones, leaving about six sturdy stems per plant. If blueberry leaves are yellowed or mottled, the soil could be too alkaline. Lower soil pH by mulching with sawdust or pine needles.

Zone 3

Use deep mulch to protect the garden from drying sun and wind;

water early in the morning to keep plants in full production. Give crops— especially tomatoes, peppers, eggplants, squash, cucumbers, and melons—an inch or more of water a week. Continue feeding melons with compost or manure tea to ensure juicy fruit. Place a board under each fruit to keep pests away and prevent rot. Harvest white potatoes after tops yellow. Cure in shade for two weeks before storing in a cool, moist, and dark place. Also, the essential oils in herbs peak as the herbs come into bloom. Pick and dry them then for best flavor. Keep a sharp lookout for pests: spider mites and hornworms on tomatoes, squash bugs on cucumbers and squash, cucumber beetles on cucumbers, and flea beetles on eggplant. Because insect pests love weak plants, clear spent crops from the garden and till the soil for fall vegetables or cover crops. Add all residue to an active compost pile, which should be kept moist and turned often for fast breakdown. Start fall crops of cabbage, Chinese cabbage, cauliflower, broccoli, and kohlrabi in flats indoors or in a shady spot outside. Later in the month, direct-seed beets, turnips, chard, bush peas, and other cool-weather crops. If the weather stays hot, pregerminate seeds in moist paper towels in the refrigerator. After planting, keep the soil moist and shade the seedbed.

Deadhead annuals to encourage continuous bloom. Mark and leave several seedpods on your favorite nonhybrid flowers for next year's seeds. Irrigation and a midsummer feeding of manure or compost tea will help prolong flowering. Mulch is the best defense against drought damage for perennials, annuals, and woody ornamentals. Soak and mulch azaleas, rhododendrons, and roses to protect their shallow roots during the heat of July. Remove seedpods from perennials so that plants can store the extra energy for bloom next year. Side-dress chrysanthemums with bonemeal and a helping of compost or decomposing mulch, but stop pinching them by midmonth. However, pinch established petunias and marigolds for renewed blooming. If you want a late display of short-season annuals like marigolds, petunias, and nasturtiums, plant them early in the month. Carefully stake tall snapdragons, phlox, lilies, dahlias, chrysanthemums, and glads for best display and easy maintenance.

As strawberry production wanes, fertilize beds and select runners for propagation. Cut out extra runners to prevent crowding. Keep blueberries watered and mulched for best harvest, and as they ripen, cover them with bird netting. As berry production on brambles wanes, cut out canes that have fruited. Water, fertilize, and mulch with an acidic material. Water fruit trees deeply once a week if rain is sparse. Remove and burn or compost all fruit drops. Remove mummified grapes from vines to slow the spread of black rot. Inspect cherry and peach tree trunks for signs of borers. If you haven't done so in the past, treat your yard with milky spore disease to kill Japanese beetle larvae. Reapply Tanglefoot around the base of trees for protection against climbing insects.

Zone 4

Keep roots cool and soil moist by spreading a thick mulch on all bare ground early this month. Vegetables will need 2 inches of water a week in hot weather. Soak, don't sprinkle, for best results. Established asparagus needs water only during dry spells. Feed melons manure tea when they begin to bloom; place a board under each swelling fruit to keep it clean and away from insects. Encourage squash plants to root at their leaf nodes (by covering the leaf nodes with an inch or so of compost) for a backup system in case of borer attack; remove borer grubs through lengthwise slits in stems where leaves wilt, or inject stems with Bt (*Bacillus thuringiensis*). Sow fall cole crops in flats. In cooler areas, make late sowings of snap beans, carrots, turnips, and rutabagas where early crops have been pulled. Prepare other beds for fall

planting as space becomes available. Turn the compost pile and keep it covered so it doesn't get dry. Remove suckers weekly from staked tomatoes.

Treat heavy-feeding perennials —bleeding-hearts, Shasta daisies, delphiniums and chrysanthemums —to manure tea or fish emulsion a couple of times this month. Mulch all perennials to conserve water. Pinch tall chrysanthemums once more before midmonth, and begin removing side branches and buds of dahlias. Remove wilted iris leaves; divide the plants if you haven't done so in the past four years, discarding borer-damaged or diseased rhizomes. Deadhead annuals to keep them in flower.

Cut back wisteria severely after bloom. Birches, elms, maples, and willows can be trimmed now or in fall. At month's end, shape evergreen hedges and trim secondary growth of deciduous ones. Remove rose suckers and feed the plants manure tea for the fall display.

Bury all windfall fruit and grape mummies in the center of a hot compost pile. Provide support for heavily laden pear and apple branches. Invite birds to patrol your orchard by providing fresh water. At midmonth, protect peach and other stone-fruit trees from borers by digging soil away from each trunk to a depth of 4 inches, spreading moth crystals, and covering them with soil. Let first-year everbearing strawberries flower for a late-summer and fall crop. Give all strawberry beds and other fruit deep soakings this month if the weather is dry. After the end of the summer raspberry harvest, cut old canes to the ground.

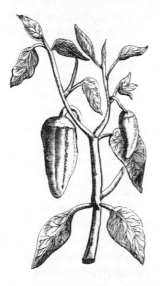

Zone 5

Harvest and remove remaining spring crops to get ready for fall plantings. Early in the month, dig up leftover potatoes and carrots. Dig in fresh manure, then wait until it rains or water once or twice before planting seeds. Except for Halloween pumpkins, hold back on succession planting of warm-weather vegetables. Fast-maturing bush beans, cucumbers, and other crops will grow better if planted later in the season when heat stress is less severe. Pick hot-weather vegetables frequently to reduce moisture stress. Water tomatoes, peppers, and southern peas when they are in flower to ensure good fruit set. Mulch heavily around all vegetables that will summer in the garden. In the East, propagate tomatoes by planting 12-inch growing tips 8 inches deep in good soil early in the month. Partial shade will benefit bush beans, winter squash, New Zealand spinach, and Irish potatoes planted this month. Where no natural shade is available, provide sunscreens to protect seedlings. Promptly remove and burn all evidence of smut in the corn patch. Help alleviate the main trouble with midseason corn—loose, sparsely filled ears inundated with insects—by hand-pollinating the ears. Better pollination results in fuller, tighter ears, which are more difficult for corn earworms to penetrate. For best results, hand-pollinate corn in the early evening to take advantage of high humidity during the cooler nighttime hours. Hand-pollination may help keep tomatoes and peppers in production straight through the summer, too. Keep these plants mulched, and water and top-dress with compost or manure late in the month.

Where nematodes are a problem, cultivate and moisten the soil, then cover it with a sheet of clear plastic for four to six weeks to cook the pests. In larger gardens, broadcast French marigold seeds in heavily nematode-infested areas if the space is not needed for food crops. Pumpkins planted now for October harvest will need protection from various sucking insects. Start them indoors if necessary, and cover the plants with cheesecloth during their first weeks in the ground. Frequently the older, open-pollinated pumpkin varieties resist insect attack better than hybrids, though old varieties require more space. Indoors, start seedlings of brussels sprouts and cabbage, followed by broccoli, cauliflower, and kohlrabi. Start fall crops of cucumber and winter squash indoors or sow outdoors where insects and drought are not severe problems.

Plant more zinnias, nasturtiums, dwarf marigolds, and other hot-weather annuals. Mulch them and other annuals already in the garden to help reduce heat stress and prolong blooming. Remove dead flower blossoms, and pinch back the earlier wave of petunias, zinnias, and other summer flowers after the first flush fades. Pinch back fall-blooming chrysanthemums one last time, too. Dig and divide irises and spider lilies. Propagate impatiens and coleus by planting stem cuttings in moist, shaded soil. Soak ornamental trees and shrubs every week to ten days, depending on rainfall. Be especially attentive to plants that have suffered winter injury. Water roses more often, and feed them with manure tea to keep them in blooming condition.

While harvesting fruit, remove and burn any fruit that shows signs of brown rot, the brown fuzz that gradually mummifies the fruit. Support heavily laden branches so they won't split in a storm. Even if fruit trees are not bearing, they need large amounts of water to mature their new wood. When watering trees, make sure the moisture penetrates well beneath the root zones of grasses and other ground covers. Continue to mow regularly beneath fruit trees to discourage insect pests. Water bearing grapes once a week if the weather is dry. This helps reduce the risk of cracked fruit later in the season. Enclose bunch grapes in small paper bags to protect them from birds and wasps. Fertilize late-bearing muscadines with cottonseed meal, manure tea, or fish emulsion sprays applied to the leaves. Nuts are filling out now, and need periodic deep irrigation along with Bt (*Bacillus thuringiensis*) applications to control leaf-eating worms. Water blueberries until the harvest is complete. Cut back tips of upright blackberry canes for the last time, and tie new branches of trailing types to trellises. Dig manure into beds to be planted with strawberries in early fall. For the rest of the summer avoid heavy fertilization of trees because new wood that develops late in the season is easily damaged in winter.

Zone 6

Plant fall vegetables this month for harvest before the first frost. Before seeding vegetables, soak the area 24 hours in advance. Plant Malabar spinach, eggplants, okra, more corn, peppers, New Zealand spinach, tomatoes, cucumbers, watermelons, and cantaloupes early in the month. Later, plant pumpkins with the next planting of corn. Plant transplants of broccoli, cauliflower, and cabbage at the end of the month. Kale and brussels sprouts should be seeded in flats now for planting out in late August. Mustard and collards also seed easily at this time. An easy way to get tomatoes planted is to root cuttings from those started in the spring. In empty beds, sow buckwheat as a green manure at a rate of 3 pounds per 1,000 square feet.

Pinch dead blooms from annuals and give a light feeding to encourage new growth and flowers. Try not to wet the foliage when watering, since this can cause foliar diseases. Water perennials more deeply and less frequently than shallow-rooted annuals. Mulch with finished compost to moderate soil temperatures, conserve moisture, and slowly supply nutrients. Chrysanthemums and poinsettias should receive their final

pinch. Plant marigolds, zinnias, spider lilies, cosmos, fall crocuses, salvias, and verbenas for fall flowers. Regularly water shallow-rooted shrubs such as azaleas, camellias, and hydrangeas and keep them mulched. Top-dress container-grown ornamentals with compost. Insect pests can be abundant at this time, so handpick or control with biological sprays.

As grape harvest nears, keep the root zone evenly moist. Protect your crop with netting if birds are a problem. Continue to tie newly planted grapes to their trellises. Give established grapes a side-dressing of compost. Water nut trees deeply during the next two months as the kernels fill out. Cut back bramble canes to make room for new wood. Tree fruit begins to ripen this month. The rule of thumb for ripe fruit is that a slight twist of the fruit should release it from the tree. Pick up fallen fruit to break insect and disease cycles. A foliar spray of seaweed will help fruit and nut trees withstand heat stress.

Zone 7

In cool Pacific coastal areas, continue to plant lettuce, beets, carrots, and blocks of corn and beans. Start fall crops of Irish potatoes, brassicas, rutabagas, endive, and fennel. Harvest garlic by midmonth, making sure that it is well dried before bringing it in for storage. In the upper tier of Zone 7, plant okra, field peas, lima beans, peppers, sweet potato sets, pumpkins, and winter squash in the first week of July. Plant the last block of corn before July 15. In the hotter southern parts of the zone, manure and mulch ground where fall crops are to be planted in August. Pick field peas, snap beans, and soybeans to keep them producing. To discourage diseases, water early in the day and avoid overhead sprinkling. In the rest of the zone, fall crops can be started after mid-July. Germinating seeds in hot weather can be a challenge. Where soils crust over, rake sifted compost into the top layer. Shade seedbeds of lettuce, parsley, beets, fennel, and carrots with plywood or burlap, removing the shading as soon as the first seedlings pop up. Start broccoli, cabbage, kohlrabi, and cauliflower in containers in filtered light. Keep beds and containers moist. Sometimes seedlings need water three times a day.

Water is critical this month. Roses want deep watering to bring them through the heat. Rhododendrons, camellias, and azaleas may not show drought stress until it's too late. Dig down in the root area of all trees and shrubs to make sure water penetrates mulch and soil. Spray with Bt (*Bacillus thuringiensis*) every week or ten days to combat budworms on geraniums, petunias, and nicotianas. In the eastern part

of the zone, plant spider lilies. Divide daffodils, daylilies, and irises from now until fall. Pinch chrysanthemums for the last time. Cut back dahlias by as much as one-third to improve shape and to stimulate fall blooms. Deadhead annuals to prolong bloom.

Give fruit and nut trees occasional deep watering in preference to frequent sprinkling. Walnut and pecan kernels will not fill out properly if the trees suffer from drought. Flood heavy soils of the West to get deep moisture penetration. In the eastern part of the zone, where sandy soils will not allow flooding, drip irrigation is the most efficient watering method. Continue to feed citrus and other subtropical fruits with liquid manure every two weeks. Many insects that attack apples, pears, and nuts can be controlled by trapping. Consult your county extension office for baits that work best in your area. Keep fallen fruit picked up to discourage insects and diseases.

To prevent sunburn on newly planted trees, paint the trunks with a special paint formulated for trees. Provide supports for limbs overburdened with fruit. Summer-prune espaliered trees to maintain shape and to increase the development of fruit spurs. Remove bramble canes that have finished fruiting. Enclose the choicest grape bunches in brown paper bags to protect them from pests and diseases as they ripen.

IN GOOD HEALTH

POISON IVY ALERT

It's summer camp, outdoor picnic, and camping and hiking season again. Along with all the fun, unfortunately, come those innocuous-looking little plants we may never notice as we plop down under a tree after a long climb up a steep trail. For dedicated campers and hikers, even those who have grown wary from past bad bouts with the weed, poison ivy is something like flies, gnats, and freeze-dried food—it comes with the territory. All experienced outdoors people know that your first defense against poison ivy and its kin is to keep an eye out for the weed at all times, but folks pulling weeds from the privet hedge in the front yard need the same wariness. Poison ivy turns up in the cultivated borders and immaculate lawns of suburbia as well as in the wilderness. If you caught a case of poison ivy during last summer's fishing trip or while weeding your tomatoes last August, arm yourself with a little knowledge now so that you can avoid a second bout this summer.

☞ Your first line of defense is to know what poison ivy and poison oak look like. If you're a novice hiker, study a field guide with photos of these plants or, better yet, get an experienced outdoorsman to show you a clump growing in the wild. The old saying "Leaves three, let it be" is a useful, if not very detailed, description of both poison ivy and poison oak. In fact, a detailed description of either of these weeds is difficult because they can assume several forms. The leaf shape of poison ivy varies with the location of the plant as does the plant form. Poison ivy can grow as a vine or a low shrub and is most common in the eastern and central parts of the United States. Poison oak usually grows as a shrub, its leaves are somewhat like oak leaves, and it is most common on the West Coast and in the Southeast.

☞ An allergy to poison ivy, oak, or sumac is much more frequent in adults than in young children who haven't had as many exposures to them yet. Sensitivity to these plants increases every time you come in contact with one of them.

☞ The chemical in these plants that causes the reaction occurs in all parts of the plant—leaves, stems, and roots—and can remain active for a full year. Be sure to wash tools, sports equipment, gloves, and clothes that touched the plants with soap and water before using them again.

☞ If you wash your skin within 10 minutes of exposure, you may prevent a reaction entirely. To wash, first flood the skin with plain water for several minutes; then use a bar of soap to wash as usual. Do not wash with alcohol or any other solvent because these agents dissolve your own skin oils, which are your first defense against the toxins.

☞ If you are in an area where exposure to poison ivy or oak is likely, wear as much protective clothing as is practical and avoid touching your face and genitalia with unwashed hands. Also avoid touching a dog that may be accompanying you on a deep woods outing. Dogs and cats pick up poison ivy toxin on their fur, and you can easily receive a dose of the poison by rubbing your hands on an exposed animal.

☞ The itchy rash *usually* appears within 24 to 48 hours after touching one of the poison plants, but the time may be as short as four hours or as long as ten days. The rash is most often at its worst five days after contact and gradually goes away within a week or two without treatment.

☞ Scratching will not cause the rash to spread, as many people believe, but it can introduce bacteria into the open sores, causing an infection.

☞ For a mild, uncomplicated case, try covering the rash with calamine lotion, which provides temporary itch relief and promotes drying of the pustules. Do not apply skin anesthetics, such as benzocaine, or skin irritants, such as lotions containing camphor or phenol. Systemic antihistamines do not alleviate symptoms, but their sedative actions may promote sleep. Some people get temporary relief from a wet dressing of aluminum sulfate solution. You can make this solution using a nonprescription powder or tablet (one trade name is Domeboro) available at many pharmacies. You should check with your doctor before using this solution, and you should only use it with an open gauze dressing so that the solution can evaporate from your skin.

☞ If you believe you have suffered a heavy exposure to poison ivy or oak, you should see a doctor immediately, especially if you are already hypersensitive to the toxins. Steroid treatments initiated within six hours of exposure can effectively reduce your allergic reaction.

☞ Researchers at the U.S. Department of Agriculture's Forest Service have developed an anti-poison ivy spray. Ivy-Block, when sprayed on skin, clothing, tools, and animals, forms a barrier that the irritating oils in poison ivy, sumac, and oak cannot penetrate. One spraying is good for 24 hours. Ivy-Block is being used by hundreds of Forest Service employees and may soon be made available commercially to the public.

Temperature and Humidity Advisory

If you exercise outdoors during the July heat, avoid the crash of heat exhaustion by following the three rules of warm-weather exercise: fluid, fluid, fluid. Conscientious fluid intake is the cardinal rule for any exertion undertaken in high heat and humidity. A simple rule of thumb is to drink enough water to cause you to urinate prior to any prolonged exertion, drink 20 ounces of water at the start of exercise, and drink 6 to 10 ounces of water every 15 to 20 minutes during exercise. You need water to maintain a normal blood plasma volume throughout the exercise. You should drink whether or not you feel thirsty, because your sense of thirst runs far behind your actual need for water replenishment. A normal stomach can pass about 10 ounces of water per hour into the bloodstream, but exercising in extreme heat and humidity can easily cause you to lose a gallon of sweat in that same time period. Waiting until you feel thirsty can put you in danger of heat exhaustion.

Heat exhaustion can be prevented with fluid intake and common sense. In the following table, "Caution" means that it may be best to scale down your normal yardwork or exercise workout. "Danger" suggests that you're probably better off skipping strenuous exercise that day. Note that high humidity is a more important risk factor than outside temperature alone; this is because moisture in the air does not permit the usual cooling effects of sweat evaporation.

Summertime Exercise Advisory

Temperature	Humidity Range (%)	Advice
70	over 65	Caution
75	over 68	Caution
80	68-75	Caution
80	over 75	Danger
85	70-75	Caution
85	over 75	Danger
90	72-75	Danger
90 and up	over 72	Danger

SOURCE: Reprinted, by permission, from "Water, Pour It On for Summer Sports Safety," by Irving I. Dardik, M.D., *Rx Being Well*, July/August, 1985.

Walking Tip for July

Keeping your body properly hydrated is the real challenge for a hot-weather walk. When walking in hot weather, you should always remember to drink *before* you feel thirsty. If you plan your walk around a circular route in which you pass the same point more than once, you can set up a convenient "pit stop" for yourself at your checkpoint. Pack a small cooler with ice and an assortment of flavored or plain bottled spring water. Stash your cooler under a bush or behind a tree at your check point. Every time you pass it, you can take a fluid break. Another way to keep up your fluid intake is to carry a plastic water bottle (the same type used by cyclists) in a small fanny pack. Your thirst quencher stays right behind you and you can make your walk without any danger of heat distress.

AT HOME

GARAGE SALE FEVER

July and August are great months to plan and execute a garage sale. The kids have been out of school long enough to be bored and will be glad to help out (for a share of the proceeds, of course); people spend more time outdoors and are more likely to be attracted to your signs and display of wares; you can use the extra money now for your vacation or save it for the inevitable Labor Day store sales; and

you'll enjoy your vacation more with the virtuous knowledge that you've cleaned out your attic and basement before you left. Here's a handy countdown to make your sale a roaring success:

A Month before the Sale

☞ Set aside items to be sold. Get the kids in on it with their own table.

☞ Think of a special use for the money you earn: A vacation? New bikes for the kids? Your favorite charity?

☞ Talk to neighbors about having a joint sale; you'll attract more people, and the sale can be more fun. And it's the way to go if you just don't have that many things you can part with.

Three Weeks before the Sale

☞ Decide on a length and date. Will you advertise a rain date?

☞ Decide where you'll hold the sale. Clean the area and remove items you don't want to sell.

☞ Clean housewares and launder clothes. Consider making minor repairs. Have the kids revamp their inventory.

☞ Start gathering boxes and bags for the convenience of customers.

☞ Call the town hall to see if you'll need a permit.

☞ Buy stickers for price tags (in more than one color for a multi-family sale); an indelible marker, poster board, and wrapping tape for signs; and 3 × 5 cards in a bright color for bulletin-board notices.

☞ Tell your friends and neighbors about the sale.

Two Weeks before the Sale

☞ Price the items.

☞ Make the signs and bulletin-board notices and post them.

☞ Call newspapers about rates and deadlines. Compose your ad.

☞ Get card tables, clothes racks, and extension cords (so that people can test appliances and tools). Consider making coffee and iced tea. Set the kids up in a concession business—cookies and beverages will encourage your customers to linger.

One Week before the Sale

☞ Place ads in the newspaper.

☞ Post direction signs around your neighborhood, and try to follow them to your house.

☞ Get plenty of change (coins and small bills) from your bank.

☞ Lay out items by category, such as clothes, appliances, tools, toys, and books.

☞ Clearly label items that are not for sale. Close off restricted areas with string and signs.

☞ Post no-parking signs as necessary to avoid inconveniencing neighbors and blocking intersections.

Sale Day

☞ Assign someone to take responsibility for the cash box.

☞ Put a large sign in front of the house. A cardboard carton will do.

☞ Be ready for the public at least an hour before your stated opening time.

☞ When the inevitable early birds show up (they're often antique dealers), resist discounting your best items.

☞ Consider radical price discounting well before your planned closing time; you can expect customers to thin out toward the end of the day.

After the Sale

☞ Take down direction signs promptly.

☞ Save the leftover items for next year's sale, give them to charity, or throw them out.

Garage sale tips above reprinted from "Garage Sale Fever" by Roger Yepsen, Practical Homeowner, September 1988.

BEAT THE HEAT WITHOUT AIR CONDITIONING

Before you reach for the switch that automatically raises your July electric bill along with the temperature, think of all the ways your house could be cooler without air conditioning. Many smart cooling strategies are simply modern reinventions of what people did in the aeons B.A.C.—Before Air Conditioning. If you're scouting for a new house, keep in mind the heat-beating design elements mentioned here. If you're staying where you are, beat the heat with cool-down additions to your present home. Some of the following home-cooling ideas are quick to implement and effective immediately, and some require time and effort on your part to install. But the time and effort always pay off—in cooler temperatures and lower summertime utility bills.

Heat-Beating Designs

If you're shopping for a new home, planning to build one, or want to analyze the heat-resistant features of your current home, keep the following basic design principles in mind.

Windows to the Wind

A house designed to beat the heat has plenty of windows on the house side facing the prevailing winds of that area (the windward side) *and* plenty of windows that open on the opposite side of the house away from the prevailing winds (the leeward side). The homeowner in such a home can keep cool by opening the leeward windows wider than the windward windows. As the air leaves the house on the leeward side it tends to draw a vacuum that pulls a steady stream of air into the house from the windward side. The effect from this type of smart window placement is similar to what you get with a room fan—continuous, gentle air movement throughout the room and greater comfort no matter how hot it is outside.

Cool Roofs and Attics

The roof in a house designed to cope well with heat will have ridge vents and light-colored asphalt shingles that reflect heat. The attic space will also be vented by soffit vents in addition to the roof ridge vents. With the combination of soffit and roof vents, hot air rising out of the attic roof ridge draws cooler air into the attic through the soffit vents. The result is a continuous air flow from the floor area of the attic through the roof.

If you live in a climate where cooling costs outstrip heating costs, you should choose a house that has light-colored roofing shingles, roof ridge vents, and soffit vents. If you live in a climate where heating is the major household utility expense, compromise by buying a home with a dark-colored roof, and ridge and soffit vents. The ridge vents will serve to direct the heat out of your attic during the summer and household moisture out

of the attic during the winter. The dark-colored roof will absorb more of the sun's heat during the winter and provide a small reduction in your heating bill.

Stay-Cool Room Layouts

Room layout in a houseplan can take advantage of the fact that in the northern hemisphere, the hottest exposures in any building are the southern and western exposures and the coolest are the northern and eastern exposures. With these simple facts in mind, a home in which the main living and sleeping areas are *not* on the south or west sides of the building will be the most comfortable during the summer. This choice of layout especially makes sense in areas of the United States where cooling costs are higher than heating.

Another factor to consider is that during the summer months, because the sun is almost directly overhead, the east and west walls of a house receive 50 percent more sun than the north and south walls. The western wall, however, will always heat up more than the eastern wall because the sun is striking it at the end of the day after the air temperature has already reached its maximum. The very best house layout for minimizing summer heat gain will always have the longest sides of the house facing north and south and the shortest sides facing east and west. Fortunately, this same layout is also great for winter warmth because it maximizes solar gain during the winter when the sun is south of its summertime path. The most efficient house shape for *maximum winter solar heat gain* and *minimum summer solar heat gain* is a rectangle with the long sides facing north and south.

A heat-resistant house will also have a porch or an extra-deep roof soffit along the southern and western sides to shade the rooms on those sides of the house from the most intense summertime heat. The traditional southern veranda was more than a romantic place in which to sit in a swing and court your sweetheart; it was a simple and very effective way to provide instant shade to the most heat-prone rooms.

If you are house shopping, your main objective should be to look for a place that minimizes the highest seasonal utility bill for your geographic area. Folks who live in cold climates should obviously shop first for a house that minimizes heating bills; extra insulation, good-quality windows and doors, and plenty of south-facing windows help here. The good news is that extra insulation helps keep the house cool as well as warm. And if you buy a house that also features good ventilation, such as windward and leeward windows and roof ridge vents, you'll be buying a home that minimizes cooling as well as heating costs.

If you live in a warm climate, look for a house that minimizes air conditioning bills. A warm-climate house should include several heat-beating features: well planned ventilation; plenty of windows on the windward and leeward sides of the house; roof ridge and soffit vents; porches or shade on the southern and western exposures; and air movement devices, such as a whole-house fan or ceiling fans.

Cool-Down Add-Ons

If your current home becomes an oven during the height of summer, spend some time on one of these cool-down projects; time and money invested here will reward you with lower cooling bills in the summers to come.

Cool Plantings

Plant deciduous trees and shrubs on the southern and western sides of your house. Deciduous trees in appropriate locations can reduce your summertime air conditioning costs by as much as 30 percent. You should choose deciduous trees rather than evergreens because the bare winter branches of deciduous trees will let the sun's heat into your south-facing windows during the coldest part of the year. In addition to blocking out the summer sun, deciduous trees increase the fresh air supply to open windows because they release oxygen and filter out dust.

Adding Attic Ventilation

If you don't have attic ventilation, install roof ridge vents and soffit vents in your house. Soffit and ridge vents are made with different vent capacities, which are measured as *net free ventilation area* (NFVA). When you purchase a ridge or soffit vent, you should find the NFVA number printed right on the vent. The rule of thumb for good attic ventilation is to have 1 square foot of NFVA for every 150 square feet of attic floor area (which is about 1 square inch of ventilation for every square foot of attic floor area). You should divide your total correct ventilation area equally between intake (which occurs at the soffit) and exhaust (which takes place out of the roof ridge).

Installing roof and soffit vents is a time-consuming, but worthwhile, job. You must remove the ridge shingles with a hook knife or flooring chisel and a small section of the roof sheathing with a circular saw. The tricky part is in cutting and removing the roof sheathing without cutting into the roof framing members. Installing soffit vents is somewhat easier, especially if you take care to locate the vents in the cavities between pairs of rafters. Also, be sure that the air flow through the soffit vents is not blocked by attic insulation.

Cool Window Treatments

For a simple and relatively inexpensive cool-down project, install heat-reflecting window treatments on the south and west sides of your house. A simple and effective window treatment that reflects heat is white or light-colored venetian blinds. To reflect heat while still allowing breezes through an open window, simply lower the blinds and tilt them in a half-open position. Old-fashioned metal or canvas awnings are also a smart choice for keeping heat out. If you live in a cold climate, choose canvas awnings because you can roll them up for the winter season and catch the warmth from the sun on the formerly shaded windows.

Another effective cooling strategy is to install solar-reflecting window screens—on all of your windows if you live in a heat-driven climate or on your south and west windows if you live in a temperate climate. Solar-reflecting fiberglass screen looks and handles just like regular fiberglass screen; it comes on bolts like cloth and costs about $1 per square foot. That's about three times the cost of ordinary fiberglass screen, but you'll save plenty of money on cooling if you replace your old screens with this new material. The manufacturer of one brand of solar-reflecting screen (Phifer Wire Products, makers of "SunScreen") claims a 70 percent reduction in heat gain through windows covered with its solar fiberglass screen. Installing solar-reflecting screen in old aluminum screen frames is just as simple as installing conventional aluminum or ordinary fiberglass screen. The only tools you need are an awl to remove the spline from the old aluminum frame, a pair of heavy duty shears to cut the screen, and a screen roller to re-introduce the spline and new screen into the spline groove.

Whole-House Ventilation

Another simple and practical way to cool an entire house without air conditioning is to install a whole-house ventilating fan. In order for this improvement to work, your attic must already be vented through ridge and soffit vents or through large gable vents. Whole-house fans work by drawing fresh air through windows and venting hot, stale air out through the attic. They range in price from about $100 to $500, and if you have easy access to your attic, you can install one in a few hours. Whole-house fans are rated by their ventilation capacity—the rate at which they can draw air (in cubic feet per minute —CFM) into your house. To determine the ventilation capacity you

need for your house, simply multiply the total square footage of your living area by three (exclude basement, garage, and attic). A house with a living area of 2,000 square feet needs a fan rated at 6,000 CFM.

Most whole-house fans come with a thermostat that turns on the fan when the attic air temperature exceeds a preset temperature (typically 90°F). Other options available include a timer switch to turn on the fan at fixed times every day, an insulated cover to block heat loss through the fan in winter, and a safety switch to shut off the fan if the motor overheats. Running a whole-house fan is considerably less expensive than running a central air conditioner. If you run your fan for six months per year and for an average of six hours per day, you'll spend from $20 to $60 per year on cooling (assuming an electric rate of 10¢ per kilowatt-hour).

YOUR JULY SHOPPER'S TIP

Peaches, apricots, beans, corn, and tomatoes are most plentiful and therefore a better buy this month. July's recipe provides a quick way to serve part of your abundant tomato crop. In addition to canning tomatoes and tomato sauce, you may also freeze garden tomatoes whole. Simply pick the ripe tomatoes, wash and dry them, and then place them on waxed paper on a cookie sheet in your freezer. After about two hours, or as soon as the tomatoes are frozen firm, pop them into plastic freezer bags and store in your freezer. During the fall and winter, you can remove as many individual frozen tomatoes as you need for soups, stews, and sauces. The frozen whole tomatoes will pop right out of their skins as soon as you drop them into a simmering stew, and you can simply skim the skins off the top of your dish and continue cooking.

Stewed Tomatoes

6 large tomatoes, peeled
2 tablespoons minced onions
2 tablespoons minced green peppers
2 tablespoons butter or vegetable oil
½ teaspoon honey

Cut tomatoes into wedges. In a medium saucepan, sauté onions and green peppers in butter or oil until slightly soft. Add tomatoes and honey, cover, and cook over medium heat for 10 to 20 minutes.

4 to 6 servings

YOUR HOME MAINTENANCE CHECKLIST

☞ Test your smoke alarms with a smoke source. See February for directions.

☞ Have your chimney cleaned if you heat your house with a woodstove.

☞ Replace filters on your central air conditioning unit.

☞ Repair cracked and broken macadam driveways.

☞ To conserve water during summer dry months, check and repair leaking faucets, shower heads, and toilets.

EVENTS AND FESTIVALS

**Pennsylvania Renaissance Faire
Manheim, Pennsylvania**
Beginning of July through the second week in October. Held at the Mt. Hope Estate and Winery, this midsummer festival features a magical re-creation of a sixteenth-century country faire in merrie olde England. Throughout the 50-plus acres of formal gardens you'll meet the likes of Queen Elizabeth I and her court, jousting knights, court jesters, jugglers, gypsies, and fortune-tellers, all of whom are played by members of the Bacchana-

lian Players, a 41-member professional acting troupe. Audience participation is one of the Faire's ingredients for success, and visitors rarely leave without having been drawn into the activities in one way or another. Information: Pennsylvania Renaissance Faire, Mt. Hope Estate and Winery, Box 685, Cornwall, PA 17016.

Fourth of July Celebration
Washington, D.C.

July 4. The grand celebration of our nation's birthday begins in the morning on Pennsylvania Avenue, at the steps of the National Archives. There the day's festivities kick off with a cannon and musketry salute, a concert of patriotic music, and a reading of the Declaration of Independence. At 12:30 P.M., the National Independence Day Parade marches down Constitution Avenue. The parade features outstanding high school bands from every state in the nation as well as beautiful floats on patriotic themes. After the parade, visit the west side of the Capitol building, and you'll be just in time to enjoy an early evening concert by the National Symphony Orchestra. The grand finale for the day is, of course, a spectacular fireworks display over the Washington Monument beginning at 9:30 P.M. All events in our national Independence Day celebration are free. Information: Washington, DC, Convention and Visitors Association, 1212 New York Avenue, Washington, DC 20005.

National Tom Sawyer Days
Hannibal, Missouri

End of June through July 4. The great American author and chronicler of life on the Mississippi, Mark Twain, is celebrated, appropriately enough, down by the Mississippi River during this festival, which was named the Number One Place to Be on the Fourth of July by the national newpaper, *USA Today*. Since Hannibal is almost Mark Twain's hometown (he was really born in the nearby town of Florida, Missouri), many of the scheduled events, such as fence-painting and frog-jumping contests, are straight out of his stories. Highlights of this five-day festival include several parades, mud volleyball games, an arts and crafts fair, a Tom and Becky look-alike contest (Tom and Becky were the two main characters in *Tom Sawyer*), nightly entertainment, and a nightly feast that includes barbecued ribs and a variety of ethnic foods as well as the traditional American hot dogs and hamburgers. All activities take place along the Mississippi waterfront. This slice of real Americana culminates in a spectacular fireworks display over the Mississippi River. Information: Hannibal Jaycees, P.O. Box 484, Hannibal, MO 63401.

Dulcimer Festival
Bar Harbor, Maine

Second weekend in July. Beginning with a concert on Friday evening, this festival celebrates the melodic sounds of the mountain and hammered dulcimers as well as other folk instruments. On Saturday and Sunday afternoons, free instructional workshops are given for those interested in learning to play a dulcimer, and neophytes can purchase a handmade instrument from any of the number of the craftsmen who display their wares at this show. If you have a song to share, bring it to the afternoon open mike session. All festival-goers are welcome at the Saturday evening, traditional New England contra dance, at which a caller teaches dancers the contra steps before the festivities begin. Information: Song of the Sea, 47 West Street, Bar Harbor, ME 04609.

Wayne Chicken Show
Wayne, Nebraska

Second Saturday in July. As the premier chicken show of the West, the Wayne

Chicken Show pays homage to all barn-yard fowl with a full schedule of events. Fly the coop for the day and participate in the fun run, the rooster crowing contest, and the free omelet feed (provided by numerous feeders and egged on by poultry). Enter the National Cluck-Off to compete for the Traveling National Cluck-Off Cup, the chicken song contest, the chicken calling contest, or the chicken olympecks. If you don't mind egg on your face, try the egg drop/catch, in which contestants attempt to catch raw eggs dropped from the Wayne city cherry picker. Fun is egg-zactly what this day is all about, and attendance at each of the events costs little or no chicken feed. Information: Wayne Chicken Show, Box 262, Wayne, NE 68787.

Garbage Day Celebration
Beech Mountain, North Carolina

Second Wednesday in July. Celebrated annually to commemorate the day the town purchased its first garbage truck, this day is Beech Mountain's way of com-memorating an important event in town history. The day starts out with the rechris-tening of the town's garbage truck. In honor of the day, residents dress up in costumes made of garbage and garbage bags to compete in the costume contest. Residents and out-of-towners line the streets for the annual garbage truck parade. Trucks from all the neighboring towns parade the streets and compete for prizes in the categories of cleanest, oldest, newest, and smelliest truck. For a mere 97¢ or one bag of roadside garbage, residents can gain admission to the town's luncheon and indulge in a birthday cake—baked in honor of the celebrated garbage truck, of course! Information: Garbage Day Celebration, Beech Mountain Chamber of Commerce, 608 Beech Mountain Parkway, Beech Mountain, NC 28604.

Circus City Festival
Peru, Indiana

Third week of July. Between 1884 and 1930, Peru, Indiana, which served as a winter headquarters for seven of the world's most famous circuses, became celebrated as the "Circus Capital of the World." To revive interest in circus his-tory and celebrate Peru's unique past, the circus festival began in 1958 and con-tinues to thrill audiences of all ages. Cir-cus performances—complete with flying trapeze and high wire acts, clowns, jug-glers, and daredevil unicycle stunts—are held every day of the festival. A tradi-tional circus parade complete with an elephant walk concludes the extravaganza on Saturday, but the spirit of the circus lives on at the Peru Circus Center Museum. After the festival visit the museum for an enjoyable tour of circus history. Informa-tion: Circus City Festival, Inc., 154 North Broadway, Peru, IN 46970.

Gilroy Garlic Festival
Gilroy, California

Last weekend in July. Gilroy celebrates its status as the Garlic Capital of the World during this midsummer harvest festival, with over 85 food booths offering a wide array of ethnic foods. Garlic gets pressed into every possible event here from the Great Garlic Cookoff to the Garlic Gal-lop (5- and 10-kilometer runs) and the Garlic Squeeze Barn Dance. As if that weren't enough, you can attend the Gar-lic Queen pageant, tee off in the Garlic Classic Golf Tournament, or pedal through the Tour de Garlique (a bicycling tour). Information: Gilroy Garlic Festival Asso-ciation, Inc., Box 2311, Gilroy, CA 95021.

AUGUST

IN THE PARCHING AUGUST WIND,
CORNFIELDS BOW THE HEAD,
SHELTERED IN ROUND VALLEY DEPTHS,
ON LOW HILLS OUTSPREAD.

Christina Rossetti

WHAT'S HAPPENING IN AUGUST?

August 1, Birthday of Francis Scott Key: The Baltimore lawyer who was the author of our National Anthem penned the lines to his poem called "The Star Spangled Banner" after observing the British bombardment of Ft. McHenry, which guarded the port of Baltimore, during the War of 1812. Key had boarded a British ship in the Chesapeake Bay in an attempt to secure the release of a friend who had been captured when the British set fire to Washington. The British detained him aboard ship during the bombardment of the fort on the night of September 13, 1814. During the night, Key suffered great anxiety and fear that the British might succeed in destroying the fort and capturing the harbor. On the following morning, he was so moved at the sight of the flag still flying over the beleaguered fortress that he composed his famous poem on the spot and submitted it the next day to a local Baltimore paper. The poem was printed by the *Baltimore American* on September 21, 1814, and soon was being sung in public to the tune of an old English drinking song. The United States did not actually have a national anthem until 1931 when the 71st Congress and President Herbert Hoover signed a bill making "The Star Spangled Banner" our national song.

August 3, Anniversary of Christopher Columbus's Departure to the New World: On this day in 1492, Columbus left the port of Palos, Spain, with a total crew of 88 aboard three ships—the *Pinta,* the *Nina,* and the *Santa Maria.* Columbus's mission was to discover a faster and more profitable route to "Cathay" (China). He was so certain of his success in this venture that he carried a letter of introduction from the King and Queen of Spain to the "Grand Khan," which was thought to be the title of the emperor of China. On the morning of October 12, 1492, at 2 A.M., the lookout on the *Pinta* sighted, in the moonlight, a limestone cliff on what turned out to be an island in the Bahamas. The explorers landed later that day on the island Columbus named San Salvador. Just prior to the return voyage the *Santa Maria* was wrecked in a storm, and Columbus returned to Spain with the two remaining ships and a firm belief that he had discovered islands off the coast of China. During the next ten years Columbus made three more voyages to the New World, each time expecting to find China, and each time landing and exploring different coasts of the Carribean islands and South and Central America. In 1504 he returned home to Spain suffering terribly from the debilitating effects of gout and another undiagnosed disease. He died two years later at the age of 55, a public flop who was despised and neglected by the Spanish court for his failure to find a route to Cathay.

August 14, VJ Day: On this day in 1945, Japan accepted the terms of surrender offered by the Allies—unconditional surrender with the safety and continuance of Emperor Hirohito guaranteed, acceptance of Allied occupation of Japan, and the return of all Japanese conquests since 1895 to their former owners. Similar terms of surrender had been offered and refused by Japan during July. As a result of Japan's refusal to surrender, President Harry S Truman approved the deployment of the first atomic bomb over the city of

Hiroshima on August 6, a move that wiped out the entire Japanese Second Army, razed four square miles of the city, and killed over 60,000 civilians.

August 10, Birthday of Herbert Hoover: As our thirty-first president, Hoover was the first president to be born west of the Mississippi River, the first to have a telephone at his desk (installed on March 27, 1929), and the first president to enter office as a self-made millionaire (with a business fortune estimated at 4 million dollars at the time of his election). Hoover was a former U.S. Secretary of Commerce, a mining engineer, and a brilliant businessman who traveled the world. He spent his single term of office overshadowed by the Great Depression and the collapse of the world economy. His subsequent defeat at the hands of Franklin D. Roosevelt in 1932 was a direct result of public dissatisfaction with the effects of the Depression and with his refusal to support federal aid to the vast numbers of unemployed Americans.

August 20, Birthday of Benjamin Harrison: Harrison, our twenty-third president, is the only president whose grandfather (William Henry Harrison) was also president. President William Henry Harrison holds the distinction of being the president who held the shortest term of office. At his inauguration on March 4, 1841, he insisted on giving a long inaugural speech outdoors in freezing weather. The day after his inauguration he fell ill with pneumonia and died on April 4, exactly one month after he assumed the presidency.

August 26, Women's Equality Day: The Nineteenth Amendment to the Constitution, which was finally ratified on August 26, 1920, was the result of decades of struggle by the women's suffragist movement. The two sole clauses of the Nineteenth Amendment, the culmination of over 40 years of feminist protest, are simple and short: *(1)The right of citizens of the United States to vote shall not be denied or abridged by the United States or by any State on account of sex. (2) Congress shall have power to enforce this Article by appropriate legislation.* As simple as women's suffrage seems, it is a right that has been purchased dearly—by countless unnamed women who defied public opinion to protest their disenfranchisement by their leaders. For example, less than 50 years before the ratification of the Nineteenth Amendment, Susan B. Anthony was arrested and fined for voting in the 1872 presidential election of Ulysses S. Grant.

The First Week of August Is National Clown Week

National Clown Week, sponsored by Clowns of America International, is a tribute to the light and laughter that clowns bring to our lives, and to the art and skill of fine clowning. National Clown Week also celebrates the healing power of laughter and the hope that volunteer clowns bring to hospitals, nursing homes, and centers for the handicapped.

If you've ever had the urge to run away and join the circus, you can indulge your fantasy by learning the art of clowning and by becoming a clown yourself. You can join the beginners, accomplished amateurs, or professional clowns who all get together to further the art of clowning at local clown clubs.

You can join a local chapter of Clowns of America International, an organization for all clowns, amateur or professional. Members receive a bi-

monthly magazine called *Calliope*, which gives information about the activities of local clown clubs, interviews with and stories about famous clowns, and hints and tips for better clowning. Membership in Clowns of America costs $20 per year, with an extra initiation fee of $5 for new members. To find out about your local clown club or to join Clowns of America International write to: Clowns of America International, Inc., P.O. Box 570, Lake Jackson, TX 77566.

IN THE GARDEN

WATER WORKS

Are your plants looking a little stressed in the August heat—or is it you who's stressed as you unroll the hoses and drag them out once again to water your garden so that it won't go limp under the summer sun? August is often the time when drought may make its presence fully known. By now you may be faced with water restrictions in your home town. Under these circumstances, you may find that keeping your garden watered by hand-holding a hose is proving next to impossible.

Your first line of defense against parching weather conditions is your old friend garden mulch. Vegetable and flower beds that were mulched by midsummer will now reap the benefits of cooler soil temperatures (a factor that helps keep plants healthy during the dog days of summer) and lower water requirements than unmulched beds. Remember the trick to using mulch is to remove it early in the season to speed soil warming but to replace it by midseason to reduce water demands.

Another way to beat the heat is through a drip irrigation system. Drip irrigation is the best way to water because it not only eliminates the drudgery of dragging hoses and sprinklers around your yard, but it also conserves water by putting every

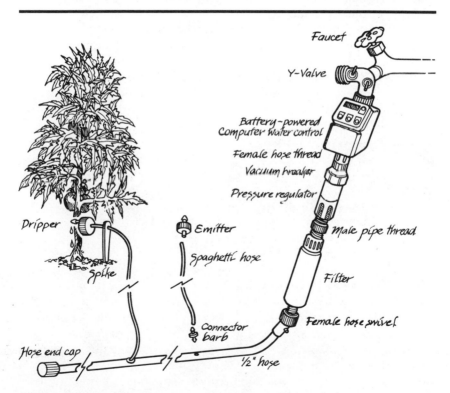

Garden Drip System
Drip systems may seem complicated at first glance, but once you understand the function of each part, you'll find it easy to snap together a system for your own use.

drop you use where it counts—in the soil. Water from conventional sprinklers is partially dispersed by the wind or evaporated from the hot soil surface as it strikes. Drip irrigation uses a little water and makes it go a long way.

For many gardeners, the switch from the bucket brigade to a drip system can be bewildering. Drip systems present a wide variety of options and a maze of terminology that seems unintelligible at first glance. It's true that setting up a drip system requires more thought than a trip to the faucet, but the concepts behind drip systems are simple. Once you've mastered the basic terminology, you can shop in confidence for a system that meets your needs.

Emitters

These do exactly what the name says—emit, or discharge, water. Emitters are designed to supply water as efficiently as possible, but they're not trouble free.

An *orifice emitter* is simply a hole sized to give a particular flow of water at a certain pressure. The holes may emit a drip, a mist, or a spray, and they're prone to two problems—clogging and water pressure changes. Soil, algae, or mineral deposits sometimes clog holes, so it's important to check orifice emitter systems periodically to make sure that water is getting through.

And because water pressure is highest at the start of the hose and lowest at the end, you will find that orifice emitters overwater in low spots and skimp water on high ground. Orifice emitters are best used in short runs on flat ground coupled with a pressure regulator.

Don't let the drawbacks of orifice emitters discourage you, because it doesn't take long (especially if you don't mind tinkering a bit) to overcome the common deficiencies of these emitters. They also have the advantage of being less expensive than the more sophisticated emitters: vortex emitters, diaphragm emitters, and labyrinth emitters. Vortex emitters, without going through the whys and whats of irrigation dynamics, self-compensate for changes in water pressure. Diaphragm and labyrinth emitters compensate for changes in water pressure, *and* they are also self-cleaning.

Tubing

Tubing is what carries the water and what emitters plug into. The standard-size tubing is a ½-inch diameter hose made of polyethylene or some other synthetic material (with the exception of porous pipe, which is made of rubber). To understand the differences among the types of tubing available, it's helpful to know that there are three different types of drip irrigation systems, each with its own type of tubing: (1) *emitter systems,* which use polyethlyene tubing with emitters inserted at intervals along the length of the tube, (2) *drip tube and tape systems,* which use a tubing or tape (made of polyethylene or other synthetic material) with holes spaced at regular intervals along the length of the tubing or tape, and (3) *porous pipe systems,* which use microscopic-size pores manufactured into lengths of flexible pipe (usually made of recycled rubber).

If you choose one of the emitter systems, you will determine yourself the number of emitters and the distance between them. Since you insert the emitters in the tubing with a hand punch, emitter systems can be set up to emit water in places exactly suited to your needs. Emitter systems also use lengths of ¼-inch diameter tubing called spaghetti tubing. Using spaghetti tubing and an appropriate connector, you can locate an emitter some distance away from your main supply tube. Before you buy an emitter system, you should discover whether or not the system accepts a device called a *goof plug.* A goof plug is simply a plug inserted into an emitter hole to block water exit. You use a goof plug to remedy any mistakes you make in installing the emitters or simply to change the location of your emitters to suit your changing irrigation needs.

If you choose one of the drip tube or tape systems, you'll find that the primary characteristic of these systems is that they emit water down the entire length of the tubing instead of at specific holes. They work best in any garden area where you want to supply a continuous band of water. Some *drip tapes* are single-walled tubes of polyethylene with sides stitched in nylon. The water drips out along the length of the hose through the stitching. These systems are simple to install and maintain, but their primary drawback is that less water is delivered at the end of the tape than at the beginning because water pressure drops as you move to the end of the tape. You can buy a drip tape that eliminates this problem because the tape (called Tyvek) is made of nonwoven, spunbonded polyethylene fibers that leak water when the water pressure is only 1 psi (pound per square inch). Most systems operate at about 25 psi. The low water pressure required to operate this drip tape system (manufactured by International Irrigation Systems) makes it possible to use drip irrigation when the only source of water is a barrel, trash can, or other water-holding container.

Drip tubes are usually dual-chamber systems composed of two hoses joined together at a common wall. One tube acts as the primary water carrier and the second tube acts as the water dispersing chamber. Water enters the system through the primary tube, leaks into the secondary tube through microscopic-size holes, and then into the ground through holes in the secondary tube. The outstanding advantage of dual-chamber drip tubes is that they are not subject to the difficulties caused by water pressure drop at the end of the tube (a primary problem with emitter systems). The water pressure is the same at the end of the line as it is at the beginning because the primary tube acts as a pressure equalizing chamber. Plants at the end of the system receive the same amount of water as those at the beginning.

If you choose a *porous pipe* system, you will find that it also delivers water in a continuous band down the length of the hose. Water flows out of the pipe through pores that are an integral part of the hose material. The water leaves the hose as a sweat rather than a spray. Because the pores in porous pipe are so small, clogging with dirt or sand is negligible. This particular feature makes it possible to bury porous pipe in the soil for long periods of time.

Pressure Regulators

Many drip irrigation systems operate at a water pressure of about 25 psi (pounds per square inch), significantly lower than the pressure of most home or city water systems. Adjusting the faucet to a lower volume of water flow will not get around this problem because you cannot control the water pressure in your irrigation system simply by setting your faucet at a trickle. Your faucet is a flow regulator, not a pressure regulator. If you operate your system at a water pressure higher than the manufacturer's specifications, you can ruin your system and void your warranty all at once. When you choose an irrigation system, you should check the manufacturer's specifications for the correct water pressure, and you should install the in-line water pressure regulator recommended by the manufacturer if it's required for your system.

Filters

To prevent clogging, filters are essential to all systems. Hose washers with screens provide a partial solution, but they're often too coarse and can allow dirt and sediment through that will plug drip emitters. An in-line 150- to 200-mesh filter, which usually screws in between the pressure regulator and the main hose, is the solution. Drip emitters can still clog unless filters are cleaned every few weeks, so use an old toothbrush and scrub the screens with a strong bleach solution. It's also a good idea to open the ends of the drip tubes and flush them with water once a month.

Timers

No system is really complete without a timer. With a timer you can enjoy the maximum advantage of drip irrigation—it's no work to water after it's installed. The simplest and least expensive timers work by water pressure and are basically waterproof versions of the classic mechanical kitchen timer. For a bit more money, you can get an electric timer that can be preset for frequency, amount, and duration of watering.

Valves

A house shutoff valve (faucet) between your water supply and the drip system is essential. In addition, you may want to install shutoff valves between various parts of your system so that you have the convenience of watering only parts of your garden if you wish. A simple ball valve will do the job here.

Backflow Preventers

If part of your irrigation system is on a ground level higher than your house shutoff valve, water in the irrigation pipes can infiltrate your household water pipes. If you install a system in which backflow is a possibility, play it safe and install a backflow preventer. These devices are required by building codes in some areas.

Putting a System Together

Before making any purchase, make a scaled drawing of your garden and sketch in the irrigation system. You can sketch several different irrigation layouts on tracing paper and lay them in succession over your original scaled drawing. This helps you see the differences in the layouts and helps you make a decision as to which design best suits your needs. You may find that one particular layout saves money by making the most efficient use of hose but that another layout provides more flexibility for adding on when you expand the garden. After you've gotten a pretty good idea of what your system should look like, your next step is to shop for irrigation kits.

If you've never installed an irrigation system before, a kit is an easy way to start because a kit provides you with all the necessary hardware and accessories as well as complete assembly instructions. Your goal in shopping for a kit is to find a package of equipment that fits your size and design needs, that gives water in the way you want (remember there are three types of systems), and that can be expanded by the purchase of extra parts and lines as your needs change. Before you purchase any kit, make sure that the manufacturer can supply you with spare parts to replace broken or defective ones and that you can get parts and line to modify the kit to suit your needs. If you decide to forgo a kit and design a system from scratch, make sure you buy from an established dealer who stocks all the standard parts for the system you buy. Buy from a dealer who is prepared to help you design your system and to give advice for any problems you encounter.

Whether you are installing a kit or starting from scratch, your first step in assembling your system is to unroll your tubing and lay it out in the sun for 30 minutes to make it pliable and easy to handle. While the hose is loosening up, connect the timer, the pressure regulator, and the filter to the main water outlet. Hand tighten all parts. To join tubing to any coupling device that uses a compression fitting, moisten and soften the end of the tubing by dipping it in hot water. Gently join the tubing to the coupling device by rocking it back and forth over the compression fitting. Never glue compression fittings together.

Before digging trenches to lay

New, Old Watering Technique

A simple, ancient watering system developed by the Chinese more than 2,000 years ago can be almost as effective as today's drip irrigation systems. The Chinese buried porous clay pots or pitchers in the soil next to plants and kept them filled with water. The water that gradually leached into the soil through the porous sides of the pots kept plants watered with little waste and little effort.

You can mimic this ancient watering technique in your garden. Simply bury clay flower pots up to their rims close to the plants you want to water. To keep water in the pot, plug up the drainage hole with florist's clay (which is waterproof). Fill the pot with water and check it daily to keep the water level high. If you don't have many clay pots, you can try plastic gallon milk jugs with just a few very small holes punched in their sides and bottoms. You must leave the tops off the jugs in order to get the water to drain. When you place your pots or jugs in the ground, be sure to leave room for the plant's roots to develop. The best strategy is to place the pots in the ground at the same time you plant your seedlings. If you try to install ground watering pots at a late stage in your garden development you run the risk of disturbing the roots of mature plants.

underground irrigation line, first lay out the entire system aboveground. This allows you to see any design problems or tubing shortages before you begin installation. To keep your trenches straight, use stakes and string to lay out the lines you will dig. If you elect to keep your irrigation lines aboveground, you can keep them along a straight or a curved path by simply driving wooden stakes into the ground every 2 feet or so, alternating on either side of the tubing as you go.

ALMANAC GARDENING CALENDAR

August is the time of harvests and peak annual blooms for cool-climate gardeners and a time of beginning again for gardeners in the warmer zones. Gardeners who are now enjoying peak harvests must keep the water coming to sustain the yields they've worked so hard to achieve. Those in the very coldest zones need to think about protection from sudden frost, which occurs as early as September and can ruin a promising tomato crop. Gardeners in the warmest zones can begin a new gardening cycle by planting warm-season crops such as toma-

toes and cucumbers for late September through October harvest.

Zone 1

Remove weeds before they go to seed. During hot weather, water regularly to sustain yields and prevent wilting. Harvest and dry parsley, basil, oregano, and thyme. Spray brassicas with Bt (*Bacillus thuringiensis*) weekly if necessary to control cabbageworms. Harvest vegetables, especially cucumbers and summer squash, every two to four days to keep them producing. Dig and cure shallots and garlic. When about half your bulb onion tops have fallen, gently push over the remainder and withhold water to speed drying. After the tops wither, dig onions and spread them to cure in a dry, shaded place. When potatoes start to die, reduce watering. Dig and store them after two weeks. If your gardening season is less than 90 days, be prepared to protect peppers, tomatoes, cucumbers, and squash from frost as September approaches. Plant overwintering spinach, Swiss chard, lettuce, and garlic during the last two weeks of the month. Pick and dry strawflowers and statice for winter arrangements. During hot weather, keep ornamentals well watered, especially those in nursery beds or near a foundation. Unless plants show nutrient deficiencies, stop fertilizing perennial flowers so that they will harden for winter.

Cover strawberries with spun-bonded polyester or blankets when frost threatens. Train strawberry runners where needed. If plants are yellow or form runners slowly, apply a quick-acting organic fertilizer. Raspberries, blueberries, and boysenberries ripen this month. Pick every three days for best quality. Cover the bushes with bird netting. After harvest, remove all canes of red raspberries that bore fruit this year to provide next year's canes with more sunlight. Renew mulches around fruit trees. Support heavily laden branches to prevent breaks. Reduce watering during the second half of the month so plants can harden.

Zone 2

Early in August, sow onion seed for scallions. What you don't eat can be kept in the ground over winter for next spring. Pick early corn daily to prevent tough kernels. Pick beans daily if succession-cropping. If you want dry beans, let the pods dry on the vine. Early August is a fine time to dig up garlic bulbs. Allow them to dry in semishade for a day or so. (August sun can "cook" the bulbs.) Late in the month, plant garlic cloves. Harvest onions when approximately half the tops have fallen over. If stalks are green, has-ten ripening by gently bending them over with a rake. Take a chance by planting out semihardy crops, such as lettuce, radishes, and beets. Plant tomato and pepper seeds in your greenhouse for winter harvest. Sow seeds now for ripe tomatoes 45 days later. If the garden has bare spaces, plant a green manure crop, such as buckwheat, to build up organic matter and cut down on weeds. Annual ryegrass comes up fast and works well as a soil builder. Spade or plow both under in late fall or spring.

Early in August trim back leggy coleus, impatiens, and begonias. Root cuttings in a pan of water. Check peonies for small, aborted brown buds, a sign of Botrytis blight; snip off and burn to prevent infection next year. Any porch pots that look ratty can be barbered now for fall show. Trim back leggy stems, and feed plants fish emulsion to promote bud formation and lush growth before fall frost. Primroses (primula), if crowded, can be divided in August. They thrive in shady spots and are ideal for naturalizing under trees.

Water deeply if the weather is dry, especially newly planted fruit tree stock. Pull or clip water sprouts from around the base of fruit trees. Keep an eye out for peach tree borers. Sawdust, sap, or gum boils are telltale signs. Pick up and destroy fallen fruit to control pests. Pick pears before they ripen so they keep longer in storage. Pick grapes before the skin bursts and attracts bees. Try your hand at bud-grafting apples now. Limit strawberry runners to about six per square foot. Keep weeds out and mulch to develop healthy plants for next year's crop.

Zone 3

Early in the month, sow one last crop of quick-maturing bush beans for prefrost harvest. Throughout the month, harvest summer crops daily to preserve freshness. Water is critical for maturing crops. If the month is dry, apply about 2 inches of water a week. Remove and compost spent plants to reduce insect populations, control disease, and make way for fall crops. At midmonth, sow spinach, beets, turnips, lettuce, radishes, peas, kale,

and other cool-season vegetables. Soak seedbeds deeply and cover with boards to keep the soil moist and cool. Check beds daily and remove boards when the first sprouts appear. In the first two weeks, transplant cabbage, cauliflower, broccoli, and kohlrabi into the garden. Water, mulch, and shade until they are established. Also, feed weekly with weak manure tea to speed growth. At the end of the month, pinch off the last few blooms at the ends of squash and melon vines so energy is spent on maturing fruit. This technique also works on tomatoes, peppers, eggplants, and zucchini.

Choose a dry, sunny day to harvest strawflowers, statice, money plants, cockscombs, baby's-breath, and artichokes for drying. Hang upside down in an airy room or shed for curing. Deadhead annuals, water with weak manure tea, and mark healthy plants for seed saving. Keep annuals picked and pruned to extend their blooming period. Keep roses well watered—at least 6 inches per week—and mulched, but stop feeding at midmonth to reduce frost-susceptible new growth. Stake glads, dahlias, and chrysanthemums; feed with manure tea or fish emulsion. Thin biennials and divide perennials such as irises and daylilies that have finished blooming. By the end of August order perennials and spring-flowering bulbs for fall planting. Watch for red spider mites, which thrive on ornamentals weakened by harsh August weather. To prevent the spread of pests, remove annuals as their blooms fade. If night temperatures fall much below 50°F late in the month, consider moving houseplants back inside.

Pests are a major problem in the orchard during August. Renew Tanglefoot around the base of fruit trees, and check mulch and foliage for pests. Pick infested fruit and continue raking up fruit drops to break insect and disease life cycles. Spray caterpillars with Bt (*Bacillus thuringiensis*) and other exposed pests with botanicals or soap. Early in the month, renovate strawberry beds. Water heavily and feed with rock fertilizers, compost, or cottonseed meal. Encourage runners from the most productive plants to take root. When they do, remove the mother plants from the bed. During August, fruit tree pests will often move into the mulch around the trees. Remove old mulch and replace it with a fresh mulch to destroy many of these pests. Check trees for disease or pest infestation. Remove damaged or diseased fruits and branches. Watch for webworms in fruit trees and berry bushes.

Zone 4

As vegetable plants cease production, pull and compost them to destroy diseases and pests. Prepare vacant beds for fall vegetables or winter cover crops. Set out Chinese cabbages and other cole crops early in the month; provide shelter from sun and hot, drying winds. Where summers are mild, sow turnips, winter radishes, and other fast-growing fall crops. Remove melon, winter squash, and pumpkin blossoms after midmonth to keep plants from expending energy on fruits that won't ripen. In hot areas, wait until the end of the month to sow spinach and lettuce. If soil temperatures are above 85°F, germinate the seeds in moist paper towels in the refrigerator. There's still time early in the month to plant potatoes for a fall crop. Continue to provide 2 inches of water to vegetables each week. When outer onion leaves turn yellow, push the stems over to speed ripening. After harvest, dry the bulbs thoroughly for storage. Stake peppers and eggplants whose heavily fruited branches could snap.

Early in the month, shape hedges for the last time this season. Prune summer-blooming shrubs when they've finished flowering. Avoid pruning most shrubs and trees between August 15 and the first hard frost; this could stimulate cold-tender growth. Feed roses once before midmonth to increase fall bloom, and give chrysanthemums one more application of manure tea. Divide Oriental poppies, peonies, and daylilies if they're crowded. Divide true lilies if the size or vigor of their blooms is declining. Cut down and burn spent hollyhock stalks to combat borers. Remove faded blooms from perennials and side-dress with bonemeal and compost. Order bulbs and peonies for fall planting. Soak lawns and shrubs periodically during dry weather. Remove suckers on grafted plants and cut out and burn webworm-infested branches of trees. Water lawns once a week. Begin preparing seedbeds for fall-sown lawns by digging in plenty of humus.

Protect ripening fruits from birds by covering plants with netting. After harvest, cut down bramble canes that have fruited and thin new growth to four or five sturdy shoots. Soak all fruit trees, especially apples and new plantings, during dry periods. Pecans will need extra water from midmonth through early September, while nuts are developing. Continue to pick up fallen fruits; when the harvest is finished, rake bare the area beneath each tree and apply new mulch to discourage pests and diseases. Eradicate stands of sweet clover and native brambles near the orchard; they can be hosts for pests.

Zone 5

Resume planting summer vegetables that mature in less than 60 days, such as cucumbers, bush beans, and squash, and make second plantings of basil and dill. At midmonth, set out seedlings of brussels sprouts, cabbage, broccoli, kohlrabi, and cauliflower in mulched, irrigated beds. Protect them from cabbage loopers with weekly applications of Bt (*Bacillus thuringiensis*). Prune back okra by one third to induce branching and increase fall yields. If summer weeds are escaping your control, at least lop off their flowers before they drop seeds. Late in the month, or whenever blister and bean beetles cease to be a problem, plant all green and sprouting potatoes culled from your spring crop. Cover them with a thick mulch. Begin direct-seeding cool-weather vegetables late in the month. Shade the young plants from full sun for two weeks. The seedlings of large-seeded snap peas and radishes will push through a thin mulch, but lettuce, carrots, beets, and spinach sprout best when partially shaded or covered with damp burlap bags. Leeks, parsley, and most hardy herbs germinate best if started indoors. When the fall rains start, direct-seed kale, turnips, and Chinese cabbage.

Give chrysanthemums a booster feeding of fish emulsion or manure tea now, while the flower buds are developing. Gather stems of statice, strawflowers, and other everlastings to keep them productive until winter. Prune dahlias to encourage new growth. Stake and fertilize tall lilies to help them store nutrients for next year's flowering. Work carefully near magic lilies and spider lilies—though the foliage is long gone, the flowers will appear any day. Daylilies and irises may be dug and divided now. Late in the month, dig and divide irises if you did not do so last year. Indoors, sow perennial and biennial flowers to set out later in the fall. Larkspurs, hollyhocks, dianthus, and Oriental poppies are excellent choices for this climate.

As fruit trees finish bearing, trim off water sprouts and diseased wood. Clean up the orchard floor, and remove and burn mummified fruit. If you cannot get at nests of fall webworms by hand, treat them with Bt (*Bacillus thuringiensis*). Use whatever means are necessary to protect ripening grapes from birds—netting, wind chimes, plastic snakes, or a transistor radio. Prune back to ground level any blackberry canes that bore this year, and tip back new canes to encourage branching. Cut back raspberry canes after the berries ripen, but wait until next month to propagate bramble fruits. Thin strawberry runners to two per plant, and place a little soil around the roots of the new plants to hasten their growth.

Zone 6

Fertilize and water peppers and okra to stimulate a fall crop. Cut okra back halfway so that it will branch and start producing pods in just a few weeks. Set out tomatoes, peppers, and celery early in the month. Sow bush beans, New Zealand spinach, limas, okra, and early maturing varieties of sweet corn, squash, and cucumbers. Later in the month, plant cool-weather crops such as daikon radishes, bok choy, escarole, lettuce, kohlrabi, Swiss chard, collards, kale, mustard, beets, leeks, and garlic. Set out transplants of broccoli, cauliflower, cabbage, and brussels sprouts in late August or early September. Order onion and spinach seeds to be sown in September. If temperatures remain extremely hot, make succession plantings of the cool-weather crops. Watch for insects for the rest of the month. Their numbers will decline with cooler weather.

Mulch and deeply water woody ornamentals to counteract heat and drought. Azaleas, rhododendrons, and dogwoods suffer the most from dry conditions. Replenish the soil with compost and sand before planting fall flowers. Add bonemeal or rock phosphate to promote healthy roots and plenty of blooms. Seed or transplant cosmos, sunflowers, calendulas, marigolds, and zinnias early in the month. At the end of the month, plant larkspurs, dianthus, sweet peas, spider lilies, and autumn crocus bulbs. Cut back dahlias and roses by about a third to encourage new growth for fall blooms. Continue to remove spent flowers from annuals. Order perennials in early August for fall planting.

Provide support for heavily laden fruit trees. Drought stress may require an additional fruit thinning. Protect grapes from bird attacks by using netting or paper bags. Clean up the orchard. Remove fallen fruit and leaves. Prune out and destroy diseased limbs, but leave major pruning for winter.

Zone 7

If your part of the zone was too hot to start fall and winter crops in July, start them this month. Sow the seeds in shade. As soon as they germinate, see that they get morning and evening sun, but shade them at midday and keep them moist. On the Gulf Coast, set out the last tomatoes, peppers, and eggplants, and sow snap beans, pole beans, and southern peas by mid-August. On the West Coast, put in Irish potatoes now to mature before frost, and plant peas by midmonth. Everywhere in the zone, start seeds of short-day onions in containers. Before the end of the month, sow seeds of endive for winter forcing.

Early in the month, sow seeds of pansies, violas, calendulas, gaillardias, foxgloves, and poppies for midwinter and early spring color. Divide daylilies, Madonna lilies, spider lilies, Shasta daisies, and marguerites after they have finished blooming. Madonna lilies want no more than an inch of soil on top of them. New plants of marigolds and zinnias put in now will produce flowers before winter. Plant autumn crocuses (colchicums) now to bloom in fall. Deadhead hydrangeas and prune lightly to keep them bushy, bearing in mind that woody stems produced this year will carry next year's flowers. Feed and lightly prune roses and dahlias to stimulate fall flowering.

Pick avocados after the fruits become dark purple. Pick summer pears when fully developed but still green. Refrigerate them until needed, then ripen at room temperature. Let Seckel pears ripen on the tree. Oriental pears are available in Asian markets on the West Coast during August. Sample the different varieties, and then order a tree of your favorite from a nursery in winter. Dry peaches, raisins, and prunes in the hot days of August and September. If your strawberry beds are over two years old, put in new plants in late August for fruit next spring. Thin established beds to five to seven plants per square foot.

IN GOOD HEALTH

HUMOR: THE BEST MEDICINE

The first week of August is National Clown Week. What better time to recognize the health benefits of humor, many of which— believe it or not— have been scientifically documented. Following the publication of Norman Cousins's book *Anatomy of an Illness,* humor became a topic of serious study in both the medical and psychological communities. In fact, humor is now being taken seriously enough as a contributor to health that some prestigious hospitals have instituted humor as an integral part of patient care. An outstanding example is New York's Columbia-Presbyterian Medical Center, which has a three-day-per-week Clown Care program for seriously ill children. A rotating team of professional clowns, complete with oversized shoes and roller skates, visits the children's wards, including the Intensive Care Unit, dispensing rubber noses, chocolate milk transfusions, and soap bubbles.

At New York's St. Luke's-Roosevelt Hospital, clowns join the monthly case-review meetings in which doctors, psychiatrists, and clowns discuss the emotional well being of children awaiting kidney transplants.

Why all this interest in humor? It's all part of the growing understanding of the mind/body connection. And the more we know about these subtle and life-changing connections, the more we can use them to help ourselves maintain good health or regain health after an illness.

The De-Stressor

A growing body of psychological research indicates that humor helps alleviate stress, particularly the stress associated with certain types of depression. In a 1986 psychological study of students at Fairleigh Dickinson University, researchers found that those students who made the most frequent use of humor and who saw humor in the greatest variety of life situations were also less likely to experience depression from stressful life events (such as leaving home for the first time, failing a test, or experiencing romantic disappointments). The researchers in this study theorize that humor allows some people to see problems as a challenge rather than a threat; they report that there is some evidence that people use humor to increase their feelings of mastery in a difficult situation and that their problem-solving abilities are enhanced by their "can do" attitude. People who feel they can overcome a problem are less likely to feel depressed about it than those who feel hopeless.

The Creative Side

Humor opens the door to your creative side. Creativity makes everyone better at solving problems because it induces the free flow of ideas and eliminates "vertical thinking"—the type of thinking in which 2 + 2 *always* equals 4. Reporting on a study of problem-solving ability at the University of Maryland, psychologist Alice Isen says that, "Research suggests that positive memories are more extensive and are more interconnected than are negative ones, so being happy may cue you into a larger and richer cognitive context, and that could significantly affect your creativity."

In the Maryland study of problem solving, two groups of students were each given an identical problem to solve. One group viewed a short comedy film of television "bloopers" and the other group saw a math film on how to find the area under a curved graph line. The researchers found that 75 percent of the students who had watched the comedy film correctly solved the problem; in contrast, only 20 percent of the students shown the math film solved the problem. The problem they were given is a classic one used in many different research projects to test the problem-solving skills of groups of people. Each subject is given a candle, matches, and a box of tacks and asked to attach the candle to a corkboard wall so that the candle will burn without dripping wax on the floor. Most people who try to solve this problem fall prey to "functional fixedness," the tendency to see everyday objects only in terms of their conventional use. Those who were in a good mood from seeing the funny film, however, were able to solve the problem by seeing that the box holding the tacks could do something else besides hold tacks. These folks tacked the box to the wall and used it to hold the candle.

The Best Painkiller

If you're told that you're sick, laugh. Or if you're told you might die, laugh harder. Although there is no scientific evidence yet that laughter can cure disease or prevent death (Norman Cousins's remission from a life-threatening disease is considered a single case report and as such is not conclusive proof to the medical community), there is compelling evidence that laughter produces at least temporary relief from pain and from the anxiety that pain produces. The reason that people experience temporary pain relief from smiling and laughing is not yet clear. One controversial theory dating back to the last century and now receiving serious scientific scrutiny is that laughing or smiling momentarily prevents blood from leaving the brain. As a result, the brain cells are bathed in an extra dose of oxygen, which causes a feeling of exuberance. If this theory doesn't satisfy the skeptics, there is also evidence that laughter produces a feeling of exuberance by causing the heart to beat faster and the blood pressure to rise. Blood becomes more thoroughly oxygenated and all cells consequently are better nourished with oxygen. In addition some scientists believe that laughter stimulates the release in the brain of endorphins, the body's own natural pain relievers.

In *Anatomy of an Illness,* Norman Cousins reports on the beneficial effects of his self-prescribed laughter treatment for his life-threatening case of ankylosing spondylitis (a disease which destroys the body's connective tissue): "I made the joyous discovery that 10 minutes of genuine belly laughter had an anesthetic effect and would give me at least two hours of pain-free sleep." This comment is coming from a man who was in such agony

when he left the hospital that contact with his own bedsheets caused him terrible pain.

Take Two Belly Laughs and Call Me in the Morning

Needless to say, you don't have to wait until you get sick to cultivate your sense of humor. The benefits of seeing the light side of life are far too rewarding to put off for emergencies only. The best time to cultivate a sense of humor is now, because then you'll always be in practice for the tough times when you really need it. You can cultivate a sense of humor even if you've never made up a joke in your life. Consciously include humor in your life every day until it becomes a part of your life like other good health habits. Among the things you can do for a start are:

☞ Laugh at something about yourself every day. The best humor always begins at home and doesn't involve hurting other people.

☞ Keep a joke journal. That's right—every time someone tells you a joke, write it down and build up a repertoire of jokes you can remember. You'll find plenty of places to use them, once you get accustomed to remembering them. Anytime you're in a tense situation or you observe an unhappy situation involving other people, you can lighten the mood and make the world a little brighter by telling a joke. You help yourself and you help others.

☞ Think of your everyday world, including your workplace, as scenes from the old television show, "Candid Camera." You'll gain an eye and an ear for the ridiculous and you'll be able to see humor where most folks miss it entirely.

☞ Consider joining a speaking club or group, such as Toastmasters, where you can practice giving presentations that include humor. You'll find that your humorous side will begin to spill over into the memos and notes you write at work; into your conversations with coworkers, neighbors, and family members; and even into tense situations like your trip to the dentist for a root canal.

☞ Become a connoisseur of humor; whenever possible, read a joke book, listen to a comedy routine, see a funny movie, or watch an old comedy on your VCR.

A small publication you might be interested in is "Laughing Matters," published quarterly by the nonprofit Humor Project of the Saratoga Institute. Articles range all over the subject of humor, from how to tell a joke to collections of original jokes sent in by readers. For information on subscription rates write to: The Humor Project, 110 Spring Street, Saratoga Springs, NY 12866.

JOKE SAMPLER

To tickle your healthy funny bone during National Clown Week, try the joke sampler here. Many of these quips come from *The Clown*, the very first magazine published by J. I. Rodale. Begun during the Depression year of 1932, these little tidbits prove that laughter is indeed the universal tonic, even for Depression-era folks facing an uncertain world and certain hardship.

Lunatics

Doctor: "Is there any insanity among your relatives?"
Lunatic: "Yes, I'm afraid so. They keep writing me for money."

Doctor: "So you think you're sane now, eh? Well, if we let you out will you keep away from women and liquor?"
Lunatic: "I certainly will."
Doctor: "Then you can't get out. You're still crazy!"

A man on trial for his life was being examined by a group of doctors for insanity. Suddenly one doctor jumped up and shouted, "Quick, how many feet has a centipede?" "For the love of Mike," the man replied, "is that all you got to worry about?"

Gangsters

A gunman, on being asked if he were guilty, replied, "I guess I am, judge; but I'd like to be tried to be sure of it."

Crooked politician: "You blamed fool, you bumped off the Governor instead of the Mayor."
Gangster: "OK. That'll be $10 extra."

If conditions continue as they are, the public will have to go to jail in order to get away from the criminals.

Kwestions and Answers

Kwestion: Can you tell me what they mean by "selling short" on Wall Street?

Answer: It means buying something you can't get with money you haven't got and then later selling what you never had and didn't pay for at more than it cost.

Kwestion: Is it possible for any man and woman to live through a long, married life without exchanging one cross word?
Answer: Yes, if both are deaf and dumb.

Kwestion: I sometimes go through my husband's pockets and take a little money without his knowing it. A friend of mine tells me this is stealing. What do you think?
Answer: Your friend is crazy. These days if you can find anything in your husband's pockets, we wouldn't call you a thief. You would be classed as a magician.

Famous Men
Benjamin Franklin

Benjamin Franklin arrived at an inn one winter's day after a tiring journey, covered with snow and half dead with cold. The innkeeper's family and several guests surrounded the fire, and no one inconvenienced himself for the stranger. Franklin sat down near a window as if to rest, and after several moments addressed the innkeeper and asked him if he had any oysters.

"Yes, excellent ones," replied the innkeeper.

"Open them and take a dozen to my horse."

"Does he eat them?"

"Just take them out and you will see."

Everybody got up to go and see the horse eat oysters. The children, the strangers, the servants all went to the stable to witness such a novelty. Franklin, in their absence, established himself near the fire, in the best place. Very soon they came back to tell him that the horse would not even look at the oysters.

"In that case," Franklin replied, "bring them to me and give him some oats."

Abraham Lincoln

Reporting on a dream he had in which he walked through a great assembly of people, the homely Mr. Lincoln recalled that in his dream someone called out, "He is a common-looking fellow." In his dream Lincoln turned to his critic and replied, "Friend, the Lord prefers common-looking people, or He would not have created so many of them!"

Calvin Coolidge

A Washington matron once boasted she could make the notoriously silent Mr. Coolidge talk. Cornering him at a dinner party, she sought to make good her boast.

"Oh, Mr. President," she said, trying to disarm him with frankness, "I have made a bet that I can make you say at least three words."

"You lose," Mr. Coolidge replied.

Did You Know? Curious Health Facts

☞ According to the American Dietetic Association, the average married American woman weighs 23 pounds more on her 30th wedding anniversary than she did when she got married. Her husband weighs 18 pounds more.

☞ The human brain contains a maximum of 14 billion cells; it reaches this maximum between the ages of 15 and 25. It's a good thing there are so many cells, because each sneeze destroys hundreds of them.

☞ Munching on a peppermint after a large meal may not have the soothing effect we think it does. Peppermint oil can be effective in relieving stomach gas created by eating too much too quickly, and some imported peppermints do contain the oil. But most mints have little or none of the essential peppermint oil, just peppermint flavoring.

☞ Heartburn has nothing to do with the heart at all but is rather a condition associated with the stomach or esophagus.

☞ Some ulcer sufferers can have an attack just by thinking about food. An ulcer occurs when the lining of the stomach or of the duodenum (the upper part of the small intestine) can no longer resist the corrosive effects of digestive juices, chiefly hydrochloric acid and pepsin. Food causes the stomach to secrete these digestive juices, but stress, alcohol, or even the thought of food can get those juices flowing.

☞ The heart beats between 70 and 80 times per minute, or about 100,000 times per day. While you rest or sleep, your heart pumps about 2½ ounces of blood with each beat, which adds up to nearly 5 quarts of blood pumped per minute, or about 75 gallons per hour. The output of the heart can vary according to the body's needs, and during vigorous exercise, the heart can increase its output to nearly five times its resting output. During exercise, a single red blood cell can make the circuit from heart to big toe and back to heart in less than 60 seconds.

☞ The most famous dentures in America—George Washington's—weren't made of wood, as legend has it, but rather of hippopotamus eye teeth.

☞ Operating rooms are often green to make it easier on the eyes of doctors and nurses. *The American Journal of Nursing* says that British army doctors complained that after looking at red blood during surgery, they saw splotches of green when they glanced up at white walls. The solution was to paint the walls green and wear white garb.

Walking Tip for August

Does August heat and humidity make your walk seem more like a trip through a sauna than a refreshing workout? Why not take up water walking? Water walking is a new exercise routine in which you walk *in* the water not *on* the water (since you're mortal, after all). It's a new program offered by many local YMCAs and health clubs. Water walking participants perform a number of strengthening and stretching routines in the water and then "walk" from one side of a pool to another. The goal of the entire water walking routine is to increase cardiovascular conditioning *without any stress or damage to joints.* Among the exercises incorporated into the water walking routine are pulling the arms through water, walking backwards, and jogging through water. Most of the water walking routines are performed in the shallow end of the pool; the few exercises performed in the deep end call for participants to wear flotation devices while they "jog" from the shallow end of the pool to the deep end. Water walking offers you a safe way to have fun in the water while you improve your cardiovascular fitness, and you *don't* have to know how to swim to participate.

AT HOME

A FRONT DOOR: YOUR SMILE TO THE WORLD

August is a good time to evaluate your home's exterior. If it's in need of a face-lift or some cosmetic changes, you still have a month or so of warm weather to perform easy tasks. One way to give your home an inviting new look is to replace your warped and leaky front door. A handsome new entry door is a quick way to perk up a plain Jane house front without a lot of investment in time or money. If you decide to replace your entry door, you'll find that you can choose from steel and fiberglass units, as well as the traditional wooden stile-and-rail front door.

Wooden front entry doors have the market cornered on warmth and tradition, but they also swell, warp, shrink, shed paint, and crack. If despite these drawbacks, you still want wood for its beauty, shop carefully. There are some top-of-the-line wood doors available that are warp-resistant because they are made with many layers of laminated wood with moisture barriers sandwiched between the layers of laminate. For a remodeling job, wood also has the advantage of being easy to trim for odd-sized openings.

Steel doors offer the biggest advantage in maintenance: There is none, save oiling the hinges and lock cylinder occasionally. Also, steel doors are usually filled with a plastic foam insulation and have an insulation value of up to R-15 versus R-3 for wood.

Fiberglass entry doors are the newest product in door development. They combine the best of steel and wood; they have a high insulation rating because they have plastic foam interiors, and they can be stained, painted, and trimmed on the edges like wood.

Before you start your door-buying excursion, we've prepared some tips for you to keep in mind.

Your Entry Door Checklist

☞ Make sure steel door skins are treated with galvanizing and a primer coat of paint. If in doubt, ask to see the specifications sheet.

☞ Look to see that a prehung door hangs straight and square in its frame opening and that the whole assembly is in good physical condition.

☞ Be sure there are at least three hinges, that they're of heavy-gauge metal, and that they have a security tab (a pin that secures the door even after the hinge pin is removed.

☞ Check that the leaves of the hinges are an even depth in the frame and in the door. Look for prefinished hinges that you won't have to paint.

☞ Check that weather stripping contacts the door evenly all around, that it's not crimped or bent, and that no daylight shines through.

☞ Make sure that the door can be bored for the lockset you plan to use.

☞ Check the glazing details to be sure that it's what you ordered.

☞ Make sure that the door passes your local building code (for example, some codes specify safety glazing or tempered glass on entry doors.)

☞ Buy from a reputable dealer who will stand by any manufacturer's warranty on the doors he sells.

Reprinted from "Entry Door Buying Tips," by David Sellers, Practical Homeowner, April 1988.

BUILD A BETTER SAWHORSE

The sawhorse is a traditional mainstay of workshops everywhere. Used in pairs for supporting long boards or as a base for a toolbench or working platform, these humble workhorses have even made their way into kitchens and living rooms as table supports.

There are plenty of designs for sawhorses. The one featured here will do equally well in kitchen or workshop. This sawhorse is as strong as any, but can fold up and be stored when it's not in use.

Construction of Sawhorse

1. Saw repeated kerfs, using a hand or power saw, to connect opposite edges of the crosspieces where legs will join. Break off waste and smooth the joint with a chisel.

2. After cutting legs to length join them to crosspieces by driving screws through crosspieces into legs. Predrill holes if necessary and use two screws per joint.

3. Brace the sawhorse upside-down with both crosspieces clamped together. Position heavy-duty butt hinges just inside the legs and attach them with screws.

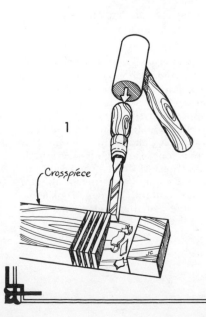

2

Crosspiece

Leg

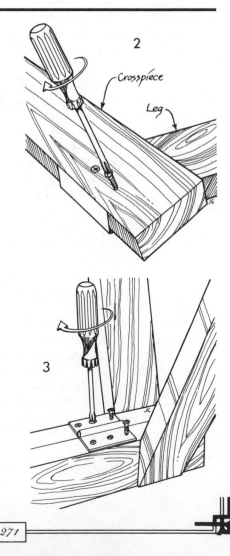

1

Crosspiece

3

You can cut the length of the legs and crosspieces to suit your own needs. One standard size is 30 inches long with 24-inch legs. Clear 2 × 4 stock, a pair of heavy-duty, three-inch butt hinges, and some drywall screws are all the materials you'll need to make each horse.

The legs fit into triangular depressions cut and chiseled into the crosspieces. Make repeated cuts, either with a hand or table saw, that connect opposite edges of the crosspiece where the leg will fit. Then use a chisel to cut out the waste and smooth the channel so that the leg will fit snugly. (See illustration 1.) Repeat this operation for each leg.

Now you're ready to cut the legs to length. Both the top and bottom of each leg should be cut on an angle of about 15°, which allows the legs to rest flat on the ground and not project beyond the top of the crosspieces. Fasten the legs to the crosspieces using drywall screws. (See illustration 2.) Predrill holes for screws if they're too hard to drive without them.

The last step is to hinge the crosspieces together. With the sawhorse braced upside-down, attach the hinges just inside the legs. (See illustration 3.) Now you're ready to put these carpenter's "assistants" to work or fold them up for storage until they're needed.

Reprinted from "Build a Better Sawhorse," by Tim Snyder, Practical Homeowner, April 1988.

YOUR AUGUST SHOPPER'S TIP

Corn, tomatoes, cucumbers, beans, berries, and melons are most plentiful and therefore a better buy this month. With this month's recipe, you can enjoy corn for breakfast, lunch, or dinner. These corn puffers can be topped with a touch of butter and honey for a delicious breakfast dish. Top them with shredded lettuce, chopped tomatoes and green peppers, and shredded cheese for a light luncheon, or serve them as a unique side dish for supper.

Welshkorn Puffers

2 egg whites
2 cups fresh corn, cut from 4 to 6 ears
3 tablespoons whole wheat pastry flour
2 teaspoons chopped fresh parsley
¼ teaspoon pepper

Beat egg whites until stiff, but not dry. Set aside. Chop corn finely with a sharp knife on a cutting board, or use a food processor or blender until coarsely chopped and slightly creamy, but not pureed. Fold into egg whites along with flour, parsley, and pepper. Drop by the teaspoon onto a hot, lightly oiled griddle in silver dollar-size dollops and cook until dry and golden underneath, about 7 minutes. Carefully turn and cook about 7 minutes on the reverse side. Serve immediately.

4 to 6 servings

YOUR HOME MAINTENANCE CHECKLIST

☛ Lubricate the garbage disposal oil ports with a drop or two of 20-weight oil.

☛ Check and clean the refrigerator.

☛ Check your fire extinguishers. See February for directions.

☛ Clean the filter in your range hood.

EVENTS AND FESTIVALS

Maine Lobster Festival
Rockland, Maine

First weekend in August. This crustacean celebration honors Rockland's status as the leader of the lobster world. Held in the harbor park overlooking Penobscot Bay, the festival features luscious lobster dinners as well as other fresh Maine seafood gathered during the Harvest of the Sea. After a Maine lobster dinner, seafood enthusiasts can stroll through the marine exhibits, cheer the coronation of the Sea Goddess, sample the winning entries in the Maine Seafood Cooking Contest, or enjoy the numerous other

activities including musical performances, arts and crafts exhibitions, a children's activities area, and a parade. Brave souls unafraid of a dunking can enter the incredible Lobster Crate Race—a test of speed and agility in which contestants try to cross Rockland Harbor by hopping onto a series of fifty lobster crates strung together to serve as a floating bridge. Information: Maine Lobster Festival, P.O. Box 508, Rockland, ME 04841.

National Polka Festival
Hunter Mountain, New York

First weekend in August. Enjoy four days of polka-filled pleasure with thousands of fellow polka fans who hoof it to the music of the most popular polka bands from Europe and the United States. Held rain or shine under a huge tent in the picturesque Catskill Mountains, this festival includes polka lessons, a Polka Queen contest, and above all, authentic European polka dance styles, such as the Rhinelander, the Czardas, and the Schotish. Information: Exposition Planners, Bridge Street, Hunter, NY 12422.

World Gee Haw
Whimmy Diddle Competition
Asheville, North Carolina

First weekend in August. What in the world is a whimmy diddle, you ask? It's an Appalachian folk toy made out of native rhododendron or laurel wood. Although it's nothing more than two sticks and a propeller, it does marvelous tricks for those skilled in the art of whimmy diddling. The skilled whimmy diddler will manipulate the toy's propeller to gee (turn to the right) and haw (turn to the left), reversing the rotations at incredible speeds. If you'd like to learn how to make your own whimmy diddle, turn out for the whimmy diddle workshop held one day before the competition. Cash prizes are awarded for the most unusual whimmy diddle and for the whimmy diddler in each category who accumulates the most rotation reversals in a given time frame. Information: Southern Highland Handicraft Guild, Folk Art Center, P.O. Box 9545, Asheville, NC 28815.

Teddy Bear Rally
Amherst, Massachusetts

First Saturday in August. Bear lovers from across the country flock to Amherst to participate in this one-day bear extravaganza! Enter your favorite bear in the Amherst Rally to compete for any one of dozens of prizes in such categories as Best Dressed Bear, Best Loved Bear, Ugliest Bear, Fattest Bear, Oldest Bear, and Best Traveled Bear (for the bear that makes the longest trip to the contest). Readings from A. A. Milne's Winnie the Pooh books take place throughout the day and set the lighthearted tone for the extensive exhibit of bear collections and bear paraphernalia. All proceeds from the Teddy Bear Rally benefit the local Amherst charities. Information: Amherst Teddy Bear Rally, Amherst Rotary Club, Box 542, Amherst, MA 01004.

Smoki Ceremonials and Snake Dance
Prescott, Arizona

Early August. Held during the "dark of the moon"(the new moon), the Smoki Ceremonials transport visitors to the ancient spiritual world of the Indians with authentic and beautiful Indian ceremonial dances, such as the War Horse Dance, the Lightning Dance, the Spider Woman Dance, and the Mexican Bird Dance. The Ceremonials end with the world-famous Smoki Snake Dance in which "Little Brothers" (live bullsnakes), are brought into the dance and then released to carry the message to the gods

that the sacred rites have been faithfully performed. All performers are magnificently costumed and made up for these dances, which are held at the Smoki Mesa, an authentic re-creation of an Indian village. Information: Smoki Ceremonials, P.O. Box 123, 143 North Arizona Avenue, Prescott, AZ 86302.

Iowa State Fair
Des Moines, Iowa

Mid- through late August. Come to Des Moines for a real old-fashioned slice of the best of the Midwest in this, the quintessential American state fair. The Iowa State Fair (first held in 1854) is one of the oldest and largest state fairs in the United States, and it has everything a state fair should have—vast agricultural and industrial machinery displays, one of the world's largest livestock shows, a 10-acre midway with games and amusements, an art show, grandstand and track events, free entertainment, and an on-site 160-acre campground. Come and bring the kids: Children, 11 and under, are admitted free. Information: Iowa State Fair, Statehouse, Des Moines, IA 50319.

Bon Festival
Delray Beach, Florida

Mid-August. Enter the world of the mysterious Orient in this re-creation of the Japanese summer ritual that welcomes ancestral spirits back to earth for a day. Folk dancing, folk music, and Japanese games and food are all part of this celebration on the grounds of the Morikami Museum. As dusk approaches, revelers bid farewell to the ancestral spirits by floating Japanese lanterns in the Morikami pond. A spectacular fireworks display tops off the day's events. Information: The Morikami Museum, 4000 Morikami Park Road, Delray Beach, FL 33445.

Crazy Day
Magee, Mississippi

Third Saturday in August. If you happen to drive through Magee on the third Saturday in August, you may notice that most of the people in town will be dressed rather oddly. Don't be alarmed! Just get out and join the festivities with the folks who are all celebrating Crazy Day, a day when people just let loose and have fun! A crazy legs contest for men, an armadillo race, a crazy "talent" show in which contestants are "gonged" for unspeakably bad performances, a fun run and state championship 5-kilometer run, music, and the Crazy Day King and Queen contest have been part of the wacky lineup since this event began in 1976. Information: Chamber of Commerce, 117 West Choctaw Street, Magee, MS 39111.

Great American Duck Races
Deming, New Mexico

Fourth weekend in August. Everything is just ducky in Deming during this quack-filled extravaganza. Serious competitors in the duck races train their ducks year-round in the art of fast waddling, because the reward for all that prerace training may be the grand prize of $2,000. The winner of the Deming Duck Derby, which is held on a 17-foot long, enclosed, dry-land track, must waddle faster than a field of more than 400 other ducks, all racing for the Deming Duck Derby Championship and the grand prize. The folks in Deming sure know how to have fun, because at the Great American Duck Races there's something silly for just about everybody—including a Darling Duckling Costume Contest (kids dressed up as ducks), the Deming Duck Calling Contest, the Duck Queen Competition, the World's Richest Tortilla Toss (tortillas thrown frisbee-style, with a $250 prize for the

greatest distance), the Chili Cookoff, the Great American Horseshoe Tournament, the Deming Outhouse Race (grown-ups racing outhouses on wheels through the streets of Deming), the Tournament of Ducks Parade, and the Best Dressed Duck Contest (ducks dressed up in people duds). Information: Deming-Luna Chamber of Commerce, P.O. Box 8, Deming, NM 88031.

Musikfest
Bethlehem, Pennsylvania

Fourth week in August. Stroll through the historic Moravian district of Bethlehem for this spirited nine-day music celebration. Each day of the festival features music at different sites (or *Platz* in German) in the historic section of the city, and visitors may choose from over 575 concerts, many of them free and all within walking distance of one another. The music offerings range from European ethnic song and dance to American folk and bluegrass, but the overwhelming influence is German in honor of Bethlehem's first Moravian settlers. Polka fanciers throng to the festival each year to dance to the music of authentic German or Austrian polka bands, and classical music lovers line up early to purchase tickets to the Bach Choir performances. History buffs may also enjoy a walking tour throughout historic Bethlehem. Information: Musikfest, 556 Main Street, Bethlehem, PA 18018.

SEPTEMBER

O SWEET SEPTEMBER!
THY FIRST BREEZES BRING
THE DRY LEAF'S RUSTLE AND
THE SQUIRREL'S LAUGHTER,
THE COOL, FRESH AIR, WHENCE HEALTH
AND VIGOR SPRING,
AND PROMISE OF EXCEEDING JOY
HEREAFTER.   *George Arnold*

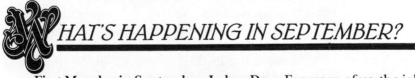

WHAT'S HAPPENING IN SEPTEMBER?

First Monday in September, Labor Day: For many of us, the job benefits we enjoy—a 40-hour work week, a guaranteed minimum wage, safe working conditions—are taken for granted. The fact that working people picketed, marched, negotiated, and, in some instances, were killed in the fight to bring humane working conditions to American workers is frequently forgotten. Congress declared Labor Day a national holiday in 1894, but the first Labor Day observance took place on Monday, September 4, 1882, when a New York City labor organization called the Knights of Labor organized a parade of more than 10,000 workers through the city. Labor marched with bands and banners up Broadway to Union Square and then to Elm Park for picnics, concerts, and orations. Given the violent history of the labor movement prior to that 1882 parade, the participants in the first Labor Day certainly demonstrated courage and conviction in the cause of organized labor.

September 6, Anniversary of the Assassination of President William McKinley: Described by historian Samuel Elliot Morrison as a "kindly soul in a spineless body," McKinley is remembered for succumbing to domestic political pressures that led the United States into the Spanish-American War—the war of Teddy Roosevelt and his horseless Rough Riders; the war that opened with the sinking of the American battleship U.S.S. *Maine* in the Havana harbor. With Americans clamoring "Remember the *Maine*!" McKinley effectively caved in to public pressure and refused a conciliatory offer from Spain to cede Cuba to the United States. Following this immensely popular though needless war, McKinley and war hero Teddy Roosevelt were an unbeatable combination for a landslide re-election. After his inauguration in March 1901, McKinley embarked on a triumphal railway journey throughout the country. In September, the trip ended tragically at a public reception in Buffalo, New York, where McKinley was shot by an anarchist. McKinley was the third president—after Abraham Lincoln and James Garfield—to die at the hands of an assassin.

September 7, Neither Snow Nor Rain Day: Most of us think the U.S. Post Office has an official motto: "Neither snow nor rain nor heat nor gloom of night stays these couriers from the swift completion of their appointed rounds." In fact, that's the motto inscribed on the New York Post Office Building on Eighth Avenue in Manhattan, a building that first opened to the public on September 7, 1914. The building's inscription was supplied by William Kendall, who worked for the architectural firm that designed the building and who translated the motto from the writings of the ancient Greek historian Herodotus. The post office really does not have an official motto, but the verse from ancient Greece makes a pretty good substitute.

Mid-September to Mid-October, Rosh Hashanah and Yom Kippur: Jews observe Rosh Hashanah as the beginning of the religious New Year. Since the time of the observance depends on the lunar cycle, the first day of the New Year may fall on any day from mid-September through early October, but it always begins with a religious liturgy that includes the blowing of a ram's horn (called a *shofar*) to call Jewish people to spiritual awakening. Rosh Hashanah is celebrated with special food delicacies prepared as omens of good luck, but it also begins a ten-day period of repentance and self-examination that culminates with the most solemn of Jewish religious observances, Yom Kippur, the Day of Atonement. Jews honor the Day of Atonement by abstaining from work, as well as by fasting, intense worship, confession of sins, and seeking forgiveness from God for wrongs committed in the past year.

September 14, Anniversary of the First Solo Transatlantic Balloon Flight: On September 14, 1984, Joe W. Kittinger, a 56-year-old balloon enthusiast, left the town of Caribou, Maine, in a ten-story-high helium balloon named *Rosie O'Grady's Balloon of Peace*. By the morning of September 17, he was over the town of Capbreton on the French Coast. He continued his journey without touching earth and landed in poor weather conditions near the town of Savonne, Italy.

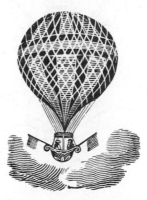

September 23, Autumnal Equinox: On this day the sun is over the equator as it continues on its journey to the Southern Hemisphere, where it will bring the summer season to those "Down Under." On the autumnal equinox there is an equal number of daylight and dark hours—about 12 hours of each for both the Northern and the Southern Hemispheres. As fall progresses in the Northern Hemisphere, the hours of darkness will increase and the hours of light, decrease, until the sun reaches its maximum latitude south of the Equator, the Tropic of Capricorn.

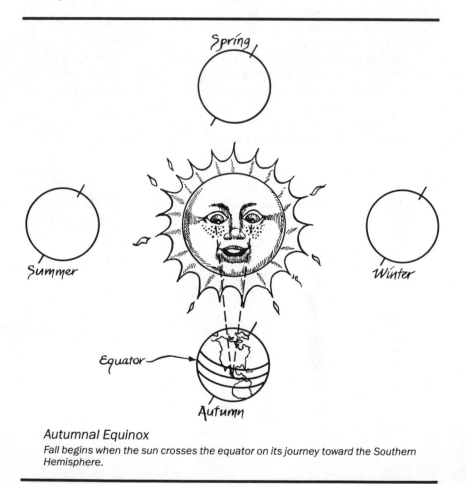

Autumnal Equinox

Fall begins when the sun crosses the equator on its journey toward the Southern Hemisphere.

Harvest Moon: The full moon nearest the Autumnal Equinox is called the harvest moon. During the harvest moon, complex astronomical forces cause the moon to rise at nearly the same time for several nights in succession. The harvest moon is so named because it typically rises near the hour of sunset and provides several additional hours of light for harvesters working the fields.

IN THE NICK OF TIME . . .

TIME HEALS ALL WOUNDS.

TIME IS MONEY.

TIME FLIES, OR IN LATIN, *TEMPUS FUGIT.*

KILL TIME . . .

HAVE THE TIME OF YOUR LIFE . . .

TIME IS OF THE ESSENCE.

TIME AND TIDE WAIT FOR NO MAN.

September Is National Clock Month

What would we do without clocks? Our universal human compulsion to keep track of time reveals itself daily in the commonplaces of our everyday speech, and the passage of time is an underlying thread in everything we read, from great literature to the front page of the local newspaper. Consider an old and commonsense view of time:

PROCRASTINATION IS THE THIEF OF TIME.

Edward Young

Or consider an ironic and twentieth-century view:

PUNCTUALITY [italics added]
IS THE THIEF OF TIME.

Oscar Wilde

Or consider our casual vocabulary of time-related phrases:

With all this preoccupation with the hours of the day, where would we be without the likes of Levi Hutchins of Concord, New Hampshire, who in 1787 invented the first alarm clock? How's that for Yankee ingenuity! The only problem with the first alarm clock was that the alarm rang only at the time set by Hutchins, and the proud owner of this newfangled clock had to get up every morning at the Hutchins-ordained time, with no possibility of changing it, ever.

Clock tinkering has been a subject of fascination for generations of basement wizards. The first clock to strike the hours was invented in 1754 by Benjamin Banneker. He was a self-educated free Negro who lived and farmed near Baltimore. He educated himself in astronomy by painstaking observation of the stars and in mathematics by reading borrowed textbooks. Encouraged by a wealthy Maryland industrialist, he pursued his scientific interests, accurately predicted a solar eclipse in 1789, and for ten years published an almanac that was distributed throughout the mid-Atlantic states and even in Europe.

Banneker's genius flowered early. At the ripe old age of 23, this nonstop tinkerer built a clock entirely out of wood that struck each hour. His only tool was a jackknife, and he had never seen anything similar except a sundial and a watch. The Banneker clock kept time and chimed the hours for 20 years after its construction, and its builder went on to become a distinguished scientist and surveyor, who was appointed by George Washington to survey the District of Columbia for the federal government.

Clock tinkering continues today, but most of the time-tinkerers are astronomers or physicists in search of completely error-free clocks to help guide scientific studies, such as making accurate observations of deep outer space or measuring nearly indetectable movements of the earth's crust. Scientists at Harvard and the Smithsonian Center for Astrophysics have built a clock that is accurate to 50 trillionths of a second a day. At that rate of accuracy, the clock will have to last 50 million years before it loses one second. In case you're interested in having one for yourself, the only thing you have to concern

yourself with is the $350,000 price tag and the size—it's as big as a refrigerator.

IN THE GARDEN

STEP RIGHT UP AND ENTER THE FAIR!

If your garden produce is picture perfect this September, maybe it's time to show off your wares at the county fair. Many county fairs are held at the end of summer or the beginning of fall, traditional harvest time when local produce is at its peak. Opening day of the county fair is a heady feast for the senses: the aroma of fresh baked goods; the colorful sparkle of home-canned jellies, jams, pickles, and vegetables; the enticing cornucopia of fresh vegetables and fruit; the lushness of garden flowers. Mix all this with the cacophony and pungency of sheep, cows, chickens, pigs, and horses on exhibit, the lurching excitement of a roller coaster ride, and the enticing call of the sideshow man, and you've got an irresistible combination.

If you've never exhibited your garden produce before, plan to visit your county fair this fall. Just by lingering for a while in the exhibit areas, you can gain some valuable pointers for winning entries at next year's fair. Visit the fresh produce displays with the aim of gathering as much information as possible. Plan your visit to coincide with judging day, which is usually opening day at most fairs. Pay particular attention to those entries that have won a prize by reading the judges' comments written on the entry card. By paying special attention to the judges' comments, you can come up with a good idea of what makes a winning entry. After you've inspected the winning entries, take a look at the other entries. Frequently judges comment on the defect or problem that caused a lost ribbon. By inspecting these entry cards also, you can get an idea of what *not* to do when you enter your own produce.

If you've never exhibited your produce or kitchen products at the county fair before but would like to take the plunge and try this year, you still have a good chance of coming up with a winner. If you've already got a superb pumpkin on the vine or some spectacular pickles in the jar, these pointers could make you a winner:

Obtain an entry schedule ahead of fair time. An entry schedule spells out the rules of entry for each class of competition. Also, if possible, obtain entry cards for your exhibit ahead of time. Study the rules for your class of competition. If the rules say three tomatoes are required, it means exactly three. If you enter four in hopes of impressing the judge, you will find yourself disqualified, even if your tomatoes are the best of the lot. It's a good idea to fill out your entry card before the fair because entry cards sometimes require you to supply information that you may find hard to recall on the spot. Typical information required for an entry card would be the complete variety name for any fruit or vegetable you enter, the complete recipe—including a list of ingredients—for any canned or baked goods, or the correct botanical name for a flower or a houseplant entered into a horticultural exhibit. Rules and entry schedules for your county fair are usually available through your county extension agent.

Read the rules on the entry schedule carefully and follow them to the letter. If you look under "Tomatoes," you will find several categories, such as "large standard," "yellow," "cherry," "pink," and so forth. Each of these categories will have its own rules. To exhibit cherry tomatoes, you may be required to provide six tomatoes, whereas you may be required to provide two tomatoes to enter the yellow tomatoes class. Never mix types or varieties unless this is specifically called for in the rules.

Keep your produce entry uniform in size and color. The overall appearance of your exhibit is what really counts. Suppose you have four large, top-quality samples of tomato "A" and also five medium-size, top-quality samples of tomato "A." The rules call for five samples of tomato "A." Don't enter the four large tomatoes plus one from your medium-size collection. Enter your five medium-size samples because they match in size and color. You may also find that some class rules call for stem or leaves to be left on (peppers usually require part of a stem, onions may require part of the greens). In this case be sure to trim the stems or greens to exactly the same length for each item in your entry.

Cleanliness definitely counts. Your exhibit should look good enough to eat on the spot. *You* wouldn't eat a tomato with dirt flecks or pesticide residue on it. Think of your exhibit as a picture you are painting—the picture should look good enough to eat. If you enter canned goods, make sure your jars, lids, and labels are sparkling clean and enticing to the eye. Be especially careful of canned goods you've kept in your basement or root cellar. Go over them with a fine, soft toothbrush to remove any trace of dust or cobwebs. Polish the glass with a dilute solution of vinegar and water to remove detergent residues that can make the contents look cloudy.

The day of the fair, rise early to give yourself plenty of time to pack your entry properly. You may have left your prize entries on the vine or branch to reach a peak of flavor on just this day. In that case, pick early in the morning, well before the sun begins to drive moisture away from the leaves and stems of plants. If you pick early, your produce will be cool and filled with water—two factors that contribute to a longer life at the exhibit. Pack the items you will exhibit in deep boxes with crumpled newspaper between each piece for cushioning. You must be extremely careful not to bruise thin-skinned items such as tomatoes or apples. You may not even see a minor bruise yourself until your exhibit has been on display for several hours. By then the heat and lights will have done their work to make any minor imperfections fully visible. If you are transporting canned goods, use plenty of packing between the jars to avoid breakage and disappointment.

Preserving Verse

While most gardeners think it's more than enough work to can and freeze the fall harvest before it spoils, the gardener here had enough energy left over to versify the steps in her effort. We don't recommend the recipe here, but we commend the originality of the cook.

To Preserve Tomatoes

Six pounds of tomatoes first carefully wipe,
not fluted nor green, but round, ruddy, and ripe;
After scalding, and peeling, and rinsing them nice—
with dext'rous fingers 'tis done in a trice—
Add *three* pounds of sugar, (Orleans will suit,)
in layers alternate of sugar and fruit.
In a deep earthen dish, let them stand for a night,
allowing the sugar and juice to unite!
Boil the syrup next day in a very clean kettle,
(not iron, but copper, zinc, brass or bell metal.)
Which having well skimmed, 'till you think 'twill suffice,
throw in the tomatoes, first adding some spice—
cloves, cinnamon, mace, or whate'er you like best
'twill add to the flavor, and give them a zest.
Boil slowly together until they begin
to shrink at the sides, and appear to fall in;
then take them up lightly, and lay them to cool,
still boiling the syrup, according to rule,
until it is perfectly clear and translucent—
your skill will direct you, or else there's no use in't—
then into the jars, where the fruit is placed proper,
pour boiling the syrup, direct from the copper.
After standing till cold, dip some paper in brandy,
or rum or in whiskey, if that is more handy;
lay it over the fruit with attention and care,
and run on mutton suet to keep out the air;
then tie a strong paper well over the top—
and now that I think on't, the story may stop.
If you'll follow these rules, your preserves never fear,
will keep in good order till this time next year.

Anonymous

Reprinted from the Ohio Cultivator, Vol. V, 1849.

Above all, enjoy the whole event. If the thought of losing even a tomato judging fills you with visions of mortification and dread, just go and enjoy the fair and forget about your entry. Remember that this is not a matter of life and death, or even your reputation around town. If your entry looks good to you, it will certainly look good to the general public. After all, even if you don't take first prize, there's always next year.

PRUNING PRIMER

This fall, before you drag out your old, rusty garden shears to cut back that forsythia that threatens to overrun your driveway, stop a moment to consider whether you really know what you're doing. Fall is a popular time for garden pruning, and many unfortunate shrubs and trees are subjected to outrageous treatment as a result of an overeager gardener's urge to solve a "problem" with a cutting tool and 20 minutes of spare time on a Saturday afternoon. The basics of pruning are simple, and a quick review before you get out your tools may spare you some embarrassment next spring when the results of your fall pruning will appear in full living color.

Timing Is Everything

The Old Testament book of Ecclesiastes offers the ageless thought that "To every thing there is a season, and a time to every purpose under heaven." Pruning falls right in that broad category of human activities described by Ecclesiastes—activities (like tennis, football, and investing in the stock market) in which timing is as important as technique. In order to select the best time to prune a tree or shrub you need to know only two things: (1) the time of the year the plant flowers or sets fruit and (2) on which kind of growth the flowers or fruits occur—on new shoots from the current season's growth, on wood one year old, or on wood two or more years old.

If your shrub or tree blooms from the *current season's growth,* prune in the early spring well before the normal bloom time. Early spring pruning of this type of plant encourages more vigorous spring growth and consequently a greater profusion of flowers. Examples of plants that bloom on current season's growth are roses, hydrangeas, and butterfly bush (also called summer lilac, *Buddleia davidii*).

If your shrub or tree blooms on *one-year-old wood,* prune in the late spring and always *after* flowering or fruiting. If you prune before bloom or fruit formation you may accidentally remove all of the one-year-old growth and have a bare plant for the season. Examples of plants that should be pruned after flowering or fruiting are forsythia, common lilac (*Syringa vulgaris*), and single-crop red raspberries (which should have all one-year-old canes removed after fruiting).

Shrubs and trees that bloom or fruit on *wood two or more years old* can be pruned in spring or fall since you will not be likely to remove all of the flowering branches when you prune. Fruit trees are the most common example of trees that may be pruned in the spring or fall.

Where Do You Cut?

Before leaves and stems become visible, they exist as "buds"—the swellings on stems and branches that really are embryonic new plant parts. In the spring, buds swell and lengthen into stems, unfurl into leaves, or open into flowers. Buds form on either terminal or lateral positions (see illustration), and flowering buds are usually fatter and blunter than leaf-producing buds.

When you prune, *always cut just above a bud.* When you prune off a stem or branch, you automatically remove the terminal bud, which is the most vigorously growing part of a plant. Removal of the terminal bud transfers this vigorous growth capability to the first lateral bud below the cut. Since you know that new growth will be initiated at the lateral bud just below the cut, select a lateral bud that points outward, away from the center of the plant. The new growth will then point away from the older growth and give an open, airy plant, a plant that enjoys greater sunlight penetration and that is not susceptible to damage from crossed branches rubbing against each other.

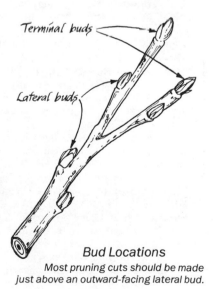

Bud Locations
Most pruning cuts should be made just above an outward-facing lateral bud.

Pruning Times for Common Trees and Shrubs

The short list here provides all you need to know about pruning a few common trees and shrubs. By familiarizing yourself with the comments in this list, you'll get an idea of the type of information you need to look up before you prune an unfamiliar plant.

American holly (*Ilex opaca*): Prune lightly any time of year; however, heavy pruning after flowering or during summer may prevent berry formation.

Azalea: Prune in the spring following flowering. For deciduous azaleas, which tend to become woody and unproductive, cut old branches off at the ground.

Birch trees (both weeping and upright are genus *Betula*): Prune late summer or fall. Cuts made during the growing season tend to bleed.

Boxwood (*Buxus microphylla*): Boxwood can be trained to a lush, compact shrub simply by pinching out the leading growth. If you'd like to shape a boxwood more extensively than pinching will allow, confine your pruning to late spring after the main spurt of growth has finished.

Bridal wreath (all species of *Spirea*): Most species of spirea flower on last year's growth. These should be pruned after flowering—midsummer or fall. A few spireas flower on new growth (notably *albiflora, bullata, bumalda, and japonica*) and should be pruned in late winter or early spring to encourage profuse new growth and flowers.

Camellia: These can be pruned at any time of year, but major work should take place in the spring.

Common lilac (*Syringa vulgaris*): Since flowers appear on last year's growth, prune only after flowering—usually in late spring or early summer.

Crape myrtle (*Lagerstroemia indica*): Since flowers appear on the current season's new growth, prune to the desired shape when the tree is dormant—late winter or early spring.

Fir trees (*Abies Nordmanniana*): Prune in the late winter and before spring growth. Don't cut back to leafless wood because the whole branch will die.

Hemlock (*Tsuga canadensis*): Prune in midsummer. Young, fast-growing hedges may require an additional early-spring trimming.

Japanese maple (*Acer palmatum*): Prune only mid- to late winter when the tree is fully dormant.

Rhododendron: Leggy, overgrown rhododendrons require a special pruning technique. Look along bare branches to find subtle swellings where leaf rosettes once existed. These swellings are called dormant buds, and if you cut just above a dormant bud, new growth will emerge at that point. The best time to rejuvenate old rhododendrons is in the winter in mild areas or in the spring where winters are severe.

ALMANAC GARDENING CALENDAR

Northern gardeners are still harvesting summer crops in September, but not for long. By the month's end, cool-climate areas are close to the first frost date, and heat- and light-loving vegetables, such as tomatoes, have stopped ripening, even if frost has not yet appeared. For northern gardeners, this month and the next are harvest times for winter squashes (the traditional pumpkins) and cool-loving crops such as lettuce, cabbage, and beets. Gardeners in the Deep South still have most of this month to harvest late-season crops—tomatoes, cucumbers, and eggplants—and to plant cool-season crops, such as snow peas and spinach.

Zone 1

In the first week of September, start cold-hardy lettuce, spinach, arugula, and other greens in a cold frame. Once the seeds have germinated, leave the frame open when the temperature is above 40°F and water regularly. Pick or cover hot-weather vegetables before the first frost. Tomatoes and peppers ripen best above 65°F. If the weather is cooler than this, pick and ripen them indoors. Cover loosely to prevent moisture loss. Pick winter squash and dig potatoes and onions before the first heavy frost (below 25°F). Store the squash at 70° to 80°F to cure for two weeks, then move to a cool, dry place. Cover head lettuce and frost-sensitive leaf lettuce when night temperatures fall below 28°F. Spunbonded polyester can be left on during the day, eliminating the nightly covering chores. Frost-hardy lettuces will survive temperatures in the low 20s.

After frost, cut back perennials so that dead foliage will not harbor diseases, insects, or mice over the winter. Cover nursery beds of perennials and biennials with a light mulch or spunbonded polyester if night temperatures fall to the low 20s. Uncover during the day to promote hardening. Lift begonia and dahlia tubers and gladiolus corms after the first frost and store in a cool place. Begin planting tulips, daffodils, and other spring bulbs. Loosen and enrich the soil with rotted manure or compost. Don't let the soil dry out after planting or the bulbs won't make adequate root growth this fall. Pick up, crack, and store fallen filberts and walnuts. Pick pears when full size but green, and store in a cool place until ripe. Cover late strawberries, bramble fruits, and grapes if frost threatens before they ripen. Pick up all fallen fruit so pests and diseases do not have a place to overwinter.

Zone 2

Before frost, pick green tomatoes and place in a cool spot to ripen. Wipe each fruit with a weak solution of household bleach to kill fungal spores. Pick winter squash and pumpkins before heavy frost and store in a cool, dry place. Leave about 2 inches of stem on each fruit to keep them longer in storage. Dig remaining onions and dry them in the sun for a day. Store in a cool garage or basement. Add compost or rotted manure to the asparagus bed. Avoid manure on rhubarb since it may cause foot rot. Pull cucurbit vines, and compost or burn them to help control squash bugs and cucumber beetles. Cool, dewy evenings and mornings make September an ideal time to patch or put in a lawn. For fast green-up, sow quick-growing perennial ryegrass along with Kentucky bluegrass, which takes about 24 days to get started. Divide perennials and replant in soil fortified with compost. Set out new roses or transplant established ones. Water the plants well and protect them so they'll pull through the winter. Plant spring bulbs as they become available. Before you plant balled-and-burlapped stock, make sure you remove plastic wrap and twine from around the soil ball. Burlap can be left on to rot.

Labor Day is a stop sign: Don't feed ornamentals from now until after dormancy in late fall or early spring. After midmonth, start cutting back any perennials that look down-at-the-heels. Tag the best chrysanthemums for dividing in spring. After frost blackens cannas and tuberous begonias, dig them up, cut them back and store in just-about-damp peat moss until next year. Pot impatiens for winter bloom. Cut back plants halfway and grow in a bright, cool window. If your fruit trees are overloaded, prop up the branches. Put hardware cloth or aluminum foil around the bases of newly planted fruit trees to thwart rodents and rabbits. Move potted fig trees into the garage for the winter. If they're planted in the ground, wrap the branches together, dig a trench, carefully bend the tree into the trench, and cover with soil and straw.

Zone 3

Early in the month, sow quick-maturing cool-weather crops such as leaf lettuce, kale, turnip greens, radishes, and spinach. Continue feeding first sowings of these crops with manure or compost tea, and mulch to trap soil heat for continued growth. Keep protection devices such as cloches, cold frames, plastic, and old sheets handy for use in case of a light frost. Pinch tops of brussels sprouts to hasten maturity. Continue to treat brassicas with Bt (*Bacillus thuringiensis*) to control caterpillars. Cultivate, water deeply, and mulch to speed growth of August-planted peas. Keep warm-weather vegetables well watered so remaining fruits will mature before killing frost. Make sure to dig sweet potatoes well before the first frost. Replace spent vegetables with quick-growing cover crops such as rye-grass or winter wheat. Toward midmonth, harvest and cure the last of your winter squash and pumpkins, leaving at least 2 inches of stem on each one. Before the end of the month, dig and pot oregano, parsley, basil, thyme, rosemary, chives, and mint for the winter windowsill.

Early September is a good time to plant container-grown or balled-and-burlapped evergreen and decid-uous trees and shrubs. Keep new plantings well watered and staked to help them get established before winter sets in. By midmonth, divide perennials such as bearded irises, daylilies, and primroses. Late in the month is best time to divide peonies. Cover their buds with 2 inches of soil, then mulch. Take root cuttings of Oriental poppies. Keep roses watered as they produce their last blooms, but don't feed them until next spring. After the first frost dig tuberous begonias, cannas, glads, and dahlias. Cut off the tops, dry the roots in the sun for an afternoon, then cure in a cool, dry place for two more weeks. Prepare beds for spring-blooming flowers such as daffodils, lilies-of-the-valley, and crocuses, but hold off planting until late September and early October.

Pick pears when full size but green, wrap in newspaper and allow them to ripen in a cool room. Leave Seckel pears on the tree until golden. Rake up windfalls and fruit drops to reduce the spread of insects such as codling moths and diseases such as fire blight, brown rot, and apple scab. Prune old canes and thin new growth on brambles. Bag grape clus-ters early to protect them from birds and bees, or harvest as soon as they ripen. Late in the month as dor-mancy approaches, spread rock fer-tilizers under trees, vines, and canes. Do not apply nitrogen, since frost-susceptible growth may result.

Zone 4

Early this month, sow radishes, lettuce, spinach, and other greens in a cold frame for a prolonged harvest. Leave the sash open until chilly weather sets in. Divide and replant Egyptian onions; they'll pro-duce a forest of sprouts for salads later this fall. Plant garlic bulbs for a late spring crop. Tie leaves around cauliflower heads when they're about 4 inches across. Pinch grow-ing tips of tomatoes at midmonth; new fruit won't have time to achieve full size before frost. Mulch vacant beds or plant a cover crop of rye, using 2 pounds per 1,000 square feet. See that the garden receives 2 inches of moisture each week throughout the month.

Start or reseed lawns before the month's end. Keep the ground moist until grass seedlings are at least 2 inches tall, then mow it. Plant groundcovers like vinca and pachysandra on shady slopes and around shrubs. Plant new evergreens now, so they'll have time to establish new root systems before freezing weather arrives. If deciduous trees have an early leaf drop (usually caused by a dry summer), water them generously. Keep spent blossoms of dahlias and roses picked, and provide plenty of moisture for these and for chrysanthemums during the fall blooming period. Plant peonies after midmonth, adding generous amounts of bonemeal and aged compost to the bed beforehand. Divide and replant other spring- and summer-blooming perennials, such as lilies-of-the-valley, Shasta daisies, and phlox, if they're crowded or bloom has decreased. Lift the corms of glads when their leaves have yellowed. Hang them up for a few weeks before husking, then let them dry completely before storing in a cool place. To prepare tuberous begonias for being lifted, give them less water. Plant Madonna lilies and spring bulbs except tulips as they become available. Store tulip bulbs in a cool place until late October.

Water pecans generously while nuts fill out during the first half of the month. Remove corrugated cardboard collars from apple trunks and burn them to destroy codling moth cocoons that have accumulated during the summer. Harvest papaws when they drop from the trees and the skin has turned yellow-brown to brown. Pick up other fallen fruits, and provide extra water to all of this year's plantings. Apples will color better if not shaded by leaves; a little judicious pruning may be in order. Remove old or weak wood from blueberry plants. Encourage tip layering of black and purple raspberries and trailing blackberries by keeping the ground watered, weed-free, and friable. Arch canes downward and anchor them with soil or stones where needed.

Zone 5

At the beginning of September, set out transplants of cabbage, broccoli, brussels sprouts, and kohlrabi. Mulch to conserve moisture, and apply Bt (*Bacillus thuringiensis*) as needed to control cabbageworms. Direct-seed kale, collards, Chinese cabbage, bok choy, and turnips. All of these brassicas need regular watering if they are to grow well in hot weather. Water tomatoes and peppers regularly too, and pinch off blossoms that appear after midmonth. Continue to succession-plant lettuce, carrots, beets, and radishes. Shade newly seeded beds or cover them with burlap bags to keep them moist. After the seeds sprout, water thoroughly and regularly to promote rapid growth. As soon as new growth appears, dig and divide garlic, multiplier onions, and chives. Sow leeks, parsnips, salsify, and parsley, which will overwinter and mature next spring. When a bed becomes vacant, plant a cover crop of annual rye, but be sure to leave space in your winter garden for a late sowing of spinach.

Direct-seed hardy flowers like Oriental poppies, sweet Williams, cornflowers, chamomile, snapdragons, and daisies. If you grew bachelor's-buttons last spring, look for volunteer seedlings and move them to where you want them to bloom next May. Dig and divide crowded perennials. As you work in the beds, add peat moss if the soil is alkaline and lime if the soil is very acidic. Begin lifting caladiums, glads, and other summer bulbs. Allow the bulbs to dry thoroughly before storing.

When warm-season grasses like Bermuda and centipede begin to turn brown, mow them low and broadcast seed of annual or perennial rye if you want better winter color. In the northern part of the zone, fertilize fescue lawns, and reseed bare or weed-infested spots. Now is a good time to replace boxwoods and other shrubs killed last winter. If boxwoods are unavailable, consider the Japanese holly as a substitute in foundation plantings. When setting out small shrubs, water thoroughly and fertilize with a little cottonseed meal. Prune shrubs that were partially damaged last winter if you have not already done so. Trim hedges late in the month. Continue cleaning up the orchard, removing and burning mummified fruit and diseased limbs. Leave pruning the healthy branches for another time when the risk of fungal infections is not so high. Late in the month begin moving young strawberries to their permanent locations. Fertilize all strawberries with compost, rotted manure or cottonseed meal. In western areas, try growing strawberries in containers filled with an acidic growing medium. Stake branches of everbearing raspberries to keep the fruit off the ground. Mow beneath nut and persimmon trees to make harvesting easier. Late in the month, begin checking beneath trees for ripe pecans.

Zone 6

Cool weather means fewer insects and diseases. There are also fewer weeds, and crop quality is higher. Eggplants, tomatoes, peppers, and beans will yield well if they're regularly harvested. Leave bell peppers on a little longer to get a crop of beautiful red bells. Plant cool-weather crops such as carrots, snow peas, lettuce, turnips, mustard, and all other cole crops. Potatoes should be in by September 1. Seed or plant garlic, shallots, and short-day onions by the middle of the month. Beets, spinach, and chard should be seeded every two weeks. Harvest and cure sweet potatoes when the vines begin dying. Work herb beds and remove summer debris. Harvest flowering herbs when ready and hang them upside down to dry. Pinch basil for the last time early in the month.

The next two months are excellent for landscaping and establishing lawns. Dig and store gladiolus corms and caladium tubers when the foliage dies. Pinch dahlias, feed, and stake to support flower heads. Order spring bulbs now. Weed and cultivate flower beds to kill insect larvae. Daylilies, oxalises, irises, and Shasta daisies can be safely divided during September. Chrysanthemums will set buds soon; feed lightly with fish emulsion. Pull off dead flowers and damaged leaves from roses, and fertilize plants with compost or a solution of fish emulsion and liquid seaweed. Plant cool-weather annuals such as dianthus, snapdragons, daisies, phlox, gazanias, and annual chrysanthemums. By midmonth plant pansies and violas. Plan now for the location of new fruit or nut trees. Prepare the area and order the trees for late-winter delivery. Order strawberries now for planting next month.

Continue to remove weeds, fallen fruit, and diseased leaves from beneath fruit and nut trees. Keep nut trees watered. Fall webworms are easily controlled with Bt (*Bacillus thuringiensis*).

Zone 7

Throughout the zone, plant cool-weather crops such as turnips, cole crops, Asian greens, fennel, carrots, beets, spinach, leeks, shallots, and peas. Plant white potatoes for new potatoes by Christmas. Plant garlic cloves now just under the soil surface and mulch with compost. Sow seeds of sweet short-day onions. In areas likely to have frost-free winters, plant heat-tolerant pea varieties, and set out eggplants, peppers, and tomatoes. Plant the last okra, cucumbers, squash, and field peas. In the cooler parts of the zone, sow the last block of green beans for harvest in late November. Sow sweet peas, calendulas, dimorphothecas, and wildflowers like bird's-eyes and California poppies. Set out cool-weather bedding plants in masses for midwinter and early spring color. Divide perennials that have finished blooming. Disbud roses, camellias, dahlias, and chrysanthemums if specimen blooms are desired. Select container-grown shrubs and trees now for fall planting. The most vigorous growth in spring comes from fall transplants. Take the containers home and spot them about to see how they look before digging in the plants. Spring bulbs need special handling in this zone. Put newly purchased hyacinths and tulips in the refrigerator and plant in late November. Some gardeners successfully keep spring bulbs refrigerated until January. This chilling period will force blooms the first year, but the plants are very unlikely to reappear the following season. In southern parts of the zone, even daffodils are treated as annuals. September is superior to spring as a time to start new strawberry beds. Dig in the best compost available. When harvesting avocados, cut rather than pull the fruit from the trees to avoid bruises that will rot in storage. Out west, dry raisins and prunes this month.

IN GOOD HEALTH

HAVE A LEAN BEAN SEPTEMBER

Men, set sail in September for weight loss. The tide is flowing and the wind is at your back. That's not poetry, but statistics, says Maria Simonson, Ph.D., D.Sc. As "captain" of the famed Health, Weight, and Stress Clinic, Johns Hopkins Medical Institutions-St. Luke Health Center, she's got it all in her log. "In the fall, men lose a higher percentage of body weight, and that loss is very consistent compared with other times of the year," she says.

Why? For one thing, come fall many men quit eating at irregular hours and settle into more of a routine, her records show. More speculative is Dr. Simonson's sartorial theory of weight loss: Men, she thinks, feel that having to stuff themselves into a winter suit makes them look sloppy. Women, on the other hand, may feel they can hide their bulges in layered clothing. Their best weight-loss season is spring—just before summer's more revealing attire appears. But we're talking psychology here—not biology. Any time is the right time for men *and* women to trim down—just fill your sails with motivation and get moving with a diet plan that includes beans!

You heard it right, beans are great ammunition in "fat combat." Any well-designed weight loss battle plan should ambush empty calories before they reach your plate, should join ranks with the low-fat and high-fiber platoon, and should call in the real ammunition—tasty foods you'd want to eat whether you're on a diet or not. Your low-fat, high-fiber "diet" foods should taste good enough to eat year-round, not just during your annual fall fat combat. And the one common item that fills the bill for great taste, high fiber, and low fat is the lowly bean. Fact is, the humble, oft-ignored bean may just be the perfect "diet" food.

Beans are classified as legumes, the dried seeds of pods. A cup of the most common varieties weighs in around 225 to 250 calories. And it's what you get for those calories that makes beans such a lean choice. After all, it's not just calories that count in a weight-loss program. What also counts is cutting fat, because dietary fat readily adds fat to your frame; boosting fiber, which fills you up, not out; and focusing on foods that pack maximum nutrition into every calorie. What foods fit that bill? Complex carbohydrates —foods like whole grains, fresh fruits and vegetables, and beans.

Yes, beans. Although beans have been a dietary staple since ancient times, they've never really gotten the respect they deserve. In fact, they are an excellent source of complex carbohydrates, as well as being low in fat and high in fiber. What's more, with a rich, meaty flavor, they can easily muscle aside the fat-heavy meat on your plate. And because they contain amino acids (which combine with other amino acids in rice, grains, or pasta to form complete proteins), your body won't miss the meat protein.

Best of all, beans are about as nutrient-dense a food as you're likely to find. They boast healthy doses of nerve-soothing B vitamins, anemia-fighting iron, and bone-building calcium and phosphorus—nutrients that fall short on many dieter's menus. Some varieties also have magnesium, manganese, and potassium.

Beans are good for the heart, too. Low in sodium and rich in potassium, they offer the ideal nutritional combination for anyone with high blood pressure. Also, legumes are powerhouses of soluble, as well as insoluble, fiber. Soluble fiber helps lower blood cholesterol levels. Add to that the fact that beans have no cholesterol and just a trace of fat, and you can see why legumes are not only ideal for weight loss—they're the perfect food for a healthy heart!

So what's the bottom line? According to Sonja L. Connor, registered dietitian and research assistant professor of clinical nutrition at Oregon Health Sciences University, most of us would do well to gradually increase our consumption to three to five cups a week. To make room, trim your diet of fatty meats and empty-calorie foods. You'll be glad you did. After all, any food with a nutritional profile like this can't help but improve your own profile.

With a little imagination, you'll find lots of ways to change your normal fare to one that favors beans. Consider a puree of cooked, seasoned beans as a spread or dip for vegetables. How about substituting chopped, cooked beans for the meat in lasagna? To get you started in a lean-bean style of eating, we've provided a simple recipe for a hearty bean gumbo.

Mixed-Bean Gumbo

Serve this hearty gumbo for dinner on the first cool evening of fall. It weighs in at only 230 calories per serving, 2.4 grams of fat (only 9 percent of total calories as fat), 5.9 grams of dietary fiber, 12 grams of protein, 259 milligrams of sodium, and no cholesterol.

⅓ cup whole wheat pastry flour
⅔ cup stock
3 cups boiling stock
1 green pepper, finely chopped
1 stalk celery, finely chopped
1 onion, finely chopped
1 14½ oz. can tomatoes, chopped
1½ teaspoons minced dried mushrooms
2 cloves garlic, minced
2 bay leaves
1 teaspoon dried thyme
2 cups cooked mixed beans (any combination, such as pinto, navy, and kidney)
½ teaspoon hot-pepper sauce (or to taste)

Place flour in a no-stick frying pan. Cook over medium-high heat, stirring constantly, to roast flour. Continue stirring until flour is medium brown, about 7 minutes. Remove the pan from the heat, and pour in ⅔ cup stock. Whisk until smooth. Transfer flour mixture to a large soup pot. Add boiling stock, peppers, celery, onions, tomatoes, mushrooms, garlic, bay leaves, and thyme. Bring to a boil, then reduce the heat to a simmer. Cover loosely and simmer for 15 minutes. Add beans and hot-pepper sauce. Continue to simmer until vegetables are tender, about 15 minutes. Serve hot.

4 servings

Prepping Beans for Easy Digestion

Beans have a bad reputation for producing gas. The problem is they contain certain water-soluble starches that the body cannot break down during digestion. But the key here is "water-soluble." By repeatedly soaking the beans in water (and discarding the runoff), much of the problem can be eliminated. Here's how:

☛ Start with a pound (2 cups) of dried beans. Discard any that are broken or discolored. Rinse until the water runs clear.

☛ Place the beans in a large soup pot with 6 cups of cold water. Boil for 2 minutes.

☛ Drain the water, and replace it with fresh. Let stand overnight or for at least 6 hours.

☛ Drain well. Add fresh water. Bring to a boil, then simmer, loosely covered, until the legumes are tender (start checking lentils after 30 minutes; others will take up to 2 hours).

☛ To save time, prepare beans on any day that's convenient and store them in the refrigerator or freezer until you need them. Beans prepared as described here will keep for a week in the refrigerator or 6 months in the freezer. Don't freeze lentils, however; they turn mushy.

Walking Tip for September

If you develop chronic heel pain during your walking program, you should be aware that recent research indicates that these pains are *not* caused by the calcium deposits called "bone spurs." According to Charles Graham, M.D., of the University of Texas Health Science Center at Dallas, the most common cause of heel pain is one or more tiny stress fractures. Since bone spurs don't usually cause the pain, they don't need to be surgically removed. Treatment for the pain-causing stress fractures of the heel is simple and inexpensive: a walking program, stretching exercises, and a heel pad in your shoe. If your doctor suggests your heel pain requires surgery get a second opinion.

AT HOME

SEPTEMBER IS WATER QUALITY MONTH

In 1986 the Environmental Protection Agency (EPA) reported that 2 percent of the municipal water in this country posed a serious health risk to the people drinking it. And 25 percent of municipal systems violated the agency's regulations for maintaining safe and healthy drinking water. Some environmental groups claim the problem is even worse than the EPA reports. As of 1987, the EPA had established standards for only 30 of the 83 pollutants required to be monitored by the 1986 Amendments to the Safe Drinking Water Act.

If municipal water system customers must be concerned about water purity, do home well-water users have any reason to feel safe? Certainly not. Well water often contains bacteria and chemicals caused by soil pollution or by improper installation of the well (such as not casing the well shaft properly). The site of soil contamination that infiltrates a home well system may not even be located on the homeowner's property. Water can travel great distances through soil and through rock fizzures, and the leaky underground gas tank ¼ mile from your house may suddenly become *your* water problem.

Because most states have only recently become sensitive to the need to protect groundwater as a precious and irreplaceable resource, the disposal of toxic substances has historically been a casual and unregulated affair of little interest to anyone. The implementation of the EPA Superfund and the well-publicized cleanup of many notorious toxic dumps should give no homeowner cause for relief. The EPA is a federal agency and is *not* responsible for maintaining the safety of home well-water supplies. Its mandate is to protect the streams, rivers, and watersheds of the nation. Protection of the groundwater supplies is entirely the responsibility of the individual states, and if you suspect you've got a well-contamination problem, you'll be looking to your own state environmental resources protection agency for help.

Bacterial contamination of a well may cause no detectable odor or change in appearance; the same is true of chemicals. Some chemical carcinogens are known to be toxic in extremely low concentrations—concentrations that give no warning odor to the water. If you own a home well, you should have your water tested twice a year because no one is looking out for your safety but you. If you're planning to buy a home with an on-site well, you should ask for a complete test of the well water as part of the agreement of sale; your agreement of sale should give you the option to walk away from the sale with no penalty if the well water tests show unsatisfactory readings either in bacteria content or in chemical contaminants.

"YOU'LL NEVER MISS THE WATER"

Testing Your Water

If your water comes from a municipal water system with more than 15 year-round hookups, the supplier is required to test it monthly for bacterial contamination and quarterly or yearly for selected organic and inorganic substances. You should be able to obtain the test results from the supplier.

To keep bacteria in check, most municipal systems add chlorine to the water, but high water concentrations of chlorine can form new, possibly carcinogenic contaminants called trihalomethanes (THMs). To find out what's in your municipal

water, ask your local water supplier for the results of government-required tests for bacteria and other contaminants. If your municipal system doesn't test for THMs or excess chlorine, you may choose to send a sample of the water to an independent testing lab.

If you've never had your water tested before, your first step is to contact your state department of environmental protection to obtain a list of certified labs in your area. It's best to stick with an independent lab not affiliated with a company that sells water treatment equipment or water treatment chemicals. Selecting a lab associated with a water treatment company guarantees that you'll get a sales pitch with your water test results, and you certainly may have reason to doubt the truth of any result that calls for you to make a purchase. You want an unbiased scientific opinion about your water, not a sales pitch.

After you contact a water testing lab, you can expect the lab to send you a test kit, with explicit instructions and containers for sending water samples to them. Follow the instructions carefully, because a poorly drawn or stored sample can invalidate the test results. Once you've dropped off or mailed in your samples, you can assume that, for most kinds of tests, it will take a few days to two weeks on the average to get results back from the lab.

The basic water test provided by most labs usually includes testing for about ten common elements and characteristics: chloride, copper, fluoride, iron, manganese, nitrate, sodium, coliform bacteria, hardness, and pH (how acidic or alkaline). However, you can also get more extensive tests that cover a whole host of possible pollutants—elements from arsenic to zinc, organic chemicals found in herbicides and pesticides, even radon gas. Since quality control in some testing labs may be poor (and you have no way of judging this), you may wish to have your water analyzed by two separate labs in order to compare the results. And if a serious problem is discovered, you should show the results to others in your neighborhood because they may have the same problem.

Deciphering Water Test Results

The results of your water test will probably look something like those in the table "Water Test Results."

The left-hand column contains those elements and characteristics that were analyzed. These items are the most common and the easiest to measure and the ones often included in a basic water analysis. Of course, you can request that your water be tested for many other contaminants.

Water Test Results

Element or Characteristic	MCL*	Your Water
Ions		
Chloride	250.0	35.1
Copper	1.000	3.503†
Fluoride	2.40	<0.50
Iron	0.300	<0.100
Manganese	0.050	0.028
Nitrate	10.00	12.00†
Sodium	none	15
Other Characteristics		
Coliform	1	3†
Hardness	250.0	327†
pH	8.5	7.3

*Maximum Contaminant Level.
†These items exceed the MCL standards for safe drinking water.

MCL, in the center column, stands for Maximum Contaminant Level. MCLs are the standards the Environmental Protection Agency has established for safe drinking water. If there has been no MCL established for an element, the column contains the word, *none;* such is the case for sodium in the table here. Primary contaminants are those that pose a health risk; secondary contaminants, on the other hand, while not dangerous, affect the aesthetic qualities of water—its color, taste, or smell. The FDA establishes MCLs for both primary and secondary contaminants, but it only enforces regulation of municipal water systems at the level of primary contaminants. The MCLs for secondary contaminants are intended as guidelines for state-established water standards.

The third column shows the results of all the tests on a single water sample. All results in the table here are in milligrams per liter, except for pH and coliform counts. The symbol < means "less than." Items with an asterisk following them exceed the MCL standards for safe drinking water. Steps should be taken to reduce the level of those items.

Here's a quick run-down of what levels greater than the MCL of each of these elements and characteristics on the table can mean to you:

☞ Chloride—A secondary contaminant. High levels can speed corrosion of pipes and heating equipment. High chloride levels are usually accompanied by high sodium levels, which can be a health concern to people who must limit sodium intake.

☞ Copper—A primary contaminant. High levels can result in gastrointestinal disturbances and other acute toxic effects. At levels greater than 1 milligram per liter, copper can stain laundry and plumbing and give a blue-green tint to blonde hair.

☞ Fluoride—A primary contaminant. At an optimum level of 1 milligram per liter, fluoride has been shown to be effective in reducing tooth decay. At levels over 2.4 it may cause mottling of teeth in those living in a temperate climate. Warmer areas have lower MCLs for fluoride based on increased water consumption.

☞ Iron—A secondary contaminant. High levels of iron in drinking water is a very common problem, and although at this time there is no known health risk from drinking elevated levels in water, too much iron can be a nuisance because it gives a rust-colored tint to laundry and plumbing fixtures.

☞ Manganese—A secondary contaminant. High levels can create brown stains on laundry and plumbing fixtures and higher levels may leave black deposits and produce an unpleasant odor and taste in water.

☞ Nitrate—A primary contaminant. High levels are particularly dangerous to infants and can cause blue baby syndrome, brain damage, and death.

☞ Sodium—A primary contaminant. A guidance level of 20 milligrams per liter is suggested by the EPA for those who have high blood pressure or heart conditions. No safe level has been set for the general population.

☞ Coliform bacteria—A primary contaminant. High levels of coliform bacteria usually indicate the presence of organisms that cause infectious diseases like pink eye, giardiasis, salmonellosis, intestinal flu, and Legionnaire's disease.

☞ pH—A secondary contaminant. pH is a measurement of the acidity of water. The lower the pH, the more acid the water. Water with a pH even slightly below 7.0 combined with a low level of hardness is corrosive to plumbing and can cause some toxic metals like lead and copper to leach into the water. High pH, by itself, is not necessarily a problem, although the cause for the high pH may be a health concern.

☞ Hardness—A secondary contaminant. Hardness is usually caused by calcium and manganese ions in water. These ions combine with soap to form a scum in water, which causes bathtub rings. More soap is needed to create a lather. Many people who have hard water prefer to use synthetic detergents in place of soaps because they aren't as affected by the calcium and manganese in the water.

Home Water Treatment

Your lab test results and the explanation and advice that will accompany them may include a recommendation that you install a home water treatment system. If you've taken care to have your test run by an independent laboratory, not affiliated with the sale of water treatment equipment, you may choose to act on that advice, or you may choose to have the test run once more by a different lab to see whether or not the results are the same. If you choose to purchase water treatment equipment, the type of treatment system you choose will vary with the type of problem you are trying to correct.

Activated carbon filter: This is the most common type of home water treament system and the one that most people think of when a home water filter is mentioned. Usually it's located right at the kitchen sink, underneath or on the counter. An activated carbon filter can filter out a host of solids and gases by trapping substances in the water as it passes through the porous carbon inside the unit. Such filters are most often used for removing disagreeable odor and taste, chloroform, chlorine, and some organic chemicals like trihalomethanes (THMs) and polychlorinated and polybrominated biphenyls (PCBs and PBBs, respectively). Carbon will also reduce, but not usually eliminate, the concentrations of heavy metals like cadmium. It won't, however, eliminate bacteria, asbestos fibers, fluoride, nitrates, or other salts.

Independent tests of several types of activated carbon units show that larger units in general do a better job and need less frequent maintenance than smaller models, although all need regular carbon replacement and backflushing of impurities that build up inside the unit. Test data also indicates that filters containing solid blocks of carbon are more effective than those using carbon granules. Filters also last longer on those systems that have a bypass valve that allows you to use unfiltered water for washing dishes. Because some studies have found that the effectiveness of most filters dropped significantly after 75 percent of the manufacturer's suggested lifetime, it's advisable to replace the filter more often than the product manual recommends.

Reverse osmosis filters: Reverse osmosis works by forcing water through a semipermeable membrane. Water can pass through but impurities cannot. It eliminates many contaminants including arsenic, asbestos, calcium, chloride, copper, fluoride, manganese, nitrates, silica, sodium, sulfates, volatile organic compounds like benzene and carbon tetrachloride,

detergents, and organic matter. It will not, however, remove some small-molecule chemical contaminants like chloroform and phenol.

Many consider reverse osmosis to be the best all-around home water treatment method; this is especially true for those units that combine reverse osmosis with activated carbon filtration (which removes chloroform and phenols and takes care of taste and odor problems). Reverse osmosis is a simple process, and the units using this method usually require no electricity or other form of energy to operate. Regular home water pressure is sufficient to force the water first through a sediment filter, which removes large suspended matter, and then through several layers of membranes that successively remove more and more impurities. Units come in sizes ranging from an under-the-counter unit for kitchen use only, to a whole-house system.

Reverse osmosis units are generally more expensive than simple activated carbon filter units, and maintenance is more involved because there are usually at least two and sometimes three elements to replace: a sediment filter, the semipermeable membranes, and an activated carbon filter (for those units that utilize both filtration systems). If your water pressure fluctuates or is not high enough to operate an osmosis system, you may need to install a pump to make the system work.

Home distillation: During the distillation process, water is heated until it turns to steam. The steam travels to a condensing chamber, leaving behind most chemicals, minerals, bacteria, viruses, and other contaminants that do not vaporize. In the condensing chamber, the water cools back to its liquid state and re-enters the house water supply. This filtering system, if cleaned periodically to remove sediment and scale, is quite effective in purifying water. Actually, it may make water too pure for some people, leaving it without even minimum amounts of healthy, essential minerals that also give water its taste. Distilled water, though quite pure, is, to many palates, flat and tasteless.

Ultraviolet disinfection: If your only water problem is elevated levels of coliform bacteria, you may want to purchase a system that utilizes ultraviolet light to kill bacteria. A home setup is simple: One or more germicidal ultraviolet lamps are sealed inside a narrow steel cylinder through which water flows. A detector constantly monitors the UV dosage.

But there are some drawbacks. The unit is pretty expensive. It uses a fair amount of electricity to keep it going. Many units require fre-

quent maintenance. And some spores and viruses aren't killed by ultraviolet light. Moreover, UV units are less effective in cloudy or dirty water, making it necessary to pass the water through a sediment filter before it enters the UV cylinder. There are some other considerations, too, that a water treatment specialist will want to discuss with you before you opt for such a system.

Water softeners: These don't purify water; they merely exchange sodium ions for the calcium and magnesium ions that give water its "hardness." If you have high blood pressure or a heart condition, drinking more sodium with your water is not such a good idea. You're better off installing the softener in such a way that it only softens the hard water that you wash clothes with, not the kitchen and bath water that you drink or use in cooking.

Food Firsts

As you trundle into your kitchen laden with brown bags full of canned and frozen food, fresh produce, and some other convenience from the grocery store (maybe a microwavable casserole), remember the generations of cooks who not only made everything from scratch, but also grew or raised the ingredients. And those cooks who didn't raise their own staples still went to several different vendors (the butcher, the baker, the candlestick maker) to provision their kitchens. A glance at these amusing food history dates shows how we got where we are today—junk food and all!

☞ 1742—The first American cookbook—*The Compleat Housewife,* by Eliza Smith—was published in Williamsburg, Virginia.

☞ 1853—Potato chips were introduced by George Crum, the chef at the Moon Lake House Hotel in Saratoga, New York. He called them Saratoga Chips. People probably enjoyed them with absolutely no guilt back then.

☞ 1879—The first milk bottle was used by Echo Farms Dairy of New York. And generations of Americans thereafter listened for the clink of the milkman as a wake-up call.

☞ 1887—Coca-Cola was first sold as a syrup to flavor carbonated water, by Dr. John S. Pemberton. The Coca-Cola trademark was registered in 1893.

☞ 1893—The first packaged breakfast cereal was sold by Henry D. Perky of Denver, Colorado.

☞ 1904—The first ice cream cone was made by a waffle vendor at the St. Louis World's Fair. The story has it that he rolled a warm waffle into a cone so that his neighboring vendor, who sold ice cream, could fill it.

☞ 1912—The first self-service supermarkets opened their doors for business. Two got their start that same year: Alpha Beta Food Market in Pomona, California, and Ward's Grocetaria in Ocean Park, California. The first major supermarket chain, Piggly Wiggly, got started a bit later, but boasted more than 2,000 stores across the country by 1923. It was started in Memphis, Tennessee, by Clarence Saunders.

☞ 1930—Clarence Birdseye sold the first packaged frozen food. It was marketed in ten grocery stores in Springfield, Massachussetts. In 1939 Mr. Birdseye began to sell the first precooked frozen foods. Chicken fricassee and steak were soon followed by a variety of entrées.

YOUR SEPTEMBER SHOPPER'S TIP

Best buys in produce this month include beets, cabbage, cauliflower, corn, pears, summer squash, and tomatoes. This quick cauliflower dish is a nifty way to use both your first garden cauliflower and the end of your tomato crop. In place of the cup of tomato juice called for in this recipe, you may substitute two or three large, peeled fresh tomatoes that have been pureed in a food processor.

Rosy Cauliflower with Onions

2 large white onions, cut into ⅛-inch slices
3 tablespoons vegetable oil
1 tablespoon mild honey
1 large head cauliflower, broken into florets
1 cup tomato juice
1 tablespoon chopped fresh parsley

In a large skillet sauté onions in oil until tender. Add honey and cook until lightly browned, about 3 minutes. Stir in cauliflower and tomato juice, cover, and cook over medium heat until cauliflower is crisp yet tender. Sprinkle with parsley just before serving.

6 servings

YOUR HOME MAINTENANCE CHECKLIST

☞ Cover or remove room unit air conditioners for the season.

☞ Seal off a whole-house fan with an airtight cover and insulate for the heating season.

☞ Clean and store the barbecue grill and outdoor furniture.

☞ Prepare storm windows for fall installation by checking and cleaning blocked ventilation holes; clean the glass with a squeegee and a solution of ammonia and water.

☞ Install clean furnace filters to be ready for the first cool night.

EVENTS AND FESTIVALS

Annual Scottish Gathering and Games
Santa Rosa, California

Early September. There are plenty of kilts and pipers at this festival, which is the largest clan gathering outside Scotland. Since 1865, expatriate Scots and those of Scottish ancestry have celebrated at Santa Rosa with Scots foods and athletic events. Work up an appetite in the caber toss and stone put; then enjoy traditional Scottish dishes such as haggis and oat cakes. Take a fling with the highland dancers, or thrill to the sound of the pipes at special bagpiping concerts. Information: Caledonian Club of San Francisco, 64 Washington Street, Novato, CA 94947.

Bumbershoot,
the Seattle Arts Festival
Seattle, Washington

Labor Day weekend. Cultural diversity and artistic excellence describe this spectacular arts festival featuring international, national, and regional artists in over 500 performances in music, theater, comedy, film, visual arts, literary art, performance art, and children's entertainment. Offering their best fare for festival-goers are over 35 of Seattle's outstanding restaurants. All events are held at the Seattle Center, site of the 1962 World's Fair. Information: One Reel, P.O. Box 9750, Seattle, WA 98109-0750.

Valparaiso Popcorn Festival
Valparaiso, Indiana

First Saturday after Labor Day. The aroma of popcorn fills the air of Valparaiso as the town celebrates one of America's most popular and nutritious snacks. Presiding over the festival is Popcorn King and Indiana native Orville Redenbacher. The Popcorn Panic 5-mile run is an energetic start for the festival, and the momentum builds with the Popcorn Festival Parade, the Mighty Popcorn Festival Drama Guild performing at the Valparaiso Opera House, and the Popcorn Bowl football game. Information: Valparaiso Popcorn Festival, 1 East Jefferson Street, P.O. Box 189, Valparaiso, IN 46384-0189.

International Camel Races
Virginia City, Nevada

First weekend after Labor Day. The ships of the desert quickly become racetrack pros when dromedary camels shipped in directly from California do the 100-yard dash around a sandy track. The camel races, which commemorate the mid-1800s use of camels for mining tasks, are just like traditional horse races, complete with saddles, jockeys, and corporate or private sponsors. The camels run heats in groups of three or four with the championship race taking place late Saturday. If you fancy feathers more than fur, catch the ostrich races in which the swift-footed birds pull chariot-like carts and drivers. Information: Virginia City Chamber of Commerce, Box 464, Virginia City, NV 89440.

Annual Bald Is Beautiful
Convention
Morehead City, North Carolina

Second weekend in September. "Morehead" but less hair is the theme of this convention. It is sponsored by the Bald Headed Men of America, a bald-is-beautiful self-help group, and all activities at this convention are for the enjoyment of men who are losing or have lost their hair and for the women who find the "topless" man attractive. Convention contests include competition for the most kissable bald head, the smoothest bald head, the smallest bald spot, and the best solardome (the best suntan on a smooth noggin). Information: Bald Headed Men of America, 3819 Bridges Street, Morehead City, NC 28557.

King Turkey Day Celebration
Worthington, Minnesota

Second Saturday after Labor Day. Since 1948, Worthington, Minnesota, and Cuero, Texas, have been feuding over which town is the turkey capital of the world. Two turkey races, one held each September in Worthington and one each October in Cuero, settle the dispute by pitting one town's turkey against the other. The times from both races are combined, and the turkey with the best overall time is the winner. Each year, "Paycheck" tries to bring home the trophy for Worthington and "Ruby Begonia" pulls out all the gobbles for Cuero. Political speakers preside over the two-block-long racecourse and also serve as referees, and turkeys are penalized for going off course or for needing human assistance to stay on the track. The festival includes a 24-hour polka marathon, a free pancake breakfast on the day of the race, turkey dinners, performances by the Turkey Trotters dance troupe, and a parade featuring 250 marching turkeys and the two star turkeys, "Paycheck" and "Ruby Begonia." Information: King Turkey Day, Inc., Box 608, Worthington, MN 56187.

World Mud Bowl
North Conway, New Hampshire

Mid-September. Men become boys once again during this world championship mud football bowl played on a field filled with 50 truckloads of loam and a few thousand gallons of water. The festivities begin with a pep rally, bonfire, and cheerleading contest on Friday evening. On Saturday, Miss World Mud Bowl is crowned, the Tournament of Mud Parade is held, and the playoffs begin. On Sunday, thousands of fans pack Hog Coliseum to cheer for their team during the championship game. An awards party is held on Sunday evening, and all proceeds benefit local charities. Information: David Cianciolo, World Mud Bowl, Box 360, North Conway, NH 03860.

International
Banana Festival
Fulton, Kentucky
and South Fulton, Tennessee

Late September. Despite the fact that there isn't a single banana tree in Fulton or South Fulton, bananas still played a major role in the economic fortunes of these twin cities until the early 1960s. Until that time, 70 percent of all bananas shipped to the United States rode the Central Gulf Railroad Line through Fulton and South Fulton. The International Banana Festival began in 1962 as a celebration of this fruity link between South America and the United States. The festival "goes bananas" with a banana bake-off, banana-rama street dances, banana bowl football, banana academic bowl, a banana parade, banana-inspired entertainment, and the world's largest banana pudding—1 ton of the creamy stuff made with 3,000 pounds of bananas, 250 pounds of vanilla wafers, and 950 pounds of pie filling, to serve 10,000 people. Information: International Banana Festival, P.O. Box 428, Fulton, KY 42041-0428.

OCTOBER

OCTOBER IS THE MONTH
FOR PAINTED LEAVES....
AS FRUITS AND LEAVES
AND THE DAY ITSELF
ACQUIRE A BRIGHT TINT
JUST BEFORE THEY FALL,
SO THE YEAR NEAR ITS SETTING.
OCTOBER IS ITS SUNSET SKY....

*Henry David
Thoreau*

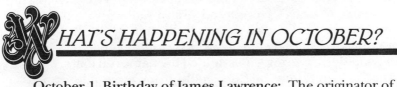

WHAT'S HAPPENING IN OCTOBER?

October 1, Birthday of James Lawrence: The originator of one of the most famous phrases in naval history, Lawrence was the captain of the U.S. frigate *Chesapeake* during the War of 1812. The British, who had blockaded almost the entire eastern seaboard by the end of 1813, challenged Lawrence to bring his ship out of the Boston harbor for a duel at sea with British Captain Broke of H.M.S. *Shannon*. Lawrence, ever glad for the chance to display his mettle and ignoring the fact that the *Chesapeake* crew was both inexperienced and mutinous, sailed out to be soundly thrashed by the British. As the ship faced certain capture and Lawrence lay mortally wounded, he enjoined his men, "Don't give up the ship."

October 5, Birthday of Robert Goddard: This irrepressible Massachusetts physics professor, who died almost 24 years before the launching of Apollo 11, was the father of modern rocketry. Backed by the Smithsonian Institution, on March 16, 1926, Goddard launched the first liquid propellant rocket (liquid oxygen and gasoline) from a farm near Auburn, Massachusetts. It only reached an altitude of 41 feet and landed 184 feet away from its launch site, but the feat was as significant to rocketry as the Kitty Hawk flight was to aviation. Three years later and after a number of spectacular and noisy rocket firings, the neighbors, the local police, and the fire department all suggested that Goddard find a more remote place to carry on his explosive hobbies. Goddard later moved his entire rocketry operation to a desert site in New Mexico.

October 8, Anniversary of the Great Chicago Fire: On this day in 1871, Mrs. O'Leary's cow kicked over a lantern in her barn on DeKoven Street, and Chicago was never the same again. Two-thirds of the buildings in Chicago were of wood, the summer had been unusually dry, and fierce veering winds fanned the flames on that calamitous day. The fire raged along the Chicago River and eventually leaped the river to burn out of control on both sides. It destroyed 17,450 buildings and left almost 100,000 people homeless, but miraculously killed only 250 people. Thousands of people fleeing the flames and firebrands rushed to Lake Michigan, and in some cases, were forced into the lake to escape the flames. Robbery, looting, extortion, orgies, and crime added to the general horror of the catastrophe. After burning out of control for almost 27 hours, the fire was finally stopped with the aid of explosives to make a firebreak, and a sudden but propitious rainfall.

October 8, Sergeant York Day: On this day in 1918, Sergeant

Alvin York, one of the greatest American military heroes of all time, performed the legendary deed for which he won the Congressional Medal of Honor and the Croix de Guerre. As an army corporal in the World War I Argonne-Meuse offensive in France, he led the seven remaining members of his decimated platoon on a charge of a German machine gun nest. Miraculously dodging a storm of machine gun fire, York almost single-handedly killed 25 German soldiers, captured another 135, and took 35 machine guns. Ironically, York, a deeply religious, fundamentalist Christian from the backwoods of Tennessee, had joined the army reluctantly because he had been twice denied the status of conscientious objector. In 1941 Warner Brothers released a popular film based on his life, starring Gary Cooper as the sergeant.

October 28, Birthday of the Statue of Liberty: On this day in 1886, the Statue of Liberty was officially dedicated by President Grover Cleveland. The idea of this colossal statue as a symbol of the friendship between the United States and France was first proposed by a French historian, Edouard de Laboulaye, just after the end of the American Civil War. The cost of the statue itself (about $250,000) was donated by France, while funds for the granite and concrete pedestal were raised by the United States. In January, 1984, a 30-month-long restoration project, which included riveting patches on her worn copper skin, completely replacing her torch, and replacing her interior support structure, was begun. Holding her new torch, the refurbished Lady Liberty greeted her admirers in a spectacular public celebration on the Fourth of July, 1986.

October 31, Halloween: Our modern-day celebration of Halloween is a continuation of the ancient Celtic holiday, All Hallows' Eve. When the early Christian Church spread to Ireland through the efforts of the legendary St. Patrick, it met there the Celts, who practiced an elaborate pagan religion. For the Celts, the year ended on Old Year's Night, a night at the end of the harvest season when the Celts believed that witches and spirits of the dead moved among men. In an effort to counteract the pagan observances of Old Year's Night, the early Church named the first day following Old Year's Night, All Hallows' Day (now called All Saints Day), and set aside this day to honor all Christian saints. The Celts converted to Christianity, but retained their fondness for the witch and ghost rituals of Old Year's Night. They simply changed the name of their pagan observances to All Hallows' Eve, which time and usage have contracted to Halloween.

October Is International Microwave Month

Cooks new to microwaving sometimes find the timing confusing. If you are one of these, the tips that folllow will help put you on the right track.

☞ Cooking times in recipes will guide you, but results will vary depending on the size, shape, and wattage of the microwave oven you're using. So when a time range is given, start checking for doneness with the shortest time given.

☞ At peak electric load times (dinnertime is one) your microwave may put out less power than usual. This is called a voltage drop and can also happen if a microwave is plugged into the same circuit as another large appliance in use, like

a refrigerator. Also, make sure your microwave is plugged into an outlet in accordance with manufacturer's instructions.

☞ Cold food will take longer to microwave than room temperature food.

☞ Microwaving in a dish that's too large for the amount of food will increase the cooking time.

☞ Loose covers like crumpled waxed paper and paper towels will increase cooking time. Tight covers, like vented plastic wrap or a snug lid, will cut cooking time.

☞ Cooking times for a given recipe will vary according to the wattage of your unit. A microwave recipe should give the wattage of the unit needed to cook the recipe in the given time. For example: A recipe may state that you are to cook a casserole on a medium setting in a

Microwave Cooking Time Chart

Watts	Cooking Time (in min./sec.)									
700	1:00	2:00	3:00	4:00	5:00	6:00	7:00	8:00	9:00	10:00
650	1:11	2:22	3:33	4:44	5:55	7:06	8:17	9:28	10:39	11:50
600	1:14	2:28	3:42	4:56	6:10	7:24	8:38	9:52	11:06	12:20
550	1:17	2:34	3:51	5:08	6:25	7:42	8:59	10:16	11:33	12:50
500	1:20	2:40	4:00	5:20	6:40	8:00	9:20	10:40	12:00	13:20

SOURCE: Reprinted from *Healthy Microwave Cooking* © 1988 by Judith Benn Hurley. Permission granted by Rodale Press, Inc.

700-watt microwave for 5 minutes. If your microwave wattage is 500 instead of 700 watts, you will need to adjust the cooking time according to the chart on the opposite page.

Microwave cooking tips reprinted from Healthy Microwave Cooking © 1988 by Judith Benn Hurley. *Permission granted by Rodale Press, Inc.*

IN THE GARDEN

THE ARRIVAL OF THE GREAT PUMPKIN

October is pumpkin month for everyone, even the cartoon characters in the "Peanuts" comic strip, who traditionally anticipate Halloween as the arrival date of the "Great Pumpkin." Cartoonist Charles Schulz uses the Great Pumpkin to play on our common fascination with anything colossal. Giant vegetables even have a special place in children's literature, as shown in the stories "Cinderella" and "Jack and the Beanstalk," or the nursery rhyme "Peter, Peter Pumpkin Eater," in which Peter keeps his wife in a pumpkin shell. This month you'll undoubtedly come across a story or two in your local newspaper that deals with a giant pumpkin of local renown—maybe even a pumpkin that makes it to the World Pumpkin Confederation Weigh-Offs, a national competition for pumpkin growers.

Pumpkin Power

If you enjoy giant pumpkin stories and wonder whether you could grow your own giant pumpkin next year, here's how you can grow one stupendous enough for Cinderella to ride in to the ball:

☞ Establish your pumpkin patch in a high, well-drained area of your garden. To give your pumpkin the longest possible growing season, avoid any spot susceptible to late spring or early fall frosts.

☞ In the spring, double dig your pumpkin patch and add plenty of compost to a depth of 12 inches.

☞ Space the pumpkin plants at least 20 feet apart and allow at least 100 square feet of area for each plant.

☞ Select a seed variety that's guaranteed to give large-sized fruit. Variety names to choose from include 'Big Max', 'Atlantic Giant', and 'Big Moon'.

☞ Give your pumpkin plants a real head start by starting seeds indoors in large containers. You should be putting six-week-old plants into the ground when you first set your plants out.

☞ Cover the pumpkin patch with a weed-free organic mulch or black plastic mulch to keep weed competition to a minimum.

☞ Cover the young plants with a hot cap or row cover if there is any danger of late-season frost.

☞ Pick all female flowers until the vine is 8 feet long. Female flowers are those with stem-end swellings resembling miniature fruit. Picking female flowers encourages vine growth needed to support and feed a giant fruit.

☞ Select one female flower on each of the plant's two main vines to bear your giant pumpkin.

☞ At least three times a week, examine the vine and pick off all other newly emerging female flowers.

☞ Feed the plant manure tea or other liquid fertilizer every ten days during late August and September. After the fruit reaches basketball size, water the vine deeply at least once a week.

☞ Don't prune the vine and don't remove any leaves except dead ones. Leaves are food producers, and each leaf can support about 4 pounds of fruit.

☞ To be sure your fruit is shapely and round, roll the fruit a quarter of a turn every week to ten days. You can only do this while the vine is green and pliable. When the stem begins to toughen, you'll have to leave the pumpkin where it is to avoid accidentally breaking the stem.

☞ For the maximum possible size, let your pumpkin grow until the vine is dead or at least nearly dry.

FALL IS FOR PLANTING

You can plant something besides bulbs in the fall. Believe it or not, the best time for planting most trees, shrubs, grasses, and many perennials is the fall. Fall's cool climate and reliable rain create excellent conditions for establishing new plantings. Roots grow the most when the soil is warm but the surrounding air is cool, and fall provides this perfect combination. Because soil does not usually freeze until well into the winter season, plantings installed in September or October have two to three months in which to grow roots before becoming fully dormant. The more developed and established a root system becomes over the fall and winter, the healthier the plant will be next spring.

Spring planting, on the other hand, does not favor root growth. In the spring, the conditions of fall are reversed. The soil is cold and wet, but the weather may be warm. These weather conditions favor vegetative growth and not root growth. Because a spring-planted tree or shrub does not have time to establish a sufficient root system to support the new top growth, a spring-installed plant is frequently a stressed plant, one that is more susceptible to drought damage and insect or disease attack.

For your fall planting spree, you'll generally be able to choose from balled-and-burlapped stock, container-grown stock, and bare-root stock. The American Association of Nurserymen recommends the procedures below for successful fall shrub and tree planting.

Container-Grown Stock

Balled-and-burlapped stock is planted the same way as container-grown stock, except that the balled-and-burlapped stock does not have to be completely removed from the burlap. You may simply loosen the burlap and leave it in the plant hole, where it will decay naturally. Be sure the burlap is real natural-fiber burlap, made from jute, hemp,

or cotton. Some "burlap" is made of polypropylene or other synthetic fiber. This will not decay and should be pulled out of the plant hole before filling with dirt.

☞ Before removing the container or loosening the burlap, thoroughly soak the plant root-ball area. Let the soaked plant sit for 10 or 15 minutes before planting.

☞ Dig your planting hole 6 to 8 inches wider and deeper than the root ball. If the ground is too dry, fill the hole with water, and let it drain.

☞ Mix mulch with soil from the hole in a 50-50 proportion, then pour some of the mix in the hole and firm it.

☞ Cut the container down its opposite sides to its base and remove the plant by grasping its soil ball rather than its trunk. For burlapped plants, remove the twine or metal staples that support the burlap.

☞ With a garden fork, score and loosen the root ball of container-grown stock. Do the same to burlapped stock, but leave the burlap under the plant root ball.

☞ Set the plant in its hole at the same depth it was in the container. Move the plant into the hole by lifting the root ball. Do not lift the plant by its trunk. Burlapped plants can be easily lifted into the hole by using the burlap as a sling to lift the root ball.

☞ Fill the hole with remaining soil, tapping down firmly with your foot.

☞ Water the plant to collapse any air pockets, and add soil to fill the depressions. Continue to water the plant regularly throughout the fall, even if it appears leafless and dormant. Water is necessary to encourage root growth.

Bare-Root Stock

Bare-root trees and shrubs should be planted as soon as possible after purchase. If you find you must delay installation of bare-root stock, dig a shallow trench in an out-of-the way place in your yard. Lay the entire plant down horizontally in the trench and cover it with a mixture of shredded leaves and dirt. Keep this mulch/dirt cover moist until planting day. On planting day, keep these tips in mind:

☞ Locate the area on the bark near the roots that is lighter than the rest of the trunk. This marks the depth at which it was growing at the nursery. Dig the hole this deep plus 8 inches, and 6 to 8 inches wider than the spread of the roots.

☞ Place a rock in the bottom of the hole on which to rest the central root mass. Mix mulch with the soil from the hole in a 50-50 proportion, then pour some of the mix in the hole and firm it.

☞ Set the plant in the hole, spreading the roots over the soil/rock mound. Place a board across the hole to ensure that the lighter part of the bark is level with the board; adjust the soil level as necessary.

☞ Fill the hole three-quarters full with soil, and firm it with your foot. Fill the hole with water, and let it drain.

☞ Add the rest of the soil, and add a ring of soil 2 to 3 inches high to act as a water well.

☞ Prune branches back by one-third to one-half their length (not all to the same length) to help compensate for any damage to the roots.

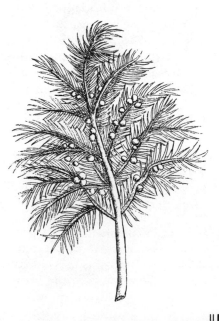

Christmas in October

October is the month to prepare for planting a live Christmas tree. Live Christmas trees are available balled-and-burlapped or container-grown. They give homeowners the pleasure of having a tree that lives on as a cheerful reminder of Christmas past. For those folks who hate to waste money or throw anything away, they serve as a "free" indoor Christmas tree before their permanent installation in the yard. It's easy to plant a balled-and-burlapped or container-grown Christmas tree, and it's easy to keep one in the house during the holidays. If you'd like to plant your Christmas tree this year, dig and prepare a hole for your tree now, while the ground is still soft and easy to work. Here are some helpful tips to prepare for December:

☞ Visit a local nursery and check out the size and price range of balled-and-burlapped and container-grown Christmas trees. You need to decide what size tree you plan to buy, even though you will make your purchase in December instead of October. Make a note of the container size or root-ball size of the tree that falls into your price range.

☞ At home, select the site for your new tree and dig the hole 6 to 8 inches wider and deeper than the container size or root ball size of the tree you will purchase. Place all of the soil in a barrel, trash can, washtub, or other suitable container. Mix an equal part of humus or finished compost with the soil, and store the soil mix in your basement or other area of your home not susceptible to freezing.

☞ Fill the planting hole with leaves or mulch so that it doesn't freeze and cover with a board to prevent anyone from accidentally stepping into the hole. Now you're ready for your Christmas tree planting ceremony. For final planting instructions, see "Tips for a Live Tree" on page 382.

ALMANAC GARDENING CALENDAR

October is a fine month for planting in all zones. Gardeners in all zones can plant bulbs this month. In addition, gardeners in the coldest zones can still plant some types of trees and perennials. Middle-zone gardeners can plant most trees and shrubs as well as perennials, and gardeners in the warmest zones can plant cool-weather vegetables, such as brassicas and spinach, as well as trees and shrubs.

Zone 1

Harvest cold-frame greens by picking older leaves, always leaving three or four center leaves on each plant. Open the frame when the temperature is above 50°F. If you must water frequently, replace leached nutrients by using fish emulsion or manure tea every two weeks. Harvest broccoli, cauliflower, cabbage, and kohlrabi before night temperatures fall to the low 20s. Harvest or cover hardy head lettuce during those nights. Protect brussels sprouts from rabbits and deer. Cover parsley with plastic tents to extend harvests into November. Root sprigs of mint in water, then pot for winter harvests. Dig and pot chives and young plants of oregano, thyme, and other herbs for growing in a cool, sunny window or under lights. Cover overwintering spinach, lettuce, chard, carrots, beets, parsnips, leeks, and turnips with 12 inches of loose mulch when night temperatures drop below 20°F. Before persistent snowfall, keep the mulch dry by covering it with clear plastic anchored with rocks or wood. Place a stake at each end of the row to help find the cache in the snow. When general garden cleanup is done, dig or till in manure.

Finish planting spring bulbs before midmonth. If your area gets subzero temperatures and little snow cover, mulch new bulb beds with 6 inches of leaves or straw. Before the ground freezes, lightly prune roses and cover with a foot of mulch.

In orchards, clean up leaves and windfalls to limit the spread of diseases and insects. If you have had trouble with scab, burn all apple leaves. Paint tree trunks with white latex paint or wrap them with burlap to prevent winter sunscald. Push mulch 6 inches away from the bases of fruit trees and wrap the trunks with wire mesh to prevent girdling by rodents. In areas with little snow cover, protect grapes and strawberries with a foot of mulch. Plant fully dormant fruit trees and bramble canes early in the month.

Zone 2

To build soil fertility, till in lime or wood ashes; spread compost and plant cover crops. Plant garlic cloves 4 inches apart and 2 inches deep for harvesting next August. Lettuce and Chinese cabbage will take light frost, but harvest them before heavy frost in November. Wait until frost has blackened the stalks of Jerusalem artichokes before harvesting. This no-care vegetable can be harvested all winter if mulched, or you can dig a few pounds to store in plastic bags in the refrigerator. Check stored tomatoes for rot. They'll keep until December if temperatures don't exceed 45°F.

Continue to plant spring bulbs. Pot up a few daffodils, tulips, hyacinths, and crocuses for January and February bloom. Keep them cool (about 35°F) and moist for at least 13 weeks before forcing. Water roses and all newly planted shrubs and trees. Finish lifting gladiolus corms. Cut off the stems, leaving a little neck; then let the corms dry for a few days before storing in wire baskets or onion bags at about 40°F. Leave the skins on to prevent drying out. As soon as frost hits tuberous begonias, cut off the stems, and store the tubers in shallow boxes of barely damp peat at 55°F. Start seeds of cineraria now for colorful, daisy-like blooms in five to six months. Give African violets more light for flower bud formation. Keep Thanksgiving and Christmas cacti in a cool room (55°F at night) to promote flowering.

Now is a fine time to plant container-grown fruit trees. Dig large holes and mulch with compost. Soak plantings once a week to encourage root growth before winter. Wrap hardware cloth or tree guards around trunks to foil rabbits and voles. Continue to pick up fallen fruit under trees.

Zone 3

You can count on killing frosts in October; keep sheets, plastic, or other coverings handy for protecting late tomatoes, peppers, eggplants, okra, and beans. As you pick the last summer vegetables, pull and compost spent plants and spread mulch or sow rye on the empty ground. Keep cool-weather crops well watered and heavily mulched to retain soil heat. Cover spinach, lettuce, and radishes with cold frames, floating row covers, or plastic tunnels for continued production. Feed chard, kale, brussels sprouts, cabbage, broccoli, and cauliflower with manure tea to hasten maturity. Begin harvesting brussels sprouts after the first heavy frost. Continue to treat fall cole crops with Bt (*Bacillus thuringiensis*) to control cabbageworms. Harvest sunflowers when the backs of the heads are yellow to brown. Leave about a foot of stem on each head and hang in a dry, rodent- and bird-free place to cure.

You can still divide and plant peonies, daylilies, and Siberian irises. It's still not too late to plant daffodils, crocuses, tulips, or hyacinths. After the first frost, dig, clean, and cure glads, tuberous begonias, cannas, and dahlias. Store in paper or cloth bags filled with dry peat, sand, sawdust, or vermiculite. Hang in a cool, dry place away from rodents. To encourage winter hardening, don't feed roses this month. Instead, lightly cut back stems and hill with a foot of compost or soil. Continue to plant balled-and-burlapped or container-grown trees and shrubs. Water deeply, mulch heavily, and stake to prepare for winter. Keep mulch at least 6 inches away from trunks to discourage rodents.

Put rodent and deer barriers around fruit and nut trees, and pull mulch at least 6 inches away from tree trunks. Apply tree wrap or white latex paint to trunks to prevent winter sunscald. Remove stakes and branch spreaders from fruit trees. Harvest the last apples and pears before hard frosts ruin their keeping quality. Rake up and compost all leaves and fallen fruit from trees, vines, and bushes. If the fall has been dry, water all fruits deeply to make them more winter hardy. Hold off on applying winter mulches until after a hard freeze. Get local birds in the habit of visiting the orchard by setting out bird feeders now.

Zone 4

Changeable weather can bring on a sudden frost early this month. By covering tender vegetables with newspapers, cloches, or row covers on clear evenings when the tem-peratures fall into the 40s you can save the plants for another month of production. After rinds are hard, cut pumpkins and winter squash, leaving 2 inches of stem attached. Cure for a couple of weeks in a warm area, then store in single layers under cool, dry conditions. Cut sunflower heads when their backs are yellow to brown and hang them up to dry.

As the average first frost date approaches, dig sweet potatoes, being careful not to cut or bruise them. Let dry briefly in the sun, then cure for a week or two at 75° to 85°F in high humidity. Store at 50° to 60°F in an airy place covered with newspapers and a towel to maintain high humidity. Pot tender herbs, such as marjoram and rosemary, for wintering indoors. Hardy parsley, chives, and tarragon can also be brought in for snipping through the cold months. When heavy frost threatens, pick all tomatoes, peppers, and eggplants and then clean up residue. In the West, protect globe artichoke plants by cutting stems to 12 inches and tying them together. Cover with overturned baskets filled with leaves. Plant rhubarb and asparagus crowns throughout the month in rich, deeply dug beds. Mulch established beds with a thick layer of aged manure. Divide older rhubarb crowns into three or more new plants.

Bring in houseplants at the beginning of the month. After frost, plant tulip bulbs in compost-rich soil. It's possible to sow lawn grass until the fifteenth. Keep mowing established lawns at 2 inches until growth stops.

Plant container-grown and balled-and-burlapped trees in large holes, and apply a thick mulch of compost. Dig in a little bonemeal around established shrubs that didn't bloom well this year, and renew mulches under azaleas and rhododendrons. Lift and dry tuberoses, tuberous begonias, and caladiums before frost strikes. Store them at low humidity—begonias at 50°F and caladiums and tuberoses at 60° to 65°F. Delay lifting cannas until frost nips tops. All month, water new plantings, evergreens, blooming roses, and chrysanthemums during dry weather.

Mow the sod around pecan trees for easier harvesting. Remove weeds and grass from other orchard plantings to keep rodents from moving in. To combat fall cankerworm in fruit trees, especially apples, place a new sticky band around each trunk. Attract woodpeckers to your orchard by providing suet.

Remove fruited canes of everbearing raspberries after harvest. Renew mulches under blueberries.

Zone 5

Early in the month, plant more spinach, kale, and leeks for spring harvest. Also, thin and mulch ear-lier sowings of them. Also thin tight stands of fall carrots, and mulch with rotted sawdust. When the tops are nipped by hard freezes, follow up with a thicker mulch that will last all winter. Mulch cold-weather vegetables to prevent emergence of winter weeds, but do not fertilize the vegetables after midmonth. As soon as cauliflower heads begin to form, gather the top leaves together and secure them with string or clothespins. Supply fall greens with plenty of water to encourage growth. Spray all leafy greens with soapy water to control aphids, which tend to congregate in the crevices between leaves. To control cabbage loopers on fall brassicas, apply Bt (*Bacillus thuringiensis*) regularly. Gather almost-ripe tomatoes before drenching rains cause them to crack. Cover tomatoes and peppers to get them through light frosts. After the first frost, quickly gather and burn all dead cucurbit foliage. This is the easiest way to get rid of lingering populations of cucumber beetles and squash bugs before they go below ground for winter. Dig and cure Irish potatoes, peanuts, and sweet potatoes. Peanuts and sweet potatoes will keep better if cured at high temperatures—80° to 90°F.

Turn under cover crops planted earlier in the fall to boost the humus content of worn soil. There is still time to plant a winter cover crop of oats, wheat, or annual rye. If you plan to mulch the garden for winter, wait until after the first hard freeze. Meanwhile, remove all plant debris and cultivate the soil to bring pests and weed seeds to the surface.

Bachelor's-buttons, alyssum, chamomile, and larkspurs will bloom earlier and better in spring if planted now and allowed to over-winter. Set out seedlings of biennials and hardy perennials, and water them thoroughly. Before the first frost, gather ripe rosehips and renew mulches around roses and other shrubs. Wait to prune roses until mid- to late winter. Keep newly planted nursery stock watered throughout the month to encourage rapid root development. Begin planting tulip, hyacinth, daffodil, and crocus bulbs after chilling them in the vegetable bin of your refrigerator for three weeks. Dig and divide crowded clumps of daffodils and magic lilies. Most of these bulbs grow well beneath shade trees because they do most of their growing in early spring before the trees leaf out. Dig and clean any remaining caladium tubers and gladiolus corms, and store them in dry sand or vermiculite in a place where they cannot freeze. Place potted poinsettias in darkness from 6 P.M. to 8 A.M. during the last half of the month.

Prune fall and everbearing raspberries after the last fruits are picked. Do not cut back green shoots that did not bear this year—these canes will bear next year. Carefully move small blackberry and raspberry plants to new areas, and mulch immediately to keep them moist. Remove runners and blooms from strawberries planted earlier in the fall to encourage development of big crowns. Check the soil level around plants to make sure the crowns are not covered. Water them thoroughly, and mulch them with an acidic material like pine straw or shredded leaves. Renew mulches around blueberries, grapes, and bramble fruits.

After the leaves fall in the orchard, set the lawnmower blade low and mow beneath the trees, then rake up the shredded debris. Trim off diseased and broken limbs, and pull up weeds growing around tree trunks. If you mulch your trees, remember to scatter needed minerals (such as lime, rock phosphate, or zinc) in the orchard before piling on the mulch. Check with your extension agent to learn about local mineral deficiencies that may affect your orchard's health.

Zone 6

Make a second planting of cool-weather vegetables as soon as garden space becomes available. Start seeds of kale, collards, chard, cabbage, Chinese cabbage, mustard, onions, and leeks in flats while you wait. Plant radishes, carrots, beets, turnips, spinach, peas, garlic cloves, and onion sets directly in the garden. Transplant thyme, sage, and comfrey early in the month, and direct-seed caraway, chervil, fennel, dill, and parsley. Sow winter rye where you're not growing vegetables. Be prepared to protect cold-sensitive crops from a frost by the end of the month. Fruits of warm-season plants don't store well if nipped by a frost, so harvest early. Dig Irish and sweet potatoes at the end of the month.

Now is the time to plant bulbs. Work compost and bonemeal into the planting area. Plant anemones, ranunculus, daffodils, Dutch irises, crocuses, amaryllises, and calla lilies as soon as you receive them. In most of the region, tulip and hyacinth bulbs must be stored for six weeks in the refrigerator before planting. Overseed lawns with winter rye to keep them green. Check for insects on houseplants that have summered outdoors and prepare to bring the plants inside. Sudden drops in nighttime temperatures may cause them to lose leaves.

Harvest pecans and store in a cool place until they can be shelled, then move them to the freezer. Apply compost lightly around the trees. While soil is still easily worked, prepare sites for fruit or nut trees that will be planted later in the winter. Before ordering trees check with local growers for varieties best suited for your area. Plant green manure crops in the orchard. Strawberries can be planted now. When leaves fall from grapevines, blackberries, and other brambles, take cuttings for rootings in sand. If you haven't cut back canes that fruited this year, remove them now.

Zone 7

All brassicas from cabbages to the newest asian greens grow best in this zone during the winter months—plant them anytime in October. In the hottest areas, plant collards, kale, the fast-maturing mustards, and heat-tolerant Asian greens. Throughout the zone, plant beets, carrots, fennel, parsley, and peas. Sow blocks of radishes, spinach, and lettuce every few weeks during fall and winter. Plant garlic, shallots, and long-day onions in early October to get the biggest, longest-keeping bulbs.

Now is the best time to add soil amendments like phosphate rock, trace minerals, and lime to your garden. On the West Coast, gardeners generally need to reduce the alkalinity of the soil by adding materials like straw, leaves, peat, and manure. Gardeners on the Gulf Coast and Eastern Seaboard often need to reduce the acidity of the soil by adding lime. Test your soil to find out what is needed. Any green manure crop planted now will be ready to turn under by January—just in time for spring planting. A combination of broad beans (favas) and annual rye is an especially good source of organic matter and nitrogen. If you don't plant a green manure crop, cover the garden with leaves to prevent weeds from taking over during the winter.

Continue to plant container-grown or balled-and-burlapped trees and shrubs. Lawns and ground covers planted now will do better than those planted in spring. Where lawns go brown in winter, broadcast annual ryegrass to bring on the green. Plant ageratums, calendulas, nasturtiums, phlox, snapdragons, stocks, sweet Williams, and sweet peas now for spring display. Stake chrysanthemums to keep them from being broken by November winds. Lift caladiums, dahlias, glads, and tuberous begonias for winter storage by the end of the month. Plant spring bulbs except hyacinths and tulips, which should remain in the refrigerator for six to eight weeks.

Don't feed your orchard now. Plant a green manure crop such as fava beans, mustard, or annual rye that will feed your trees when tilled under in February. Trees like nectarines, apricots, and peaches that are sensitive to wet, cold soils are a problem in the West, where the soils are heavy and the winter rains sometimes relentless. A few ditches dug through the orchard now while the ground is dry will carry off excess water and prevent the soil from becoming sodden. Stop feeding subtropical fruits like citrus and avocado to prevent them from producing frost-tender growth, but keep watering through dry periods.

Container-grown or balled-and-burlapped fruit trees have a greater survival rate than bare-root trees and get off to a better start in spring. Citrus, avocado, and subtropical fruits can be planted as soon as they are available.

Start new strawberry beds in South Florida, Texas, and California. Buy only plants certified to be disease free, and make sure to plant them with the crowns above soil level. Avoid planting them in areas where potatoes, tomatoes, eggplants, and peppers grew for the last three years. Renew the acid mulch around blueberries. Cut out all bramble canes that bore fruit.

IN GOOD HEALTH

COUGH COMFORTERS

This October may find you feeling impatient because your end-of-summer ragweed allergy continues unabated even as the pollen count drops. Your upper respiratory system may be so sensitized by prolonged allergen contact that even very low pollen counts may set off a new round of symptoms. In addition, many asthmatics find their symptoms worsening in the fall, possibly due to the molds present on the fallen leaves. Unfortunately, prolonged allergic reactions in the fall predispose many sufferers to early season colds.

One of the most annoying symptoms of a cold is a persistent dry cough, which may wake you up a dozen times at night and make you feel miserable, distracted, and impatient because the coughing doesn't relieve your chest congestion. But you don't have to suffer through your cold in dry, hacking silence. You have several options for making yourself feel better and making your cough work to clear your chest of all its congestion.

Dry-Cough Blues

During a cold or other respiratory infection, mucous membranes (which line your entire respiratory tract) don't release as much liquid as they normally do. So the mucus that is there in the tract changes from its benign, thin, watery consistency to a thick, gummy consistency —what we call phlegm.

Any aid you use to help you cough up phlegm and get it out of your chest and your life is called by a fancy name: expectorant. Many people think that expectorants work by stimulating your cough reflex so you'll cough more. That extra coughing, they believe, helps bring up the phlegm. "But that's probably not how expectorants operate at all," says Branton Lachman, Doc-

tor of Pharmacy and clinical assistant professor at the University of Southern California School of Pharmacy. "Instead, they do their job by attempting to thin out phlegm so it's easier to cough up."

Which expectorants work? That's a hard question to answer, experts say. Expectorants are tough to test under rigorous scientific conditions because everybody's phlegm is different and difficult to measure. Despite these problems, there are some types of expectorants doctors think are worth trying—and some worth forgetting. Here's a rundown:

Extra Fluids: From Water to Chicken Soup

Medical opinion is almost unanimous in recommending extra fluids as the most effective expectorants to reach for, especially as a first line of defense. "Extra fluids go into all compartments of the body, including your respiratory tract, where they help to liquefy hardened mucus so it's easier to cough up," says Dr. Lachman. How much extra fluid is enough? Dr. Lachman recommends six to eight 8-ounce glasses a day. Patients on fluid restriction should check with their physicians first.

Does chicken soup, that oldest of folk remedies for a cold, have any magical qualities as an expectorant? Probably not, say our experts, although it's a delicious, nutritious way to take in extra fluids. One famous study, conducted at Mt. Sinai Medical Center in Miami Beach, Florida, found that chicken soup made volunteers' noses run faster than did other hot or cold liquids. But the researchers didn't attempt to measure the soup's effect on phlegm deeper in the respiratory tract, the kind that needs to be coughed up.

And what about that oft-quoted piece of wisdom that says avoid drinking milk during a cold because it increases the amount of phlegm in your system? Not true, says Dr. Lachman. "Milk does not produce phlegm, infection does," he says. "It may be that milk is a coating liquid. It gives you a feeling of more phlegm in your throat but the milk isn't really increasing the amount."

Camphor/Menthol Chest Rubs

The Food and Drug Administration (FDA) says it doesn't have enough information to rate camphor/menthol chest rubs, such as Vicks VapoRub, as effective expectorants. But it did recently decide that camphor and menthol can individually be effective to calm a cough. So if you're coughing a lot, and all that hacking is unproductive (that is, you're not getting up phlegm

with your coughing), you might use one of these rubs, especially at night so you can sleep better. One caution, however: Chest rubs should never be taken internally in any amount.

Over-the-Counter Drugs

The most common expectorant ingredient in most over-the-

counter cough remedies is guaifenesin (found in some formulations of Robitussin, Benylin, Sudafed, Triaminic, and other products advertised as containing expectorants). Guaifenesin stimulates your stomach to release body fluids that are supposed to travel to your chest and go to work to thin out phlegm. But does it really do the job?

Many experts think that studies have been inconclusive about whether guaifenesin actually does have an effect on phlegm. But apparently the FDA begs to differ. Sources at the FDA say that it has analyzed new evidence about guaifenesin's effectiveness and that the agency is "likely" to move the drug into its "safe and effective" category as an over-the-counter expectorant sometime soon. Until now, the FDA has said it didn't have enough evidence to make a decision on guaifenesin's effectiveness.

If guaifenesin's status does change, it will be the one and only expectorant the FDA categorizes this way. The agency has judged all other over-the-counter expectorants as either not effective or not tested enough to provide evidence to rule one way or the other.

What about cough medicines that combine expectorants with other cold remedies? Many doctors and pharmacists would probably be reluctant to recommend such "combination" drugs if all you need is an expectorant. But a lot of physicians would also agree that in some situations a cough suppressant/ expectorant is justified. "Some people have an incredibly sensitive cough reflex, which the suppressant could help tone down so they're not coughing all the time," says Dr. Lachman. "Then, if the expectorant is doing its job, you'll only cough when there's something actually ready to be coughed up."

Other Home Remedies

Lozenges containing licorice, horehound, or aromatic oil such as peppermint or spearmint are often linked with increased breakdown of phlegm, says Varro E. Tyler, Ph.D., a professor of pharmacognosy (the study of drugs derived from plants and animals) at Purdue University. As they dissolve in your throat, they help liquefy the mucus, he says.

And hot, spicy foods—the kind that make your eyes water or your nose run—may also be modestly effective. "They help mucous membranes all over, not just in your nose, to secrete more liquid, which can help thin mucus," Dr. Tyler says. So you might want to add foods containing hot peppers, curry, and other hot, spicy flavorings to your menu when you have a cold. If you're not used to such foods, be careful to use them sparingly at first. "There's a great deal of difference in the sensitivities of people's palates when it comes to things like hot peppers—so be cautious," says Dr. Tyler.

Exercise

If you're careful to wait until the acute stage of your cold is over (after you're through battling the infection and your temperature is normal again), exercise just might help you loosen up phlegm left in your respiratory tract. So say several experts, including Bryant Stamford, Ph.D., director of the Health Promotion and Wellness Center, University of Louisville School of Medicine. "It may be that the jarring effect of exercise helps to break up mucus," he says.

Vaporizers and Humidifiers

Some doctors also recommend humidifying the air you breathe to help thin mucus. Other doctors say you have to drink extra fluids in order for humidifying devices to have an effect on deep-down congestion—just breathing in moisture through the air isn't enough. Since moistened air can keep dry nasal passages comfortable, however, there's certainly no harm in keeping a humidifier going during a cold. (See "Humidifier Report," below.)

Whatever expectorant you use,

Humidifier Report

If you'd like to increase the humidity in your home, you have four devices from which to choose: *evaporative humidifiers,* which work by driving a spongy material through a water-filled tank and blowing air through the wet sponge as it emerges from the water; *steam vaporizers,* which work by boiling water and emitting the vapor as steam; *cool-mist vaporizers,* which have a rotating impeller that breaks up water into droplets that are ejected into the room; and *ultrasonic humidifiers,* which use high-frequency sound vibrations to turn water into mist.

The ultrasonic humidifier, developed in Japan, is the most recent device and also currently the most popular. Ultrasonic devices have two advantages over the other, older types of machines: (1) They're quieter than any of the other devices, and (2) they don't emit the molds and bacteria that frequently grow in humidifier water. However, they may emit particles of nonviable molds and bacteria as well as airborne particles resulting from the minerals in hard water. Using softened water in an ultrasonic humidifier doesn't help because the sodium in artificially softened water forms a white dust of particles so small they're easily inhaled.

No humidifier currently on the market is without drawbacks. People can experience allergic reactions to airborne particles emitted by humidifiers or become ill from bacteria and molds that inhabit humidifier water. Cold-mist vaporizers often emit live molds and bacteria in the water droplet spray as well as the same mineral particles emitted by ultrasonic devices. Evaporative humidifiers can encourage microorganisms to grow on surrounding surfaces if too much humidity is added to the air.

If you use a humidifier for comfort or to combat a cold, be sure to clean and disinfect the water reservoir daily. If you purchase either a cold-mist or an ultrasonic humidifier, choose a model that includes a demineralization filter to eliminate airborne mineral particles.

it's a good idea to see a doctor if you keep coughing up a lot of phlegm for several days. You could have a more serious respiratory infection, such as pneumonia. Also, any cough that's unrelated to a cold, or a cough that seems to be getting better then gets worse again, should be checked out by a professional.

Walking Tip for October

To relieve blisters, cut two patches of moleskin, one small and one large, and stick the patches together sticky side to sticky side. Then, putting the nonsticky side of the small patch against the blister, stick the cushion in place. You can remove the cushion without tearing off the blister's top.

AT HOME

ARE YOU LOCKING IN HOME POLLUTANTS AS YOU TIGHTEN UP FOR WINTER?

October is the month of pre-winter rituals—putting up the storm windows, caulking around the door and window frames, sealing off fan or air conditioner openings, stacking firewood, and pulling out the old woolen comforter. We perform these annual chores with a sense of closure and comfort. As the year is coming to an end, we're preparing a snug nest for retreat from cold weather, and we're looking forward to evenings at home near a fireplace or wood stove. Unfortunately, we're also closing ourselves in with the all-time, most unwanted guest of the twentieth century—indoor air pollution.

An Environmental Protection

Agency (EPA) study released in late 1987—the first large-scale, direct measurement of personal exposure to a variety of chemical pollutants—revealed that people are exposed to higher levels of toxic substances inside their homes than outside them. But it didn't take a government study to convince some people that the air they were breathing indoors wasn't clean. They knew it already by the discomfort they were feeling: They suffered from one or a combination of such complaints as dizziness, nausea, nagging coughs, rashes, irritated eyes and nose, headaches, sleeplessness, and depression. There's even a term for what these people have; it's called Sick House Syndrome. Ten years ago it was thought that only highly sensitive people were susceptible to this malady. We now know that many more people are affected by common household products in both obvious and subtle ways. The 1987 EPA study on indoor air pollutants indicates that indoor levels of toxic substances are much higher than outdoor levels, even in highly industrialized areas.

There are a number of potential contributors to indoor air pollution. Pesticides and fungicides, for example, can be found in everything from carpeting to wood preservatives. Fumes from solvents used in paints and sealants make some people sick. Another significant and controversial culprit, formaldehyde,

is used as a binder in wood products and carpet backings and as a component in the now banned urea-formaldehyde insulation foams. Formaldehyde gas, in addition to being a suspected carcinogen, makes many people sick—with symptoms ranging from merely annoying eye irritation to downright incapacitating nausea, lethargy, and shortness of breath. And finally, radon, a gaseous pollutant that you can't smell or see, can significantly increase your risk of lung cancer.

Fighting Formaldehyde

Formaldehyde resins are used as binders in a number of wood products, notably particleboard and plywood. When the product is new, the binder contains excess free formaldehyde that can be given off as a gas—a process called *outgassing*. As the wood product ages, the amount of formaldehyde outgassing decreases, and the smell and discomfort associated with free formaldehyde gas also decreases. But the real question is: Is it reasonable to be exposed to *any* formaldehyde gas, even at a low level?

No one knows yet what the *safe* level of exposure to formaldehyde is. But the U.S. Department of Housing and Urban Development (HUD) has established formaldehyde emissions standards for the hardwood plywood and particleboard used in manufactured housing. Manufacturers of these products have been able to come up with ways to reduce the formaldehyde outgassing of wood products by 60 to 90 percent, mainly by using nonformaldehyde-based resins and by adding special chemicals that absorb free formaldehyde.

If you suspect you have a sensitivity to formaldehyde, or if you know you're allergic to it, here are some steps you can take to minimize your exposure:

☞ If you're not sure whether formaldehyde is causing you to feel ill, purchase a home formaldehyde monitor. Home formaldehyde monitors cost about $40 and are made to be hung in your house for a few hours, then returned to the laboratory for analysis. One tester that's widely available is the 3M 3720 Formaldehyde Monitor. For information, write to 3M Occupational Health and Environmental Safety Division, Marketing Communications Building 220-3E-04, St. Paul, MN 55144.

☞ Before you purchase new upholstery, draperies, or carpet, make sure that the product you've chosen does not have a formaldehyde-based resin included as a binder (for example as part of a carpet backing). In addition, you *can* remove formaldehyde, fungicides, bactericides, and stain-resistant coatings from wall-to-wall carpet. First, rent a commercial carpet steam cleaner (not a rug shampooer) and a supply of steam-cleaning concentrate *without* deodorants. Weigh an empty container. Mix the concentrate plus water according to the "heavy soil" directions and add to the empty container. Weigh the container plus the newly mixed cleaning solution and subtract the weight of the empty container to determine the *weight of your cleaning solution.* Add sodium bisulfite (available in many drugstores) to your cleaning solution to neutralize the formaldehyde from the carpet backing. To determine the weight of sodium bisulfite to add, multiply the weight of your cleaning solution by 1 percent. Steam clean the carpet with this mix. Then, mix the steam-cleaning concentrate according to "light scrub" directions and clean the carpet again. **Note:** Some asthmatics are allergic to the sodium bisulfite solution recommended. If anyone in your household suffers from asthma, steam clean the carpet with clear water instead of cleaning concentrate/sodium bisulfite solution, ventilate the room for a week, and steam clean with clear water again.

☞ Avoid medium-density fiberboard (MDF) in your next construction project or furniture purchase. MDF gives off about three times more formaldehyde than particleboard and is the most commonly used core material underneath plywood or veneers in cabinets and furniture. Before you buy a piece of furniture, ask if MDF has been used in any part of its construction. In the lumberyard, MDF is sold in ⅝-inch-thick sheets and should be clearly labeled.

☞ If you use plywood for an indoor construction project, use exterior-grade plywood, even for indoor finish work. Exterior plywood uses a phenol-formaldehyde resin, which gives off less formaldehyde gas than the urea-formaldehyde resin used in interior-grade plywood.

Bucking the Other Indoor Polluters

Among other common indoor pollutants are the chemicals and additives in paints, varnishes, caulks, and adhesives.

If you must finish a hand-crafted furniture or remodeling project with a solvent-based finish, plan to complete the finishing process in the late spring or early summer. With proper timing, you can have up to six months of open-window weather while your new finish dries. Apply solvent-based finishes only in a well-ventilated space (use a large ventilating fan) and keep the room where your new project is drying shut off from the rest of your house. Also wear an OSHA-approved face mask for protection from solvent vapors while you work on the project.

If you're bothered by paint fumes, switch to a less-toxic type of paint. Many people are allergic to either the chemical solvent or to the bactericides and fungicides in the paint. Most paints contain cellulose thickeners, which are subject to bacterial attack, and bactericides are necessary to prevent this. Paints include fungicides to resist mildew in areas of high moisture. If you are allergic to either bactericides or fungicides, select a low- or non-toxic product such as Negley's Fungicide & Biocide-Free Paint Products, Casein-Based Milk Paint, Safecoat Paint, Auro Brand, and Livos Plant Chemistry paint. If you are allergic to solvent (some brands of oil-based paint contain up to two quarts of solvent for every gallon of paint), switch to a water-based paint.

Switch to a water-based adhesive or glue if you're allergic to construction adhesives, glues, or mastics. You may be allergic to the organic solvents found in many of these products. If you have a solvent allergy, white glue (polyvinyl acetate) and carpenter's glue (yellow aliphatic resin) are safe after they've dried. Products made especially for low toxicity include Dyno Flex water-based synthetic rubber sealant, Linami Cork Adhesive, Auro Brand Adhesives, and Solomon Brand non-toxic wood glue.

Avoid using building products that contain asbestos. Asbestos is used in thousands of building products including vinyl tiles and sheet flooring, siding, and wood stove insulation boards. In solid form, asbestos is not hazardous, but if it's sawed, drilled, sanded, or broken, invisible fibers can stay in the lungs and can cause respiratory illness.

What About Radon?

Radon is a colorless, odorless, radioactive gas that is given off from some types of soil and rock (notably granite and shale). The gas is harmless to people in the outdoors because it quickly becomes diluted by the surrounding air. But if the gas leaves the soil and enters a house through cracks in the basement or ground level slab, it is not diluted with outdoor air and can be a serious health problem. High-level exposure to radon over 20 or 30 years can cause cancer, but no short-term symptoms warn of the threat. Though millions of homeowners are exposed to radon in their homes, only a fraction of them are aware that the air in their house could increase their risk of contracting lung cancer.

Scientists haven't yet devised an accurate method of predicting which houses will be radon contaminated. From the testing done so far, it's clear that the extent of the problem varies not only from area to area, but also from house to house on the same street. Houses that have flunked radon tests, however, do have some things in common. Researchers have found that:

☞ Airtight homes have higher indoor radon levels then leaky ones.

☞ Home well-water is more likely to contain radon than municipal water.

☞ Buildings with slab-on-grade construction collect more radon than those with basements or crawl spaces.

☞ Single-level houses test higher than multi-level ones.

☞ Clay soil beneath a house blocks more radon from entering the home than sandy soil does.

The only sure way to tell if your house has radon problems is to test it. The EPA recommends a multistage testing procedure. It suggests that homeowners do a quick and simple test first, and if that gives a high radon reading, follow up with a long-term test that monitors radon levels over weeks or months. The first, simple test is a charcoal monitor, which you set up in your living area or basement for three to seven days and then send to a laboratory for analysis. Such tests cost under $20. The longer, follow-up test is called an alpha-track monitor, and without going into the whys and wherefores of radon chemistry, this detector "counts" radiation (which is produced by radon gas) in your house for at least 60 days. The detector is then returned to a laboratory for analysis.

In order to understand the results of a radon test, you need to know that radiation levels from radon gas are measured in units called picocuries of radiation per liter of air (pCi/l). Although there is no clear consensus among experts on how many pCi/l of radiation constitute a health hazard, the EPA has calculated that living with 10 pCi/l carries about the same lung cancer risk as smoking a pack of cigarettes a day. It urges homeowners to take measures to reduce radon levels in all homes in which the radiation level measures 4 pCi/l or higher.

Radon Remedies: How to Safeguard Your Home

Simply opening basement windows on all sides of your house to insure good ventilation can sometimes reduce radon levels significantly, by as much as 90 percent. In cold weather this will raise your heating bills, but it might be worth the extra money since it's such an easy solution. You can also install an air-to-air heat exchanger. This device brings outside air into the house through one channel and releases indoor air to the outdoors through another. The unit is de-signed to recover the heat from the indoor air before allowing it to escape.

Another remedy is to block the pathways the radioactive gas follows into your home. Plug cracks and crevices in the basement with a concrete silicone sealant (available at most home centers). Radon also enters the basement through floor drains, and these should be sealed unless they're necessary to keep the basement dry.

In addition, some contractors specialize in radon incursion problems and can install a variety of systems to eliminate radon from your house. Usually these systems are a little too difficult for the average do-it-yourselfer to install alone. One of the commonest contractor-installed systems involves drilling two or more holes through the entire thickness of the basement floor. The holes are connected by means of sealed pipes to a small exhaust fan that blows air out of the house, usually through an opening in the basement foundation wall. When the exhaust fan is turned on it creates a vacuum that draws radon gas from beneath the basement floor, through the connecting pipes, and through the exhaust fan to the outside of the house.

Fresh Air Indoors

All indoor air pollution problems can be at least partially eliminated using one simple remedy—

ventilation. As a rule of thumb, the *average* home needs a fresh air supply in the range of 100 to 200 cubic feet per minute (CFM), depending on indoor air quality. Anything that creates stale or stuffy air—supertight construction, heavy smoking indoors, or a fume-producing workshop, for example—increases your ventilation needs. Although there is no national code for home ventilation rates, the U.S. Department of Housing and Urban Development recommends an air exchange rate of at least 150 CFM. To reach that 150 CFM minimum you can use a combination of four different types of ventilation systems: (1) local exhaust fans, which remove moisture and odors from kitchen and baths, (2) whole house fans (see "Beat the Heat without Air Conditioning" in the July section), (3) a central exhaust system with wall ports for air exchange (a system that is useful only in warm climates), and (4) a heat-recovery ventilation system, which ventilates your home without losing the heat supplied by your furnace.

FIRE PREVENTION WEEK

The second week in October is National Fire Prevention Week.

Fire Prevention Week, first proclaimed in 1922 by President Warren G. Harding, was established in memory of the Great Chicago Fire of 1871. (See "What's Happening in October.") The National Fire Protection Association, an international, nonprofit organization devoted to the study and prevention of fire fatalities, supplies the following information on home fire prevention:

☞ The majority of fatal fires in the home occur at night, when occupants are asleep, and the majority of victims are the very young and the very old. Since an early warning can prevent many of these unnecessary deaths, every home should be equipped with properly placed and maintained smoke detectors.

☞ You should have at least one smoke detector on each floor of your house, including the basement; in addition, you should have one detector located ouside each bedroom door.

☞ You should also have a smoke detector in these fire-prone areas: attic, garage, home shop, kitchen, and near your furnace or oil burner.

☞ Test the operation of your smoke detectors once a week.

☞ If you use a woodburning fireplace or a wood stove, have your chimney cleaned by a professional cleaning service at least once a year.

☞ Mark your calendar annually for a whole-house fire hazard inspection. A good time to perform this routine is at the beginning of the heating season in your area.

Home Fire Hazards

During your home fire inspection, check for the following:

☞ Dead smoke detector batteries

☞ Insufficient airspace around televisions, portable heaters, ranges, and other appliances

☞ Placement of portable heaters near curtains, draperies, or upholstery

☞ Creosote buildup in chimneys

☞ Overloaded electrical circuits

☞ Frayed electrical cords

☞ Electrical cords under rugs, pinned tightly against walls by furniture, or on the floor in high-traffic areas

☞ Improperly sized or bypassed fuses

☞ Unsafe storage of flammable liquids or oily rags

☞ Matches or lighters kept within the reach of children

☞ Grease buildup on ranges or kitchen hoods

YOUR OCTOBER SHOPPER'S TIP

The best buys in produce this month include apples, beets, broccoli, cauliflower, leeks, and pears. This month's recipe uses the abundant broccoli crop. For tips on getting the most from your own garden broccoli harvest, see "Picking at Prime Time" in the July section. Broccoli should never be overcooked because it develops a cabbagey flavor and olive coloring when it's cooked too long. In cooking broccoli for the recipe here, you should cook the vegetable rapidly and remove it from the broth as soon as it is crisp yet tender and still bright green. The best way to cook broccoli to a crisp, tender, bright green stage is to first remove the broccoli florets from the stems and then slice the stems into 1-inch lengths. Cook the stems first because they take longer; add the florets last because they cook very quickly.

Broccoli au Gratin Soup

1½ pounds broccoli
4 cups chicken stock
1 cup cottage cheese
1 teaspoon curry powder
2 cups milk
   grated Parmesan cheese

Wash and trim broccoli. Break into florets and slice the thick stems into 1-inch pieces. Add chicken stock to a 5-quart soup pot and bring to a boil. Add broccoli stems to stock, lower heat, and cook, covered, for 3 to 4 minutes. Add florets and continue cooking uncovered until they turn bright green. With a slotted spoon, remove broccoli from broth at once. Keep broth in the soup pot but remove it from the heat and set it aside. Puree cooked broccoli and cottage cheese together in a blender until smooth. Return puree to soup base. Add curry powder and milk. Reheat on a low burner setting. Do not allow soup to boil. Serve hot, sprinkled with Parmesan cheese.

6 to 8 servings

YOUR HOME MAINTENANCE CHECKLIST

☛ Check and clean your home heating system according to the manufacturer's instructions, or have it done by an authorized serviceman.

☛ Vacuum the baseboard elements of an electric heating system monthly during heating season.

☛ Check and clean dehumidifier. See March for directions.

☛ Check the operation of the fireplace damper and clean the fireplace. If you didn't have your chimney cleaned in July, do it now.

☛ Clean the wood stove pipe between the stove and chimney. Check for corrosion and holes and replace if necessary. *Do this every few weeks during the heating season and then as often as experience tells you there is creosote buildup.*

☛ Put storm windows in place.

☛ Close off shutoff valves to outside faucets and water lines and drain the water lines leading to these faucets to prevent freezing during cold weather.

EVENTS AND FESTIVALS

Any and All Dog Show
Tryon, North Carolina

Early October. Dog owners of all ages enter their pet pooches in this off-the-wall dog show with categories like, "The Dog Who'd Really Rather Be at Home," "The Dog Who Looks Most Like His Master," "The Dog with the Most Doubtful Ancestry," the cutest dog, and the best-dressed dog. In addition to the fun categories for beloved, ordinary mutts, the Any and All Dog Show features a bloodhound show and obedience trials. Information: Tryon Riding and Hunt Club, Box 1095, Tryon, NC 28782.

Irmo Okra Strut
Irmo, South Carolina

Early October. South Carolinians celebrate one of the staples of "soul food" in this festival that features the luscious pods fried, steamed, frittered, and gumboed for the thousands of out-of-towners who flock to Irmo in October. This festival, which was voted one of the Top 20 Festivals in the Southeast by the Southeastern Tourism Society, starts out with a street dance and goes on to include the Dam Run to Irmo (a 10K run across the Lake Murray Dam), an okra-eating contest, a grand parade, and a variety of entertainment. Information: Irmo Okra Strut, P.O. Box 406, Irmo, SC 29063.

The Whole Enchilada Fiesta
Las Cruces, New Mexico

Early October. Over 100,000 people come out to watch the creation of the world's largest enchilada, a process that requires a two-story crane and two steel plates to transport it to the pot. Add to that spectacle a parade, entertainment, arts and crafts, a children's area, and more food, and you'll experience a fiesta like no other in celebration of an enchilada. Information: Las Cruces Chamber of Commerce, P.O. Box 519, Las Cruces, NM 88004.

West Virginia Black Walnut Festival
Spencer, West Virginia

Second weekend in October. Spencer celebrates West Virginia's black walnut heritage with a kickoff parade. What follows is a truly nutty weekend that includes an art show, agricultural exhibits, wrist-wrestling competition, 2-mile Nut Race, antique car show, quilt show, turkey-calling contest and Harvest Hoedown. Information: West Virginia Black Walnut Commission, P.O. Box 27, Spencer, WV 25276.

Scarecrow Contest
Waterbury, Vermont

Mid-October. All you corn-patch artists now have a chance to display your true talent. The only contest rules are that scarecrows must be made primarily of all-natural materials and must be a minimum of 5 feet tall. Bring your old clothes, household castoffs, straw or cornstalks, as well as your creativity, and build a scarecrow to compete for prizes in several categories—Adult Creative, Adult Traditional, and Children's Scarecrows. If your talents lie in creative carving, enter the jack-o'-lantern contest. Cash prizes are awarded in every competition, and there's free Ben & Jerry's ice cream for everyone who attends. Information: Ben & Jerry's Scarecrow Contest, P.O. Box 240, Waterbury, VT 05676.

Bean Fest and Great Arkansas Championship Outhouse Race
Mountain View, Arkansas

Third Saturday in October. Build yourself a water closet on wheels and come on down and join the Championship Outhouse Race. There are free beans and cornbread for everyone who shows up to watch the race down Main Street, and all the festivities are set to the pickin' and grinnin' of bluegrass music. A tall-tales contest, children's games, talent show, and bean-cooking contest round out the fun. Information: Tourist Information Center, Main Street, Box 253, Mountain View, AR 72560.

Wooly Worm Festival
Banner Elk, North Carolina

Third Saturday in October. Bring your own wooly worm or buy one from a roadside worm dealer to enter in the Wooly Worm Race. The stripes on the winning worm forecast the coming winter in Banner Elk. The blacker the stripes, the harsher the winter. Everyone in Banner Elk hopes the winner will sport brown stripes, a sure predictor of a mild winter. Traditional music and mountain arts and crafts provide a lively scene for this southern fall ritual. Information: Banner Elk Chamber of Commerce, P.O. Box 335, Banner Elk, NC 28604.

Annual Goose Festival
Fennville, Michigan

Third weekend in October. Fennvillians use the over 300,000 migrating Canada geese that stop over in Fennville as an excuse to have a rip-roaring good time. During this weekend of food, fun, frolic, and foolery, you can get a front row seat at the Great Lakes Canada Goose Calling Championship, the 10K Wild Goose Chase Run, or a wildlife art show featuring nation-

ally known artisans. Saturday evening, get out your party duds for the Goose Ball and enjoy a foot-stomping good time. Information: Chamber of Commerce, Box 484, Fennville, MI 49408.

Peanut Valley Festival
Portales, New Mexico

Third weekend in October. Portales is the number one producer of the tasty Valencia peanut, an extraordinarily large and delicious peanut. Celebrate the peanutiest harvest in the West with peanuts prepared in every imaginable way, even plain and unsalted. The Peanut Valley Festival includes live entertainment, an arts and crafts show, and the Peanut Olympics featuring such events as the Peanut Toss and the Peanut Roll. Information: Peanut Valley Festival, Station 39, Eastern New Mexico University, Portales, NM 88130.

World's Championship Chili Cookoff
Rosamond, California

Second to last Sunday in October. Contestants who have won state and regional chili contests come from all over the world to compete for the title of World Champion Chili Chef *and* the top prize of $25,000. Now that's a lot of chilis! In addition, continuous entertainment and the traditional bombing of the outhouse by World War II bomber planes from nearby Edwards Air Force Base guarantee a hot time for all. Information: International Chili Society, Box 2966, Newport Beach, CA 92663.

NOVEMBER

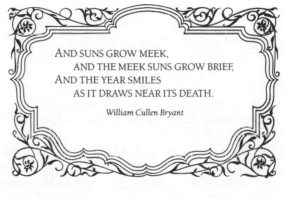

AND SUNS GROW MEEK,
AND THE MEEK SUNS GROW BRIEF,
AND THE YEAR SMILES
AS IT DRAWS NEAR ITS DEATH.

William Cullen Bryant

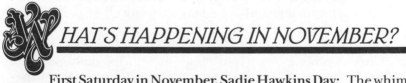

WHAT'S HAPPENING IN NOVEMBER?

First Saturday in November, Sadie Hawkins Day: The whimsical creation of cartoonist Al Capp (1909-1979), Sadie Hawkins Day was the day of last resort for all unhappily single females who lived in Dogpatch, U.S.A. Dogpatch, that mythical place of backwoods innocence and sly political humor, was the home of Li'l Abner, his wife Daisy Mae, Mammy and Pappy Yokum, and all the assorted yokels, preachers, and politicians that Al Capp created as satire on modern day life. Al Capp fans will doubtless remember that Li'l Abner evaded the pursuit of the determined Daisy Mae for 17 years before he finally succumbed to the lures of matrimonial bliss. For the aid and comfort of all the other unwed females of Dogpatch, Al Capp created Sadie Hawkins Day. On this special day, all the spinsters of Dogpatch could pursue the unmarried males, and any man caught by such a girl was obliged to marry her.

November 11, Veterans Day: Originally celebrated in the United States and in Europe as Armistice Day, this day was first established in 1918 as a day to remember the official end of World War I, which occurred on November 11 at 11 A.M. Armistice Day tradition dictated a moment of silence at the eleventh hour on the eleventh day of the eleventh month to honor those who died in World War I. In the United States the original Armistice Day eventually became Veterans Day, a day to honor veterans of all wars.

November 18, Screen Debut of Mickey Mouse: Although Mickey was probably "born" in the mind of Walt Disney while on a train en route to Los Angeles from New York, his early life is something of a secret. Mickey's successful entertainment career began years later when he went to work at the Disney Studios as an animated film actor. He had made a few silent films, including one with his leading lady Minnie Mouse, but his first real smashing success was in the very first talking animated picture, "Steamboat Willie," which opened in New York on November 18, 1928. Mickey is now over 60 years old and has enjoyed a stellar career as an animated film actor. The highlight of his acting career was his thoroughly convincing portrayal of the "Sorcerer's Apprentice" in the 1940 Disney film *Fantasia*. During World War II, Mickey left film acting and joined the war effort: The password for the Allies on D Day was "Mickey Mouse." Following his wartime service, Mickey went on to conquer television and the hearts of a new generation of postwar American children with his daily television program, *The Mickey Mouse Club*. Today as the official host for Disneyland in California and for Walt Disney World in Florida, he's busy shaking hands, leading parades, and having his picture taken with charmed visitors to the "Magic Kingdom."

November 19, Anniversary of the Gettysburg Address: On this day in 1863, before a crowd of 20,000 on a battlefield that was to mark the turning point of the Civil War, President Lincoln delivered the Gettysburg Address. The speech was simple and short, only 270 words long. Contrary to legend, Lincoln had not scrawled the speech on the back of an envelope while on the train to Gettysburg. He had worked on the speech before he left Washington and also after he arrived in

Gettysburg. On the morning of the ceremony, he wrote the final version of the speech on two pieces of paper, which he rolled up and placed in his coat pocket before joining the parade to the cemetery. Most of those in the crowd had come to hear a famous orator, Edward Everett, who obligingly delivered a long-winded, two-hour address in honor of the Union dead. Today, no one except curious historians reads Everett's overwrought, tortured rhetoric, but people all over the world know and love the simple, straightforward remarks made by President Lincoln. His moving phrases touching on equality, dedication to duty, and the completion of unfinished tasks have been chiseled in shrines throughout the United States, scrawled on posters as far away as China, and memorized by generations of schoolchildren.

November 22, Anniversary of the Assassination of John F. Kennedy: On this day in 1962, at 12:30 P.M., President John Kennedy was shot while riding in a parade in downtown Dallas, Texas. Riding in the 1961 Lincoln convertible with President and Mrs. Kennedy were Texas Governor John Connally and his wife, Nellie. Governor Connally was also hit—by a bullet that had first passed through the president's body. Although the president's car reached Parkland Memorial Hospital just 5 minutes after the shooting, the president was already near death as he entered the emergency room and was declared dead at 1:00 P.M. John Kennedy, who committed America to visiting the moon and who initiated the Peace Corps, was the youngest man ever elected president, the first Roman Catholic, and the first president to have served in the U.S. Navy. He was the fourth president to be assassinated and is one of two presidents buried at Arlington National Cemetery (the other is William Howard Taft).

Fourth Thursday in November, Thanksgiving Day: The first Thanksgiving was probably a celebration of miraculous survival rather than a feast of plenty. Out of the original 102 Pilgrim settlers of the Plymouth Colony in Massachusetts, only 50 survived illness and starvation the first year to celebrate the first Thanksgiving feast. The Pilgrims held that first Thanksgiving in October 1621, and they invited a small group of friendly Wampanoag Indians to be their guests. These same Indians had doubtless contributed to the survival of the few remaining colonists by teaching them how to plant corn.

Thanksgiving was not associated with the month of November until President George Washington appointed the last Thursday in November as a national day of thanksgiving. But most states ignored the presidential proclamation and continued to celebrate the end of harvest on various days according to their local customs. President Abraham Lincoln revived Washington's holiday in an effort to promote national unity during the Civil War. Following Lincoln's proclamation, Thanksgiving remained set as the last Thursday in November until 1939, when President Franklin D. Roosevelt changed the holiday to the fourth Thursday in November.

Sunday Nearest November 30, Beginning of Advent: The Advent Season is by tradition the true beginning of the Christian year (except in the Greek Orthodox Church). Advent begins either on St. Andrew's Day (November 30) or on the Sunday nearest to it and lasts for four weeks. It takes its name from the Latin word *adventus,* meaning "arrival," and is traditionally a season of penitence and reflection as Christians prepare for the arrival of the Christ child.

November 30, Birthday of Mark Twain: Born in Florida, Missouri, in 1835 and raised along the banks of the Mississippi, Mark Twain, whose real name was Samuel Clemens, personified the wanderlust, the down-home humor, and the ridicule of social convention that Americans associate with Yankee ingenuity and independence. He spent almost half of his life as a wanderer, writing articles for various local newspapers and doing odd jobs, including four years on the Mississippi River as a steamboat pilot. His career as a successful author was launched by a story he wrote for an obscure literary journal; the story, "The Jumping Frog of Calaveras County," was based on a true incident (a frog race in which one competitor loaded the other's frog with gunshot so that it couldn't jump) that Twain had witnessed while visiting a California gold mining camp. From this single enormously popular story, Twain went on to enjoy a stellar literary career, which reached its peak with the 1885 publication of *Huckleberry Finn,* a novel that Twain published himself in partnership with a nephew. Twain had anticipated selling 40,000 copies of the book, but to his delight, the book was banned by the Concord, Massachusetts, public library. Twain exulted over this news: "That will sell 25,000 copies of our book for sure!" In fact, his prediction was an incredible underestimate: Total sales reached over 500,000 copies.

November 21 Is World Hello Day

Founded in 1973 by Harvard student Michael McCormack, World Hello Day celebrates the value of personal communication in fostering world peace and in resolving international conflict. To celebrate World Hello Day, greet ten people in the name of peace; greet your old friends in person, by mail, or by telephone; or visit a shut-in, a nursing home resident, or a hospital patient. Schools can celebrate World Hello Day through activities and programs that promote world awareness.

Since the establishment of World Hello Day, volunteers have translated World Hello Day information into 40 languages. Founder Michael McCormack and his brother Brian have mailed World Hello Day information to every country in the world, and the day has been celebrated in 131 countries, including the Netherlands, Great Britain, the Soviet Union, Hungary, and the People's Republic of China. For a packet of information on World Hello Day write to: The McCormack Brothers, P.O. Box 993, Omaha, NE 68101. And on November 21, remember to say, "Hello."

World Hello Day

November 21

Hello	English
Bonjour	French
Buenos días	Spanish
哈 囉	Mandarin
Guten Tag	German
привéт	Russian
Ciao	Italian
صَرْ	Arabic
בָּא שָׁלוֹם	Hebrew
Goddag	Danish
Pozdrawiam	Polish
Morn	Norwegian
Kia Ora	Maori
Salamu	Swahili
Dai duit	Irish
Nabad	Somali
Hälsningar	Swedish
నమస్కారం	Telugu
Thân Chào	Vietnamese

Greet Ten People for Peace!

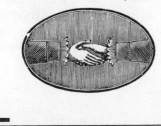

IN THE GARDEN

EVERLASTING PLEASURES

November is the month when everlastings begin to shine. From now until the last gray days of February, you can fill your home with an endless array of colors, textures, and shapes, all from the world of everlastings. Everlastings are exactly what the name implies—flowers, leaves, pods, and cones that dry easily, look as beautiful in the dried state as they did when they were growing, and last forever. If you buy everlastings in a specialty shop, you'll find they're expensive. If you grow them yourself, you'll find they cost very little but provide pleasure worth a king's ransom. Most beginning gardeners discover everlastings in November and December, the season when they're most often displayed in door wreaths, holiday nosegays, table arrangements, and even Christmas tree decorations.

Everlasting Sampler

Although experienced gardeners frequently preserve flowers using a number of complicated drying techniques, the simplest technique—air drying—can give perfect results. The trick is to select those plants that dry easily with no special treatment. Included here is a selection of both annual and perennial everlastings that will air dry perfectly. As the seed catalogs begin to arrive next month, use this list to order seeds for next year's garden of everlastings.

Annuals

Ammobium: A pure white flower with a button yellow center, this everlasting can be grown as a perennial in areas where winter temperatures seldom fall below 20°F. To preserve the bright yellow color of the center, gather these for drying before the flowers are fully open.

Celosia: These annuals should be started from seed indoors and transplanted after all danger of frost is past. Also known as cockscomb, celosia comes in two forms, crested and plumed. The colors of the fresh flowers are brilliant and a bit garish, but as they dry they change to subtle, attractive shades.

Globe amaranth: A low-growing, tough little annual whose flowers resemble the flowers of sweet clover, this everlasting requires almost no care once it's started. Seeds can be started indoors, or they can be direct-seeded into the garden.

Larkspur: Once established this annual form of delphinium is much easier to grow than traditional hybrid delphiniums. Larkspur self-sows easily, but the choice hybrid colors of the original planting will disappear into the nonhybrid purple color of the offspring. Larkspur is difficult to germinate. Many gardeners have good luck with sowing the seed in the fall so that it germinates in the early spring. If you'd like to try a spring sowing, sow outdoors quite early—at least a month before your normal last frost date.

Salvia: This extremely large genus includes over 700 species of flowers in annual, biennial, and perennial forms. The vertical spiked shape of these flowers make a beautiful contrast to the more common flat or rounded forms of other common everlastings. Colors range from fiery red to deep blue or purple, as well as white. Start seeds of the annual forms indoors and transplant to the garden after all danger of frost has past.

Statice: There are at least a half-dozen varieties of statice and a rainbow of colors to choose from. Two types of statice, sea lavender and German statice, are perennials suitable for cold-climate gardens. The perennial varieties are difficult to start from seed and are most easily grown if purchased as started plants from a nursery. The annual varieties should be started indoors under lights and transplanted into the garden in late spring.

Strawflower: Although the plants themselves are ungainly and unattractive, the strawflower annual is worth growing. It's an extremely easy flower to grow and will produce an abundance of flowers despite almost any insect or disease attack. For greatest variety, pick flowers in all stages of development, from closed bud to almost-mature flower.

Perennials

Artemesia: Once established, this perennial is easy to grow and will produce an abundance of silver-toned foliage that dries easily. If you want to grow this as an everlasting, choose an upright variety rather than a creeping type. Creeping varieties have foliage only on one side of each branch.

Baby's-breath: This light, airy plant sports a veil of tiny white flowers that air dry quite easily. Baby's-breath is available also as an annual, but the annual variety does not air dry well. Stick to the perennial varieties for best results.

Chinese lantern: Plant this perennial in an obscure part of your yard and check it frequently to make sure it isn't spreading out of its allotted space. In its early stage of development, Chinese lantern resembles a potato plant and certainly is no more decorative than a potato. It comes into its glory in early autumn with the production of brilliant orange, lantern-shaped bladders, which hang from the stems just like miniature lanterns. The plant spreads via underground runners and is difficult to eradicate once it is established. Make sure you like it before you plant it.

False indigo: This perennial does double duty. Its flower spikes resemble lupines, but these don't air dry easily. Keep the flowers unpicked and enjoy them in the garden until fall. The flowers leave branches laden with large, dark brown, decorative pods on vigorous upright stems. You can finish drying the pods by standing the stems in an empty container. If you want them to appear even more dramatic, spray the dried pods lightly with varnish. **Oriental poppy:** While the flowers of all poppies are extremely fragile and not suitable for air drying, the seed pods of the oriental poppy resemble miniature ginger jars and make a worthwhile addition to any collection of everlasting flowers. The pods are woody, durable, and beautiful. To collect pods simply allow your poppies to bloom and drop petals; then pick the pods from mid-summer on as they dry on the plant. **Tansy:** A vigorous, 4-foot-tall perennial sporting brilliant yellow button-shaped flowers, this everlasting can be invasive. In fact, in some parts of the United States, it's a wildflower. For drying, pick the flowers when they are a fresh, brilliant yellow, but leave some flower clusters on the plant to turn deep brown. Harvest these in the early fall at the end of the growing season. **Yarrow:** This perennial is easy to grow and comes in several forms including types suitable for a rock garden. For air drying, choose an upright golden or white variety. The pink varieties do not air dry well.

Drying the Easy Way

You can preserve everlastings in several ways: by air drying; by drying in silica gel, sand, or a mixture of cornmeal and borax; or even by drying in your microwave. Air drying is by far the easiest way to preserve everlastings, but there are a few tricks to this method:

Gather everlastings when they are not fully opened from the bud stage. They will continue to mature during the drying stage. If you pick flowers that are already fully mature, they will deteriorate as they dry.

Air dry everlastings in a dark, warm, dry place. Because of its periodic high moisture levels, the kitchen is the last place in the world you should air dry flowers. Moisture encourages mildew, and sunlight causes a definite loss of color. A good place to dry everlastings is a clean, well-ventilated attic or an unused closet.

Air dry flowers as soon as possible after they're picked. For almost all flowers, remove the leaves, which usually don't dry well, and gather the stems in a small bunch secured with a string or a rubber band. Secure the stems tightly because they shrink as they dry.

Wire the heads of weak-stemmed flowers before drying. Some flowers have stems that, when dry, are not strong enough to support the dried flower head. Expe-

Fall Grapevine Wreath

One beautiful way to display your everlasting flowers is by wiring or gluing them to a grapevine wreath. If you don't have your own grapevines to make a wreath, visit a nearby vineyard. Most vineyard owners will gladly give away or sell prunings for a nominal cost. If you have access to undeveloped land, you can also gather prunings from wild grapevines, honeysuckle, or Virginia creeper (also called woodbine). These all make fine wreaths, as do prunings from willow and forsythia. Caution: If you choose to prune wild vines, make certain you do not include poison ivy in your pruning. Poison ivy can assume the form of a shrub or a vine. Before venturing into the woods, be sure you know what poison ivy looks like. Wear clothing that covers your arms and legs, and wear gloves.

After you've gathered your vine prunings, you will probably find that some of them are thick, stiff, and woody, and others are thin and pliable. The thick, woody trimmings make a fine base for a vine wreath, but you will find them much easier to work with if you soak them in water first. Before you begin work on your wreath, gather the woody, stiff vines and soak them overnight in a washtub or trash can filled with water.

To assemble your wreath you will need four stakes, a light sledge hammer, a spool of lightweight wire, wire cutters, and pruners to remove unwanted portions of vine. Begin your wreath by pounding the four stakes into the ground to form a square. Choose the longest of the woody vines that you've soaked in water. Wire one end of this vine to a stake and wrap the entire length of the vine in a circle around the four stakes. Secure the end of this vine by tucking or wiring the end to the circle. Add successive vine pieces beginning with the thicker pieces and ending with the lightweight pliable pieces. Secure the vines by tucking the beginnings and ends into the emerging wreath. Usually the friction of the surrounding vines will hold a new piece in place, but if you encounter a piece that won't stay in place, simply attach it to the wreath with wire. If the vines you've gathered have curled climbing tendrils, take care to keep these attached. Tendrils are fragile and easily broken off, but including them adds a natural beauty to your creation.

Before removing your wreath from the stakes, bind the entire wreath together by adding a tight circle of wire at four separate intervals around the entire wreath. Clip the wire that held your starting piece to the stake, and remove your wreath, which is now ready for a wire hanger. For best results, add a wire hanger to the back of the wreath *before* decorating the front. As you decorate, let your imagination fly. Choose anything gathered from nature—for example, dried everlastings, cones, nuts, berries, abandoned birds' nests, sea shells, moss, dried seed pods, unusual pebbles. Finish off your creation with a jaunty bow.

rience will teach you which flowers work best with wire for stems. Common everlastings that need wiring include globe amaranth and strawflowers.

Dry most everlastings by hanging the bunches upside down so that the weight of the flower pulls the stems straight. This method works for most common everlastings, such as statice, celosias, and salvias. Everlastings that don't dry well upside down include flat-faced flowers, some grasses, and some unusual everlastings, such as money plants and Chinese lanterns.

Dry flat-faced flowers, such as Queen Anne's lace or yarrow, with the flower facing upward. If you dry these flowers by hanging them upside down, the flower face tends to form a cup shape. A simple way to air dry flat-faced flowers is to insert the stems through a window screen that is supported horizontally like a table. The stems drop toward the floor and the flower faces are held facing upward.

Dry a few selected everlastings by simply standing them upright in a container. Chinese lanterns, money plants, and most ornamental grasses assume a more natural shape if dried in an upright position. In choosing which everlastings to dry in a standing position, think about how the plant looks in nature. If it assumes a bending, drooping shape in the garden, it will look best if it dries in this form.

ALMANAC GARDENING CALENDAR

As winter spreads its icy fingers from the northernmost zones toward the south, the differences between the garden climate zones become more pronounced. For most cold-zone gardeners, the most exciting gardening event on the horizon is the late December arrival of the new seed catalogs. Gardeners in the middle zones can still plant balled-and-burlapped nursery stock as well as bulbs. Gardeners in the warmest zones can begin an entirely new gardening season by setting out cool-temperature-loving crops.

Zone 1

Keep cold-frame lettuce, spinach, rocket (arugula) and other greens moist, and open the frame on days when the temperature is above 50°F. When temperatures fall below 10°F, bring container-grown greens inside and place in a sunny window or in a window supplemented with grow lights. To overwinter parsley, remove cloches so the plants go dormant, then cover them with mulch when night temperatures regularly fall below 20°F. Clean the garden for winter. Drain and store hoses and other irrigation equipment. Empty the gas and oil from tillers, mowers, shredders, weed whips, and any other machines you won't be using until next spring. Clean the earth from the blades and tines of all your hand tools.

To prevent conifers from spreading under the weight of heavy snow, tie ropes around them or enclose in chicken wire staked in place. Prepare pots of bulbs for winter forcing. Place them in the basement or anywhere that the temperature is 50°F or lower (but not freezing) to let the roots grow. When the bulbs poke through the soil surface, put the pots on a sunny windowsill.

If you are going to plant new strawberry beds next spring, put in everbearers. Zone 1 gardeners frequently have late frosts and rainy Junes, which can cause the berries to be small, poorly flavored, or diseased. Start researching now in catalogs and with your extension agent to learn which varieties have proven themselves in local trials. All through the month check stored fruit for spoilage.

Zone 2

Do a final garden cleanup. After fall chores are over, winterize garden tools—clean off mud and wipe metal parts with oil to prevent rust. Check stored squashes and tomatoes for rot. Wipe sound fruit with a weak solution of household bleach. Discard squashes subjected even to a light frost—they won't keep. Cover carrots and parsnips left in the ground with 12 inches of straw.

Both vegetables store best at about 55°F. If you want to store cabbages, select solid, disease-free heads with a heavy, waxy bloom. Mid-November is a good time to sow seeds of compact tomatoes for indoor growing.

Clean up and spade or till the annual bed so that it's ready for spring planting. Give your lawn one last mowing if the grass is more than 3 inches tall. Short stems mean less disease. Houseplants recently brought indoors need good light while they readjust to their environment. Check the pots for slugs, snails, sow bugs, and other pests. Cut coleus plants back halfway and water regularly. Start new plants from the tip cuttings.

Fertilize fruit and nut trees now for fast growth next spring. Gather and dispose of mummified and fallen fruit to control insects and diseases. There's still time to whitewash trunks to prevent southwest injury. Remove sod and mulch from the base of fruit trees and apply hardware cloth or tree guards to prevent animal damage. Dry hulled hickory nuts and black walnuts on a screen in the basement so that they'll stay sweet and keep longer. When dry, store in onion bags at 50°F or lower.

Zone 3

On subfreezing nights, remember to close cold frames containing spinach, collards, lettuce, and endive. These crops won't grow much, but will stay fresh for harvest through the month. After cleaning up residues of late crops, take soil samples for testing and till under mulch, manure, and compost. Spread mulch over exposed soil to reduce erosion. Cover compost piles with tarps, boards, or other waterproof material to keep winter rain from leaching valuable nutrients. If you plan to store crops such as carrots, turnips, and salsify in the garden, cover them with at least a foot of mulch before the first heavy freeze. Mark rows so you'll know where to dig after snowfall.

As chrysanthemums die back, prune to ground level. Cover with a loose mulch after the ground freezes. Dig geraniums, clean soil off the roots and hang in a cool cellar for the winter. Cut down and compost the foliage of perennials, and top-dress with manure or compost after the ground freezes. Mark those that need to be divided next spring. Plant hardy annuals such as sweet alyssum, larkspurs, and snapdragons in well-marked beds for an early start next spring.

It's still safe to plant balled-and-burlapped evergreens early in the month. Water deeply, mulch, and stake for the winter. If you plan to buy a live Christmas tree, dig a hole for it before the ground freezes. Evergreens and other woody ornamentals planted this year should receive their last deep watering just before the ground freezes. As shrubs, trees, and perennials reach full dormancy, mulch with an inch or two of well-rotted manure or compost.

Harvest all nuts as they fall. Destroy diseased and wormy nuts to break pest life cycles. Rake up the last leaves and fruit drops from trees, bushes, and vines. Prune limbs that may not bear up under accumulations of ice and snow. Once trees are dormant, spray with dormant oil on a day with temperatures above freezing as an early attempt to keep scale and other overwintering pests under control. Balled-and-burlapped fruit trees can still be planted. Water deeply, stake, and mulch heavily. Wrap trunks to protect them from rodents and sunscald. If the month is dry, water first-year fruit trees, bushes, and vines deeply to insulate roots. Protect blueberries with a loose, acidic mulch of pine needles or rotted sawdust.

Zone 4

Apply straw or any other airy mulch to hardy vegetables, such as beets, kale, and spinach, to keep them harvest-ready into colder weather. Harvest Jerusalem artichokes, parsnips, and brussels sprouts after they've been sweetened by frost. Horseradish can be dug now or left until spring. Apply 12 inches of mulch to garlic beds, carrots, parsnips, and other ground-stored root crops. Top-dress asparagus and rhubarb beds with compost or manure. In mild-winter areas, plant garlic, onions, and radishes. Burn diseased or insect-infested plants and add the rest to the compost pile. Cover the pile with leaves, but don't turn it. In cool weather, turning only retards decomposition. Till vacant beds and leave them open a few days to expose pests to predators before applying winter mulch. Bring in soil and compost to make potting mixes this winter. Before filing this year's garden notes, evaluate the yield of each vegetable variety to guide your purchases for next season.

Plant tulips early in the month, making sure they have good drainage. After frost, cut down dahlia tops to 3 or 4 inches, but leave the tubers in the ground another week or so before digging them, taking care not to break the necks. Let them dry a week or two before storing in sand or vermiculite in a cool, frost-free place. Cut down cannas and apply a thick mulch if you leave the roots outdoors. In the last half of the month, remove lily tops and pile 2 inches of soil over beds to keep mice from nibbling bulbs. Wait to mound soil around roses until their leaves have begun to fall. To prevent loosening of roots, cut tall canes to 30 inches and thin small branches that create wind

resistance. Cut back and clean up perennial beds. Give the lawn a final mowing and soaking when growth has stopped, and water all woody ornamentals, especially new evergreens, before the ground freezes. Wrap trunks of young thin-barked trees with burlap to protect against sunscald. Pick bagworm cases off shrubs.

Harvest pecans as soon as possible after shucks are killed by frost, and store in the freezer. Keep pecan trunks wrapped in burlap until they're six years old. Protect fruit tree trunks from rodents with hardware cloth or plastic tree guards. Dig holes early in the month for new stock that could arrive during bad weather. Fill the planting holes with leaves or straw. To avoid root damage when planting new stock, insert support stakes before filling in planting holes. Tie up plants only if necessary, and only for one year.

Zone 5

This month will bring a couple of sneak freezes, but if you can nurse cool-season vegetables through the frigid nights they may continue to grow for several more weeks. Cover broccoli and other brassicas with plastic sheeting or cardboard boxes during brief cold spells. To minimize frost damage to the hardy brassicas (broccoli, cauliflower, cabbage, and brussels sprouts), flood the rows with water just before nightfall. Tying leaves over the heads of almost-ripe broccoli and cauliflower will protect them from moderate frosts. In the lower elevations of the West, use plastic tunnels or other cloches to extend the season for lettuce, radishes, and other semihardy vegetables.

Dig new potatoes, and pick through leftovers from your spring crop. Plant those that are soft and sprouting, but be sure to insulate them from winter with a deep mulch. Dig sweet potatoes, being careful not to poke them with your fork or shovel. Cure them for 10 days at about 85°F—most varieties taste better after curing than fresh from the ground. As carrots and other root crops reach full size, mulch with a foot of chopped leaves or other material. Mulch kale and spinach, too. Plant garlic cloves, or dig and divide clumps left from last year. Sprinkle bonemeal beneath cloves to provide phosphorus. In areas with mild winters, set out winter onions for big, sweet onions next spring. Late in the month, cut back asparagus and mulch the bed with manure and straw. Cultivate open soil to expose insect larvae to birds. Plant a winter cover crop of cereal rye, which grows faster than annual rye this late in the year.

This is the ideal time to plant daffodils, tulips, crocuses, and hyacinths. Prepare beds with compost, and plant in clumps for best effect.

All bulbs will grow better if bonemeal or cottonseed meal is mixed into the soil at planting time. Also plant new lilies, and cut back iris leaves to 4-inch fans. Mulch around roses, but wait until later in winter to prune them. If you prune too early, new growth may appear just in time to be winterkilled. Cut back chrysanthemums after the flowers fade, but wait until spring to dig and divide them. If you have big, healthy seedlings of biennials and perennials, set them out now. Be prepared to cover them if a hard freeze strikes before they have adjusted to outdoor life. Direct-seed sweet peas, but sow pansies and other hardy annuals indoors.

Renew mulches around grapes and berries. Add leaf or pine-straw mulch to strawberries and blueberries, which thrive in acidic soil. Raspberries and blackberries do better with a hay or straw mulch. Replace wrappings around the trunks of young trees before hard freezes. If insects or molds have set in, leave the trunks bare for a short time before rewrapping. If you use white latex paint instead of wrappings, put an extra coat on the south side of every trunk for more protection against sunscald.

Zone 6

Harvest the last fruits of frost-sensitive vegetables and replace them with cool-season crops. Put in transplants of cabbage, broccoli, and brussels sprouts early in the month, and sow seeds of English peas, kale, carrots, and radishes. Follow these at midmonth with turnips, mustard, beets, and spinach. Use a portable cold frame to keep lettuce protected. Put in onion sets and plants. Onion plants smaller than a pencil will form large bulbs. Also plant chives, shallots, and garlic. Cut back asparagus fronds after they turn brown, and cover the beds with compost. Plant new asparagus beds now. Sow coriander, parsley, caraway, chervil, and fennel. Plant yarrow at the end of the month. Keep an eye out for worms in the garden—especially cabbage loopers. Bt *(Bacillus thuringiensis)* will keep them in check.

Chill hyacinths, narcissi, tulips, and crocuses in the refrigerator for four to six weeks before planting. Other bulbs can be planted now without precooling. Sow pansies, delphiniums, poppies, and larkspurs in flats for spring planting. Direct-seed sweet peas. Ornamental cabbage and kale make for good color. Planted in a large grouping, these plants are showy all winter.

Before freezing temperatures set in, dig holes for planting trees. Add compost and other amendments to holes and allow them to sit before planting. Plant strawberries. Root blackberry cuttings and grow them in containers. Mark diseased or damaged tree limbs while the leaves are still on, but hold off pruning until later in the season.

Zone 7

Make succession plantings of the cool-weather crops you started last month. Asian brassicas, such as bok choy, tend to bolt if transplanted, crowded, or otherwise stressed. Sow them in your richest soil. Keep them thinned and weeded. Feed with manure tea and mulch in hot weather. In south Florida, the southern tip of Texas, and the desert valleys of southern California, continue planting beans, celery, corn, onions, parsley, white potatoes, turnips, and tomatoes. Frost can occur in some of these areas during December and January, so keep protective covers handy.

Set out perennials and cool-season bedding plants. Direct-seed larkspurs, cornflowers, and nigellas. Sow wildflowers in those patches where a spring show is wanted without a lot of effort. Plant narcissus bulbs that have been refrigerated for six to eight weeks. Wait until December to plant tulips. Order bare-root roses and other ornamentals. Prune to shape some evergreens, such as junipers, arborvitae, pines, spruces, pittosporums, and magnolias, but don't prune camellias, spireas, or azaleas because spring blossoms will be lost. Renew the acid mulch on camellias, rhododendrons, *Daphne odora,* and azaleas. Continue to plant lawns, ground covers, shrubs, and trees while the soil is warm enough to promote root growth. Divide Shasta daisies, geraniums, daylilies, and agapanthus. After bloom, cut back chrysanthemums to about 5 inches. Divide irises, cut back the leaf fans to about 4 inches, and replant in a bed enriched with compost and bonemeal.

Plant new strawberry beds in all but the hottest parts of the zone. Plant balled-and-burlapped fruit and nut trees as they become available. These are far superior to bare-root trees, which become available later. On the West Coast, keep watering fruit and nut trees, especially citrus. Break down catchment basins under peaches, apricots, and nectarines to allow winter rains to drain away. Sow an orchard cover crop of annual rye and mustard for plowing down in early spring.

IN GOOD HEALTH

TO DRINK OR NOT TO DRINK

November signals the start of the year-end holiday season, the traditional time to break out the champagne or have an extra cocktail at a family Thanksgiving or Christmas gathering.

Perhaps you've found yourself drawn in recently by the enticing news that moderate alcohol consumption may actually be good for your health. Headlines over the past several years have spoken of a reduced mortality from heart disease, lower risk of stroke, and even weight loss as a consequence of moderate drinking. But before you bend your elbow, let me bend your ear a bit.

First the good news. Several surveys carried out about 10 years ago indicated that people who drank small amounts of alcohol had a lower mortality from heart disease than those who did not drink at all. This observation suggested that alcohol, consumed in moderation, somehow protected against heart disease.

Considerable evidence has stacked up since then to show exactly *how* small intakes of alcohol might confer protection against heart disease: by increasing the high-density lipoprotein (HDL) fraction in the blood. HDL is the beneficial type of cholesterol.

In one study with seven normal men, HDL cholesterol increased significantly when they were drinking moderately. Levels of LDL cholesterol (the "bad guy" responsible for deposits in the blood vessels that ultimately lead to heart attacks) and triglyceride (another damaging blood fat) were unaffected, though. In a group of 24 healthy men, the HDL-cholesterol level fell when the men abstained from drinking and rose again when they consumed modest amounts of alcohol.

In an investigation with 100 subjects, both men and women, it was again shown that the HDL

cholesterol increased. In this study, the amount of alcohol consumed was fairly small: about 18 grams of alcohol per day (a pint of beer, two small glasses of wine, or about a jigger of whiskey).

In a more recent study of almost 8,000 men, however, British researchers found that while moderate drinking raised HDL, it did not significantly lower the risk of heart attack. The effects of the well-known risk factors, such as cigarette smoking and high blood pressure, far outweigh those of moderate drinking, the researchers conclude.

Fewer Strokes, Fewer Pounds

It was recently reported in the *New England Journal of Medicine* that the risk of strokes was lower in light drinkers than in nondrinkers. But in heavy drinkers, the risk from stroke was four times as high as in nondrinkers. Light drinkers were defined as those who consumed between 10 and 90 grams of alcohol per week (there are about 10 grams in a small—3½ ounce—glass of wine) and heavy drinkers, those who consumed more than 300 grams per week.

One nutritionist has reported that the metabolic rate (the rate at which the body expends energy) is increased following modest alcohol consumption. Another research group found that people given a diet that included wine or alcohol lost weight, while a similar group of people consuming the same total number of calories but with food taking the place of alcohol calories didn't lose any weight. This suggests that alcohol is utilized less efficiently as an energy source than other "foods."

In that same study, pure alcohol was compared with alcohol from wine. The researchers noted that the minerals calcium, phosphorus, and magnesium were better absorbed and utilized when wine was consumed rather than an equivalent amount of pure alcohol.

But beware. As with so many other facets of our complex lives, moderate alcohol intake has another side. In an investigation comparing food and nutrient intake in two groups of men in a Veterans Administration center in Wisconsin, men who drank regularly consumed about 11 percent fewer total calories from food than nondrinkers. In other words, they were filling up on alcohol and depressing their appetites. As a result, they had somewhat lower intakes of other nutrients.

But by far the greatest concern about moderate alcohol consumption is the recently discovered link to breast cancer. Two major studies

on that subject were published in the *New England Journal of Medicine.* One study, from the National Cancer Institute, included more than 7,000 women. It showed that a woman who drank about three drinks a week had a 40 to 50 percent higher risk of developing breast cancer in her lifetime. An American woman is believed to have about a 10 percent chance of developing breast cancer in her lifetime. A 50 percent increase in that risk would increase her chances of getting the disease to 15 percent.

The other report, from Harvard Medical School, showed essentially the same results: a 50 percent increase in risk in those women who drank moderately. That was defined as three to nine drinks per week.

What should we conclude from all of this? Current information suggests that men may benefit from moderate drinking of alcoholic beverages—say, an occasional drink during the course of a week. But women appear to be at increased risk for breast cancer, even from the very modest intakes of alcohol that may reduce the risk of heart disease. On balance, then, evidence right now dictates extreme caution when it comes to imbibing more than an occasional drink. And of course, you should make every effort to prevent a pattern of continuous drinking.

Close Encounters of the Holiday Kind

Thanksgiving is traditionally family reunion time. This is the time of year when you get to hear Aunt Grace tell about her gall bladder operation for the tenth time; it's the time of year when your brother-in-law always gets tipsy and insults the other guests; it's the time when the dog will chew up Cousin Al's new gloves, and the kids will tell Grandma something you definitely don't want her to know. Even the most affectionate families find family reunions stressful. To keep yours affable, break the tension with some of these strategies:

☞ Be realistic in your expectations; accept the fact that personalities don't change dramatically. You'll be better able to deal with problem family members if you remind yourself ahead of time what to expect.

☞ Include nonfamily members in your family celebration. Most family members naturally become reluctant to renew old quarrels in the presence of an unfamiliar face. Nonfamily guests give everyone a chance to forget family problems and concentrate on "polite" conversation.

☞ Enlist children to help other family members using the buddy system. If anyone in your family is in need of special assistance or care, such as an elderly member who is hard of hearing, assign a child to be a buddy to that person and to look out for his needs. Assign an older child to entertain a younger child.

☞ Plan an easy outing immediately following your holiday meal. If everyone leaves the dinner table to take a walk to the park or to the local high school football game, there's less chance for conflict to arise.

Walking Tip for November

Before snow, slush, ice, or freezing rain become a fixture in the weather forecast, equip yourself for winter walking. Your regular sneakers or walking shoes won't keep your feet warm and dry, and you'll need something for balance before tackling an icy sidewalk. For winter walking comfort, choose a lightweight hiking boot lined with Gore-Tex to keep out moisture. Don't bother to buy insulated boots because uninsulated models are lighter and more flexible and can be used in warm weather as well as cold. After you've purchased your boots, invest in a few pairs of wool socks with a polypropylene liner. The liner wicks away sweat and prevents it from freezing on your feet. If you don't already own a favorite walking stick, try one of the collapsible models from a hiking supply shop. An old ski pole also makes a handy walking stick. If you decide to buy hiking boots through a mail-order catalog, make a tracing of each foot (wearing the wool socks you've purchased) and send it to the mail-order company as a size check on the boot you've ordered.

AT HOME

SHOPPING FROM HOME

November is a good month to shop at home. With a few hours of free time and a stack of catalogs you can complete all of your holiday gift shopping without fighting the post-Thanksgiving crowds and without searching for a parking space in an overloaded parking lot. If you're doing your holiday gift buying through mail order this year, order early in November. Early ordering gives you plenty of time to shop elsewhere if an item you ordered is out of stock or proves to be unsatisfactory in any way.

At-home shopping, which includes shopping through catalogs, television shopping services, and computerized electronic shopping, is big business—close to $65 billion in sales in 1987. And it's been growing steadily in recent years. Currently the dollar value of home shopping is increasing at the rate of about 12 percent a year. This growth is at least in part due to the simple fact that today, people have more money to spend but less time to spend it in. Some experts believe that a third of all retail purchases will be made from home by the year 2000, a development that could raise the annual total dollar sales of home shopping to half a trillion dollars.

While many people still enjoy the excitement of shopping malls and department stores, others are discovering that catalogs are looking better and better. They're slicker, more sophisticated, and sometimes even enlightening. Sears is the granddaddy of them all, but Spiegel, Bloomingdale's, L. L. Bean, Neiman-Marcus, Brookstone, Conran's, and many other trendy newcomers have contributed greatly to the fashionability of buying by catalog. And toll-free 800 numbers and credit cards have made it almost effortless to shop at home—at least until the bills come!

If TV, rather than the printed page, is your preferred media, welcome to shopping via the tube. In 1985 TV home shopping accounted for $90 million in purchases; a year later that figure had jumped to $450 million—no small leap. Nationally, about 40 cable networks offer shop-at-home broadcasting. Now, with J.C. Penney and Sears involved in television shopping, and with the growth of cable stations that mix TV shopping with game shows and other forms of entertainment, look for enormous growth in TV shopping.

Some Advice for Shopping by Mail or Phone

Although shopping by mail and phone are convenient, there are some drawbacks you should know about. Because you don't actually get to see and touch the item before you order it and because you're communicating with the merchandiser by long distance, you're forced to place a lot of trust in the seller. Unless you've previously bought from a particular company, you have no way of judging the quality of the merchandise or service. Here are some precautions to keep in mind:

☛ Before you order an item, check to see if there is a charge for postage and handling. Postage and handling may increase the total price you pay by several dollars. After adding these charges to the original cost of the item, you may discover that the item you're considering is not really a good buy.

☛ Keep the catalog or ad after you've placed your order. You may need to refer to it if the item you receive is not quite what you expected.

☛ If an order you've placed and paid for seems to be taking an unusually long time to arrive, you may have some recourse. Companies that do business through the mail are regulated by the Federal Trade Commission (FTC). The FTC enforces a code of conduct for mail-order businesses under a federal regulation called the Mail-Order Rule.

Your Mail-Order Rights

Advertisements for mail-order goods may designate a shipping date somewhere in the advertisement; for example, the ad may say, "Allow five weeks for shipment." The FTC Mail-Order Rule requires the seller to ship the merchandise within the advertised time. If *no* shipping time is given in the ad, the FTC requires the seller to ship the merchandise to you within 30 days of receiving your properly completed order form and complete payment for the goods (either by cash, check, money order, or credit card).

If the seller finds that he cannot ship to you within the time he advertised or within 30 days of receiving your order and payment, he must notify you of the delay and give you a choice between two options: (1) to cancel your order and receive a refund or (2) to agree to accept your item at a later date. In sending your option notice, the seller must provide a free way for you to reply (usually a postage-paid card). If the *delay* in shipping your merchandise will be 30 days or less, the seller may assume that *your failure to reply to the delay notice means that*

you have accepted option (2). For all delays of 30 days or less, you must notify the seller in writing if you wish to select option (1), cancellation of the order.

If the seller finds that the shipping delay will be longer than 30 days from the promised delivery date, he must inform you of the two options mentioned above, *but he must assume that you wish to cancel the order unless you notify him otherwise.* For all delays of more than 30 days, you must inform the seller in writing if you wish to select option (2) above, acceptance of your merchandise at a later date.

HELP FOR THE UNHAPPY CUSTOMER

The telephone you just bought doesn't ring loud enough? Your new stereo speaker has an annoying buzz? Your electrician just sent you a shockingly high bill for a simple service? You may be angry but you needn't feel helpless. There are more people out there ready to assist you than you probably realize.

If you're unhappy with goods or services you've purchased, the U.S. Office of Consumer Affairs has a very useful booklet, *Consumer's Resource Handbook,* that tells you what to do. You can get a copy for free by writing *Handbook,* Consumer Information Center, Pueblo, CO 81009.

In the handbook, the U.S. Office of Consumer Affairs provides free advice to folks who are dissatisfied with a purchase. The first recommended step is the obvious one: Go back to the store or person you did business with and try to get your problem resolved.

If that doesn't work, write a letter of complaint. If your complaint is about a defect in merchandise, write to the consumer contact or customer service representative associated with the product's manufacturer. If your complaint is about a service you received, write to the customer service representative of the company that delivered the service. The *Consumer's Resource Handbook* gives you letter-writing tips and shows you a sample letter of complaint that you can revise for your particular situation. If the address of the company or manufacturer is not in your local telephone directory, see the listing of corporate consumer contacts in the *Consumer's Resource Handbook,* or check *Standard & Poor's Register of Corporations, Directors, and Executives* in your library. If you don't know the name of the company that made your product, look in the *Thomas Register;* it lists the manufacturers of thousands of products.

And if *that* doesn't work, you don't have to give up. There's more help. If you've tried to settle a business dispute using the strategies given so far and had no success, here are some other options open to you:

Third-Party Resolution Programs

These programs have been set up solely to deal with unresolved problems between customers and industry members. Your case will be referred first to an informal mediator, and if he or she can't solve the problem, then to a panel or independent person who will make a decision in your case. A list of such programs can be found in the *Consumer's Resource Handbook.*

Better Business Bureaus

You're probably already familiar with these nonprofit organizations. They're organized by local businesses and can provide general information about member companies to any interested caller. But many Better Business Bureaus also handle consumer complaints and may even mediate and arbitrate complaints. A list of the 170 BBB's across the country can be found in the *Consumer's Resource Handbook.* You can also contact the Council of Better Business Bureaus for the BBB nearest the company or person you have a complaint against. Its address is 1515 Wilson Boulevard, Arlington, VA 22209.

Newspaper, TV, and Radio Action Lines

Check out local TV or radio stations for programs that help consumers with problems. Check local newspapers for an Action Column that deals with citizen complaints. Although the media have no legal powers, their persuasive powers can be very strong because of the publicity they can generate for or against a company.

State, County, or Local Consumer Offices

First contact your city or county consumer affairs office; if there isn't one in your area, then call the state consumer affairs office. They talk to consumers with problems all the time and can either help you directly or refer you to the proper agency. The government section (blue pages) of your phone directory lists consumer offices; the *Consumer's Resource Handbook* also has a listing of them.

Industry and Trade Associations

Many industries and professional groups have trade associations that promote their businesses. Some of these associations can help you with a problem you're having with a company within that industry or profession, *even if the firm in question is not a member of the association.* Several of those that will handle complaints are listed in the *Consumer's Resource Handbook;* you'll also find listings in a directory called *National Trade & Professional Associations of the U.S. and Canada and Labor Unions.* You'll find a copy of this directory at your library.

Occupational and Professional Licensing Boards

If your problem isn't about a toaster or TV but concerns a service you received—from a plumber or a doctor, for example—you can contact a state licensing or regulatory board. There are about 1,500 state boards that license or register more than 550 professions and occupations, including such diverse professions and services as lawyers, doctors, funeral directors, plumbers, auto repair facilities, and employment agencies. Your local or state consumer affairs office can help you find the right licensing board for your problem; you can also look in your telephone directory under government offices or professional listings.

Federal Agencies

Some government agencies can handle individual complaints. Call the Federal Information Center in your state and they'll tell you which agency can help you. The *Consumer's Resource Handbook* also lists specific agencies and the services they have for consumers.

Small Claims Court

Legal procedures here are generally simple, the fees are nominal, and you usually don't need a lawyer. Check under municipal, county, or state government listings for small claims courts, and call yours to find out if your problem can be settled there.

Private Lawyers

Obviously, you can hire a lawyer to handle your problem. Consider this option if the problem is serious, if you don't have the time to handle it yourself, or if you aren't getting satisfaction through other channels. The Lawyer Referral Service through your local or state bar association can help you find a lawyer if you don't know of one.

YOUR NOVEMBER SHOPPER'S TIP

Apples, broccoli, cabbage, cranberries, and sweet potatoes are most plentiful and therefore a better buy this month. The sweet potato recipe here makes a quick and easy appetizer. You can also serve sweet potato munchies as the main dish for an evening meal; served with brown rice and bright green broccoli, this sweet potato dish makes a colorful and appealing dinner platter.

Sweet Potato Munchies

sweet potatoes
vegetable oil
cheddar cheese, sliced

Peel sweet potatoes and slice crosswise. Sauté in a small amount of oil and drain quickly on paper towels. While still hot, place a slice of cheddar cheese between 2 slices of sweet potato. (Hot potato slices melt cheese.) If your munchies cool off a little between preparation and dinner time, reheat them in your microwave.

YOUR HOME MAINTENANCE CHECKLIST

☞ Check and clean air filters in forced-air heating systems; this should be done monthly during heating season.

☞ Drain your hot water heater. See January for directions.

☞ Vacuum the baseboard elements of an electric heating system monthly during heating season.

☞ Test your smoke alarms with a smoke source. See February for directions.

☞ Check and clean your humidifier according to the manufacturer's instructions.

☞ Check and clean your washing machine. See March for directions.

☞ Clean the filter in the range hood.

EVENTS AND FESTIVALS

Queen Kumquat Sashay
Orlando, Florida

Early November. Join the fun in Orlando at the Kumquat Sashay, a parade that pokes fun at the lavish, highly staged Citrus Bowl Parade. Opening ceremonies for the sashay begin with the crowning of the Kumquat Queen, who must be a redhead selected at random from the parade spectators. No conventional clubs, groups, or bands need apply for the Kumquat Sashay, because this parade is reserved for all those groups of people who would never be asked to march in an ordinary parade. Among the marchers in past parades are handicapped paraders performing synchronized wheelchair drills, a riding lawn mower brigade, a whale rescue team dispensing slushed ice to the crowd, a group of lost liberals in bleeding heart tee shirts, a group of five guys who never got to march in a parade, a group of folks who claim to have seen Elvis recently, and just about any other wacky group you can think of. As if all this silliness weren't enough, marchers throw the pecan-sized, sour, orange-colored kumquats to spectators throughout the parade route. Information: Bob Morris, Queen Kumquat Sashay, *The Orlando Sentinel,* 633 North Orange Avenue, Orlando, FL 32801.

Buffalo Auction
Custer, South Dakota

Mid-November. If you have a few extra acres out back, you too can have a buffalo herd. All you need is some ready cash and a cattle truck to haul home your prize buffaloes. Each year Custer State Park auctions off 300 buffaloes from the park's resident herd. Most folks who bid are supplementing private herds, but anyone is welcome to bid. The average buffalo goes for about $950, and all proceeds go to the park. Information: Custer State Park, HCR 83, Box 70, Custer, SD 57730.

Alascattalo Day
Anchorage, Alaska

Third Sunday in November. The alascattalo, *Walroosurous moosticus alaskatorus,* is the genetic cross between a moose and a walrus. Originally bred and used by miners during the Gold Rush, it died out with the mining industry. Whether you believed that story or not, you've just been exposed to your first bit of "absurding" as Alaskans call it. Absurding is the Alaskan custom of inventing tall tales that incorporate the ridiculous beliefs tourists have about Alaska. Alaskan humor stems from the constant need to set tourists from the Lower 48 straight about Alaskan life. For example, a tourist might ask an Alaskan where to find the igloos, penguins, and blubber stew. Instead of explaining that there really are no igloos in Alaska, that penguins are native to Antarctica, and that Alaskans don't eat blubber stew, an Alaskan will often invent a tall tale that confirms the tourist's beliefs. In any case, the absurd alascattalo has become a popular part of Alaskan folk humor, and on the third Sunday of November, Alaskans honor the art of absurding by holding the shortest parade in North American history. It begins promptly at 12:03 and ends at 12:07, meandering down one block of an alley in Anchorage. Rowdy behavior is expected, and the parade often receives national television coverage. Information: Steven C. Levi, 8512 East Fourth Avenue, Anchorage, AK 99504.

Mother Goose Parade
El Cajon, California

Sunday before Thanksgiving. Bring the kids! This larger-than-life rendition of Mother Goose rhymes and fairy tale characters sure beats television. Mother Goose leads the parade followed by an all-star line-up of characters: Old King Cole, the Queen of Hearts, Humpty Dumpty, Old Mother Hubbard, Simple Simon, and a host of others. Over 500,000 people line the streets of this suburban San Diego town to watch this storybook extravaganza. Information: Mother Goose Parade Association, Box 1155, El Cajon, CA 92022.

Macy's
Thanksgiving Day
Parade
New York, New York

Thanksgiving Day. Since 1926, this extravagant procession of floats, helium balloons, and bands from across the country has ushered in the holiday season for New Yorkers. Appearing every year just in time to delight the spectators, Santa Claus greets all the kids from his sleigh full of toys. Cartoon characters in the form of huge and colorful helium balloons fill this larger-than-life parade, which is televised from coast to coast on the morning of Thanksgiving Day. Information: Special Productions Director, 151 West 34th Street, New York, NY 10001.

Chitlin Strut
Salley, South Carolina

Late November. A true southern delicacy, chitlins (that's southern talk for "chitterlings") are hog intestines which are cleaned, boiled, battered, and fried. Every year 40 to 50,000 visitors flock to this tiny town (population 584) to pig out on chitlins. This festival, originally a fundraiser to buy Christmas decorations for downtown Salley, has now expanded to include a hog calling contest, a beauty pageant, a parade, clog dancing, and a strut dance contest. Information: Salley Town Council, P.O. Box 484, Salley, SC 29137.

Pasadena Doo Dah Parade
Pasadena, California

Late November. As a satire on the Annual Tournament of Roses Parade, the Doo Dah Parade has no theme, no judges, no prizes, no animals, and no order of march. However, it does have something that no other parade in the country has—the Synchronized Briefcase Drill Team, a wacky group of bankers and financiers who grab their attachés and let loose for the Doo Dah Parade. This is one of the original wacky parades in the United States, and though it's intentionally disorganized, marchers always seem to get it together in time for its usual coast-to-coast television coverage. Information: Peter Apanel, Czar, Pasadena Doo Dah Parade, P.O. Box 2392, Pasadena, CA 91102.

Holiday River Festival
San Antonio, Texas

End of November through December 31. This festival begins with the lighting of over 70,000 lights illuminating trees and bridges along the San Antonio River, and the arrival of Santa Claus on the river. The Holiday River Festival includes the Fiesta de Las Luminarias—a Mexican tradition in which thousands of luminarias are lit along the River Walk and Las Posadas. The luminarias (brown paper bags holding lighted candles) light the way for singers who parade along the River Walk to commemorate the Holy Family's search for lodging. Information: Convention and Visitors Bureau, Box 2277, San Antonio, TX 78298.

DECEMBER

IN COLD DECEMBER
FRAGRANT CHAPLETS BLOW,
AND HEAVY HARVESTS NOD BENEATH
THE SNOW.

Alexander Pope

HAT'S HAPPENING IN DECEMBER?

Early to Mid-December, Hanukkah: Also known as the Festival of Lights or the Feast of Dedication, Hanukkah commemorates a miraculous event in the history of the Jews. The story of Hanukkah originated in the year 167 B.C. when the King of Syria, who also governed Judaea, declared the practice of Judaism illegal. To make good his intention to stamp out Judaism, this same king dedicated the Temple of Jerusalem to the Greek god Zeus and instituted pagan rites there. A devout family of Jewish patriots, the Maccabees, led the Jews in revolt against the Syrian repression. Of the five sons of patriarch

Mattathias Maccabee, two were killed in battle with the Syrians, but three lived to lead the Jews through 20 years of war and intrigue that finally banished the Syrians from Judaea. The most famous of the five sons, Judah Maccabee recaptured the Temple of Jersualem from the Syrians in 164 B.C. and rededicated it to the God of Abraham. At the feast of dedication, a lamp was lit with sufficient oil to burn for one day; however, as a sign of divine favor, God caused the ceremonial lamp to burn for eight days. During Hanukkah, Jews celebrate the rededication of the Temple of Jerusalem and the sign of the miraculous lamp by lighting a special candelabra (a menora) for eight consecutive nights. Included also in the celebration are festive meals, songs, games, and the exchange of gifts.

December 6, St. Nicholas's Day: Most Americans associate St. Nicholas with Santa Claus; in reality, Santa Claus (a purely American invention) is an American corruption of the Dutch name for Saint Nicholas (*Sinter Claes*). Although there is no historical documentation of his actual existence, Saint Nicholas was one of the most popular saints of the ancient Christian Church. He was most probably a fourth-century bishop of the ancient Turkish town of Myra; accounts of his many miraculous deeds first appeared in a Greek text dating from the sixth century. His best-known legends involve saving children from tragedy and sailors from drowning. He is the patron saint of Russia, as well as the special protector of children, scholars, merchants, and sailors. A favorite legend involves his rescue of three little girls, whose parents had no dowry with which to procure them a fit marriage. Secretly visiting the home of the impoverished girls at night, Nicholas, according to legend, tossed three bags of gold through a window to supply the needed dowries. From this legend grew the old custom of giving presents in secret on the Eve of Saint Nicholas's Day. This old custom eventually was transferred to Christmas Eve and thus began the association of Saint Nicholas with Christmas.

December 7, Pearl Harbor Day: At 7:55 A.M. on a Sunday in 1941, the first Japanese dive bomber appeared over Pearl Harbor, Hawaii. It was followed by nearly 200 aircraft, including torpedo planes, bombers, and fighters. At 8:50 A.M. a second wave of attack began, and shortly after 9:00 A.M. the Japanese withdrew. In little more than an hour the Japanese had destroyed or severely disabled more than 200 of the 300 aircraft stationed at Wheeler Field near Pearl Harbor and had inflicted heavy damage to the naval fleet of nearly 100 vessels stationed in the harbor. Of the eight battleships at rest in

Pearl Harbor on that morning, five were sunk, and three were damaged. The most famous battleship to go down in the attack, the U.S.S. *Arizona,* blew up in a tremendous explosion. Eleven other ships were either sunk or severely damaged. Fortunately, the Pacific fleet's three aircraft carriers were not in the harbor that day. These three carriers proved invaluable in launching the coming war in the Pacific.

Despite the sudden, unprovoked nature of the attack, historians note that it really should not have been that much of a surprise. At about 3:00 A.M. on December 7, the U.S. destroyer U.S.S. *Ward* sighted a Japanese submarine in the waters just outside the harbor, but made no report of the sighting. At about that same time, an army private practicing on a radar set after its normal closing time, noted and reported to his lieutenant a large flight of planes on his radar screen. He was told to forget it, for a flight of B-17s was due to arrive from the United States at about the same time.

December 17, Anniversary of the Flight at Kitty Hawk: On this day in 1903 at 10:25 A.M. at Kill Devil Hills, a spread of sand dunes just outside of Kitty Hawk, North Carolina, Orville Wright crawled into a prone position between the wings of a biplane he and his brother Wilbur had built in their bicycle shop. He opened the throttle of their homemade 12-horsepower engine and took to the air. That first flight covered the grand distance of 120 feet and lasted all of 12 seconds. Nevertheless, the daring inventors were not discouraged. During the course of the day's fun, Wilbur took his turn on the new flying machine and achieved the day's distance record—852 feet.

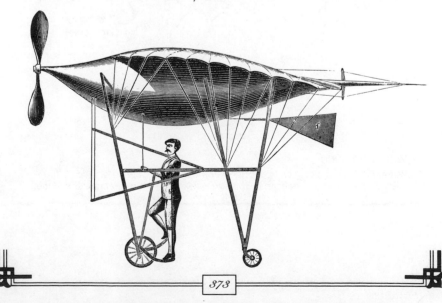

December 21, Winter Solstice: In the Northern Hemisphere, today marks the official beginning of winter, and in the Southern Hemisphere, today is the beginning of summer. On this day the sun is over the Tropic of Capricorn, its southernmost latitude on the earth. For the Northern Hemisphere, today represents the shortest number of daylight hours of the entire year, ranging from about 12 hours over the Equator to zero hours of daylight over the Arctic Circle.

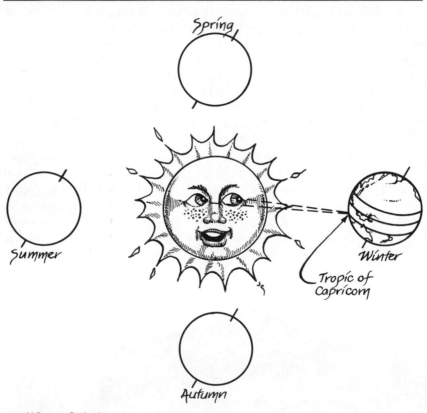

Winter Solstice

Winter begins when the sun is directly over the Tropic of Capricorn, which is the southernmost latitude reached by the sun in its annual journey across the globe.

December 25, Christmas: Also called the Feast of the Nativity, Christmas takes its name from the early Christian designation of this day as Christ's Mass, the day on which the Mass (to Protestants, the Lord's Supper or the Eucharist) was celebrated in commemoration of Christ's birth. During the early centuries of the Church, Christ's Mass was celebrated as a movable feast set by the phases of the moon, much as Easter is set today. This early custom makes a lot of sense in light of the fact that no one really knows the date of Jesus' birth. Seventeenth-century English Puritans were opposed to the celebration of Christmas and even enacted a Parliamentary decree forbidding its celebration. The English, being sensible sorts, celebrated anyway.

December 26, St. Stephen's Day: As the traditional Christmas carol goes

GOOD KING WENCESLAS LOOKED OUT
ON THE FEAST OF STEPHEN,
WHEN THE SNOW LAY 'ROUND ABOUT
DEEP AND CRISP AND EVEN;

Contemporary Christmas carolers can take pleasure in the knowledge that there really was a King Wenceslas; he was a tenth-century King of Bohemia who was martyred for his attempts to introduce Christianity into that pagan country. The day on which he looked out his window was St. Stephen's Day, a day to be celebrated with as much solemnity as Christmas. The ancient Christian Church chose St. Stephen's Day to be celebrated on the day immediately following Christmas; the purpose was to remind Christians to give thanks for the sacrifices of the saints, whose lives make the celebration of Christmas possible. The story of St. Stephen is told in the New Testament book of Acts; he was the first Christian martyr.

December 31, New Year's Eve: The revelry we associate with New Year's Eve has its origins in the ancient Roman festival of Janus, a god with two faces who looked both backward and forward in time, but the actual date of the first day of the year has been the subject of controversy and change for centuries. During medieval times, most of Europe celebrated New Year's Eve on March 24, while England celebrated it on December 24. The Gregorian Calendar (see page 1) established January 1 as the first day of the year for most European countries, but England didn't accept this new date until 1752, nearly 200 years after its adoption in Europe.

December Is a Time to Remember
Poor Richard

On December 28, 1733, Benjamin Franklin first published *Poor Richard's Almanack* under the pen name of Richard Saunders. Published for 25 consecutive years following its first issue, the almanac became the most commonly owned book, save the Bible, in colonial America. Franklin, observing the popularity of his little creation with the common folk, "considered it as a proper vehicle of instruction among the common people, who scarcely bought any other books." Franklin, taking note of the needs of his audience, filled the spaces between the remarkable days of the calendar with proverbs, verses, and sentences that were chosen specifically to encourage the virtues of frugality and industry. Genius that he surely was, Franklin did *not* originate all of the sayings in *Poor Richard's Almanack*. Franklin was a great reader and doubtless read the works of earlier philosophers and satirists, such as Sir Francis Bacon and Rabelaise, from whom he took many of the ideas for his almanac. That he was an astute observer of human nature is indisputable, but Franklin's real genius lay in the ability to take great philosophical and ethical themes and transform them

through his own native wit to ideas easily grasped and appreciated by the common man. What follows here are some samples of Franklin's favorite themes:

Frugality

HE THAT WOULD HAVE A SHORT LENT,
LET HIM BORROW MONEY
TO BE REPAID AT EASTER.

A PENNY SAVED IS TWO PENCE CLEAR.
A PIN A-DAY IS A GROAT A-YEAR.
SAVE AND HAVE.

NECESSITY NEVER MADE A GOOD BARGAIN.

WHAT MAINTAINS ONE VICE
WOULD BRING UP TWO CHILDREN.

Industry

LITTLE STROKES, FELL GREAT OAKS.

WELL DONE, IS TWICE DONE.

HE THAT WAITS UPON FORTUNE,
IS NEVER SURE OF A DINNER.

EARLY TO BED AND EARLY TO RISE,
MAKES A MAN HEALTHY, WEALTHY,
AND WISE.

GOD HELPS THEM THAT HELP THEMSELVES.

Human Nature

THREE MAY KEEP A SECRET,
IF TWO OF THEM ARE DEAD.

HE THAT LIETH DOWN WITH DOGS,
SHALL RISE UP WITH FLEAS.

LOVE YOUR NEIGHBOR;
YET DON'T PULL DOWN YOUR HEDGE.

HE THAT CANNOT OBEY, CANNOT COMMAND.

MANY HAVE QUARREL'D ABOUT RELIGION, THAT NEVER PRACTICED IT.

HE THAT FALLETH IN LOVE WITH HIMSELF, WILL HAVE NO RIVALS.

A Clear Conscience

LET NO PLEASURE TEMPT THEE,
NO PROFIT ALLURE THEE,
NO AMBITION CORRUPT THEE,
NO EXAMPLE SWAY THEE,
NO PERSUASION MOVE THEE,
TO DO ANY THING
WHICH THOU KNOWEST TO BE EVIL;
SO SHALT THOU ALWAYS LIVE JOLLILY;
FOR A GOOD CONSCIENCE
IS A CONTINUAL CHRISTMAS.

ing on the eve of January 6, the Feast of the Epiphany, which commemorates the visit of the Magi to the Christ child. This year, in the spirit of the twelve days of Christmas, celebrate by sending twelve gifts from the garden to a loved one.

IN THE GARDEN

TWELVE GIFTS FROM THE GARDEN

A popular Christmas round song depicts the giving of twelve gifts beginning with a partridge in a pear tree and ending with twelve lords-a-leaping. The twelve gifts in the song really depict the ancient custom of presenting a gift to a loved one on each of the twelve days of Christmastide, an old festival beginning at the Feast of the Nativity on December 25 and end-

The twelve garden gifts here are easy to make:

1. A collection of heirloom seeds. As you explore the realm of heirloom and open-pollinated seeds in your garden, collect enough seeds at the end of the gardening season to share with friends as well as with any seed exchange program to which you belong. Heirloom seeds make a unique and thoughtful gift because they are seeds for varieties of flowers and vegetables that usually are not available through normal commercial seed catalogs. As an attractive way to package your gift from the garden, fold and glue

sheets of stationery into a "seed packet." Decorate the seed packet with pressed flowers (see page 379 for instructions on pressing flowers). For information on obtaining heirloom seeds, see page 97 of the almanac.

2. Potpourri in a decorative container. For a traditional potpourri, collect petals or whole flowers from your garden; roses and lavender flowers should be the primary ingredient, but other fragrant flower petals that work well are sweet pea, lily-of-the-valley, lilac, and honeysuckle. Place the flowers on a nonmetal screen or a cookie sheet with a nonstick coating and air dry them in a dark, dry place. To your dried flowers add one or two dried herbs, such as rosemary, mint, thyme, or marjoram. Add two special ingredients to your dried mixture, an *essential oil,* which enhances the natural fragrance of your potpourri, and a *fixative,* which prolongs the shelf life of your fragrant mixture. Both of these items are available through craft shops. A basic recipe for potpourri includes 4 cups of dried flowers and herbs, 10 to 20 drops of an essential oil, and 2 to 4 tablespoons of a fixative. After your initial mixing of the ingredients, your potpourri should age for at least four weeks to fully develop a subtle, sweet scent. Simply store your potpourri in jars with screw lids in

a warm, dark place, and shake the ingredients every few days. At gift-giving time, pour your fragrant gift into individual containers. Be sure to choose containers with lids, so that the scent can be contained or released.

3. Sachets. Surprise! From your original potpourri (see above), you can make another easy but thoughtful gift. Simply crush your finished potpourri into a fine powder. A simple mortar and pestle helps here. Sew individual cloth bags or buy decorated handkerchiefs and sew up the sides to make a cloth bag. Fill the bag with your ground potpourri, and tie with a colored ribbon or bit of lace. Sachets tucked into linen closets or clothing drawers provide a subtle, sweet scent to the stored items.

4. Pomanders. This old-fashioned decoration just shouts "Christmas!" Use any citrus—with the exception of grapefruit, which is a little too large—and a bottle of whole cloves to make your sweet-scented pomander. Simply insert the whole cloves all over the fruit until you have completely covered its surface. Use a thimble to spare your fingers, or pre-pierce the fruit skin with an ice pick. About 2 ounces of cloves will cover a medium orange. After you've covered the fruit with cloves, first dust it with cinnamon, nutmeg, or

ginger for added scent; then dust the pomander with a powdered fixative, such as orris root (found in craft shops). Place your pomander in a dark, dry place to age for about four weeks. Decorate the finished gift with lace or ribbon. Tie a few sprigs of fresh fir or spruce into the bow to make it more festive.

5. A dried herb wreath. This fragrant wreath can decorate a front door from the Christmas season right into spring. Unlike traditional evergreen or holly wreaths, it keeps its beauty long after Christmas is over. Purchase an undecorated base wreath of straw or Spanish moss (available in craft shops). Select a background dried herb or foliage that you have plenty of. Artemesia and sage both work well. Insert this herb stem by stem into your base until the whole wreath is covered. Now add colored accents to your basic wreath. Choose from pyracantha berries, fresh holly, brightly colored everlastings, sprigs of bittersweet, varnished clusters of nuts, or bundles of cinnamon sticks tied with bright ribbon.

6. Herbal tea. If you've a nice herb collection in your garden, blend one of the following combinations of dried herbs and present it to your favorite tea drinker in a decorative container: tansy, sage, and rosehips; rose petals, rosehips, and raspberry leaves; basil, lemon verbena, lemongrass, and lemon thyme; chamomile and valerian.

7. Flavored vinegars. Pull out all of those interesting bottles you've saved throughout the year and stock them with an inexpensive but elegant herb vinegar. Buy any type of generic vinegar that suits your fancy —white wine vinegar, white vinegar, apple cider vinegar, or rice vinegar. Heat the vinegar, but don't boil it. Pour it into a glass bottle or jar to which you've added several sprigs of fresh herbs or other ingredients. Cool the vinegar, seal the bottles, and store in a dark place for up to a year. Some interesting flavor combinations to try include: rosemary, raisins, orange peel, garlic, and white wine vinegar; sage, parsley, shallots, and red wine vinegar; rose petals, violet petals, and rice vinegar.

8. A grapevine wreath. Follow the instructions on page 351 to make a grapevine wreath. To make the wreath more Christmassy, decorate it with dried baby's-breath and tiny red velvet bows, or with evergreen cuttings, pinecones, and varnished nuts.

9. Pressed-flower stationery. If you've never pressed flowers, a simple stationery project is a great way to learn the craft without investing money in a flower press. The easi-

est flowers to press with no special equipment are small, fine, and flat—such as pansies, violets, primroses, and buttercups. Grasses and ferns also press easily. Avoid large bulky flowers, such as snapdragons, foxgloves, or lilies, and flowers with many petals, such as dahlias and chrysanthemums. To press small flowers and leaves, you need only a heavy book. The flowers will discolor the book pages, so choose a book you don't value highly. Place a piece of blotting paper on a page, arrange flowers on the paper, and cover with another sheet of blotting paper. As you place the flowers cut away thick stems or awkwardly placed leaves. Secure some flower parts to the paper with adhesive tape if they are unruly. Place a heavy weight, such as a dictionary or several telephone books, on your book press. Most flowers will be dry and ready to handle after six weeks. Do not add any new material to the press during the six weeks because this will add moisture to your partially pressed flowers. If you are in a real hurry, you can experiment with pressing flowers between two sheets of blotting paper with a medium hot iron. Remove flowers dried with an iron to a dry, dark place for a day or so before using.

To decorate your stationery, you need only tweezers, an artist's paintbrush, and glue. Arrange your flowers in a pleasing pattern on any stationery. Use tweezers and the paintbrush to avoid touching the flowers while you work. Don't apply any glue until you're completely satisfied with your design. Apply the glue quite sparingly to the backs of the flowers and press into place.

10. A pressed-flower candle. To create a floral candle, select candles at least 2 inches in diameter. In addition to the candle, you will need tweezers, an artist's brush, white craft glue that has been thinned with water to the consistency of light cream, and pressed flowers, leaves, and grasses. See the instructions above for pressing flowers. Arrange your dried material on the candle without glue. Use tweezers to avoid handling the flowers directly. When your design pleases you, lift each piece individually and use the paintbrush to coat the back of it with the thinned glue. After you've applied your entire design, let it dry overnight. Make up a new batch of thinned glue, and paint it over the pressed design, extending the glue beyond the edges of the design. This last step seals the design with a clear glue covering.

11. A garlic braid. If you've a nice garlic patch, share your bounty with your favorite culinary friend. To make this gift all you need are a dozen or more garlic bulbs with the tops still intact, scissors, a ball of jute string, glue, and some dried everlastings (see page 350 for instructions on drying everlastings). Gather three garlic bulbs, and tie the tops together with one end of the ball of string. Begin braiding the three tops as in plaiting hair, working the string as one unit with one of the garlic stems. After making several crosses, work in an additional bulb, and continue in this manner, spacing the bulbs out evenly. When the braid is finished, the string will extend over the entire length of the braid, but no one garlic stem will extend throughout the braid. Use the twine to make a hanging loop at the end. Decorate the braid by gluing on dried everlastings in a design that pleases you. For extra drama, attach a big bow at the top to conceal the hanging loop.

12. Fire starters. If you give a set of these to friends who have wood stoves or fireplaces, they'll thank you every time they light up this winter. To make fire starters, you'll need to collect pinecones that will fit into the cups of a muffin tin. Other supplies you'll need include a box of paraffin (available in supermarkets with canning supplies), an old saucepan, a double boiler, newspaper, an old muffin tin, paper muffin cups, scissors, candlewicking (available at craft shops), and a red or green crayon. Melt the paraffin in the old saucepan set over a double boiler. Dip each pinecone into the melted paraffin to coat it completely; cool on newspapers. After dipping all of the cones, add a single red or green crayon to the remaining melted paraffin to color it. Place the paper muffin cups in the muffin tin and add about ½ inch of colored paraffin to each muffin cup. Add a 2-inch length of candlewicking to the liquid paraffin. Allow the paraffin to partially harden, then press a pinecone into each cup. Let the cone harden completely and remove from the muffin tin. For a rustic look give a collection of fire starters in a recycled, old produce basket decorated with a Christmas bow.

Tips for a Live Tree

In selecting your live Christmas tree, you'll have a choice between balled-and-burlapped stock that has been dug from a field nursery, and container-grown stock. Although container-grown trees are more expensive than field-grown trees, they have a slightly better rate of survival. In selecting your tree, look for a tree with a good green color, no dead branches, and no signs of recent heavy pruning. If you select a balled-and-burlapped tree, shake the trunk slightly, and pass up any tree whose trunk wobbles easily. A trunk that's easily moved usually indicates that the soil around the root ball has become dry and loose. The root ball of a burlapped tree should feel solid and moist.

When you take your tree home, be careful to pick it up by the container or the root ball. Never pick up a balled-and-burlapped tree by the trunk. If the tree is too heavy to lift from your car trunk, use a car jack and a board to lift the root ball; then slide a sheet of heavy cardboard or canvas under the root ball and use this as a sling to lift the tree from the trunk.

Before bringing the tree into the house, keep it in an unheated garage or basement for at least a week. Water the root ball or the container daily and apply a heavy water mist to all of the branches. Your goal is to keep the soil evenly moist but not soggy. You will have the best chance of successfully transplanting your Christmas tree if you keep its exposure to indoor heat to a minimum; therefore plan to keep your tree indoors for no longer than a week. When you finally bring the tree indoors, place a balled-and-burlapped tree in a washtub, sawed-off barrel, or other ample container, and place a container-grown tree in an ample saucer to catch water. Continue watering the tree daily and keep the room temperature below 70°F.

After the holidays, harden off the tree by returning it to the garage or basement for a week, then plant it. See "Christmas in October" on page 319 for instructions in preparing a planting hole. See "Fall Is for Planting" on page 316 for instructions on planting trees. Decorate your live Christmas tree with popcorn and cranberry strings. Leave these decorations on your tree. When you plant it outside, you'll provide a feast for the birds with no extra trouble on your part.

ALMANAC GARDENING CALENDAR

Cold-climate gardeners can look forward to spending the next few weeks dreaming over the new mail-order seed catalogs. Gardeners in the warmest zones can look forward to the start of the camellia blooming season. December is also a prime time for gardeners in Zones 5 though 7 to start seeds for crops to be set out in February.

Zone 1

Grow indoor herbs and greens at 65°F or cooler, especially under low-light conditions. Keep the soil moist to counteract low humidity. More than 13 hours of light may cause winter lettuce and other greens to bolt; place supplemental grow lights on a timer. As gardening comes to a halt, begin planning next year's garden. If you have had trouble maturing tomatoes, peppers, and eggplants, review the catalogs you ordered from to identify earlier ripening varieties. Make a note of these, and look for other early varieties when the new crop of seed catalogs arrives. After harvesting brussels sprouts, replace wire or netting to protect plants from deer and rabbits. Store wood ashes for next year's garden in a covered container to prevent leaching of nutrients.

Check potted spring bulbs weekly to make sure they don't dry out. When sprouts appear, place in a sunny window until flowering. Replace the top inch of soil in pots of amaryllis with compost, and water lightly until growth begins. To prevent heaving of perennials, shovel snow over them. Before heavy snowfall, make sure fruit trees and bushes are mulched and barriers against deer and rodents are in place. Check them periodically for feeding damage to make sure that your preventive measures are sufficient. Where the cold is severe, shovel snow over the strawberries and the lower portion of blueberry plants. If snowfall is lean, use hay or leaves.

Zone 2

Harvest the last batch of kale before a killer freeze sets in. If you've never grown this nutritious vegetable, sow seeds of kale next spring for harvest in late fall and winter. If you have an empty south window, fill a flower box with soil and sow bush beans, lettuce, and onions for a midwinter novelty. Keep an eye on vegetables in storage. Cabbages store best at close to 32°F and 90 percent humidity. Potatoes prefer 40° to 45°F and high humidity. Onions and garlic like 32° to 50°F and dry, airy conditions.

Cut tops off cured gladiolus corms (leave skins on for protection). Store glads, cannas, and dahlias (45°

to 55°F); cover with a thin layer of peat moss. Cut back leggy impatiens and coleus. Root new plants in jars of wet perlite. If you brought geraniums indoors, cut them back for winter blooms. If you just want to store them, pack five or six in a tub with soil or peat moss. Keep them near a window in a cool basement until February. Sprinkle with water now and then. Apply an antidesiccant to newly planted evergreens and those growing in a windy spot. Water deeply once more before the ground freezes. Mulch with wood chips or sawdust to prevent heaving and to help hold moisture in the soil.

Plant strawberry seeds now in a loose mixture of sand and peat moss. Cover seeds with ¹/₁₆ inch of vermiculite or sphagnum moss, soak thoroughly, and slip the container into a plastic bag. Uncover immediately after germination. Transplant seedlings at the three- or four-leaf stage, and grow in good light at 60°F.

Wrap aluminum foil or tree guards around young fruit trees to ward off voles and rabbits. Stake and mulch them to prevent heaving, which kills young trees. Begin pruning apples and other fruits now. Look for egg masses of tent caterpillars (varnished brown bands clustered on twigs and branches). Mash them with a piece of burlap. Scrape off and burn the feltlike brown egg masses of gypsy moths. Check your supply of apples and pears for spoilage.

Zone 3

This is the month to begin planning next year's garden. Send for catalogs now so you'll have time to order seeds and tools before next spring's rush. Extend the harvest of hardy crops such as kale, collards, endive, and spinach by protecting them at night and uncovering them on warmer days. Early in the month, harvest the last Chinese cabbage, corn salad, brussels sprouts, and parsley.

Make sure the mulch over ground-stored crops, such as carrots, parsnips, Jerusalem artichokes, and salsify stays at least 12 inches deep. Dig those you plan to store in a root cellar or refrigerator before a heavy freeze. Check root-cellared produce weekly for signs of decay. Keep a careful eye on fragile fruits such as tomatoes. When the last greens and radishes have been harvested from the cold frame, dig in compost and rock fertilizers to enrich the soil for spring planting. Clean and store cages, stakes, trellises, and irrigation systems. If you're planning to renovate your asparagus bed next spring, dig 18-inch-deep trenches before the soil freezes. Line them with compost for easy digging when spring arrives.

If you're planning to buy a live Christmas tree, remember to dig the hole before the ground freezes.

Choose a small tree—it will transplant better than a large one. Keep the root ball moist and the boughs misted before carrying the tree inside a day or two before Christmas. Immediately after, return the tree to the garage or shed for at least two weeks before planting. Spread well-rotted manure around biennials and perennials. To prevent heaving and foliar damage, use a light mulch of straw or evergreen boughs to cover fall-planted stock and biennials that overwinter as leaf rosettes, such as foxgloves and sweet Williams. Check stored bulbs and corms regularly for deterioration. Swelling indicates too much light or heat.

As soon as cuttings of Joseph's coat, begonias, and other bedding plants develop roots in jars of water, transplant them into pots. Provide as much light as possible.

Check trees, bushes, and vines at least once a week for signs of rodents, storm damage, or other problems. Taking corrective action now will reduce stress and increase production next spring. Before snow arrives, clean up fallen fruit that was missed earlier and burn or compost it. After the ground freezes, spread manure, compost, and rock fertilizers around all fruits. When the ground freezes an inch or more, mulch strawberries and other fruits loosely with pine needles, straw, or spoiled hay held in place with branches. If you haven't already done so, wrap the bases of fruit trees with chicken wire and pull back mulch to keep gnawing rodents at bay. Paint the trunks of young fruit trees white to protect them against sunscald. Set out feeders, suet balls, and water in the orchard to keep birds working on insect control. Check stored fruit for spoilage.

Zone 4

In the West and other mild areas, direct-seed radishes, peas, lettuce, and spinach. Sow cabbage and broccoli in pots or flats about midmonth for setting out in February. In the rest of the zone, prepare beds for early peas and other cool-season crops now to save time and work next spring. Mark rows of ground-stored crops with tall stakes.

Rhubarb can be planted in mild areas until December 21. Provide rich soil with good drainage. Established beds should be divided if stalks were thinner this year. In colder areas, pot up rhubarb plants before the ground freezes, leave them outdoors for a few weeks, and then bring them into a cool cellar for forcing.

Early in the month, give irises a feeding of bonemeal. Mulch beds thickly to prevent heaving. New shrubs and trees can be planted as long as the soil isn't frozen. Water all plantings well, especially those under eaves, before winter sets in.

After the ground freezes, cover chrysanthemums and other perennials with a springy mulch such as leaves or evergreen boughs. Mulch evergreens with salt hay or oak leaves no more than 3 inches deep. Mound soil over roses before temperatures fall to 10°F. Scrape oystershell scale from the bark of lilacs, maples, and willows, and spray with dormant oil when the temperature will remain above 40°F for several hours.

Spray the orchard with dormant oil now, and again in February, to control scale and other sucking insects. Spread a half-inch layer of compost under fruit trees, beginning 2 feet out from each trunk and going beyond the dripline. Keeping the ground clear near the trunk helps prevent rodent damage. Mulch all plantings with straw or shredded leaves.

Zone 5

Harvest cool-season greens after they have been sweetened by a few frosts. Cold weather also improves the flavor of Jerusalem artichoke tubers, which should be in peak condition this month. Place a thick mulch over those left in the ground for later harvest. Mulch carrots, parsnips, and other root crops to keep them from freezing. Do not mulch rhubarb; in this climate, it needs all the cold it can get. Chop and turn compost, and add as much new material as you can find. Set aside manure that may

contain weed seeds, especially manure from pasture-fed animals. Most weed seeds must be exposed to temperatures of 120°F or higher to be killed, and winter composts don't usually run that hot. Avoid manures that may contain seeds of Johnsongrass, bull thistle, or other rampant weeds. If the soil is dry enough to till, start turning under cover crops and prepare a few beds for early spring planting. This is a good time to double-dig raised beds. Work fresh manure into the soil, and cover prepared beds with mulch, burlap, or plastic to keep them in top condition for spring planting. Indoors, plant seeds of cabbage, parsley, chives, and bunching onions. This is the last month to divide crowded clumps of daffodils and magic lilies. Sprinkle a little bonemeal into planting holes when you move the bulbs to their new locations. Continue to set out prechilled bulbs of crocuses, tulips, and hyacinths. Late in the month, seed sweet peas and alyssum in prepared beds. If your hollies are bothered by scale, apply dormant-oil spray now and again in late winter. If freezes threaten your long-awaited camellia blossoms, cover the buds with plastic bags until the cold weather passes. Set the mower blade high to cut annual rye that has been seeded into warm-season lawn grasses. Indoors, continue planting seeds of hardy flowers such as pansies, baby's-breath, hollyhocks, and all types of daisies.

Check your trees for signs of insects and winter injury. Flaking bark may be evidence of codling moths. Scrape affected areas clean, but be careful not to gouge the tree. Peeling cracks in small branches are usually caused by sudden cold snaps. Wait until later to prune these limbs—this year's damage has just begun. Apply dormant-oil spray to fruit trees to kill insects in bark crevices. In locations where the soil is naturally acidic, apply lime to maintain the pH between 6 and 6.5. Mulch deeply around figs to protect the roots from freezing.

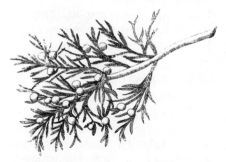

Zone 6

December is a good time for soil building. Work in amendments specified by a soil test so that they have time to weather before spring planting. Sow cereal rye on unused garden space. Till under rye planted in September so that it breaks down by early spring. Start seeds of broccoli, cabbage, onions, and leaf lettuce in cold frames for setting out next month. Prepare beds for planting asparagus in late December or early January.

Harvest carrots, parsnips, Jerusalem artichokes, and horseradish this month. Root crops are tastiest after the first few frosts. Prepare soil for flowers as you would for vegetables. Work in good amounts of bonemeal and compost. Plant seeds of calendulas, alyssum, dianthus, bluebonnets, sweet peas, larkspurs, and pansies before December 15. Transplant lantanas and petunias for spring bloom. Transplant ornamental cabbage and kale. Remove tulips, hyacinths, and crocuses from the refrigerator and plant in full sun.

Order fruit and nut trees after finding out what varieties do best in your area. Buy from local nurseries if possible. Clean up orchard debris to break pest and disease cycles. Spray trees with dormant oil to kill eggs laid in cracks and crevices. Locate sources for beneficial insects to help control pests next year.

Zone 7

If soil and weather conditions permit, continue planting cool-weather crops such as carrots, beets, spinach, peas, and the cabbage family. In the southern tier of the zone, choose early maturing varieties —warm weather can come on rapidly after December. If your soil is heavy clay, plant peas in raised beds to keep the seed from rotting. Where the ground is cold and wet, brassicas will often germinate when nothing else will. For instance, mustard and turnips will make a crop by January if sown now. In the northern tier of the zone, sow peppers, tomatoes, and eggplants indoors late in the month. In the southern parts of Florida, Texas, and California, set out seedlings of these same crops any time this month. Top-dress asparagus, globe artichokes, and rhubarb heavily with manure. It's not too late to plant a cover crop, which can be turned under in early spring. Winter annual rye is the hardiest and germinates well in cold, wet ground. Fava beans (broad beans) will take freezes only if they have been gradually hardened off. At midmonth, divide dormant herbs such as mint, tarragon, chives, oregano, and marjoram.

Early in the month, plant spring bulbs that have been refrigerated for six to eight weeks. Bulbs sold now at reduced prices are a poor value because of the need to chill them before planting. Continue to plant cool-weather annuals for spring color, massing the plants for best effect. Many wildflowers, as well as alyssum and forget-me-nots, will germinate even in cold, wet ground; sweet peas, on the other hand, demand good drainage. Sow lobelia, ageratums, candytufts, and petunias in containers indoors. Bareroot perennials such as bleedinghearts, columbines, delphiniums, peonies, lilies-of-the-valley, and Oriental poppies are available for planting now. Plant ranunculus, anemones, callas, amaryllises, glads, and various lilies before the month is over; the soil will warm up in January and they will start to grow. Feed roses at the beginning of the month to bring on blooms by New Year's Day. When the soil is dry enough to work, anticipate new rose plantings by digging holes and adding compost. This is an excellent time of year for transplanting trees and shrubs or putting in new ones. In the cool, moist ground, their roots will become established in time to support spring leaf growth. Evergreens especially seem to adapt well if planted in December. Needle and broadleaf evergreens take best to pruning at this time. Use the cuttings for Christmas wreaths.

Fruits, nuts, and berries are as dormant as they will get in zone 7, making this the prime time to move them or to put in new ones. Start new bramble beds by dividing roots from existing plantings. Till and compost beds for strawberries to go in next month. If you plan to grow strawberries as annuals, choose a variety that fruits early and massively. When the plants have finished fruiting in May, pull them out and plant something else for the summer. Spray the orchards with dormant oil to kill insect eggs and lingering adults. To rid peaches and nectarines of peach leaf curl, spray with lime-sulfur early in the month as soon as all the leaves have dropped. Late in the month all trees and vines should be thoroughly dormant and ready to receive their winter pruning. Leave citrus and avocado unpruned. Don't pull off Japanese persimmons until they are bright orange. Dry surplus persimmons in a food dehydrator.

IN GOOD HEALTH

EIGHT KEYS TO A HAPPY HOLIDAY

It may be the season to be jolly, but you may be feeling that everything's stacked against you. For some people, the holidays bring more anxiety and depression than any other time of the year. The annual Christmas or Hanukkah festivities bring on feelings of sadness, longing, fear of family conflict, and both physical and financial fatigue. For many people, the holidays bring on feelings of sadness because they are a graphic reminder that time is passing. This sensation of time flying by provides ample opportunity for regret and sadness over missed opportunities, past mistakes, or the loss of loved ones through death or separation. Others find the hype and commercialism of this season a source of pressure to spend more than they can reasonably afford and do more than they have the time or energy to do. Yielding to these pressures only heightens feelings of anxiety (the bills will surely come in January), anger (the kids might not appreciate the fact that you stood in line for an hour to buy that special gift), and depression (all this spending doesn't erase long-standing personal problems).

This holiday time, resolve to bypass the negative thoughts that can arise this time of year by adopting some strategies that make this season joyful and meaningful for you. What is meaningful for you may not be in the tradition of "White Christmas" and "Jingle Bells," but don't feel guilty about that. The important point is to make this holiday season a time of rejuvenation and hope for yourself and for those you love. Here are eight ideas to get you started:

1. Start a new tradition. You may have always gone caroling with your neighbors on Christmas Eve, but

perhaps this year you think of this upcoming event with dread. It doesn't matter why you feel this way; it does matter that you do something about it. Arrange a new activity for yourself, even if it doesn't seem like a traditional or Christmassy activity. Perhaps you'd rather walk on a deserted beach with your spouse or a special friend, or maybe treat yourself to a weekend away from home this time of year. Maybe you'd rather arrange a Christmas covered-dish supper with some new acquaintances, or buy a plane ticket to visit someone you really love. The point is to respond to your real needs instead of the expectations of others.

2. Give yourself the gift of guilt-less giving. Spend only what you feel comfortable spending. Don't buy gifts for people out of a sense of guilt or misplaced obligation. If someone gives you a gift you cannot afford to reciprocate, allow that person the pleasure of being the giver and allow yourself the pleasure of writing a heartfelt, personal note of thanks, something that costs you almost nothing yet makes the giver feel appreciated.

If you feel sad because of the loss of a loved one this season, make a donation to a favorite charity in the name of your loved one. It's a way of giving thanks for that person's life, and it puts you in the position of doing something about your sadness instead of just succumbing to it.

3. Shop at home. Shopping malls are the common scene for the onset of a tension headache. The reason—too much to buy and too many decisions to make in a short amount of time. Unless you're the type of person who finds a day of shopping a relaxing trip into a dream world, Christmas is an excellent excuse to shop at home through mail-order catalogs or by phoning in an order for an advertised item at a local store. Mail-order shopping saves you the most time if you're shopping for friends and family members who live out of town, because you can have the gift sent directly from the store to the recipient. If you have many gifts to buy, another smart holiday strategy is to shop at home through mail-order catalogs for most of your gift list and then make a pleasant excursion to shop for only a few special gifts. You can relax and enjoy the holiday music and the gaily decorated stores if your shopping agenda is short and simple.

4. If you're lonely, volunteer. If you find yourself alone this holiday season, don't wait for the full weight of it to dawn on you on December 24. Check your local newspaper for charitable groups, hospitals, or nursing homes that could use some helping hands during the holidays. Being with other volunteers in a

task-oriented activity may not alter your current life situation, but it sure helps you to forget it for a few hours. There's no better antidote to being blue than helping someone who's worse off than you are.

5. Celebrate with someone new. Just because you always have your in-laws for Christmas dinner doesn't mean that you can't include someone new in your old circle. Include nonfamily friends in a family gathering, especially people new to your area or people who are alone. Including others opens up the possibility of friendship and intimacy with people other than your family; it also forestalls a rehash of old family quarrels that can break out all too easily during the high-stress holiday season.

6. Consider skipping the holiday altogether. If you've already had a stress overload this past year (perhaps a major illness or a divorce), why add insult to injury? No one says you *have* to celebrate. If you need quiet and a chance to recuperate this holiday season, consider taking a trip to areas where Christmas and New Year's are just days on the calendar. You may feel more relaxed in a backwoods cabin in Maine, or you might enjoy a vacation at the resort areas of the Caribbean, Mexico, South Florida, Arizona, California, or Nevada. Be forewarned that you'll pay top dollar for R and R during this popular vacation season, but it may be an expense you're willing to pay to get the rest you need.

7. Prepare for flare-ups of chronic health problems. High-stress holidays usually provide a great stage for the flare up of arthritis, back troubles, headaches, old athletic injuries, angina, asthma, or digestive troubles. If you recognize that you'll be challenged to meet all of your obligations during the holiday season, make sure you have your doctor-prescribed medication on hand before the season reaches full pitch. Use every means you can think of to cut back on your stress and thus forestall an outbreak of an old health problem. Simple measures include making time for your regular exercise no matter how tight your schedule, avoiding late-night hours, eating and drinking modestly at parties, and making simple choices that cut down on your stress. For example, do you really need to attend each of the three Christmas parties you were invited to?

8. Avoid the typical high-fat, high-salt, high-sugar, high-alcohol consumption of holidays past. This holiday, give yourself the gift of health. An easy way to forestall a bout of party binging that you'll regret the next day is to eat dinner at home before you go to a holiday bash, and once you're at the party, drink alcohol sparingly or not at

all. If you eat a complete, healthful meal before you make your grand entrance, you certainly won't be tempted by hunger to overindulge. If you keep your alcohol consumption to a minimum, you won't lose your normal appetite inhibitions and find yourself grabbing hors d'oeuvres by the armload every time a tray passes by.

IN THE SPIRIT OF THE SEASON

December is the season of hope. It's been nearly 2,000 years since the first Christmas, and modern science is finally coming up with tangible proof that the experience of hope is more than a sign of spiritual health—it has physical value in combating disease and possibly in keeping us well to begin with. Reporting on a study of over 200 terminally-ill cancer patients at the University of Texas Health Science Center at Dallas, Dr. Jeanne Achterberg, Ph.D., found that some patients

significantly outlived their predicted life expectancy. When she compared the psychological profiles of these outstanding survivors, she found that they shared a whole host of psychological traits, including a rejection of their role as invalids, self-reliance, an openness to new ideas, and *an utter refusal to give up hope*.

In this season of the year, when our popular culture pays lip service to hope and optimism, why not take the value of hope seriously by spending some time exploring your own personal optimism? Use the Positive Person Quiz as a quick, fun way to find out how optimistic you really are.

POSITIVE PERSON QUIZ

To find out how positive you are, answer these 15 questions as honestly as possible, using this scoring system: Give yourself a 5 if your answer is *Always* or *Almost Always;* 4 if it's *Usually;* 3 for *Sometimes;* 2 for *Rarely;* 1 for *Never.*

1. When the unexpected forces you to change your plans, are you quick to spot a hidden advantage in this new situation?

5   4   3   2   1

2. When you catch a stranger staring at you, do you conclude it's because he or she finds you attractive?

5 4 3 2 1

3. Do you like most of the people you meet?

5 4 3 2 1

4. When you think about the new year, do you tend to think you'll be better off then than you are now?

5 4 3 2 1

5. Do you often stop to admire things of beauty?

5 4 3 2 1

6. When someone finds fault with you or something you've done, can you tell the difference between useful criticism and "sour grapes," which is better off ignored?

5 4 3 2 1

7. Do you praise your spouse/best friend/lover more often than you criticize him or her?

5 4 3 2 1

8. Do you believe the human race will survive into the twenty-first century?

5 4 3 2 1

9. Are you surprised when a friend lets you down?

5 4 3 2 1

10. Do you think of yourself as happy?

5 4 3 2 1

11. If a policeman stopped you for speeding when you were quite certain you *weren't*, would you firmly argue your case and even take it to court to prove you were right?

5 4 3 2 1

12. Do you feel comfortable making yourself the butt of your own jokes?

5 4 3 2 1

13. Do you believe that, overall, your state of mind has had a positive effect on your physical health?

5 4 3 2 1

14. If you made a list of your ten favorite people, would you be on it?

5 4 3 2 1

15. When you think back over the past few months, do you tend to remember your little successes before your setbacks and failures?

5 4 3 2 1

Scoring: If you scored 65 or over, consider yourself a "superstar" —someone whose optimism is a powerful healing force.
60–64: Excellent—you're a genuine positive thinker.
55–59: Good—you're a positive thinker . . . sometimes.
50–54: Fair—your positive side and your negative side are about evenly matched.
49 and below: Do you see any consistent negative patterns? Where could you improve?

The "Positive Person Quiz" reprinted from Prevention's *Regeneration Project* booklet, *"Regeneration of Health and the Human Spirit."*

Walking Tip for December

Since it's the season of gift giving, why not buy a walking-related gift for someone you love? Or purchase a special piece of walking gear for yourself, wrap it in gift wrap, and open it on New Year's Eve as an incentive to keep up with your walking program in the coming year. Walking is just about the least expensive activity you can engage in. Still, there are a few items that can make a walking program more fun or more comfortable. Check out the items listed here, all of which are available at hiking and camping specialty stores: a pedometer, for those who love numbers and want to know exactly how many miles they've covered; thick wool socks with polyethylene liners, for keeping feet dry and warm during the winter walking season; a walking stick, either a collapsible stick or a beautifully carved and decorated wooden model; a fanny pack, the best way to carry small items, such as a water bottle, a map, or a camera; a light-reflecting vest, a thoughtful safety item for those walkers who usually take their walks in the dim hours before or after work; an all-weather nylon suit, a great gift for the enthusiast who frets about a day missed because of rain; a gift certificate for a pair of walking shoes.

AT HOME

SIX STEPS TO GETTING GREAT RESULTS FROM A CONTRACTOR

As the holiday season draws to a close, you may be thinking of some long-delayed household project that you'd like to complete in the upcoming year. If your plans call for some extensive remodeling or addition to your home, you may find yourself hiring a professional building contractor or tradesman to do your work. The relationship between you and your building professional should satisfy both of you. Give some thought to the following guidelines before you hire someone for any project, large or small.

1. Do your homework. Whether you plan to build a house, reroof

your garage, or construct a deck, spending time to research your project will pay off in less wasted time and money. If you are not familiar with the various building trades, go to the library and check out as many books as you can on the trades that relate to your project. If you are planning to build a house, a year or so of serious research into this subject is a good investment. When you begin to talk to a contractor or building tradesman, you should be able to talk his language. If your recently hired mason asks you how deep you want the footers for your brick garden wall, you should know what he is talking about. Begin talking to prospective contractors only after you have a clear idea of what you want—the more detailed your plans, the better.

2. Get competitive bids. Unless you really need to give the job to your cousin to keep peace in the family, you should never overlook this step. Each contractor or tradesman will have his own unique way of approaching your project. Ask each contractor for a bid in writing, and ask that each bid contain all the particulars of how the project will be done, including a description of the method of construction and a list of the amount, the grade, and the type of materials the contractor will supply for your job. Also inquire

about how many helpers or tradesmen will work on your project, and ask for proof that all workers are insured against accidental injury on your job—you do not want to be liable for the injury of a workman. After you have received a number of bids (at least three, better yet four or five), sit down with all these written specifications and numbers and do some comparison shopping. You may find that even though Contractor A bids 10 percent more than Contractor B, you like his ideas more and have a higher level of confidence in his abilities. As a courtesy, let every contractor know that you are getting competitive bids. This knowledge may inspire some creative pencil sharpening, and it also lets contractors know that you are serious about getting your job done.

3. Visit other satisfied customers. Before making your final choice, inform your lead candidate that you would like to consider him further and would appreciate seeing some of his most recently completed work. Any reputable contractor will maintain good relationships with his past clients, and he should be able to show you a sample of his work. Whether he builds garages or installs aluminum siding, he should make arrangements for you to visit a job he has recently completed. You should be able to talk

to the owner yourself and ask any questions about how satisfactorily the work was performed.

4. Get a written contract. Now you will be glad that you got your competitive bids in writing. The bid you select will form the basis of your written contract with the professional tradesman or contractor. For all projects, be sure that the amount and type of materials and the manner of construction are all written into the contract. The contract will specify the time and manner of payment for the work, usually in installments as stages of the job are completed. It may include a clause that specifies the time limits during which the work is to be performed. After you have gone over every clause of the contract several times, don't sign it—sleep on it. It doesn't hurt to be cautious and you may find that new ideas and concerns occur to you that you hadn't considered before. A good rule of thumb is to consult an attorney before signing any contract. A contract is a binding legal obligation between you and another party. Signing today and discovering problems in the contract later will cost you money and time. Never sign a contract that requires you to pay the entire cost of a job before the work is completed to your satisfaction.

5. Get all change orders in writing. As work proceeds on your project, you may encounter problems that

force you to make changes in your plans: The siding you specified for your family room addition is no longer available, you saw a dandy freestanding wood stove that you'd like to incorporate into the floorplans, the single window you ordered really would look better if it were a sliding glass door. Before asking for any change in your original plans, discuss it with your contractor or tradesman. Ask for a detailed account of how much the change will cost in labor and materials. Negotiate this price as you would any other bargainable item. If your contractor comes up with a price and a solution you can accept, get a description of the change (called a change order) in writing. You and your contractor should both sign and date the change order, and you should each receive a copy. Keep this with your original contract. In some cases, the contractor may owe you money or credit because he is unable to perform some aspect of your job due to materials shortage or unexpected job site conditions. Be sure to get your credit due statement from him and keep it with your contract.

6. Inspect all work daily. If an error occurs in completing your job, the sooner you find it the better. Know exactly what materials you are paying for as well as exactly what construction methods will be used in your project. If you find an error, report

it to the contractor immediately. It is always best to assume that building professionals are like everyone else —they make honest mistakes. Obviously, an error committed by your contractor in the completion of your work should not cost *you* more money. If you have taken appropriate care in selecting the best person for your job, you will find it relatively easy to get mistakes corrected.

Home for the Holidays

Robert Frost described home best in his poem, "The Death of the Hired Man":

> HOME IS THE PLACE WHERE, WHEN YOU HAVE TO GO THERE,
> THEY HAVE TO TAKE YOU IN.

In Frost's simple description, there's no mention of lace curtains on the windows, no department-store-perfect furnishings, no silver or bone china on the table, and no shining brass doorknockers. For this poet at least, home is something far more elemental than the shiny goods we see in advertising circulars. Home is a place where pretense is put aside, where we are fully known and loved for who we really are and not for who we would like to be.

"Not home" is all those places in our lives where we assume a role or play a part, where we are regarded for what we *seem* to be. "Not home" places are public places, like department stores or hotel lobbies, or business places, like bank lobbies or office buildings. Most of us spend most of our waking hours in places that are "not home" because of the simple necessity of earning a living.

This holiday season, go home for a while—in your dreams, over the telephone, through a letter, in person, any way you can. Home may be a real house, where the front door always sticks and the faucets leak; it may be an apartment in Brooklyn, where the radiators always clank and the doorbuzzer doesn't work; or it may be the top floor of a two-flat in the Chicago suburbs, where the old lady downstairs plays the television loud enough to blast your ears out. No matter. We all know home wasn't meant to be perfect. It's just the place where we can be who we really are and where we can love and accept others for who they really are. As Dorothy says in *The Wizard of Oz:* "There's no place like home. There's no place like home."

YOUR DECEMBER SHOPPER'S TIP

The best buys in produce this month are apples, broccoli, brussels sprouts, cabbage, cranberries, grapefruit, oranges, and pears. This colorful and tasty brussels sprouts recipe is low in fat and includes the pleasant contrast of crunchy almonds.

Brussels Sprouts with Yogurt

2 to 2½ pounds brussels sprouts
1 medium-sized tomato, chopped
2 teaspoons chopped fresh chives
½ teaspoon ground nutmeg
¼ teaspoon pepper
1 cup plain yogurt, whisked
¼ cup grated Parmesan cheese
¼ cup blanched almonds, toasted

Preheat oven to 350°. Steam brussels sprouts until tender when pierced with the tip of a knife, about 7 minutes. Place cooked sprouts in a buttered ovenproof casserole. Sprinkle tomatoes and chives over top, add nutmeg and pepper, and then pour yogurt over all. Sprinkle with cheese and almonds and bake for 15 minutes.

6 to 8 servings

YOUR HOME MAINTENANCE CHECKLIST

☞ Clean or replace air filters in forced-air heating systems; this should be done monthly during heating season.

☞ Vacuum the baseboard elements of an electric heating system and the fins of baseboard radiators monthly during heating season.

☞ Check areas around windows and doors for cold air leakage; the first warm day (40°F or above), apply caulk to stop leaks. Tack felt weather stripping to old, leaky wooden windows.

☞ Lubricate door hinges and window glides with silicone spray or wipe with a light oil.

EVENTS AND FESTIVALS

Elgin Catfish Stomp
Elgin, South Carolina

First weekend in December. Help yourself to catfish stew! Or how about a mess o' fried catfish, hushpuppies, and all the trimmin's for a down home, strictly southern catfish supper? The big "cats" are fresh out of the Wateree River and as savory as freshwater catfish ever get. (Southern fried chicken is available for those poor folks who don't like catfish.) The folks in Elgin play host to thousands of visitors who come for the fabulous food, the catfish parade, and the coronation of the Elgin Catfish Queen. After you've taken in the sights and cleaned your plate, spend some time at the country music and bluegrass concert, take a stroll through the midway of the country carnival, or do a little Christmas shopping at the dandy arts and crafts displays. The folks in Elgin have just one thing to add to this description of the Catfish Stomp: "Ya'll come!" Information: Elgin Catfish Stomp, P.O. Box 850, Elgin, SC 29045.

Sinterklaas Festival
Lynden, Washington

First weekend in December. This holiday festival honors the traditional December 6 Dutch celebration of St. Nicholas's Day. The Dutch believe that on St. Nick's Day, Sinterklaas (that's Dutch for St. Nicholas) returns to earth to bring gifts to children. At the Lynden Sinterklaas Festival, Sinterklaas arrives in downtown Lynden on a white horse with his helper, Zwarte Piet, to give out cookies and candy to children. According to Dutch tradition, it is Zwarte Piet who does the dirty work of hauling toys down the chimneys for Sinterklaas. There are Dutch carols and carolers, Dutch *klompen* (clog) dancing, and a chance for the children of this predominantly Dutch community to sit on Sinterklaas's lap and tell him their Christmas wishes. Information: Lynden Chamber of Commerce, P.O. Box 647, Lynden, WA 98264.

Army-Navy Football Game
Philadelphia, Pennsylvania

First Saturday in December. An American tradition since 1890, this game is a battle between cadets and midshipmen for the Commander in Chief's trophy. Navy enters the fray led by its stubborn goat mascot, and Army leaps to the challenge with the bray of its equally stubborn mule. And fabulous martial music supplied by the top-notch Army and Navy bands adds excitement and color to this tradition-bound contest. As of the end of the 1988 contest, Navy and Army both have 41 wins, and seven contests have ended in a draw. Past players in this gridiron classic who have gone on to

bigger battlefields include Generals Eisenhower, Bradley, and MacArthur (he was actually a manager, according to Army sources), and Admirals Halsey, Byrd, and Ewen. Information: Army Athletic Ticket Office, West Point, NY 10996.

Christmas at the Zoo
Asheboro, North Carolina

Mid-December through January 1. This natural-habitat zoo honors the ancient legend that on Christmas Eve, all the beasts in God's creation receive the power of speech. In keeping with this view of the sacredness of the natural world, the zoo puts on a Christmas celebration for the animals. Among the zoo's Christmas traditions are a tree trimmed with edible ornaments for wild birds and a Christmas caroling party in which the carolers sing to the animals. Children's activities include storytelling, a class in animal art, and trimming gingerbread houses. As its gift to the community, the zoo offers free admission on Christmas Day. Information: North Carolina Zoological Park, Route 4, Box 83, Asheboro, NC 27203.

Christmas Sing in the Cave
Mammoth Cave National Park, Kentucky

Mid-December. In 1883, guests at a nearby hotel held a Christmas party in the cave, and this event re-creates that evening with old-fashioned barbershop quartet singing, choral concerts, and caroling. A lighted Christmas tree decorates the cave, and all activities take place by lantern light. The acoustics of the cave are excellent, and at the end of the program, each spectator lights a small candle as a symbol of the hope and joy of the season. Participants are invited to enjoy hot apple cider and cookies after the Christmas Sing. Information: Mammoth Cave National Park, Mammoth Cave, KY 42259.

Chester Greenwood Day
Farmington, Maine

Mid-December. In 1873 Farmington's most famous citizen, Chester Greenwood, invented something the folks in Maine can't do without—earmuffs. Tiny Farmington still proclaims itself the Earmuff Capital of the World during its annual Chester Greenwood Day celebration. Chester Greenwood Day is just the ticket for folks who love down-home Maine humor, because the folks in Farmington go all out for this zany, fun-filled day. To keep the spontaneity of the event intact, sponsors don't reveal the plans for Chester Greenwood Day until almost the day itself; among the past shenanigans were a Chester Greenwood look-alike contest, an ice cream sculpture contest, a road race with only earmuffed contestants allowed, a backward dogsled race, and a few other wacky events. Information: Farmington Town Hall, Candy Targett, 147 Lower Main Street, Farmington, ME 04938.

Re-enactment of Washington
Crossing the Delaware
Washington Crossing, Pennsylvania

December 25. Thousands of spectators line the river banks to see this re-creation of George Washington's 1776 Christmas Day crossing of the Delaware River. In a strategic stroke of genius, Washington surprised Hessian mercenaries in Trenton, who were sleeping off a long Christmas celebration, and captured the town from British hands. For the re-enactment, 120 participants authentically dressed and outfitted as colonial soldiers cross the river in replicas of the original Durham boats. An authentically costumed and made-up "Washington" leads the party as it departs from the Pennsylvania side of the river. Before the re-enactment, visitors may tour the park and visit the Memorial Building to enjoy a life-sized painting of Washington's historic crossing. Also available at the Memorial Building is a regularly scheduled documentary film that examines the important events of that Christmas Day. Even though Washington actually crossed the river at 7:00 P.M., the re-enactment takes place for the convenience of spectators at 2:00 P.M. on Christmas Day. During the half-hour preceding the re-enactment, the colorfully garbed and outfitted participants parade from the park entrance to McKonkey's Ferry, the actual site of the original crossing. Information: Washington Crossing Historical Park, Washington Crossing, PA 18977.

First Night Arts Celebration
Boston, Massachusetts

December 31. Boston welcomes the New Year with this annual celebration of the arts throughout its historic Back Bay, Beacon Hill, South End, and Downtown areas. Sixty sites—including many of the city's historic churches—host performances and exhibitions of almost every form of the visual, performing, and literary arts— including dance, music, mime, storytelling, film, puppetry, poetry reading, theater, and environmental art. The First Night Arts Celebration offers a spectacular evening jam-packed with over 150 events, including the Grand Procession. The gala celebration concludes with a midnight fireworks show at Boston Harbor. Information: First Night, Inc., Box 573, Back Bay Annex, Boston, MA 02117.